ARCHAEOLOGICAL HERITAGE MANAGEMENT IN THE MODERN WORLD

TITLES OF RELATED INTEREST

Animals into art
H. Morphy (ed.)

Archaeological approaches to cultural identity
S. J. Shennan (ed.)

Avebury reconsidered: from the 1660s to the 1990s
P. J. Ucko *et al.*

Centre and periphery: comparative studies in archaeology
T. C. Champion (ed.)

Chalcolithic, Bronze and Iron Age cultures in South Asia
M. Lal (ed.)

Conflict in the archaeology of living traditions
R. Layton (ed.)

Domination and resistance
D. Miller *et al.* (eds)

The excluded past: archaeology in education
P. Stone & R. MacKenzie (eds)

Food, metals and towns in African history: African adaptations in subsistence and technology
T. Shaw *et al.* (eds)

Foraging and farming: the evolution of plant exploitation
D. Harris & G. Hillman (eds)

From the Baltic to the Black Sea: studies in medieval archaeology
D. Austin & L. Alcock (eds)

Hunters of the recent past
L. Davis & B. O. K. Reeves (eds)

The meanings of things: material culture and symbolic expression
I. Hodder (ed.)

The origins of human behaviour
R. A. Foley (ed.)

Pleistocene perspective: innovation, adaptation and human survival
A. M. ApSimon & S. Joyce (eds)

The politics of the past
P. Gathercole & D. Lowenthal (eds)

Signifying animals: human meaning in the natural world
R. G. Willis (ed.)

State and society: the emergence and development of social hierarchy and political centralization
J. Gledhill *et al.* (eds)

The walking larder: patterns of domestication, pastoralism, and predation
J. Clutton-Brock (ed.)

What is an animal?
T. Ingold (ed.)

What's new? A closer look at the process of innovation
S. E. van der Leeuw & R. Torrence (eds)

Who needs the past? Indigenous values and archaeology
R. Layton (ed.)

The world at 18 000 BP: high latitudes
O. Soffer & C. Gamble (eds)

The world at 18 000 BP: low latitudes
C. Gamble & O. Soffer (eds)

Archaeological Heritage Management in the Modern World

Edited by Henry Cleere

London and New York

First published in 1989 by Unwin Hyman Ltd
First published in paperback in 1990 by Unwin Hyman Ltd

Reprinted 2000 by Routledge
11 New Fetter Lane, London EC4P 4EE

Simultaneously published in the USA and Canada
by Routledge
29 West 35th Street, New York, NY 10001

Routledge is an imprint of the Taylor & Francis Group

Typeset in 10 on 11 point Bembo by Computape (Pickering) Ltd,
Pickering, North Yorkshire
Printed and bound in Great Britain at the University Press, Cambridge

British Library Cataloguing in Publication Data
A catalogue record for this book is available from the British Library

Library of Congress Cataloguing in Publication Data

ISBN 0–415–21448-36

List of contributors

Gabebah Abrahams, South African Cultural History Museum, Capetown, South Africa.

Peter V. Addyman, York Archaeological Trust, York, UK.

John Alexander, St John's College, Cambridge, UK.

Margareta Biörnstad, Riksantikvarieämbetet, Stockholm, Sweden.

Henry Cleere, Council for British Archaeology, London, UK.

Jon S. Czaplicki, Cultural Resource Management Division, Arizona State Museum, Tucson, Arizona, USA.

Hester A. Davis, Arkansas Archaeological Survey, Fayetteville, Arkansas, USA.

Evan I. DeBloois, USDA Forest Service, Washington, DC, USA.

Josephine Flood, Australian Heritage Commission, Canberra, ACT, Australia.

Javier García Fernández, Universidad Complutense de Madrid, Spain.

Francis N. Golding, English Heritage, London, UK.

Ann Hamlin, Historic Buildings and Monuments Branch, Department of the Environment for Northern Ireland, Belfast, UK.

Florante G. Henson, National Museum, Division of Archaeology, Manila, Philippines.

Joachim Herrmann, Zentralinstitut für Alte Geschichte und Archäologie, Berlin, German Democratic Republic.

Kristian Kristiansen, Center for Research in the Humanities, Copenhagen University, Denmark.

Robert M. Laidlaw, Bureau of Land Management, Sacramento, California, USA.

V. M. Masson, Institute of Archaeology, Leningrad, USSR.

William J. Mayer-Oakes, Department of Anthropology, Texas Tech University, Lubbock, Texas, USA.

Kwasi Myles, Organisation of Museums, Monuments and Sites of Africa, Accra, Ghana.

Presley Norton, Programa de Antropología para el Ecuador, Quito, Ecuador.

Robert J. Pearce, Museum of Indian Archaeology, London, Ontario, Canada.

David Rasamuel, The University of Madagascar, Antananarivo, Madagascar.

Mario Sanoja, Academia Nacional dela Historia de Venezuala, Caracas, Venezuela.

Andrew Saunders, English Heritage, London, UK.

Curtis F. Schaafsma, Museum of New Mexico, Sante Fe, New Mexico, USA.

Kent A. Schneider, USDA Forest Service, Atlanta, Georgia, USA.

Roland Silva, Ministry of Cultural Affairs, Colombo, Sri Lanka.

Nicholas P. Stanley Price, The Getty Conservation Institute, Marina del Rey, California, USA.

B. K. Thapar, The Indian National Trust for Art and Cultural Heritage, New Delhi, India.

Gustaf Trotzig, Riksantikvarieämbetet, Stockholm, Sweden.

Iraida Vargas, Departamento de Arqueología y Etnografía, Universidad Central de Venezuela, Caracas, Venezuela.

Geoffrey Wainwright, Engish Heritage, London, UK.

Zhuang Min, State Administrative Bureau for Museums and Archaeological Data, Beijing, People's Republic of China.

Foreword

This book is one of a major series of more than 20 volumes resulting from the World Archaeological Congress held in Southampton, England, in September 1986. The series reflects the enormous academic impact of the Congress, which was attended by 850 people from more than 70 countries, and attracted many additional contributions from others who were unable to attend in person.

The *One World Archaeology* series is the result of a determined and highly successful attempt to bring together for the first time not only archaeologists and anthropologists from many different parts of the world, as well as academics from a host of contingent disciplines, but also non-academics from a wide range of cultural backgrounds, who could lend their own expertise to the discussions at the Congress. Many of the latter, accustomed to being treated as the 'subjects' of archaeological and anthropological observation, had never before been admitted as equal participants in the discussion of their own (cultural) past or present, with their own particular vital contribution to make towards global, cross-cultural understanding.

The Congress therefore really addressed world archaeology in its widest sense. Central to a world archaeological approach is the investigation not only of how people lived in the past but also of how, and why, changes took place resulting in the forms of society and culture which exist today. Contrary to popular belief, and the archaeology of some 20 years ago, world archaeology is much more than the mere recording of specific historical events, embracing as it does the study of social and cultural change in its entirety. All the books in the *One World Archaeology* series are the result of meetings and discussions which took place within a context that encouraged a feeling of self-criticism and humility in the participants about their own interpretations and concepts of the past. Many participants experienced a new self-awareness, as well as a degree of awe about past and present human endeavours, all of which is reflected in this unique series.

The Congress was organized around major themes. Several of these themes were based on the discussion of full-length papers which had been circulated some months previously to all who had indicated a special interest in them. Other sessions, including some dealing with areas of specialization defined by period or geographical region, were based on oral addresses, or a combination of precirculated papers and lectures. In all cases, the entire sessions were recorded on cassette, and all contributors were presented with the recordings of the discussion of their papers. A major part of the thinking behind the Congress was that a meeting of many hundreds of participants that did not leave behind a published record of its academic discussions would be little more than an exercise in tourism.

Thus, from the very beginning of the detailed planning for the World Archaeological Congress, in 1982, the intention was to produce post-Congress books containing a selection only of the contributions, revised in the light of discussions during the sessions themselves as well as during subsequent consultations with the academic editors appointed for each book. From the outset, contributors to the Congress knew that if their papers were selected for publication, they would have only a few months to revise them according to editorial specifications, and that they would become authors in an important academic volume scheduled to appear within a reasonable period following the Southampton meeting.

The publication of the series reflects the intense planning which took place before the Congress. Not only were all contributors aware of the subsequent production schedules, but also session organizers were already planning their books before and during the Congress. The editors were entitled to commission additional chapters for their books when they felt that there were significant gaps in the coverage of a topic during the Congress, or where discussion at the Congress indicated a need for additional contributions.

This book results from discussions at the Congress on 'Public Archaeology and Cultural Resource Management', discussions which were organized under the headings 'The History and Development of Cultural Resource Management', 'Archaeology in Legislation, Government and Planning', 'Training and Qualification of Archaeologists for Cultural Resource Management', 'Data Management and Cultural Resource Management', 'Cultural Resource Management of Stonehenge', and 'Archaeological Heritage Management at the International Level'. An additional morning's session was devoted to 'Contemporary Claims about Stonehenge' when participants to this overall theme on 'Public Archaeology and Cultural Resource Management' joined with participants of another of the main Congress themes on 'Archaeological "Objectivity" in Interpretation'.

One of the reasons for the choice of this topic at the Congress was the realization of the unique mix of participants who would be attending the meetings. Here, it was felt, was an exciting chance for people from a very diverse set of nations to learn about the legislations of others, as well as the problems, and solutions, which occurred in a variety of countries. Another reason was the feeling that behind many of the concerns of Fourth World participants (and see *Who needs the past?* and *Conflict in the archaeology of living traditions*, both edited by R. Layton) would be misunderstanding, and even fear, of imposed legislations and, at the same time, genuine desire to see the evidence of the past adequately protected for posterity. Finally, although difficult to believe, this would be the first major international occasion which would be devoted to discussion of the issues involved rather than mere formal descriptions of what already exists.

The successful outcome of these expectations can be seen in part at least from the fact that this book contains chapters by authors from 18 different countries, including China, the USSR, Madagascar and Ghana, Venezuela and Ecuador, Australia, Canada, India and Sri Lanka, the USA, and several European nations. The result is the first compendium of information which *should* be common knowledge to all archaeologists, in whatever areas they work. It is significant that, despite the variety of their backgrounds, all the authors are agreed that education of as wide a population as possible is the only real hope for the future.

This book makes it abundantly clear that archaeology as a discipline would be foolish to allow the current divisions which exist in many countries between the academic, the field worker and the legislator, to continue. It also brings to everyone's notice the common need to respond in a coherent and well-planned way to the potentially destructive threats of development and tourism.

Successful and coherent action, however, depends on a clear analysis of the vital question regarding the ownership of a people's heritage. Who is it who should have the right to make decisions about the heritage – the 'owners' of land, the dispossessed with traditional claims, the local community, the nation or state, or even the world? This book reveals how little public discussion appears to have taken place about fundamental questions such as this. On the contrary, legislation is often haphazardly imposed in the wake of colonialism or is revised under the influence of other forces by central governments. Characteristically, those involved in the implementation of such legislation rarely appreciate the real nature of the problems, nor the full import of their actions. In Australia, for example, as revealed by a chapter in this book, the *nature* of cultural 'significance' is not felt to warrant examination, not even who should determine what is deemed to be of significance (nor to whom). Land Rights are taken to be of less long-term interest than site protection by archaeologists and legislators who have not consulted the Aborigines about their wishes in this regard. The enforced handing over of Aboriginal Land to create a Park for tourism and archaeology is presented as some sort of a triumph, and the whole problem of disturbance of burial grounds is simply ignored. In several other cases populations or cultures are simply assumed to be either dying out or to be 'prehistoric' (and see *Conflict in the archaeology of living traditions*, edited by R. Layton). As such, heritage management legislation and its practitioners are often in the same class as at least two other areas of related concern to heritage management (and see *State and society*, edited by J. Gledhill, B. Bender & M. T. Larsen) – site recording and education – which have often also been attacked for their manipulative and imperialist rôle in disenfranchising whole groups and societies from their own pasts, and hence from their identities. The South African decision to choose the arbitrary date of 1652 before which all monuments are deemed to be prehistoric is an extreme example.

Archaeological heritage management in the modern world brings many of the elements of the world situation for the first time into sharp focus. Legislation, in fact, mirrors the political and social conditions of each country in striking but complex ways – intricate balances between notions of private

property, political ideologies, the status of academia in the country concerned, as well as the existence and status of any minority groups. What is
considered appropriate legislation to protect the archaeological heritage at
any one time and place is liable to swift, and even dramatic, change
depending on circumstances. Often these circumstances involve the tourist
industry and, in Third World countries, the need to attract foreign currency.
The sites selected for conservation and protection may often not be those
considered to be the most important by the archaeological community. In
many cases the archaeologists may not be consulted about the choice of site,
and even less about the appropriate way to conserve and display it. But,
ironically, in many instances, it is only through such tourist developments
that any money at all becomes available for the protection of sites. In some of
these instances, as described in this book, the problems and plight of the
archaeologists concerned are both moving and heart rending. The unique
world emphasis of this book brings out these often unrealized aspects of
legislation in a very novel and forceful way.

Central to all the problems of such legislation is the inherent assumption
by archaeologists and national legislators that 'the past' is a national asset
whose rights and interests must take precedence over the more particularized
rights of groups which are often called ethnic (and see *Archaeological
approaches to cultural identity*, edited by S. J. Shennan). There is often an
apparent assumption that governments have the right to some monopoly of
'cultural identities' (and see *The politics of the past*, edited by P. Gathercole &
D. Lowenthal), with the consequent power and entitlement to claim unto
themselves (through land acquisition and financial penalties) the nature and
even the number of sites and areas which will come under their control, and
thus receive public and symbolic national acknowledgement. It is not
surprising, therefore, that this book reveals that what is deemed 'appropriate
legislation' will often vary from a 'nationalistic' and 'patriotic' decision to
present and display only selected kinds of past evidence, to the actual
sanctioned destruction of others – with the 'colour' of the national government in power thus requiring frequent revisions to statutes or acts, as
governments change and as public opinion develops in various ways
through travel, education and the media (and see *The excluded past*, edited by
P. Stone & R. MacKenzie, *The politics of the past*, edited by P. Gathercole
& D. Lowenthal, and *Conflict in the archaeology of living traditions*, edited by R.
Layton). There is little doubt that those most directly affected by such
changes to legislation are rarely consulted in advance, and there is often
considerable tension involved in the application of the law. Those most
clearly touched by such legislation often have great difficulty appreciating
the nature of the 'legitimate interest' asserted by national or state governments. Moreover, the complexities of many of the bureaucracies and of
many of the often complex statutes which may be involved in such situations
discourages genuine involvement and understanding in such legislative
activities. As many chapters in this book emphasize, such legislation is
intimately related to the creation and/or maintenance of cultural identity,

and such depersonalization and compartmentalization of heritage activities is therefore dangerous in the extreme. In this context, the concept of the *world* heritage, now embodied in a set of international conventions and recommendations, has not received adequate public discussion; its impact has yet to be fully appreciated outside a restricted tourist and developmental context. For those whose traditions involve the correct performance of rituals at sacred localities to ensure their continuation, the assumption of rights by 'the world' will be seen as shocking and will be accompanied by little, if any, understanding of such developments or of the supposedly related concepts of 'serene joy and pleasure of the national and international public' (Ch. 21).

It is therefore fundamental to all analysis of cultural heritage legislation to determine not only who should decide what is worth legislative protection and what is not, but also what levels of protection are appropriate. Here again, as this book clearly reveals, the archaeological profession is currently ill-prepared for its legislative rôle. In one sense at least, as the editor discusses in his Introduction, any archaeologist would have to claim, just as does the Australian Aborigine, that *all* sites are at least potentially significant. But it is clear that legislators and governments are, by definition, seeking to grade sites according to some criteria of relative importance since, they insist, total preservation can not be afforded and would, in any case, see the end of 'development' as they define it. Legislation is therefore intimately linked to questions about the appropriate levels and detail of site recording pro- grammes, environmental impact statements, and rescue excavations. These are such vital questions that they need to be addressed in detail, and indeed it has been announced that they will form the basis of future meetings of the World Archaeological Congress.

Meanwhile, this book takes the first vital step forward, namely the open recognition of the problems involved in this aspect of archaeological enquiry and activity. It contains material which must form the basis of ongoing discussions and its world-wide coverage exemplifies the nature of the necessary debate. It is a sign of the growing maturity of archaeology as a discipline that it is beginning to recognize its responsibilities to the wider community. Attempts to understand and analyse its role in the public domain is only belatedly being recognized in most countries within tertiary education, at least as far as undergraduate and postgraduate training in archaeology is concerned (and see *The excluded past*, edited by P. Stone & R. MacKenzie). Hopefully this development will serve to break down some of the barriers between academic archaeologists and those whose prime task is heritage management. Nevertheless, this is only the beginning of the necessary exercise; in many countries strict divisions of responsibility are enshrined in different ministerial portfolios and the problem of intercom- munication will be difficult to achieve. All too often 'culture' is considered the football of politicians, to be switched arbitrarily from ministry to ministry.

This book forces relevant debate into the open, on a world-wide basis. In

such debate lies the only hope for future effective and sophisticated legislation about the cultural heritage, a sophistication which must reflect the
various, and often potentially conflicting, nature of the interests of the people
affected by such legislation. Those involved in archaeological heritage
legislation must be fully informed not only about the nature of archaeological enquiry, not only about development, tourism and educational
needs, but also about the complex and often political interests that all questions of heritage ownership and legislation necessarily entail.

P. J. Ucko
Southampton

Contents

List of contributors   page   vii
Foreword   P. J. Ucko   ix
Preface   Henry Cleere   xxiii

Introduction: the rationale of archaeological heritage
management   Henry Cleere   1

   Historical introduction   1
   Why manage the archaeological heritage?   5
   How should the archaeological heritage be managed?   10
   Who should manage the heritage?   15
   References   17

APPROACHES TO HERITAGE MANAGEMENT

1 Perspectives on the archaeological heritage: history and
  future   Kristian Kristiansen   23

   The archaeological heritage – from political ideology to
     scientific ideology and back   23
   Protection – from private property to general regulations   24
   Walking on a knife-edge: CRM and world history   26

2 World archaeology – the world's cultural heritage
  Joachim Herrmann   30

   References   36

3 Significant until proven otherwise: problems versus representative
  samples   Curtis F. Schaafsma   38

   Relevant until proven irrelevant   48
   Significant until proven insignificant   48
   References   50

4 Science, service and stewardship – a basis for the ideal archaeology of
  the future   William J. Mayer-Oakes   52

   The philosophy: broadened responsibilities   52
   Stewardship   53

US experience in a nutshelll 54
Basis for a universal or holistic archaeology 55
A recommendation 56
Conclusion 57
References 57

5 *The 'cultural dimension of development' – an archaeological approach* Gustav Trotzig 59

References 63

6 *Cultural resource management and environmental education in Venezuela* Mario Sanoja and Iraida Vargas 64

Cultural property and natural resources 64
The rôle of the ecological museum 65
The aims of the ecological museum 66
The ecological museum and environmental education in Venezuela 67
The ecological museum and social aims 69
Reference 69

7 *The ICOMOS International Committee on Archaeological Heritage Management (ICAHM)* Margareta Biörnstad 70

REGIONAL AND COUNTRY STUDIES

8 *'Tread softly for you tread on my bones': the development of cultural resource management in Australia* Josephine Flood 79

The development of heritage protection 79
Aboriginal sites legislation 80
Consultation and involvement 83
Human skeletal remains 87
References 89
Appendix 1. Australia ICOMOS: Objectives for Legislation to Protect the National Estate and Guidelines for Discussions with State Governments 90
Appendix 2. The Australia ICOMOS Charter for the Conservation of Places of Cultural Significance (The Burra Charter) 92
Appendix 3. Guidelines to the Burra Charter 96

9 *The administration of China's archaeological heritage* Zhuang Min 102

10 *Historical development and attendant problems of cultural
   resource management in the Philippines*   Florante G. Henson   109

   Introduction   109
   Laws pertinent to cultural resource management   111
   Major problems   112
   Conclusions   116
   References   116

11 *Cultural resource management in sub-Saharan Africa: Nigeria, Togo
   and Ghana*   Kwasi Myles   118

   Introduction   118
   Nigeria   119
   Togo   123
   Ghana   125
   Acknowledgements   127

12 *Problems in the conservation and restoration of ruined buildings in
   Madagascar*   David Rasamuel   128

   Legislation relating to the cultural heritage   128
   Conservation and restoration practices   132
   Policies for training and research   136
   References   141

13 *Archaeological rescue and conservation in the North Andean
   Area*   Presley Norton   142

   Background   142
   So, who cares?   143
   The Italian caper   144
   It really does matter   144
   Conclusion   145

14 *Cultural resource management at the federal, provincial, municipal
   and corporate levels in southern Ontario, Canada*   Robert J. Pearce 146

   Introduction   146
   Federal level   146
   Provincial level   147
   Municipal level   148
   Corporate level   149
   Conclusion   149
   Notes   150
   References   151

15 *Heritage management and training in England*   Andrew Saunders   152

Definitions   152
Legislation   152
Heritage management   153
Heritage managers   157
Qualifications for heritage managers   160
Training   161

16 *The management of the English landscape*   G. J. Wainwright   164

Objectives   164
The protection of monuments   164
The management of monuments   168
Preservation by record   168
Conclusion   169
References   170

17 *Government archaeology in Northern Ireland*   Ann Hamlin   171

18 *The new Spanish archaeological heritage legislation*
Javier García Fernández   182

Legislation before 1985   182
The importance of the 1978 Constitution for the archaeological
    heritage   184
Archaeological aspects of Law No. 16/1985   184
The organization of archaeological heritage management in
    Spain   190
Legislation in the *Comunidades Autónomas*   192
Notes   192
References   193

19 *Archaeological heritage management in the USSR*   V. M. Masson   195

Bibliography   206

20 *A review of the South African cultural heritage legislation,*
1987   Gabebah Abrahams   207

Historical development   207
Current legislation   208
Discussion   215
Acknowledgements   217
References   217

CASE STUDIES

21 *The Cultural Triangle of Sri Lanka*   Roland Silva 221

Strategies for excavation, conservation and the layout of sites 222
International effort 222
National effort 223
Implementation 223
Excavation 224
Conservation 224
Administration 224
Steering committees 225
Publicity committee 225
Conclusion 226

22 *Cultural resource management in the USDA Forest Service*
Evan I. DeBloois and Kent A. Schneider 227

Introduction 227
The current CRM programme 228
Future directions 231

23 *Cultural resource planning and management in a multiple-use
agency*   Robert Laidlaw 232

Introduction 232
Inventory 232
Management and planning issues 234
Synthesis 234
Conclusion 235

24 *A contractor's perspective of two approaches to cultural resource
management in Arizona*   Jon S. Czaplicki 236

Pertinent Federal legislation 237
The Bureau of Reclamation's Tucson Aqueduct Project:
scheduled cultural resource management planning 238
The Bureau of Land Management's Navajo-Hopi Land
Exchange Project: cultural resource management and crisis
planning 245
Different approaches to cultural resource management 248
Concluding comment 249
Acknowledgements 250
Appendix. Views from 'the other side' 250
References 255

25 *Stonehenge – past and future*   F. N. Golding 256

Note   264

26 *The Stonehenge we deserve*   Peter V. Addyman   265

    Problems of presentation at Stonehenge   265
    The real opportunity at Stonehenge   267
    The HPL scheme for Stonehenge   267
    The presentation philosophy   270

TRAINING AND QUALIFICATION OF
ARCHAEOLOGISTS FOR HERITAGE MANAGEMENT

27 *Learning by doing: this is no way to treat archaeological*
    resources   Hester A. Davis   275

28 *A suggested training scheme for archaeological resource managers in*
    tropical countries   John Alexander   280

29 *Policies for the training and recruitment of archaeologists in*
    India   B. K. Thapar   285

    Early history   285
    Specialized training   287
    Courses for professional training in heritage management 288
    Recruitment   290

30 *Archaeology and conservation training at the international*
    level   N. P. Stanley Price   292

    Introduction: conservation and archaeological management 292
    International training in conservation   294
    Archaeologists and international training   297
    Ethics and professional qualifications   297
    Notes   299
    References   299
    Appendix. ICCROM, ICOM, ICOMOS and IIC   300

31 *The rôle of the professional institution*   Peter V. Addyman 302

    The need for a professional archaeological institution in Great
        Britain   302
    Moves towards the formation of a British archaeological
        institution   303
    The Institute of Field Archaeologists   304

Other professional institutions in Great Britain and the
   problems of regionalism 307
The future for professional institutions in the provision of
   cultural resource management services 307
Reference 307

Index 308

Preface

When it was announced that the XIth Congress of the International Union of Prehistoric and Protohistoric Sciences was to be held in the UK, at Southampton, in 1986, the Council for British Archaeology undertook the organization of a three-day symposium on 'Public archaeology and cultural resource management' as its contribution to the work of the Congress. In the view of the Council, a non-governmental body which has a broad remit connected with every aspect of archaeology and archaeological heritage management in the UK, the presence in Southampton of archaeologists from every part of the world would provide the first truly international forum for discussions at the interface between the academic discipline of archaeology and its public face, a view that was reinforced when the intention of the organizers to ensure participation from every corner of the world was made known. This interface is an ill-defined one, the problems of which had never been discussed at an international gathering before, a circumstance that was both surprising and regrettable in the light of the symbiotic relationship that must exist between the academic and public faces of archaeology.

In the event, the Council for British Archaeology withdrew its support from the World Archaeological Congress. Happily, the recently formed International Committee on Archaeological Heritage Management of ICOMOS (International Council on Monuments and Sites) assumed responsibility for the Symposium, and archaeologists from some 40 countries took part in the three days of discussions based on contributions from nearly 20 countries in all parts of the developed and developing world.

Most of the chapters in this book are based on contributions to the Southampton Symposium, with the addition of five especially commissioned chapters to fill certain regional and conceptual lacunae in the Symposium programme – those by Abrahams, Herrmann, Rasamuel, Thapar and Zhuang. The Editor has also contributed an introductory chapter. The selection of authors from the contributors at Southampton was not easy; it was necessary to ensure a reasonable level of representation to different regions, political systems and administrative structures. It is perhaps worth recording that the chapter on the Philippines was radically revised after the Congress, and reflects the greater freedom of speech that now obtains in that country. The chapter on South Africa was invited from a Cape Malay archaeologist who came to the UK in 1986 at the invitation of the British Council.

It is hoped that the result will be acceptable to as wide a spectrum of readers as possible. Any apparent bias towards Europe and North America should be recognized as inevitable, given that the new discipline of archaeological heritage management was evolved in the USA and spread first to Europe. To avoid too heavy a dependence on US authors, the chapter on professional institutions was commissioned from the UK rather than the USA, where the first regulatory body of this kind was set up. The international level of activity is represented by chapters on the Unesco-sponsored Cultural Triangle Project in Sri Lanka (Ch. 22) and the work of ICCROM and other international agencies in training for conservation and other aspects of heritage management (Ch. 31). The chapters are grouped into four sections, dealing with approaches to heritage management, regional and country studies, case studies, and the training and qualification of archaeologists for archaeological heritage management.

Archaeological heritage management is a new field of professional endeavour, a child of the years since the end of World War II. It is still striving to define its objectives in the context of the social and economic imperatives of the later 20th century, and to establish a basic philosophy and a common methodology. It is hoped that this book will make a positive contribution to the resolution of these problems, and will assist in the creation of a new generation of archaeological heritage managers.

The Editor is deeply grateful to all those friends and colleagues who responded to his call to take part in the Symposium and to write chapters for this book. His thanks are also due to those colleagues who shared the chairmanship of the Symposium sessions with him – Joachim Herrmann and Roland Silva – and to Lyn Greenwood who compiled the index. Finally, he welcomes the opportunity to express his infinite debt to the Series Editor, Peter Ucko, for his many constructive suggestions during the planning of both the Symposium and the book, and for his forbearance in the face of so many delays in the production programme.

Henry Cleere
London

ARCHAEOLOGICAL HERITAGE MANAGEMENT IN THE MODERN WORLD

Introduction: the rationale of archaeological heritage management

HENRY CLEERE

Historical introduction

The academic discipline of archaeology and the administrative function of archaeological heritage management are twins that have developed at different rates. As a number of treatises on the history of the subject (for example, Daniel 1981) have demonstrated, archaeology owes its origins to those peripatetic scholars like William Camden, William Stukeley and Ole Worm who travelled their native lands, recording the material remains of their ancestors, and to the collectors, many of them royal, who began creating the 'cabinets of curiosities' that formed the basis of so many famous national and university museums – in Copenhagen, London, Oxford and many other European cities.

Archaeological heritage management may be deemed to have begun with the Swedish Royal Proclamation of 1666, declaring all objects from antiquity to be the property of the Crown. This was a departure from the widespread medieval fiscal prerogative of Treasure Trove, or the Royal Fifth of the Spanish monarchy that operated in the Americas, which saw gold and silver objects from antiquity solely in terms of their financial convertibility; for the first time the intrinsic importance of the remains of the past was acknowledged in a national legal code. The despoliation of the remains of Herculaneum in the mid-18th century provoked the Bourbon king of Naples to issue a decree to bring the buried heritage of his realm under juridical control a century later (D'Agostino 1984), and Denmark followed suit in the first decade of the 19th century (Kristiansen 1984). By the end of the century the ancient monuments of most of Europe were covered by protective legislation of varying degrees of efficacy, and the USA enacted its first Federal Antiquities law in 1906 (McGimsey & Davis 1984). The UK passed its first Ancient Monuments Protection Act in 1882 (Cleere 1984), although this was, somewhat surprisingly, a relatively toothless measure compared with the earlier (1863) law that had been enacted in Imperial India (Thapar 1984).

Although legislation was in force over much of the world by the outbreak of World War II, the profession of archaeological heritage manager was still embryonic in many countries. The few names which come immediately to mind from the 19th century – J. J. A. Worsaae in Denmark, General Pitt Rivers in the UK, Prosper Merimée, the saviour of Carcassonne, in France, and Auguste Mariette in Egypt – were all full-time directors of antiquities services, but they were usually working either alone or at best with a handful of paid and largely untrained assistants. Excavation was a part-time activity, for the most part in the hands of university teachers, museum curators or gentleman amateurs, and the maintenance and presentation of great monuments, particularly those outside Europe, was generally entrusted to officials with little, if any, awareness of or concern for archaeology (it is interesting to note that this is a complaint voiced by Rasamuel in respect of contemporary Madagascar in Ch. 12). Decisions regarding excavations or presentation were often taken for ideological reasons – witness the archaeological policies of Italy during the Mussolini regime in, for example, Rhodes (or Rome, for that matter). Few countries outside Scandinavia had developed policies towards the archaeological heritage, based on equal concern for public interest and academic priorities.

The end of World War II saw the beginnings of archaeological heritage management as an integral component of social and economic planning. The devastation of 1939–45 provided boundless scope for archaeological initiatives in many countries. Excavations took place in many of the war-torn cities of Europe, of which the work on Roman Cologne around the Dom is probably the most outstanding. Many opportunities for the investigation of historic town centres in Europe were lost: in London, for example, municipal avarice meant that much of its history was obliterated without any recording (Grimes 1968). Nevertheless, the concept of 'rescue' or 'salvage' archaeology in advance of development or redevelopment became firmly rooted in the archaeological consciousness – and, more reluctantly perhaps, in that of officialdom.

It has been, however, the immense economic, political, social and technological changes since 1945 that have done most to foster the development of archaeological heritage management. Postwar reconstruction was followed by the worldwide economic boom of the later 1950s and 1960s. This was accompanied by the coming to nationhood of many colonial territories, notably in Africa and Asia. Economic prosperity in the older nations resulted in substantial investment in and aid to the developing countries, making use of the technological and scientific advances triggered by the strategic exigencies of the war years.

Suddenly, in the 1960s, development became the dominant theme. In the developed countries major highways spread in all directions, historic town centres became the prey of property developers and speculators (not infrequently the civic authorities themselves), mineral extraction tore gaping holes in the landscape, the new 'agribusiness' converted areas of traditional countryside or wilderness into cereal prairies, and new towns were built to house expanding populations. With the growth of affluence tourism became a major industry, long stretches of quiet coastlines were submerged under ribbon hotel development, and the visitor pressure on major historic sites such as Stonehenge (the subject of Chs. 25 and 26) and the Athenian Acropolis began to put the monuments themselves in jeopardy from sheer physical attrition. Affluence, along with the availability of relatively inexpensive detection and earth-moving equipment, also created a new form of threat to the archaeological heritage: the long-established *tombaroli* of Etruria and the *huaqueros* of Central and South America (see Ch. 13) were joined by legions of pot-hunters, often working with mechanical back-hoes, in the American Southwest and the treasure hunters of Europe, with their electronic metal-detectors, and international financial backing became available for the underwater despoliation of historic shipwrecks in the Caribbean, the China Seas and the Mediterranean. (It is interesting to observe that scientists have been guilty of what amounts to looting in South Africa, as indicated in Ch. 20). The spoils of this commercialized looting has swelled the illicit trade in cultural property, which was the subject of a Unesco Convention in 1971 (still to be ratified by many of the richer developed nations).

In the developing countries the exploitation of natural resources resulted in widespread deforestation and mineral extraction, and industry and highway construction devastated large tracts of hitherto undisturbed natural and historical landscapes (see Ch. 5): this is typified by Brazil, where so much of the virgin Amazon jungle has been destroyed in recent years, and where iron-ore mining has turned large areas into lunar-type landscapes. In certain of the better-endowed developing countries large-scale programmes of industrialization were put into effect – in India and Brazil, in particular – without any regard for their impact on the environment, whether natural or historic. At the same time there was a demographic explosion throughout the entire Third World, thanks to improvements in medical science, which created a further source of threat to the heritage.

The end of the period of unremitting economic growth in the early 1970s did little to relieve this pressure. The need to maximize agricultural yields all over the world meant that erosion of the non-urban environment continued apace, while the demand for alternative sources of energy to replace oil stepped up mineral extraction in certain areas: the fate of the medieval town of Most in northern Bohemia, sacrificed to reach the rich deposits of lignite on which it was built, is a paradigm of this situation (though in fairness to the Czechoslovak Government it should be recorded that the state energy organization financed a long and detailed archaeological investigation as the town was being quarried away). The availability of abundant natural gas from the North Sea and the need to build long pipelines created a new source of threat to the archaeological heritage (Catherall *et al.* 1984).

Suddenly environmental protection became a major international preoccupation. Following a major conference in Helsinki in 1972, the United Nations established the UN Environmental Programme (UNEP), and funds became available to mitigate the impact of development. The USA had enacted its National Environmental Policy Act (NEPA) in 1969, and this was followed by a series of measures, one of which, the Archaeological and Historic Preservation Act of 1974, provided substantial funding for archaeological work in advance of all Federally financed projects (McGimsey & Davis 1984). The operation of these policies is discussed in Chapters 22, 23 and 24. The official adoption of environmental protection policies had followed a swell in grass-roots public opinion, which has now become a significant political force in some countries as the Green Movement.

In most countries, however, the importance of archaeological conservation as the historical dimension of the heritage was largely overlooked. It had long been conceived as such in countries such as Denmark, where the archaeological heritage managers constitute one branch of Fredningsstyrelsen, the environmental agency, alongside their wildlife and landscape conservation colleagues (Kristiansen 1984), and the USA adopted the historical element as an essential component of all Environmental Impact Assessment in respect of Federal projects. Over much of the world, however, antiquities services stand apart from other governmental environment protection agencies: see, for example, Chapter 11, which discusses the administrative systems in three West African countries. It is significant that the breakthrough in the UK which led to significantly increased funding for rescue excavations, under sustained pressure from the archaeological community, both amateur and professional through the ginger group Rescue, was directed almost exclusively to urban archaeology (Schofield & Leech 1987, see also Ch. 15).

Nevertheless, the development pressures of the 1960s and the environmental movement of the 1970s had a profound effect on archaeological heritage management. It is significant that almost every European country enacted new antiquities legislation during the 1970s, to replace the outdated and ineffectual statutes of a less stressful pre-war era; the most recent is the Spanish legislation of 1985, which is the subject of Chapter 18. To meet the increased demands of this legislation, there was a substantial increase in personnel to carry out the necessary operations of recording, designation and excavation, while the pressures of increased tourism led to a radical reappraisal of presentation methods in several countries. All of these changes took place, however, under extreme pressure; only in the USA was there initially any apparent awareness of the growth of a new profession with a need to establish its own philosophical and ethical framework, to identify its academic and social relationships and obligations, and to evolve its own methodologies. For the most part archaeologists were plunged headlong into routines that were laid down in a more leisurely age and woefully inadequate to cope with the pressures of the later-20th century. The implications of this new situation are discussed in several country studies in this book (China in Ch. 9, the Philippines in Ch. 10, Madagascar in Ch. 12, Ecuador in Ch. 13, Canada in Ch. 14, England in Chs. 15 & 16, Northern Ireland in Ch. 17 and the USSR in Ch. 19). As a result archaeological heritage management is still confused and disorientated, in search of an identity.

The concepts of 'cultural resource management' (CRM), 'public archaeology' and 'conservation archaeology' (which are largely synonymous, or at least overlapping) were developed in a series of important studies published in the USA in the 1970s (McGimsey 1972, Lipe & Lindsay 1974, McGimsey

& Davis 1977, King *et al.* 1977, Schiffer & Gumerman 1977, Dickens & Hill 1978), all based almost exclusively on US practice. These were to a large extent practical manuals on how to deal with the US system, but Lipe (1974) published a seminal paper setting archaeological heritage management in its wider context, which he brought up to date 10 years later in a classic paper (Lipe 1984). Chapters 1–4, by one Danish, one East German and two leading US conservation archaeologists, are important new contributions to this debate. The ethical problems associated with heritage management have been tackled by the professional bodies established in the USA (the Society of Professional Archaeologists) and the UK (the Institute of Field Archaeologists) in their respective Codes of Conduct (see Chs 26 & 30), but the most extensive treatment of this important subject so far to appear in print again emanates from the USA (Green 1984).

The first attempt to study archaeological heritage management on a supranational, comparative level was in 1978, an initiative taken by archaeologists and heritage managers in the German Democratic Republic (Herrmann 1981). At the same time valuable work was being done by the International Council of Museums (ICOM) and the Council of Europe (Burnham 1974, Hingst & Lipowschek 1975, Council of Europe 1979) in bringing together legislative texts relating to the protection of antiquities and monuments, with commentaries. Unesco is currently publishing the texts of legislation relating to the protection of movable cultural property from all of its member countries (Unesco 1985 onwards), but the most important publication in this field is probably the ambitious series of volumes being produced by two distinguished Australian jurists (O'Keefe & Prott 1984).

The value of international consultation and comparison in the field of archaeological heritage has been slow to be realized by its practitioners. Apart from the pioneer East German volume (Herrmann 1981, see also Ch. 2), only one other publication has attempted to deal with this subject (Cleere 1984), and that was restricted to critical papers on the systems in operation in 12 countries around the world, owing to financial constraints. The regional initiative represented by the three New World Conferences on Rescue Archaeology held in Ecuador (1981), the USA (1984) and Venezuela (1987) have so far produced two volumes of proceedings (Wilson & Loyola 1982, Wilson 1987) which contain much that is of value about the diverse facets of heritage management extending beyond the 'rescue archaeology' of their titles. So far the American example has not been followed in other regions, but the ICOMOS International Committee on Archaeological Heritage Management (see Ch. 7) is planning a series of regional conferences, starting with a major symposium in Stockholm in 1988.

Why manage the archaeological heritage?

An awareness of the past is a characteristic that is unique to *Homo sapiens*. In less-developed societies myth and history intermingle to create a tradition that is a living reality – the Dreamtime of the Australian Aborigines (Flood 1983) is a vital element in creating social awareness and cohesion, for example, whereas ancestor worship is an important component of many religions. This is not to imply that in such societies there is no awareness of the linear dimension of time: it is highly developed and continuously renewed through oral transmission. The past is a living component of present-day life in such societies. This identity of past and present is often closely associated with specific locations and structures, which may be devoid of any tangible human artefacts, such as many Aboriginal ritual sites (see Ch. 8). However, even without this spiritual foundation, an interest in the past is manifested widely among contemporary 'developed' societies. Many treasure-hunters are genuinely motivated in this way, robbing archaeological sites not for financial gain, but solely to build up personal collections of 'relics' – not dissimilar to the 17th and 18th century 'cabinets of curiosities' that formed the basis of so many great European museums. The greater mobility of modern developed societies leads to a search for roots, which may take many forms – an interest in the previous owners of a dwelling-house or in the history of an adopted community, or a concern to delve into family history.

The formation of attitudes towards the past has been the subject of several recent studies in the UK (Lowenthal & Binney 1981, Lowenthal 1985), but these attitudes are so ill-formulated in the minds of most individuals that it is difficult to draw any valid analytical conclusions. The one element that seems to be common to them all involves the concept of identity or identification – a sense of belonging to a place or a tradition.

In less-developed societies this is enshrined in religious or spiritual beliefs. The members of a tribe or clan are bound together by their religion, which embodies the corporate traditions of the group and is usually expressed in tangible terms by association with certain sites or constructions. In such cases, however, the identification is restricted to those material elements that have a direct significance in connection with the spiritual apparatus; thus a ritual or funerary site may be sacrosanct and inalienable, but other manifestations of the group's social development, such as dwellings or fortifications, or elements of this kind lying within their territory that have no cultural associations with the group, may be demolished or neglected as having no significance, even though from an archaeological point of view they are equally meaningful.

This restricted concern for archaeological and historical artefacts can, of course, be identified in more developed societies. In Europe the remains of classical antiquity were used as quarries for the great medieval palaces and cathedrals; the medieval and Renaissance pontiffs ransacked Imperial Rome to bedeck their constructions, only the Pantheon surviving intact, and that by virtue of being converted into a church. The Reformation in England saw a similar disregard for the magnificent abbeys and monasteries of the outlawed Roman Catholic orders, which were for the most part deliberately slighted to provide building materials for their new secular masters, where they were not used as the cores of new private dwellings. It is change of use that has ensured the survival of many of the masterpieces of antiquity, the most famous being perhaps Constantine's Santa Sophia, in Istanbul. This lack of concern for earlier cultures is not confined to Europe and the Mediterranean lands: the successive masters of Delhi showed scant heed for the works of their predecessors – using those works as sources of raw materials, or simply allowing them to subside into ruins.

It was probably the Renaissance and the ensuing Enlightenment, with the revival of historical studies as a branch of learning, stemming from the classical historians, that created the relatively modern notion of cultural continuity – the linear view of history – as distinct from the spiritual continuity of other communities. Contemporary societies were perceived as having cultural links extending back over time, so the relics of earlier phases were seen to be important documents in recording that continuity, and as such they became worthy of care and preservation. This concept was slow to achieve recognition: the debates in the British Parliament during the passage of the first Ancient Monuments Protection Act in 1882 were notable for some remarkably reactionary views. One Conservative aristocrat queried the concept of 'national monuments', which he dismissed as the 'absurd relics' of the 'barbarian predecessors' of the English, 'who found time hanging heavily on their hands and set about piling up great barrows and rings of stones' (Kennet 1972, p. 25)! Nevertheless, this basic philosophical tenet is now widely accepted in many countries of the world, and it underlies much modern heritage management.

Few, if any, countries can, however, lay claim to unbroken cultural continuity of any kind. In some there is a serious problem stemming from traumatic cultural discontinuities. For example, in the USA a European culture was abruptly and fiercely imposed upon an indigenous culture. The earlier European settlers were openly contemptuous of the Native Americans, and they made every effort, either deliberately or out of indifference, to erase the monuments of the pre-contact societies. Of the many thousands of earthworks of all kinds in the Mississippi valley that were surveyed by early antiquaries such as Caleb Atwater or the famous partnership of Ephraim Squier and Edwin Davis in the 19th century, only a minute proportion have survived to the present, and even the Great Serpent Mount, nearly 400 m long and 4 m wide, was only saved from obliteration by the dedication of an archaeologist, Frederick Putnam (Fagan 1977). Further south many great pre-Columbian monuments in Central and South America were either obliterated for political motives (as was the case with Moctezuma's great capital of Tenochtitlán) or slighted and left for the tropical forests to engulf.

A situation of this kind can be exacerbated by political considerations. Ex-colonial powers often left their newly independent ex-colonies a legacy of excellent heritage management legislation (see, for example, Chs 10, 11 & 21). During their two centuries of rule the British endowed India with excellent protective legislation and a well-organized antiquities service, both of which continued after Independence in 1947 (Thapar 1984). India's record in protecting and preserving its monuments stands comparison with that of any country in the world at present, with one exception. The British were in India for more than two centuries and, whatever the ethical considerations involved, this period constitutes a significant phase in the history of the subcontinent, one that left its mark in the form of tangible monuments. Sadly, until comparatively recently monuments of the Raj have been accorded the lowest priority in heritage management in India, except where they have been taken over for contemporary functions, as in New Delhi or in military cantonments. As a result the task of conservation involved in dealing with the surviving colonial monuments is of considerable proportions. A comparable situation obtains in many other ex-colonial territories, such as Togo (see Ch. 11).

The end of colonialism in the postwar period and the birth of new nations has seen the promotion of archaeological heritage management in a more positive sense, however. Colonialism created a discontinuity in many of these countries, which is being counteracted by the use of monuments to demonstrate a continuous cultural identity within which the colonial period was no more than an irrelevant episode. The supreme example of this phenomenon must surely be that of the former British colonial territory of Southern Rhodesia, which elected on achieving its independence to take the name of its greatest archaeological monument, Zimbabwe. This use of the archaeological heritage to establish cultural identity in former colonial territories is widespread, and not solely a 20th century phenomenon; the Spanish ex-colonies of Latin America, notably Mexico, have made extensive use of their precolonial antiquities to consolidate the sense of cultural continuity and identity, as a visit to the Anthropological Museum in Mexico City quickly confirms. The importance of archaeological remains in establishing cultural identity in Latin America has been powerfully stated by Sanoja (1982, see also Ch. 6).

With older nations which have survived as discrete political entities for many centuries, such as France or England in Europe, the innate awareness of cultural identity is such that material symbols of this kind are perhaps hardly needed. The average French or English man or woman does not need archaeological or historical monuments as a reminder of his or her Frenchness or Englishness; this is inborn and reinforced daily in many ways. Language is perhaps the primary and most obvious carrier of this tradition. The secure cultural identity of such nations contrasts with that of others, such as the Poles or the Jews, for whom monuments are potent symbols of nationhood: one only has to think of the reconstruction of the Old City in Warsaw, or the excavations at Masada.

This inward awareness of cultural identity, coupled with the increasingly materialistic nature of modern society in most of the developed countries, puts monuments in such countries at especial risk. Paradoxically, it is probably a form of revulsion against this very materialism and an inchoate desire to return to older values, however illusory, that lies behind much of the popular appeal of monuments of the past.

Another important factor underlying the protection of monuments is their educational value. The teaching of national history is universal, and modern teaching methods call for the use of aids of many kinds. Especially for younger children, the appeal of an historic site or structure visited in connection with formal classroom teaching of a specific period or topic is strong. The imagination of the child can be stimulated much more effectively by ruined castle walls or ancient burial mounds than by any amount of formal teaching or reading. The value of archaeological sites and monuments is now recognized universally as being an incomparable teaching aid (PACT 1985, 1986, 1987, Cracknell & Corbishley 1986, Council of Europe 1988) which is widely used in all parts of the world. It is interesting to note that official policy in Northern Ireland is directed primarily towards the presentation of monuments for the benefit of the local population and for schoolchildren.

At a less-elevated level but of rapidly growing importance is the rôle of monuments in tourism. Mass tourism is a feature of modern economic life, both nationally and internationally; although much of it is directed exclusively towards sunny beaches or snow-covered pistes, historical and archaeological monuments and sites form an important element in much tourism. 'Cultural tourism', visiting primarily monuments and art galleries, represents only a minor proportion of the visitors to such monuments: for every 'cultural' tour group visiting Ephesus or the Pyramids at Teotihuacan and spending several hours studying them in detail there are 20 groups arriving by bus *en route* between one visit and the next, spending half an hour in a hurried and unprepared tour before buying their souvenirs and boarding their buses for their next destination. The value of such tours is debatable; for the individuals concerned it is probably minimal, since they will have little time to absorb even the basic facts about these important and complex sites. Nevertheless, there is an intangible benefit in that many of them will be almost subconsciously influenced by a feeling of respect for the past and for the human achievement that such monuments represent – though few are likely to be able to articulate these feelings in such terms – and as a result they may well be instinctively sympathetic to 'archaeology' when they are confronted with it in their home environments, whether in a television programme or an excavation in their home town. Archaeological heritage managers should not be too dismissive of mass tourism of this kind, since it can only serve to improve public attitudes towards their work, at the same time probably contributing financially to their continued work. It is vital, however, that the quality of presentation at monuments should be high and that it should be directed at more than one level of visitor, otherwise it may prove to be counterproductive by sending visitors away with a sense of disgruntlement and dissatisfaction.

The final justification for archaeological heritage management – at the same time by no means the least important, but equally not the most important – is the protection of the database for the academic discipline of archaeology. Archaeologists are always avid for data, both qualitative and quantitative. Without any form of heritage management the stock of sites and monuments would dwindle rapidly: the rate of destruction from all sources of prehistoric monuments in the UK in the past decades has led some heritage managers to estimate that all save the most outstanding, such as Stonehenge or Maiden Castle, would have disappeared by the end of this century through the usual processes of destruction without the protection of the legislation and its administrative infrastructure. The intensity of industrial and agricultural development in the *Land* of Nordrhein-Westfalen, in the Federal Republic of Germany, and the difficulties of achieving preservation under the *Land* land-use planning and monuments legislation have meant that the annual expenditure on rescue excavation in recent years has regularly exceeded the total rescue budget for the whole of the UK. Inadequate or underfunded archaeological heritage management in a country with a high level of development can quickly result in the almost total disappearance of the archaeological database without record, an ever-present danger in the Third World, as Trotzig cogently points out in Chapter 5.

To summarize, therefore, archaeological heritage management has an ideological basis in establishing cultural identity, linked with its educational function, it has an economic basis in tourism, and it has an academic function in safeguarding the database.

How should the archaeological heritage be managed?

Since the archaeological heritage is governed by legislation, which must be deemed to have been enacted in the public interest, and is in most countries in the ownership of the state or other public institutions, it must be accepted as axiomatic that it should be managed in the public interest. This concept of management for public benefit or stewardship is treated at length by Mayer-Oakes in Chapter 4.

There are, however, many problems in defining that public for whose benefit the heritage is being managed, which is multifaceted. In its broadest sense the public must be seen as the body of taxpayers whose money is being used in its name to finance antiquities services, survey and excavation, compensation for taking monuments out of cultivation, the conservation, presentation and promotion of monuments, and much more. Then there is the tourist public, whose entrance fees and purchases of souvenirs and guidebooks make a substantial contribution to maintenance and promotional costs. There is the public that visits monuments and sites for educational purposes – schoolchildren, students and avocational archaeologists. In many countries there is that public for whom archaeological sites and monuments are potent symbols of an indigenous culture that is threatened or submerged by an alien intrusive culture (see Ch. 8). There is the academic public for whom the archaeological heritage forms an essential resource base. The demands of these disparate groups on the archaeological heritage differ in quality and in degree, and not infrequently they come into conflict with one another.

In many countries further complications are introduced by the existence of property rights under the law. Those countries with fully socialist constitutions experience no difficulties in this respect: all land and property are owned by the state, which can manage them in any way that it sees fit (see Ch. 19). In the Common Law countries such as the UK and many of its former dominions and colonies (including the USA), however, property rights in land are absolute, without the fundamental legal concept of all of the territory of a sovereign nation being vested in the state which exists in other legal systems. A frequently recurring motif in debates on successive protection measures introduced into the British Parliament is encapsulated in the description by a Conservative landowner of the 1882 Act as 'a measure of spoliation . . . legalising burglary by daylight . . . invading the right of private property' (Kennet 1972, p. 24). García Fernández (Ch. 18) rightly stresses the revolutionary nature of the recent Spanish legislation, which overrides entrenched property rights. Only in the Scandinavian countries, with their long traditions of heritage protection, does the ideal enunciated by Lord Curzon in a Parliamentary debate on the 1913 UK Ancient Monuments Act seem to have become deeply rooted in the national consciousness: 'Owners now recognise that they are not merely owners of private property, but trustees to the nation at large' (Kennet 1972, p. 35).

Given the differing constraints under which archaeological management organizations have to work, it is not an easy task to lay down general principles. Certain common determining factors can, however, be identified.

The basis for all archaeological heritage management must be the identification and recording of that heritage. In some countries the mere act of registration constitutes legal protection, but this is an exceptional situation. There are archaeological managers who take the view that all archaeological resources must be considered to be relevant until they are proved to be irrelevant (see Introduction & Ch. 3), and so some form of protection must be given to all antiquities. By far the majority of national heritage management services are compelled by legal, political or financial constraints to operate some form of selectivity in respect of monuments protection and management. If the selection is to be valid in academic and cultural terms, then it must be representative, and a representative sample can only be decided on the basis of a knowledge of something approaching the total stock, which can then be evaluated according to carefully formulated objective criteria for selection (see Ch. 16, Darvill 1987). Fundamental to this process is systematic and comprehensive field surveying and recording, of the type begun in Denmark by Worsaae as early as 1873 (Kristiansen 1984, p. 22).

The popular perception of archaeology is that of excavation, and that of the archaeologist as excavator. This is hardly surprising, since major excavations such as the tomb of Tutankhamun, the terracotta warriors of

Xi'an or the 16th century English warship, the *Mary Rose*, provide the 'stories' so beloved of the media. For archaeologists themselves excavation is perhaps the most enjoyable aspect of their work, too. Excavation must obviously continue to be a major source of basic archaeological data, but its rôle in heritage management is a somewhat ambivalent one. The pressures of modern society have created a demand for 'rescue' or 'salvage' excavations that soak up most of the available archaeological manpower, whether in major international projects such as those in Sri Lanka (Ch. 21), in Nubia (Säve-Söderbergh 1987) or at Carthage, prestige excavations such as those at the Louvre in Paris or the Parliament building in Stockholm, or the more run-of-the-mill mitigation excavations occasioned by pipeline projects or urban redevelopment (Ch. 24). Government finance for non-rescue excavations, initiated with solely research objectives, is severely limited in every part of the world, and the obligatory funding of excavations by developers that is an expanding feature of the world scene is by definition applicable only in a rescue context.

It has been argued that all rescue excavation is research, in that its results contribute to the overall archaeological research database (Rahtz 1974, pp. 55–6). Again, financial constraints impose selectivity in rescue archaeology, and many heritage managers take the view that the research potential of a threatened site should be the primary criterion in selection. This view is not universally accepted, however, Kristiansen (Ch. 1) argues strongly against research potential being given priority in any decisions relating to protection or any other aspect of heritage management. Nevertheless, in pragmatic terms, given the constraints under which heritage management operates in so many countries, and the importance of the heritage as a resource database, it is difficult to support this purist argument, however worthy it may appear in idealistic terms. The implementation of any form of selectivity must inevitably be conditioned by several extraneous factors – legislative, administrative, economic, political and ideological – and it is difficult to enunciate general principles in this respect.

The second determining factor in relation to heritage management that does seem to have universal applicability is the need for it to be closely integrated with land-use planning. The Danish system (Kristiansen 1984) is an admirable paradigm of this aspect of heritage management, and similar systems apply in the UK and in Federally owned territories in the USA (Newcomb 1979 contains a perceptive comparison of the three systems). In each of these countries – and, indeed, in several other countries – all planning decisions are passed in review to determine their impact on the archaeological heritage, and appropriate action is taken to mitigate that impact. This may take the form of intensive survey and selective excavation, as exemplified by the Unesco-sponsored Nubia Project (Säve-Söderbergh 1987) or on a slightly more modest scale by the Cache River project in Arkansas (Schiffer & House 1975). The involvement of archaeological heritage managers at an early stage of the planning of projects of this kind can, however, serve to lessen their impact on the sites and monuments on their provisional routes, which are varied so as to avoid as many of these as possible, only those that come to light during construction or which cannot be avoided for technical reasons associated with the project demanding rescue excavation. In such cases the involvement of heritage managers with planning should not cease at the feasibility stage, but should continue with line management throughout the relevant phases of the project, so as to avoid the undesirable 'crisis management' situations graphically described by Czaplicki in Chapter 24.

Land-use planning as practised in most countries relates to every aspect of the landscape, and man has left his imprint over much of the world's surface. The current environment must be conceived of as possessing more than one dimension. It is inhabited not only by man, but also by countless biological species, living in a state of delicate balance. It also has aesthetic qualities of especial significance to modern man. Human operations of all kinds – forestry, agriculture, road-building, mineral extraction, industrial activity, etc. – can disturb this balance and degrade these aesthetic qualities, to the detriment of future generations. It is often forgotten – not least by archaeologists – that the sites and monuments of antiquity constitute the historical dimension of this global environment, and that their interests are intimately bound up with those of the wildlife and aesthetic dimensions. Ancient woodland may preserve high-standing archaeological remains of an ancient landscape that has everywhere else been obliterated by ploughing, for example, whereas certain types of ruined archaeological site may form havens for endangered species of animals and plants. There is thus a strong community of interest between the different conservation agencies, yet in so many parts of the world this interdependence has not been appreciated and the conservation agencies operate in isolation from one another. A third significant factor in any archaeological heritage management operation must therefore be the establishment of close links and common policies between the different facets of environmental protection. The Danish model is admirable, with the ancient monuments protection service completely integrated into a conservation agency that covers every aspect of environmental heritage protection, including wildlife, landscape, coastal protection, and much more (Kristiansen 1984).

So much for the less-visible, though nonetheless fundamental, aspect of heritage management. Its more conspicuous face, in terms of the general public, is represented by the sites and monuments that are managed and promoted for public enjoyment and edification. It has to be assumed that these are adequately conserved and maintained, out of respect to the monuments to themselves as much as in the interests of their potential visitors. The debate on the level of restoration and reconstruction that is permissible is an endless one. The philosophy behind the stringent criteria applied for over a century in the UK is admirably summarized by Thompson (1981), and will not be recapitulated here. The Venice Charter, which enshrines the basic doctrine of ICOMOS (see Ch. 7), sets its face resolutely against any level of reconstruction beyond anastylosis (the replacement of elements in locations from which they can be demonstrated to have derived).

It is undeniable that reconstruction of archaeological monuments has proceeded considerably further in many parts of the world, from the Wilhelmine excesses of the Saalburg in western Germany to that triumph of scholarly re-creation, Colonial Williamsburg. Although the academic objections to high levels of reconstruction on inadequate evidence are wholly valid, it cannot be gainsaid that many archaeological sites make impossible intellectual and imaginative demands on the lay visitor. Little effort is required to appreciate Chichén Itzá, Herculanaeum or the Great Wall of China, perhaps, but many visitors with high expectations must leave Troy, Carthage or the Roman Forum with a sense of disappointment coupled with bafflement and, even more serious, a loss of sympathy towards the archaeological heritage.

The onus upon archaeological heritage managers to make those components of the heritage of which they are public guardians accessible, both physically and intellectually, to the whole range of needs that the public embraces is therefore another common factor. This obligation to present and interpret is overriding, and it should involve making the fullest use of modern techniques of mass communication. There is the thinnest of dividing lines here between effective interpretation and the creation of what have been described as 'archaeological Disneylands'. This does not mean that the methods of Orlando have no place in archaeological interpretation: the remarkably effective Jorvik Viking Centre in York has successfully adapted the electric cars of Disneyworld to take visitors around its re-created 10th century street and the excavations upon which this was based. The York experiment has succeeded, largely thanks to the predominant rôle assigned to professional archaeologists in its conception and execution, and it does not merit the implied criticism in a recent diatribe against 'the heritage industry' (Hewison 1987, pp. 83–4). In less-sensitive and responsible hands, however, attempts to emulate the success of the Jorvik Viking Centre may prove disastrous.

The two chapters on Stonehenge in this book (Chs 25 & 26) represent two approaches to the problem of presenting and interpreting a great prehistoric monument which attracts nearly a million visitors each year. The English Heritage approach (Ch. 25) is cautious in its innovations; conscious of the fragility of the monument under the impact of increased visitor numbers, it has chosen to remove its interpretation centre and parking facilities some distance from the monument itself, and to require visitors to proceed to the monument on foot, a solution which will inevitably result in a constraint being placed upon visits (and consequently on potential revenue). The emphasis in the proposals from Heritage Projects (whose experience was gained with the Jorvik Viking Centre) is placed, by contrast, on maximizing visitor numbers by ensuring a smooth and rapid throughput (though allowing for a more leisurely and extensive tour by more-serious visitors). There is no doubt that the English Heritage solution will be more in harmony with the ambience of the monument itself: it may prove worthy of study by those heritage managers wrestling with the problem of other 'honeypot monuments', such as the Athenian Acropolis or the Taj Mahal.

The interpretation of the heritage has wide ramifications, going beyond the presentation of monuments. It requires the archaeologist involved in its management to ascertain the requirements of the public in its many different guises, and to ensure that there is printed and audio-visual material available to explain the significance of the heritage and to help visitors, whether tourists or local residents, schoolchildren or professionals, to understand what they are seeing. The excavation monograph must be prepared for the scholar, the worksheet for the schoolchild, the card guide for the general tourist, and the works of synthesis and survey for the informed layman and the 'cultural tourist'. It is too much to expect professional heritage managers to produce such a broad spectrum of publications, but their expertise must be available to the professionals in the field of communications who have the requisite skills.

Who should manage the heritage?

Archaeological heritage management as a distinct professional technique has developed in an unco-ordinated way: heritage managers had been in post and hard at work all over the world for many years before the need was belatedly recognized for the establishment of a methodological and ethical framework within which they should work. The UK system (Ch. 15) is typical of the way in which recruitment and training have operated in the older-established services. The system was essentially that of apprenticeship as used in the traditional crafts – 'sitting alongside old Charlie' and learning-by-doing under the tutelage of an old hand. Young graduate archaeologists have been entering antiquities services straight from their academic university studies, without any training in the special skills needed in management and administration.

The expansion of heritage management in the 1970s that is described above resulted in the creation of many new posts in several countries, and the traditional system of training proved inadequate to produce a properly trained new generation: there were just not enough 'old Charlies' available to look after the myriads of apprentices. In the developing countries the situation was even worse, under the impact of industrial and agricultural development: in many cases new antiquities services had to be formed from the handful of available indigenous archaeologists who had been trained in the academic discipline of archaeology and had no tradition of heritage management, but who could not be spared to spend periods in developed countries to study their methods. As a result, in all but a handful of countries, a great deal of bad heritage management resulted during the 1970s in both the developed and the developing world – and, indeed, continues to be carried out. Mitigation projects were carried out in the USA, for example, by hastily formed teams in order to meet the statutory obligations laid upon Federal agencies (Chs 22 & 23). Rushed and underfunded 'implications surveys' and inadequately prepared sites and monuments records proliferated in the UK, and these were incapable of providing a sound basis for planning decisions affecting the heritage. The loss of important archaeological evidence without any record in much of Latin America and Africa accelerated disastrously (Wilson & Loyola 1982, Wilson 1987).

Although the blame for much of this must be laid at the door of the reluctance of governments and officials to divert adequate public funds for archaeological heritage management, the profession itself cannot be exculpated for its own failure to respond to the challenge. As Davis (Ch. 27) cogently points out, archaeological heritage management is distinct from the discipline of archaeology. Even though a high proportion of archaeology graduates make careers in heritage management, there have been no formal training courses in this speciality until comparatively recently. During the 1970s many US universities began to introduce postgraduate courses in cultural heritage management, but few other countries have followed their lead. The best example is probably that of Italy, where recent reforms of university studies have resulted in a bifurcation of students into research or heritage management at an early stage in their archaeology courses (D'Agostino 1984, p. 80). D'Agostino rightly draws attention to the dangers of such a system, which runs the risk of the 'devaluation' of archaeological heritage managers compared with research archaeologists. This is a real issue in Poland, where archaeologists working for the State Conservation Ateliers (PKZ) feel themselves to be looked down upon by their colleagues working at universities or for the Institute for the History of Material Culture, and some British archaeologists working on rescue excavations have voiced similar feelings. This situation is directly attributable to the failure so far on the part of archaeological heritage managers to recognize that the vocation that they have chosen is a profession in its own right, of equal standing with research or teaching in social terms. Until they do so, these feelings of resentment and injustice will persist, to the detriment of the heritage as much as of its managers.

Who, then, should the members of this new profession be, and what skills should they offer to the public in their heavy task of protecting a precious human asset? By definition they must have an extensive knowledge and understanding of the archaeological record and its interpretation, which bespeaks a primary training to university or equivalent level in the academic discipline of archaeology. This must include a solid practical grounding in the techniques of modern archaeology – survey and prospecting, excavation, the use of computers, and the like. In addition, archaeological heritage managers must acquire basic general management skills such as financial control and budgeting, personnel management, communication, project planning, human relations, etc. It is important that they also receive training in the legislative framework of heritage protection, land-use planning, health and safety, etc., and understand the workings of government at all levels, and of commerce and industry. Conservation must also be an integral element of training for heritage managers, and ICCROM has made a valuable contribution in this field at the international level (Ch. 30). It is arguable whether these elements should form part of the first university degree course or should be acquired after the initial academic archaeology degree in the form of postgraduate studies. Alexander (Ch. 28) sets out an excellent basic training syllabus for heritage managers, which is of general application. It is worth pointing out, however, that the creation of a trained cadre of archaeological heritage managers must go hand-in-hand with the establishment of a monuments service that gives due acknowledgement to their skills; as Rasamuel (Ch. 12) cogently points out, there is little point in training heritage managers if there are no places for them or if they are to be excluded from decision-making.

The creation of a new profession of archaeological heritage manager imposes an obligation for peer recognition and review of the type embodied in the professional institutions set up in the USA, in the UK, in Ireland, in Australia and in other European countries in recent years (Ch. 31). If the new profession is to command the high social profile that its work justifies, then it must demonstrate to its employers and to the general public, in whose name it is managing the heritage, that it is capable of establishing acceptable standards of performance and of regulating its practitioners.

It is asking too much of archaeologists to expect them to acquire all of the manifold specialist skills that heritage management requires. The legal aspects of the work, financial management, communication in all its manifestations, and marketing all require specialist training, and an effective heritage management or antiquities service will ensure that it includes at least some of these on its staff, or is prepared to expend some of its funds to acquire such services from consultants. This does not free the archae-ologically trained manager from the obligation to receive training in all of these fields, in order to be able to evaluate specialist advice or services and to make use of this training in certain aspects of his or her work. All too often antiquities services are headed by specialist administrators, archaeologists being relegated to subordinate rôles in management and decision-making. Until the situation is reached when it is unthinkable that top-level management in any antiquities service should be in the hands of anyone other than a professional whose basic training was in archaeology, archaeological heritage management will not have reached maturity and the heritage will remain at risk.

References

Burnham, B. 1974. *The protection of cultural property: Handbook of national legislations.* Paris: International Council of Museums.

Catherall, P. D., M. Barnett & H. McClean 1984. *The southern feeder: the archaeology of a gas pipeline.* London: British Gas Corporation.

Cleere, H. F. (ed.) 1984. *Approaches to the archaeological heritage.* Cambridge: Cambridge University Press.

Council of Europe 1979. *Monument protection in Europe*. Deventer: Kluwer.

Council of Europe 1988. *A future for our past* **31**, 3–21 (issue devoted to the theme 'Young people and heritage').

Cracknell, S. & M. Corbishley 1986. *Presenting archaeology to young people*. CBA Research Report No. 64. London: Council for British Archaeology.

D'Agostino, B. 1984. Italy. In *Approaches to the archaeological heritage*, H. F. Cleere (ed.), 73–81. Cambridge: Cambridge University Press.

Daniel, G. 1981. *A short history of archaeology*. London: Thames & Hudson.

Darvill, T. C. 1987. *Ancient monuments in the countryside: an archaeological management review*. London: English Heritage.

Dickens, R. S. & C. E. Hill (eds) 1978. *Cultural resources: planning and management*. Boulder, Colorado: Westview Press.

Fagan, B. W. 1977. *Buried treasure: the story of early archaeologists in the Americas*. London: Macdonald & Jane's.

Flood, J. 1983. *Archaeology of the Dreamtime*. Sydney & London: Collins.

Green, E. L. (ed.) 1984. *Ethics and values in archaeology*. New York: Free Press.

Grimes, W. F. 1968. *The excavation of Roman and mediaeval London*. London: Routledge & Kegan Paul.

Herrmann, J. (ed.) 1981. *Archäologische Denkmale und Umweltgestaltung*, 2nd edn. Berlin: Akademie Verlag.

Hewison, R. 1987. *The heritage industry: Britain in a climate of decline*. London: Methuen.

Hingst, H. & A. Lipowschek 1975. *Europäische Denkmalschutzgesetze in deutscher Übersetzung*. Neumünster: Karl-Wachholz Verlag.

Kennet, W. 1972. *Preservation*. London: Temple Smith.

King, T. F., P. P. Hickman & G. Berg 1977. *Anthropology in historic preservation: caring for culture's clutter*. New York: Academic Press.

Kristiansen, K. 1984. Denmark. In *Approaches to the archaeological heritage*, H. F. Cleere (ed.), 21–36. Cambridge: Cambridge University Press.

Lipe, W. D. 1974. A conservation model for American archaeology. *The Kiva* **39**, 213–43. (Reprinted in revised form in Schiffer & Gumerman 1977, 19–42.)

Lipe, W. D. 1984. Value and meaning in cultural resources. In *Approaches to the archaeological heritage*, H. F. Cleere (ed.), 1–11. Cambridge: Cambridge University Press.

Lipe, W. D. & A. L. Lindsay (eds) 1974. *Proceedings of the 1974 Cultural Resource Management Conference, Federal Center, Denver, Colorado*. Flagstaff, Arizona: Northern Arizona Society of Science and Art.

Lowenthal, D. 1985. *The past is a foreign country*. Cambridge: Cambridge University Press.

Lowenthal, D. & M. Binney (eds) 1981. *Our past before us: why do we save it?* London: Temple Smith.

McGimsey, C. R. 1972. *Public archeology*. New York & London: Seminar Press.

McGimsey, C. R. & H. A. Davis (eds) 1977. *The management of archaeological resources: the Airlie House report*. Washington, DC: Society for American Archaeology.

McGimsey, C. R. & H. A. Davis 1984. United States of America. In *Approaches to the archaeological heritage*, H. F. Cleere (ed.), 125–31. Cambridge: Cambridge University Press.

Newcomb, R. M. 1979. *Planning the past*. Folkestone: Dawson/Hamden, Connecticut: Archon Books.

O'Keefe, P. J. & L. V. Prott 1984. *Law and the cultural heritage*. Vol. 1: *Discovery and excavation*. Abingdon: Professional Books.

PACT 1985. Acts of the First Meeting on 'Making children aware of the existence, study and conservation of the archaeological cultural heritage', Ravello, 11–13 June 1985. *PACT News* **15**, 23–100; **16**, 14–82.

PACT 1986. Communications of the Second Meeting on 'Making adolescents (10–16 years old) aware of the existence, study and preservation of the archaeological heritage'. *PACT News* **17**, 36–104.

PACT 1987. Communications of the Second Meeting on 'Making adolescents (10–16 years old) aware of the existence, study and preservation of the archaeological heritage'. *PACT News* **18**, 33–148.

Rahtz, P. A. 1974. Rescue digging past and present. In *Rescue Archaeology*, P. A. Rahtz (ed.), 53–72. Harmondsworth: Penguin.

Sanoja, M. 1982. Cultural policy and the preservation of Latin America's national heritage. In *Rescue archeology: papers from the First New World Conference on Rescue Archeology*, R. L. Wilson & G. Loyola (eds), 21–8. Washington, DC: Preservation Press.

Säve-Södebergh, T. (ed.) 1987. *Temples and tombs of Ancient Nubia: the International Rescue Campaign at Abu Simbel, Philae and other sites.* London: Thames & Hudson/ Unesco.

Schiffer, M. B. & G. L. Gumerman 1977. *Conservation archaeology: a guide for cultural resource management studies.* New York: Academic Press.

Schiffer, M. B. & J. H. House (eds) 1975. *The Cache River Archeological Project: an experiment in contract archeology.* Fayetteville, Arkansas: Arkansas Archeological Survey.

Schofield, J. & R. H. Leech (eds) 1987. *Urban archaeology in Britain.* CBA Res. Rep. No. 61. London: Council for British Archaeology.

Thapar, B. K. 1984. India. In *Approaches to the archaeological heritage*, H. F. Cleere (ed.), 63–72. Cambridge: Cambridge University Press.

Thompson, M. W. 1981. *Ruins: their preservation and display.* London: British Museum Publications.

Unesco 1985 onwards. *The protection of movable cultural property: collection of legislative texts* (23 published to December 1987). Paris: Unesco.

Wilson, R. L. (ed.) 1987. *Rescue archeology: proceedings of the Second New World Conference on Rescue Archeology.* Dallas, Texas: Southern Methodist University Press.

Wilson, R. L. & G. Loyola (eds) 1982. *Rescue archeology: papers from the First New World Conference on Rescue Archeology.* Washington, DC: Preservation Press.

APPROACHES TO HERITAGE MANAGEMENT

1 Perspectives on the archaeological heritage: history and future

KRISTIAN KRISTIANSEN

The archaeological heritage – from political ideology to scientific ideology and back

Until the mid-19th century, when archaeology gained a foothold as an independent discipline, the preservation of monuments was used as a means of legitimizing existing ruling dynasties. However, it would be a mistake to believe that archaeology since then has been freed from the influence of political ideology. The development of archaeology, and especially the idea of protecting the archaeological heritage, is intimately linked with various political ideologies, whether national, colonial or imperialist.

Since archaeologists are themselves members of society, however, such ideologies have been concealed and represented as natural. It is in an historical perspective that we learn how the development of archaeology and the protection of its heritage was linked with the transformation of Europe from a static agricultural–mercantile society to a modern industrialized society. This transformation resulted in the destruction of natural landscapes and archaeological monuments on an unprecedented scale, and it gave a new depth to history, since it can be seen to be occurring before our very eyes. These profound economic and social transformations, which triggered both revolutions and severe political upheavals, led to the development of national ideology as a means of stabilizing and legitimizing dominant political groups.

It was this turmoil of economic and political change that gave birth to archaeology, not merely as a scientific discipline but also, from the outset, as a testimony of the historical heritage of the nation and its people. During the same period archaeology developed its own scientific ideology which set standards and objectives that were supposed to be independent of political and economic interests. With respect to methodological standards this did not pose any problems; the situation was very different so far as theoretical frameworks were concerned. Ethnic interpretations were framed so as to match perfectly with national and political ideology.

Although it may be said that archaeology lost its political and theoretical innocence in Europe during World War II, when ethnic and theoretical archaeology was abolished, it would be wrong to conclude that this was the end of *political* archaeology. With the global expansion of archaeology during the last generation and the transformation of traditional colonialism, archaeology is no longer used solely in a search for historical roots and identity. In many regions it has become part of a struggle to recapture a cultural identity that was lost during colonization and industrialization. Moreover, it has also become part of claims for rights over land and resources. This is not the case in Africa or America alone. In Scandinavia, too, the Lapps are employing archaeology in their struggle to maintain their traditional rights and ways of life. Conflicts of this kind can be revealed indirectly in the selection of priorities for excavation or protection – Nordic interest in the Vikings, the Slavs in Eastern Europe, colonial history versus aboriginal history, etc.

At the same time the 'New Archaeology' re-established theory, but in doing so once again tried to separate archaeology from political ideology and historical reality by choosing as its objective the explanation of universal cultural laws, independent of history and geography, of time and place. However, this simply transfers the problems to somebody else, mainly museums and cultural resource managers (at best). The question, then, is not whether archaeology and political ideology can be separated – they cannot – but, rather, how we can cope with the situation in a responsible way. This question is especially urgent for cultural resource management, since it is part of the political system.

Questions about what should be protected, and why, are linked with legal, economic and political problems in a very complex way. In order to deal with these problems, two approaches have developed: one asserts that preservation should be determined by scientific relevance, whereas the other maintains that each piece of archaeological heritage has a value in its own right. In principle, therefore, protection should not be selective, but should embrace everything.

The belief that scientific and political ideology can be separated and the question of selective versus total protection raise difficult problems. Let us first consider various approaches towards protection of the archaeological heritage.

Protection – from private property to general regulations

Legislation forms part of a cultural and historical pattern of development. Throughout the ages ancient monuments and antiquities have been regarded from many different angles, ranging from reverence to the assessment of their monetary value, from national sentiment to detached research.

Within the European context we can observe that as early as the Germanic tribal societies severe penalties were prescribed for those who dug up and robbed buried corpses. In Scandinavia the first provisions appeared in the early medieval laws, which laid down that gold and silver found in the ground belonged to the king. By the mid-18th century the medieval provisions of Treasure Trove had been extended by regulations that reflected the viewpoint of early archaeologists. The prime concern was to ensure that finds of old treasure were handed over to the royal collections, and in particular to the king's art collection. A decree of 1752 contains special rules relating to the payment of rewards to finders.

Provisions concerning prehistoric monuments, however, reflect entirely different attitudes. These monuments, particularly barrows and megaliths, have always been regarded as integral parts of the Scandinavian landscape. Because of their historical significance as ancestral monuments, they appealed to the patriotic sentiments of the monarchies of the Renaissance and Baroque periods.

In Sweden legal protection of ancient monuments was in force as early as 1667, whereas Denmark had to wait until almost three centuries later before similar protection was ensured. This is attributable to the interests of the private ownership of land in the intensively farmed Danish countryside. In Sweden, with large tracts of common untilled land, monuments constituted less obstruction to farming.

Scandinavia thus exemplifies both some of the earliest legal considerations and the statutory protection of finds and monuments from antiquity. It further demonstrates the two traditions that are still to be found in many parts of the world, those of private ownership versus state ownership, which have led to different legal traditions of protection. However, in both countries, the early legal regulations were clearly linked to the patriotic or nationalistic ideologies of the ruling monarchies, providing them with historical legitimization and glamour.

During the 19th and early 20th centuries attitudes towards monuments changed. They were still regarded as part of the nation's history, but they came to be interpreted as testimony of the people as a whole, in accordance with the growing democratic movements. As a result, they were increasingly thought of as belonging to the people as a whole, represented by the state. From the mid-19th century onwards excavation and preservation were regarded as responsibilities of the state. From that time grants were given on the authority of the finance act for these activities, and archaeologists were employed as state officials.

In Denmark legal protection was still voluntary. With the expansion of archaeology and national history to wider segments of the population, however, a general political demand arose for all monuments to be protected by law. These movements ran parallel to the destruction of monuments, due to the expansion of modern agriculture. In 1937 all remaining archaeological monuments were automatically protected without any compensation to landowners: they were, in effect, nationalized. There are now more than half a million protected monuments in Scandinavia.

The Scandinavian development exemplifies a general historical trend. Today it is generally accepted throughout the world that the protection of archaeological monuments is a responsibility of the state. Legal protection is now in force in most countries. In that respect, therefore, the situation may be seen as a satisfactory one. As in Scandinavia, legislation and administration are directly related to historical traditions. In most of Europe protection is accorded to individual monuments, the types often being detailed in the legislation. Outside Europe (in North American for instance) protection is ensured in National Parks, and in this way a total sample of the monuments in a landscape is preserved. However, outside the Parks there is little or no control or protection.

In many countries a strong legal tradition of protecting private property has made the protection of monuments difficult to implement. For example, in the UK monuments proposed for statutory protection ('scheduling') have to be evaluated both archaeologically and (in a covert sense) politically. This is obviously not a satisfactory situation, since the resulting administrative burden means that only a relatively small number of monuments will be protected. In most countries the protection of monuments is therefore selective in one way or another. The imbalances resulting from this selectivity gradually led to the recognition that all other unprotected monuments and sites deserved at least the negative form of protection given by archaeological excavation if their destruction was inevitable. This awareness developed during the strong urban and industrial growth after World War II. Archaeologists were able to demonstrate that the protected monuments represented only a minor part of the total historical and prehistoric settlement pattern.

Most countries consequently now also have some form of legal protection for monuments that are found during construction work; in most cases the archaeological excavations are financed either by the state or by the developer. This recent legislation has resulted in the largest economic boom in the history of archaeology throughout the world. However, it has also resulted in a failure to recognize the problems of protected monuments, the care, restoration, registration and administration of which is often considerd to have a lower priority than excavations, except when they represent major tourist attractions.

Today all types of archaeological monument have some form of statutory protection in most countries, either *in situ* or through excavation. It is the balance between *in situ* protection and excavation that determines the profile of cultural resource management (CRM) in individual countries. The fundamental consequences of these two opposing strategies of conservation, however, have not been sufficiently recognized and dealt with. Despite such discrepancies, I believe that some general objectives for CRM must be maintained, and I will conclude by discussing these.

Walking on a knife-edge: CRM and world history

What conclusions, if any, can be drawn from this short outline of the political, scientific and legal aspects of the archaeological heritage in historical perspective?

First of all, it must be recognized that they represent interrelated and interlocking aspects of the management of the heritage. Administration, research and political ideology cannot be separated. To recognize this is the first condition for handling them in a responsible way. The archaeological heritage contributes to the historical identity of nations, people and local communities. It is part of the sum of knowledge and experience from which the decisions for tomorrow are taken at all levels in society. It represents an irreplaceable contribution to what has been termed the collective memory of mankind. This memory is stored mostly in the landscape. It is in the landscape that the heritage should be protected, and only as a last resort, after excavation, in museums. This is the major historical and political reason why the archaeological heritage should be (and is being) protected in most countries in the world today as a responsibility of the state.

Since each age has its own conception of what is important, and since science is constrained by its own history and by the limitations of methodology, protection should never be assessed either on the basis of research priority or on political considerations. The basic principle in all protection should be that monuments and sites are to be protected in their own right and in all their variety, as far as possible. In legal terms this implies that protection should be based on general regulations relating to ownership on a national level. The determination of which types or groups should be covered by such general regulations, however, remains a political and governmental decision that will be based on historical, archaeological and political traditions. Thus, protection should not be based on political or scientific considerations relating to the individual site. Although this may and should be done in specific cases, it must be regarded as an exceptional practice.

Given acceptance of these basic principles, their application to diverse historical and legal traditions throughout the world will result in different profiles of conservation. We Europeans should take care not to moralize on this subject on behalf of the rest of the world. We should remember that CRM is directly dependent on political systems and the laws of social evolution. Europe exploited both man and nature with little regard for the archaeological heritage during the 19th and early 20th centuries. Modern history would not have been possible if our current regulations, which apply to a situation where both nature and monuments have become scarce resources, had been in existence at that time. Many countries in various parts of the world are going through transformations that in some respects equal those of Europe 100 or 200 years ago. What can be protected in such a situation may be different from what can be protected in Europe today.

With non-selective *in situ* protection in the form of general regulations as our major objective, excavation should be a last resort. Here, by contrast, priorities must be decisive, although they should be used with great restraint. The random excavation of different types of monument in various parts of a region will, in the long term, provide a more representative sample of the past than a strategy based solely on research priorities, with a tendency to allocate all the available funds to a few highly important and prestigious key sites. I therefore recommend a combination of random small-scale excavations and a few large-scale projects.

Let me end by proposing three objectives of cultural resource management for the future. The first is that *systematic field survey* must be seen as a major and independent objective of CRM. What can be excavated will never represent more than a tiny fragment of the total heritage. The reconstruction of cultural systems and their dynamics demands systematic regional and national recording and inventorization of all archaeological monuments and sites in the landscape. This is a long-term strategy that will take generations to accomplish. It is, in fact, a never-ending process which has been more or less accomplished in Scandinavia and partly accomplished in Great Britain. It should be a major objective of CRM, since it serves as a basis for both research and protection.

The second objective is that *the research environment should contribute to history* – not only global history, but also regional and local history. This includes migrations and questions of identifying tribal groups, because these were once historical realities. I do not propose that the New Archaeology should be abandoned. However, its emphasis on samples of universal cultural laws out of time and out of history is of little interest and value if these are not linked to local and regional sequences of historical processes.

Archaeologists have a responsibility to write history and to show how laws may eventually penetrate and manifest themselves in history at the local level. Consequently archaeologists have a responsibility to popularize their knowledge instead of leaving this to commercial authors. This is a first priority for CRM, since it is the general understanding and awareness of the past that makes it possible. It is, furthermore, a precondition for protection and excavation, and thus indirectly for the work of two-thirds of all archaeologists in the world today.

Finally, CRM should *develop a high profile as a profession*. Since CRM provides most of the money for archaeology in the world today, it is astonishing how modest a role CRM archaeologists play in the archaeological environment, which is still dominated by traditional university research. We should be much more determined in our efforts to expand our rôle as a profession in its own right, just as museum work, teaching and excavation have their own profiles. Cultural resource management, too, has a profile of its own, combining historical and administrative experience with research. It thus holds an important position for developing a better-integrated understanding of the past in the present. The only way to develop our discipline is by initiating and achieving respectability for research in CRM – research in administration, planning, methods of fieldwalking, information systems, restoration and – not least – research on the rôle of archaeology in society. There is a whole sector of applied research waiting to be developed within CRM.

Cultural resource management, or heritage management, holds a central position for the future direction of archaeology, bridging the political, social and archaeological environments, and controlling decisions and money. Such a position implies that critique is a permanent condition of our work, which we should learn to handle constructively. Therefore, CRM should engage in a constant dialogue both with other archaeological sectors and with those social and political sectors or groups whose heritage is being protected and administrated. It places high demands on our ability to maintain an open and reflective strategy rather than to retreat into dogmatism. In this chapter I have tried to sketch some of the components of such a strategy.

2 *World archaeology – the world's cultural heritage*

JOACHIM HERRMANN

(translated by Katharine Judelson)

The protection of the world's archaeological heritage is far-reaching in its implications, touching upon science, culture, academic politics, legislation and education, and having important connections with public awareness and publicity. Since some of these questions touch upon the relationship between historical knowledge and the historical and cultural heritage, they are treated in more detail below.

The problems of archaeological research and the management of monuments and sites (archaeological heritage management, or conservation archaeology) vary between one region of the world and another, and from one epoch in the history of human culture to another. In many countires important focuses of monument management have resulted directly from archaeological work – think of the antiquities of Egypt or Nubia, the pyramids of Meröe in the Sudan, Kasanlyk and Plovdiv in Bulgaria, Pompeii in Italy, Mycenae or Vergina in Greece, Petra in Jordan, Xi'an in China, etc. The durability of the inorganic building materials of these monuments makes it possible to restore and reconstruct them on the basis of the abundant material apparatus that has survived. In the lands of the north and in parts of the tropical zone in Africa, by contrast, another situation obtains. The predominant use of organic building materials during the early histories of these regions has meant that archaeological research primarily involves first the gathering of evidence and the exploration of historical sources. Human artefactual material in these regions has almost completely perished and can at best only be reconstructed on the basis of detailed study and then be exhibited in open-air museums especially set up for this purpose.

The fundamental difference between these two situations is reflected in the different methods of official organization and in different types of legislation. In southern countries the same institution will be responsible both for the conservation of monuments and for archaeology, within an Antiquities Service. In more-northerly regions, however, it is more usual for there to be separate institutions, one for the conservation of monuments (concentrating on artistic and architectural monuments) and the other for archaeology and the conservation of archaeological sites. The latter focuses on archaeological research and the protection of prehistoric and protohistoric remains of former settlements, burial and ritual sites, fortifications, etc. In many countries the service is provided by state or scientific institutions. For example, in the USSR the upkeep of monuments is a ministerial responsibility, exercised through bodies with a responsibility for cultural matters, whereas archaeological research is the task of the USSR Academy of Sciencies or the All-Union Academies (Krasnov 1981, and see Masson, Ch. 19, this volume). A similar situation is to be found in Bulgaria, Romania, Hungary and Poland. In the German Democratic Republic the upkeep of artistic and architectural monuments and the administration of museums are under the jurisdiction of the Ministry of Culture. The Ministry for Higher and Vocational Education and its Scientific Museums section is responsible for the upkeep of archaeological sites. Overlapping research projects are co-ordinated by the Academy of Sciences in accordance with the arrangements for the upkeep of sites. To this end the Academy of Sciences in the GDR has set up a Council for Archaeology and Ancient History, the members of which are representatives of all of the major institutions concerned with the upkeep of sites and archaeological research (*Mitteilungen* 1987, *Archäologische Denkmale* 1981, p. 233, Coblenz 1981).

Most of the member states of the United Nations or Unesco have enacted laws and regulations to protect cultural monuments, often linked with others designed to protect sites of natural interest (Burnham 1974). Broadly, these consist, wholly or in part, of measures and regulations that can be summarized under the following headings:

protection and preservation of monuments;
use of monuments to promote education of the general public;
inclusion of monuments in national and international tourist programmes;
archaeological excavations and further scientific investigation of monuments.

These four main aspects of this work have links with a number of widely different interests; they can sometimes prove to be mutually exclusive, particularly when there are separate institutions representing the specific areas. Unrestricted and excessive tourist activity, for example, can lead to the physical destruction of monuments and their surroundings, thereby depriving researchers of their source material. The solutions that have been put forward or are being sought can differ widely. Three main courses of action are emerging.

First, *restriction* and regulation of public access within designated reserves and areas under official protection by virtue of their archaeological interest. This includes measures to ensure protection of the environment, such as the limitation of air pollution in the surrounding area by restricting the flow of motor traffic and the effect of other sources of harmful substances. Regulations of this type involve considerable sociopolitical and financial commitments. They are often introduced in conjunction with an international project that has the backing of an organization such as Unesco.

Secondly, *denial of access* to certain endangered monuments and the provision of replicas of them in the immediate vicinity. This means that part of the atmosphere inspired by the original is inevitably lost; the cultural and educational experience is nevertheless still assured, and the original itself is preserved. One of the first sites where this solution was adopted was the Thracian grave at Kasanlyk in Bulgaria (Velkov 1981, p. 98). The painted cave at Lascaux dating from the last Ice Age had to be closed to the stream of tourist visitors, to prevent it from deteriorating completely. A copy of large parts of the cave and the wall paintings in it was created at great expense. In northern European and American countries reconstructions of monuments, either as models or in open-air museums, are being set up on a wide scale, since the originals may be difficult for the amateur to distinguish. Examples of large-scale arrangements of this sort are Pliska and Preslav in Bulgaria, open-air museums in Chernigov, Kiev, Novgorod, and elsewhere in the USSR (Sedov 1981), Biskupin and Opole in Poland (Dąbrowski 1981), Mikulčice and Staré Mésto in Czechoslovakia, etc.

In the GDR an open-air museum has recently been opened in Gross Raden, near Schwerin (*Ausgrabungen und Funde* 1988, **1**). A further open-air museum is currently being built at the site of the fully excavated Tilleda Palace at Kyffhäuser. The open-air museum at Tilleda, which occupies about 5 ha, is part of an extensive educational and tourist complex which provides an introduction to the history of feudal society in Central Europe, and which incorporates the Kyffhäuser castles about 2 km away and Schlachtenberg, near Bad Frankenhausen, about 8 km distant. Tilleda represents the formative period of the feudal system and the castles of Kyffhäuser the heyday of that system. In 1525 Thomas Müntzer's peasant army was slaughtered on the Schlachtenberg hill. On the slope of the hill a panoramic monument is being erected, in which the sexton Tübke is depicted leading the revolt of the oppressed medieval peasants and the struggle to usher in the bourgeois era of human society.

Thirdly, *removal* of selected endangered monuments *and reconstruction* at new, more-accessible sites. This process, which has been used for more than 100 years, began with excavations in the Near East. At first the newly discovered monuments were removed to the great museums of London, Paris and Berlin. The Pergamon Museum in Berlin was, in fact, originally built specifically for such a purpose. The normal procedure nowadays is for reconstruction to take place in the land of a monument's origin, involving the partial imitation or at least a suggestion of the original setting. This was the method used for the temples of Sudanese Nubia, which were threatened with inundation by the Aswan Dam reservoir; they were moved some 1000 km up the Nile to the National Museum in Khartoum, where they were re-erected in the museum gardens, which were laid out like a park on the banks of a small-scale model of the Nile (Hinkel 1981, 1985).

This handful of examples, chosen more or less at random, make it clear that the problem of archaeological monuments can only be solved if the four aspects of this work are approached as a whole, starting from their specific character and significance, and how they can best be utilized. This is the issue at the very heart of the debate: it is a question of opening up monuments as vehicles of culture and human cultural creativity.

In the Mondiacult Declaration at the Unesco World Conference on culture-related politics, a definition of the concept of 'culture' was set out which, on the one hand, treats the subject as such and, on the other hand, addresses the underlying objectives of the management and preservation of cultural monuments, as follows (*Mondiacult* 1983, p. 53):

> Culture today, in the fullest sense of the word, can be viewed as the totality of the intellectual and material landmarks, which may albeit differ in the level of understanding and emotion they represent, but which nevertheless characterize a society or social group. Apart from art and literature it also embraces ways of life, man's fundamental rights, systems of values, traditions and convictions.
>
> Culture enables man to contemplate himself. It is through culture that we first became specifically human beings, that is beings which are endowed with reason and critical faculties and live in accordance with ethical principles.

Yet how should we define cultural identity, which provides the justification for the examination, preservation and designation of archaeological and cultural monuments?

Cultural identity makes use of the historical heritage in its entirety: that is the premise from which Unesco starts. The Argentinian novelist Julio Cortazar described the connection in the following words: 'What we call culture is, in fact, nothing more than the presence and exercise of our identity in its full vigour' (Unesco 1985, p. 21). Three essential components can be distinguished within the historical–cultural heritage that has survived (Hermann 1986):

> First, the intellectual cultural heritage, which finds expression in the achievements of science, literature, fine art, and the overall concept of humanity;
> secondly, the material cultural heritage which finds expression in concrete statements of human creativity, ranging from tools and objects in daily use to great intellectual achievement, manifested in material form as architecture and fine art;
> thirdly, the ideological tradition moulded by historical circumstances and events, a chain which spans the centuries.

In the present context it is the material cultural heritage that is of particular interest. This question as a whole has been discussed in detail elsewhere (Historisch–kulturelles Erbe 1981).

The discovery and preservation of the intellectual cultural heritage depends primarily on the intellectual efforts of individuals and society. The discovery and preservation of the material cultural heritage also often involves considerable expenditure. The objects which make up this material heritage are often neglected, not merely as objects of intellectual interest, but also as physical entities: works of architecture and art fell victim to remorseless social progress, and were deliberately eliminated. Examples of this can be found in all regions and in all countries. This process took on a new dimension in Europe with the advent of bourgeois–capitalist society. Monuments were destroyed wherever they stood in the way of the capitalist economy or where profit was to be gained from such steps. In the then-remote little university town of Greifswald, for example, the Chancellor gave the Gothic monastery building in Eldena, part of the university's property, to its professors so that they might use it as a cheap source of bricks (Möbius 1979).

Whereas in the past the increasing scale of the destruction of monuments was a solely European problem, it has subsequently become a world problem. In their colonies the colonial powers often put a stop to the traditional utilization and maintenance of the material cultural heritage, and in so doing dealt blows to the native population's sense of its own identity. Capitalist exploitation of these countries and the introduction of industrialization brought in their wake further dangers and destruction, particularly in centres of high population density. The increasing industrial and agricultural transformation of these countries after they had achieved cultural independence gave further encouragement to the tendency to do away with the material cultural heritage, a policy that was represented as an inevitable by-product of economic progress. At the same time state services were set up in most countries of this kind to preserve the surviving antiquities services which saw themselves as intellectual cultural institutions, but which also regarded both the practical protection of the objects forming part of this material heritage and the intellectual cultural mastery of such objects as their concern.

In many cases, however, the massive financial outlays involved are more than a single country can cope with. Consider for a moment the scale of some of the projects involved: the construction of the Aswan dam reservoir threatened several hundred monuments both in Egypt and in the Sudan, among them the temple of Ramesses II at Abu Simbel and the temples of Philae. Rescuing the monuments from the Philae site alone cost approximately US$15 million (*World Cultural Heritage* [Unesco] 1976, p. 4. Rescue projects on a similar scale have been, and are being, carried out on the banks of the Euphrates, the Indus and the Red rivers, and below the dams on the Volga, Don and Danube.

The deliberate efforts that have been going on for decades to preserve and make full use of mankind's material heritage have now become a focus for direct action on the part of Unesco. In 1956 a recommendation calling for the establishment of international principles for archaeological excavations was accepted by the 18th Convention of the General Conference, in New Delhi. The recommendation had been drawn up on the basis of the conviction that the emotions which the contemplation of and knowledge about works of the past can further, of the conception that the history of mankind includes knowledge of the separate cultures and that it is therefore very important that in the general interest mankind's archaeological finds be investigated, perhaps saved and exchanged in view of the fact that the most certain guarantee for the preservation of monuments and works from the past is the respect for and attachment to them that the peoples themselves manifest.

(*Archäologische Denkmale* 1981, p. 257)

The recommendation concerning the preservation of treasures which the XVth Convention of the Unesco General Conference agreed upon in 1968, emphasized, among other things (*ibid.*, p. 265), 'that cultural treasures are the result and manifestation of various traditions and that they therefore represent one of the fundamental factors which determine the specific identity of a given people', that a people is 'in this way able to consolidate its consciousness of its own worth'. Later the notion is propounded that the preservation of cultural treasures from all periods of the history of a people contributes directly to the creation of 'a favourable and stimulating environment' for the well-being of any people. Finally, mention is made of the rôle that tourism has to play, and also to the contribution that can stem from the utilization of mankind's treasures to social and economic development. In 1972 the XVIIth Session of the Unesco General Conference adopted the Convention on the Protection of the World's Cultural and Natural Heritage (the World Heritage Convention), in order to find solutions in the face of urgent ecological problems. The concept of 'cultural heritage' is applied in this Convention to monuments and finds, complexes of buildings and cultural treasures, as well to cultural sites. This heritage was acknowledged by the signatories to the Convention as the 'world heritage' 'for whose protection in toto all peoples should feel themselves obliged to co-operate' (*ibid.* p. 274f). From this approach to the world's tangible cultural heritage there then ensued theoretical and practical measures undertaken by Unesco. Since 1956 Unesco has called for international co-operation more than 100 times, for the investigation, protection, preservation and presentation of that material cultural heritage in Asia, Africa, Europe and America (a map of the relevant sites is published in *Archäologische Denkmale* 1981, p. 33).

Among the various points of view regarding the preservation and utilization of the historical heritage, a key rôle is clearly assigned to that involving the research for national identity. Indeed, in states that are inhabited by a variety of tribes or ethnic groups, a category into which the majority of former colonial countries falls, the material cultural heritage is particularly suited to helping to develop the population's awareness of a shared historical identity. Although the intellectual cultural heritage in its form and content is influenced by ethnic attributes, at least insofar as oral traditions are concerned, these characteristics are far less prominent (or are missing altogether) in respect of the material cultural heritage. It would be more appropriate to say that in this case it is rather the general, civilizing-cum-cultural character that finds expression, and one that is determined by environmental factors. From this it follows that it is possible for members of diverse and different peoples to identify with a single tangible cultural heritage. One of the best-developed manifestations of this type of a people's relationship with its heritage is that provided by Poland in connection with the reconstruction of buildings of architectural value destroyed during World War II in former German towns such as Szczecin (Stettin), Wrocław (Breslau) or Gdańsk (Danzig). Attention might also be drawn to the management in Bulgaria or Hungary of monuments dating back to the classical and Byzantine periods, to the investigation and display of monuments from the Indus Valley culture, from the ancient cultures of Iraq, Syria, Jordan, etc. Unlike the intellectual cultural heritage, the material cultural heritage to a certain extent provides an anonymous foundation on which a people's self-awareness and international recognition can develop.

Another important consideration is the fact that an awareness of history is closely connected with archaeological and architectural monuments, and that such monuments constitute important landmarks in the transmission of historical knowledge, understanding and awareness. Monuments of this type encourage the visitor to acquire new historical knowledge and under-standing, or to come to terms with the historical knowledge with which he or she is being confronted. It is to this end that Marxist theory and practice have long been addressing the question of how best to approach and benefit from the material cultural heritage. Lenin gave instructions immediately after the October Revolution for a decree on the subject of the protection of monuments to be drawn up, which he was to sign on 5 October 1918. It was promulgated 'with the aim of preserving and promoting the study of treasures from the world of art and the ancient past that have survived in Russia and to acquaint the broad masses of the people with them on as wide a scale as possible' (*Ochrana* 1973).

Archaeological and cultural research, as well as the conservation, preser-vation and display of monuments from past epochs of human history, are without doubt important tasks of our time. William Faulkner was to write (quoted in Holzer 1978, p. 9): 'The past is never dead, it has not even passed on'. In a Unesco declaration the situation was aptly summed up as follows: 'Historic monuments . . . teach every man reverence for the creative genius, which unites the nations and generations on a plane above their conflicts' (*Sites and Monuments* [Unesco] 1970, p. 9).

References

Archäologische Denkmale 1981. *Archäologische Denkmale und Umweltgestaltung*. Berlin: J. Herrmann.
Burnham, B. (compiler) 1974. *The protection of cultural property: handbook of national legislation*. Paris: ICOM.
Coblenz, W. 1981. Ergebnisse und Probleme der Ur- und frühgeschichtlichen

Bodendenkmalpflege in der DDR. In *Archäologische Denkmale und Umweltgestaltung*, 45–53. Berlin: J. Herrmann.

Dąbrowski, K. 1981. Archäologische Reservate als Elemente der Umweltgestaltung in der VR Polen. In *Archäologische Denkmale und Umweltgestaltung*, 89–92. Berlin: J. Herrmann.

Herrmann, J. 1986. Historisch–kulturelles Erbe vorkapitalistischer Gesellschaftsformationen in unserer Zeit: Erforschung, Darstellung, Wirkung. In *Wege zur Geschichte*, 99–110. Berlin: B. Tesche.

Hinkel, F. W. 1981. Die Rettungsarbeiten an den Tempeln Sudanesisch-Nubiens und deren neuer Standort. In *Archäologische Denkmale und Umweltgestaltung*, 125–30. Berlin: J. Herrmann.

Hinkel, F. W. 1985. *Exodus from Nubia*. Berlin.

Historisch–kulturelles Erbe 1981. Das historisch–kulturelles Erbe vorkapitalistischer Gesellschaftsformationen und seine zeitgenössische Bedeutung. *Abhandlungen der Akademie der Wissenschaften der DDR* 2. Berlin.

Holzer, M. 1978. *Evolution und Geschichte*. Köln.

Krasnov, J. A. 1981. Die Erfahrungen in der Organisation archäologischer Untersuchungen bei den großen Bauvorhaben in der UdSSR. In *Archäologische Denkmale und Umweltgestaltung*, 77–81. Berlin: J. Herrmann.

Masson, V. M. 1989. Archaeological heritage management in the USSR. In *Archaeological heritage management in the modern world*, H. Cleere (ed.), ch. 19. London: Unwin Hyman.

Mitteilungen 1987. *Mitteilungen zur Archäologie und Alten Geschichte ab Jg. 1, 1972 bis Jg. 14, 1986*. Berlin.

Möbius, I. 1979. Eldenas Erbewert. *Kunstwissenschaftliche Beiträge: Beiträge der Zeitschrift 'Bildende Kunst'* 8, 1ff.

Mondiacult 1983. *Mondiacult: Weltkonferenz der UNESCO über Kulturpolitik, Mexiko 1982: Dokumente*. Berlin.

Ochrana 1973. *Ochrana Pamjatnikov istorii i kultury. Sbornik dokumentov*. 18–20. Moscow.

Sedov, V. V. 1981. Die Archäologie und die Bildung archäologischer Reservate in den Städten der Alten Rus. In *Archäologische Denkmale und Umweltgestaltung*, 71–6. Berlin: J. Herrmann.

Unesco, 1985. *Culture and the future*. Paris: Unesco.

Velkov, V. 1981. Museumsstädte und archäologische Reservate in der VR Bulgarien. In *Archäologische Denkmale und Umweltgestaltung*, 97–101. Berlin: J. Herrmann.

3 *Significant until proven otherwise: problems versus representative samples*

CURTIS F. SCHAAFSMA

Managing cultural resources is like managing any other resource. It represents a balance among competing forces, and it is subject to changing political and financial climates. For at least the past 15 years cultural resource management has been guided by the conservation ethic as applied to archaeological remains by a group of concerned archaeologists in the early 1970s. The process of conserving and protecting these resources is buttressed and defined by a series of important laws, the most basic being the National Historic Preservation Act, as amended (P.L. 96–515) and the Archaeological Resources Protection Act of 1979 (P.L. 96–95). For background on the historic development of these laws and the emergence of the significance concept which is central to them all, refer to the excellent paper by Tainter & Lucas (1983). The fundamental sentiment that is expressed in these laws and the conservation ethic is that the public has an interest in the information contained in all archaeological sites, and the loss, damage, or misuse of sites constitutes an irreplaceable loss to the public. The public has a right to the knowledge of the past that we can derive from them. From this perspective, archaeological sites or the collections and records derived from them, or both, are like historical documents: they are the archives of archaeology.

I would like to address recent trends in the principles behind cultural resource management in the USA that I believe are an affront to the conservation ethic, inconsistent with existing legislation, and decidedly detrimental to the wellbeing of the archaeological resources. At issue is the *rigid* application of the 'Hempelian' hypothetico–deductive method in archaeology. For years a few zealots have insisted that the only permissible method of scientific research entails defining the hypothesis to be tested *before* the data are gathered. This opinion has long been seen as flawed when dealing with archaeological materials, and it must be addressed because there are good reasons for thinking this opinion will be amplified into general Federal policy (King 1981). I wish to say something about what actually is generally accepted scientific methodology, and to make explicit the paradox that emerges when dealing with finite, non-renewable archaeological resources. The focus of my concern is the *insistence* that archaeological data cannot be gathered without *previous* identification of its relevance. I will also propose an alternative to the trend, which is concordant with the suggestion of Tainter & Lucas (1983, pp. 716–7) on the same matter.

Archaeologists have traditionally been rather casual about methodology (in the philosophic sense), and were unprepared for the sudden insistence in the 1960s and early 1970s that they had to adopt an explicit version of the logical positivist method or they were not doing 'science' (Leone 1972, King 1971, Martin 1971). It is important here briefly to explore current ideas about what constitutes scientific methodology.

To begin with, I would like to call attention to the singular success of quantum mechanics (Rohrlich 1983, Heisenberg 1958). There are two attributes of quantum mechanics which intrigue me and which have direct relevance to archaeology. One is the insistence on confirmation of theoretic assumptions by recourse to experimental data, and the other is the unsettling manner in which quantum mechanics was forced on researchers because it was the only solution that fitted the data satisfactorily. Heisenberg's *Physics and philosophy* (1958) explores both of these characteristics. The experience of the quantum theorists emphasizes the primary fact that any science has to have reliable recourse to experimental data in order to allow the testing of hypotheses that are developed by various means. Secondly, the history of quantum mechanics clearly demonstrates that it evolved *in spite of* the initial preferences or inclinations of the researchers who developed it. The people who developed quantum mechanics did not know the answers beforehand by some subtle recourse to hidden information, some hidden agenda that let them know the answers before they began their research. In fact, Heisenberg and Bohr were appalled that nature should be as absurd as their research indicated (Heisenberg 1958, p. 42). They also found themselves bitterly opposed by colleagues who objected to some of the implications of quantum mechanics (Heisenberg 1972, pp. 70–81).

Northrop wrote an instructive introduction to Heisenberg's book in which he analysed the method behind quantum mechanics. It is obvious that simple inductivism has been rejected for a long time, and '. . . that we know the object of scientific knowledge only by the speculative means of axiomatic theoretic construction or postulation; Newton's suggestion that the physicist can deduce our theoretical concepts from the experimental data being false' (Northrop 1958, p. 9). In choosing which theoretical constructions we are to use, the primary criterion must be which survive the encounter with empirical data. Quantum mechanics is presently held in high regard for the reason that, of all the theoretical constructions that have been advanced, it best fits the data (Rohrlich 1983). This is so despite the fact that latent within quantum mechanics are assumptions about the nature of things to which many scientists objected very strenuously, the most notable being Albert Einstein and David Bohm. Like it or not, 'the epistemology and the ontology of quantum mechanics must now be taken more seriously than ever before' (Rohrlich 1983, p. 1251). The message from quantum mechanics is clear – no science can survive without data, science in general is a process of exploration into the unknown, and we may well be confronted with knowledge that nobody could have anticipated beforehand.

Exploration has always been an appealing characteristic of archaeology. Exploring the unknown is a characteristic of all science and the need to retain that was well stated metaphorically by Heisenberg (1972, p. 70):

> If I were asked what was Christopher Columbus' greatest achievement in discovering America, my answer would not be that he took advantage of the spherical shape of the earth to get to India by the western route – this idea had occurred to others before him – or that he prepared his expedition meticulously and rigged his ships most expertly – that, too, others could have done equally well. His most remarkable feat was the decision to leave the known regions of the world and to sail westward, far beyond the point from which his provisions could have got him back home again.

Perhaps because archaeologists have become wary of being labelled as 'treasure-hunters', they have run to the extremes of 'rigging their ships' in grasping at the Hempelian method. In doing so, they may be in danger of discarding an essential quality of the discipline – exploration.

Conservation archaeology originally grew out of an inductivistic milieu. However, the contradictions between the inductive method in archaeology and the hypothetico-deductive method were already well understood and actively being addressed in the early 1970s (King 1971, Martin 1971). At the most simplistic level the narrow inductivist method (Hempel 1966, Hill 1970, King 1971) can be compared with putting a jigsaw puzzle together. All of the pieces fit together (one hopes), and when all of the pieces are put together they make a larger picture that transcends what we can discern from any one piece or a small set of the pieces. When some aspect of the archaeological record is destroyed, those concerned with the emerging picture developed by archaeological research feel just as thwarted as one who had some pieces of a jigsaw puzzle destroyed or stolen. The analogy with map-making should be obvious. The practitioners of the method constantly refer to 'filling-in the gaps'. Viewed in this manner, all of the pieces have relevance and none of them should be allowed to disappear. However, the inductivist claim that bits of data eventually add up to a coherent picture is discarded in the hypothetico-deductivist view.

Historically the attack on narrow inductivism in archaeology was largely made with reference to Hempel's (1966) discussion on the philosophy of natural science. Hempel's position is clearly stated (1966, p. 13):

> In sum, the maxim that data should be gathered without guidance by antecedent hypotheses about the connection among the facts under study is self-defeating, and it is certainly not followed in scientific inquiry. On the contrary, tentative hypotheses are needed to give direction to a scientific investigation. Such hypotheses determine

among other things, what data should be collected at a given point in a scientific investigation.

Several archaeologists were involved in introducing the Hempelian hypo-thetico-deductive method to American archaeology (Leone 1972). By 1970 Hill was able to present a cogent and compelling case for following Hempel's method in archaeological research. Hill (1970, p. 26) also defined some of the points that are part of the current trend in cultural resource management:

> If one generates a series of propositions ahead of time, he will be aware of the kinds of data that must be collected to test them. If he does not do this, he will fail to collect the relevant test data (and collect a great deal of 'data' that are not relevant to anything in particular). This amounts to wasted time and money and is inefficient from a scientific point of view.

Over the years archaeologists have proceeded from this general starting point to the idea that there is no such thing as 'data', there are only data relevant for testing some hypothesis that relates to a problem (Hempel 1966, p. 12). As an intellectual nicety this is an interesting notion, and it was certainly developed by Hempel. However, this position can become troublesome when it is translated into cultural resource management poli-cies. King (1981) has expanded upon the points made by Hill (1970) to insist that collecting 'data' simply because it exists is unacceptable, inefficient and a waste of money. This subject is addressed below.

In the course of evaluating 'Inductivism' versus 'Deductivism' (King 1971), very few archaeologists have considered the status of the hypo-thetico-deductive method within the larger scientific community. It is truly instructive to read accounts such as those of Heisenberg (1958, 1972) of how something like quantum mechanics came about, and what the reasons were that precipitated its development. Things are rarely as tidy as Hempel would have us believe. In addition there is the issue of to what degree philosophers can adequately tell scientists what to do. Heisenberg, Bohr and Pauli were most suspicious of the positivists and their presumption of not only knowing what the scientist is doing but of being in a position to lay down ground-rules for the practice of science (Heisenberg 1972, pp. 205–17). My interest here is not to refute Hempel – his call for methodological rigour is well taken. However, it is essential to realize that Hempel's method has to be balanced against many other considerations, and it is not universally accepted as *the* guide to scientific research.

The paradox attendant upon following Hempel's directive in archaeo-logical research emerges when it is realized that the data upon which the science of archaeology depends are limited and non-renewable, not infinite like electrons or essentially infinite like the grains of sand to which Hempel (1966, pp. 11–12) referred. The difficulty becomes very acute when one considers the nature of most contract archaeology and a great deal of all archaeological research. We are always confronted with archaeological materials that are not immediately relevant to some research problem.

Experience has shown that many of the new directions in research come from unanticipated finds or observations. In any field of science new directions often emerge from observations that are inconsistent with existing concepts (Hempel 1966, p. 40). Many grand concepts have come tumbling down because they were shown to be inconsistent with observations. In science our concepts need to be in agreement with our percepts, and research must be open to new perceptions. Indeed, the edifice of Newtonian physics required massive reassessment because of inconsistencies in the radiation of black bodies that eventually led to the formulation of quantum mechanics (Heisenberg 1958, p. 30).

Dealing with unanticipated finds or observations is really the essence of the present paradox in cultural resource management: what do you do with the archaeological remains that are not relevant to a guiding research design?

Many sciences such as geology, botany, palaeontology and even astronomy have gathered a great deal of useful data without any guiding antecedent hypotheses, and data-gathering seems to be essential to any science. Flannery (1982, p. 275) handles the problem nicely in his parable for the archaeology of the 1980s:

> But suppose an archaeologist were to say, 'I'm only interested in Anasazi myth and symbolism, and I'm not going to collect data on subsistence.' Off he goes to a prehistoric cliff dwelling and begins to dig. He goes for the pictographs, and figurines, and ceremonial staffs, and wooden bird effigies. What, then, does he do with all the digging sticks, and tumplines, and deer bones that he finds while he's digging for all the other stuff? Does he ignore them because they don't relate to his 'research problem'? Does he shovel them onto the dump? Or does he pack them up and put them in dead storage, in the hope that he can farm them out to a student some day to ease his conscience? Because, unlike the situation in ethnology, no archaeologist will be able to come along later and find that stuff in its original context. It's *gone*, son.

Kidder (1932, p. 7) made essentially the same point while complaining about archaeology being guided by the quest for museum specimens, instead of the quest for 'relevant data'. The quests may differ, but somehow the effect on the archaeological resources remains very much the same:

> Sites are thus at best only partly examined, at worst ruinously mangled. It is as if a historian were to tear the illuminated pages from a unique manuscript and cast its text unread into the fire.
>
> This would not be so disastrous if we were dealing with almost any other sort of material. An entomologist, for instance, may collect only handsome and showy beetles, he may draw false deductions and his

publications may be utter rot. Unfortunate, indeed, but not irreparable, for there will always be a fresh supply of beetles awaiting the attention of more competent observers. And the same is true of nearly every other branch of science. But materials for the study of man's past are limited, expendable. Once pillaged, a prehistoric site is ruined for future investigators; another page has been ripped from the already mutilated volume of history.

The discussions developing the conservation ethic in American archaeology (McGimsey 1972, Lipe 1974) began with the realization that the archaeological record is a scarce non-renewable resource which is fast disappearing. This is not a new observation. You cannot grow another archaeological site, or an atl-atl point someone lost on the Arizona desert 5000 years ago. The archaeological record is a fragile entity (if we can regard it as an entity for discussion) that is composed of things in their context. In this regard, context is one of the most important aspects. Better yet, things and their context are different sides of the same coin so far as usefulness as scientific data is concerned. The basic issues were well developed by McGimsey (1972) and Lipe (1974). The American Society for Conservation Archaeology Plenary Session at the 1984 SAA meeting in Portland affirmed the fundamental soundness of most of the original ideas developed by 1974 (Mayer-Oakes & Portnoy 1984). The essence of the conservation ethic is that we should make every effort to preserve and use wisely what we have left. This includes stringent conservation measures during research (or 'treatment') which wring the maximum information from the archaeological record each time we utilize any of it, regardless of the purpose (Lipe 1974, 1984). This includes proper curation of specimens and records for future researchers not yet born who will be asking questions we have not yet even begun to anticipate (Cantwell *et al.* 1981).

Lipe considered these difficulties at length as early as 1970 when he suggested some ground-rules for what many of us have been doing since then (Lipe 1970, p. 86):

It seems to me that the philosophy behind the field work of the Glen Canyon Project was something like this: A salvage project cannot focus on any single specific problem, ignoring data not relevant to that problem. Because the sites under study will be irrevocably lost, the salvage archaeologist must collect the specimens and make the observations that will serve the greatest variety of important archaeological problems of which he is aware. Further, he must do his best to predict what kinds of problems, and therefore what kinds of data, will be important in the years to come. He is, in effect, working for the whole profession of archaeology rather than just for himself.

Implementing Lipe's suggestion means dealing with archaeological materials that have not been deemed relevant to some research problem. This relates to the simple fact that the 'salvage' archaeologist does not have the option of choosing those materials being dealt with; society in general chooses the location because of some desired development. As Lipe (1974; p. 242) wrote, 'the salvage archaeologist thus differs from the academic or "pure" problem-oriented researcher in that he must adapt his problem requirements to the body of sites made available to him by society's decision to destroy them'. The archaeologist in this context does not have the option of being faithful to Hempel's dictum that the problem, hypothesis and deduced test implications must precede the selection of the relevant data.

Virtually all of cultural resource management is predicated upon an implicit acceptance of Lipe's (1974, p. 234) solution that '. . . in the long run, however, it does not matter in what sequence the problem, hypotheses and data get together. What matters is that they be logically appropriate to one another and that significant results be obtained'. A strict refusal to accept Lipe's solution would prohibit any possibility of 'mitigating the impact' on archaeological resources, since the data would always be selected on the basis of considerations other than the data requirements relevant for testing a particular hypothesis.

I am not developing a case for non-problem-oriented archaeology; however, I *am* defending Lipe's solution. I am addressing the paradox that Kidder brought out with his reference to beetle-collecting. We are dealing with a scarce non-renewable resource and not one that is essentially infinite, and clearly not one that is renewable. I am concerned about those aspects of the archaeological record that have not been deemed relevant to a particular research problem. Flannery's illustration emphasizes the fact that they have to be properly considered.

Whenever possible one should strive to follow some version of the methodology that was well developed by people like Hill (1970). While conducting research on the Piedra Lumbre Phase in northern New Mexico, I followed Hill's method very closely (Schaafsma 1979). This is the only sensible manner in which to approach archaeological materials in any context of research, but especially so in research not precipitated by some pending impact (i.e. non-'salvage archaeology'). Describing 'data' *ad nauseum* is a guaranteed route to stagnation, and much 'salvage archaeology' has been mired in this trap. Anyone who has ever excavated a large site has found that the 'data' or potential observations are so voluminous as to become impossible to manage. Hill and others (Leone 1972) were trying to avoid the hopeless tangle of observing and recording *all* of the 'facts' (Hempel 1966, pp. 11–12) latent in archaeological research. They were correctly trying to make archaeology 'a science worthy of the name' (Kidder 1932, p. 6). They were also in agreement with the general realization that simple induction is an illusion (Northrop 1958). Martin (1971, p. 6) sketched the interplay and feedback between induction and deduction that has been the basis of most archaeological methodology over the past 15 years.

Kidder's experience at Pecos has been a classic example for those of us working in Southwestern USA. Although Kidder's fieldwork was conducted between 1915 and 1929, it was not until 1958 that he published *Pecos Archaeological Notes*, his only comprehensive summary of the excavation of Pecos Pueblo. In his preface he made it clear that he would never be able to report at length on the field data and collections that he had recovered (Kidder 1958, p. xi). By the early 1970s many of us were all too aware that Kidder's problem was the norm, and not the exception. There was a desperate need to organize and make systematic our archaeological research. The Hempelian method applied to archaeology (Leone 1972, Hill 1970) was most welcome. Some guiding research design was a necessity, and nobody today would endorse excavating a ruin simply because it was there. However, most of us soon found out that there were problems.

It became obvious that Hill's recommended method could not be followed strictly during the excavation phase, especially in impact areas or during 'salvage' archaeology, if we were to adhere to the conservation ethic. I confronted this dilemma while working with the Piedra Lumbre Phase. As mentioned above, there was a clear acceptance of Hill's method, and it was utilized throughout the excavation and analysis programme (Schaafsma 1979). The problem was how to handle all of the recovered materials that were *not* relevant to the research design:

> While the research problem being discussed was the focus of the current project, it must be recalled that this was also a salvage project intended to mitigate the impact on the site of a proposed campground as well as heavy public use of the area. Accordingly, the research was not free to merely select those aspects of the archaeological record that would address the problem and leave the rest intact. To paraphrase Hill, in salvage archaeology it is necessary to collect a great deal of 'data' that are not relevant to anything in particular (1970, p. 26). One is not free to pick and choose according to the needs of a preconceived research design. Any salvage excavation has the obligation to collect and adequately preserve certain basic classes of data as well as all ancillary archaeological materials for which we can reasonably anticipate any future usefulness . . . . It was the goal of the field procedures to adequately recover the archaeological materials at the site as well as the contextual information that relates these materials to their proveniences. Consistent with Lipe's discussion, all classes of archaeological remains for which there are presently any relevance were collected and recorded.
> (Schaafsma 1979, pp. 6–7)

Following Lipe's (1974) study, it became apparent that the place to be selective is during analysis where only a fraction of the recovered materials are utilized for a focused analytic programme that emphasizes those materials that are relevant to a definite research design. Economizing and addressing a definite research problem had to be accomplished during the analysis phase. I addressed this problem in the Piedra Lumbre report (Schaafsma 1979):

As Lipe has stated (1974), it is impossible to examine in depth all the material recovered from a site. This is particularly true of outside analyses. Selection of what materials to analyse must be guided by an overall research design which focuses on some problem or set of problems that can be addressed with the excavated materials. The need for critical selection that conforms with some research problem is the inevitable result of funding limitations and the cost of various analyses. The present study presents the results of analyzing those aspects of the materials from the site that potentially can inform on the question of the ethnic identity of the site. The materials and information not discussed here are available for future research.

Lipe's solution means that selecting the data can *precede* developing the hypotheses to which the data would be relevant. The 'data' can be 'selected' by society's decision to destroy a site or set of sites. The purists have never accepted this solution, on the basis that it is an affront to the hypothetico-deductive method. It has nevertheless been the basis for most cultural resource management decisions over the past decade. It also means that a great deal of material will be collected and not analysed in depth because it was found to *not* be relevant to the research designs that were developed, after some other process (e.g. society's decision to build a campground) had selected the materials to be excavated. As mentioned above, the materials and records are curated for future research. This obviously put a tremendous obligation on museums and repositories (Cantwell *et al.* 1981, Schaafsma 1984). The problem of curation has to be addressed in another forum, but implicit in Lipe's solution is a long-term programme of curation of collections and records, and ensuring that these materials are accessible for researchers that want to utilize them. In a functional sense the essence of Lipe's solution is that a *representative sample* of those materials *not* deemed relevant to the research design will be collected and curated, as I did with the Piedra Lumbre site. I suppose that, in doing this, we archaeologists have been doing something that is more appropriate for squirrels than for scholars (King 1981).

King's recent comments on this topic (King 1981, p. 54) stand in marked contrast with Lipe's solution:

> If we *cannot* preserve in place, however, . . . then the decision not to preserve is a decision to invest the archaeological property in the investigation of those research questions we are able to address today. It is *not* a decision to recover some arbitrarily defined sample of information against tomorrow's postulated research needs. It should be your business as professionals to define research questions well, and to execute efficient, well-organized research projects to address them. It should *not* be your business to bicker about how big or what kind of sample to take, without thought about what purpose the sample is to serve.

This position is in direct conflict with Lipe's solution and the practice of obtaining representative samples of all aspects of the archaeological record, the potential relevance of which we can reasonably anticipate (Lipe 1974). To retain or even re-establish the practice of obtaining representative samples is going to demand a revision of the dogmatic stand that sites will *not* be dealt with (excavated, tested, etc.) simply because they exist (King 1981). The whole philosophy of conservation archaeology assumes that, in addition to those materials relevant to a guiding research design, a representative sample of the resources in an impact area (as well as those aspects of an archaeological site being dug in any context) that are not directly relevant to a research problem will be carefully excavated, properly recorded, studied as much as possible, reported, and curated for future use.

The earlier quote from Hill (1970, p. 26) should now be recalled in the light of King's (1981) position. Those who watch over the public purse become very excited when they become aware of a practice that is inefficient *and* a waste of money. For example, the General Accounting Office, in their 1981 study of archaeology, stated that:

> federally funded archaeological protection efforts are now proceeding in an unsystematic manner with little assurance that anything other than redundant information on already well-known cultures will result from archaeological salvage work.
>
> (GAO 1981, p. 26)

Eventually we obtain policies such as that stated by Aldrich (1982, p. 4):

> To require . . . that every site be salvaged regardless of learning anything important, would be wasteful and inefficient, and I am advised that such requirements produce bad archaeological research as well.

What this all seems to come down to is a philosophy of cultural resource management which states that one must have a problem and an explicit hypothesis (or hypotheses) before 'data' are gathered. If one does not have a problem that establishes the research relevance of the archaeological materials, then one will not be allowed to spend public money on their retrieval. No problem and no clearly stated hypothesis (or hypotheses), then no money.

As things are developing now, all of those resources that are not proven to be relevant beforehand (i.e. even before going into the field) to some preconceived research design can be ignored in a 'treatment plan'. I contend that this is in direct conflict with all of our laws which protect sites simply because they exist. However, it is clearly consistent with Hempel's argument. From this perspective things become relevant, and therefore worth spending public money on, only in the context of a research design. By themselves ('simply because they exist') they can be as irrelevant as Hempel's grains of sand (1966, pp. 11–12). The question as examined by the GAO

(1981) becomes very important: why spend public money on irrelevant activities? The GAO has a point, and we as a profession must be able to respond. Those who watch the public purse strings are not likely to sanction the expenditure of funds on 'bad archaeological research' (Aldrich 1982, p. 4).

The 'conflict of values in American archaeology' (King 1971) is still with us and, without many of us being aware of it, one side seems to have gotten the upper hand. As I put things together, inductivistic 'salvage' archaeology that is not preceded by a problem-oriented research design to establish relevance is equal to 'bad archaeology' (Aldrich 1982). Lipe's solution seems to have been lost in the shuffle. Some middle ground has to be found, or we are going to have problems.

Relevant until proven irrelevant

Concordant with Lipe's original solution, I would like to propose the principle that archaeological resources should be treated as relevant until proven irrelevant. This is rather like being innocent until proven guilty. If something is proven irrelevant, then it can be discarded (destroyed). In all fairness to the potential research interests of other researchers and future researchers we should develop cultural resource management policies which assume that the resources are relevant until a proper trial has demonstrated that they are irrelevant to all reasonably anticipatable present and future research. One aspect of this is the demonstration that the resources being considered are *not* relevant for the research design being used, and that they are among those things *not* needed to form a representative sample of the remaining materials. The process of having to *prove* archaeological resources are relevant *before* they can be dealt with is backwards, and very much the same as assuming they are guilty until proven innocent.

Significant until proven *in*significant

The key word these days is 'significance'. However, I would propose that when we are dealing with significance under section (d) of the National Register criteria, significance cannot be separated from relevance. 'Significance' becomes a legal label that something is relevant and therefore worth spending public money on. 'Significance' and 'relevance' become synonymous and are different words to use in different contexts. By extension of the above argument, then, archaeological resources should be regarded as significant until a fair trial has demonstrated that they are *in*significant.

Tainter & Lucas (1983) have explored the link between relevance and significance in a most productive way. The basic point is that, just as relevance is relative and changes with the research goals of the times, so significance also has to be relative and able to change with the needs of the times. That means that our significance- (relevance-) determining procedures must be dynamic, up to date and truly in concert with research trends. We simply *cannot* say, once and for all, that 'these are significant and those are not'. The determination has to be made each time a new set of resources is being considered. They have equally well argued that the only logical position is to determine the significance of sites according to today's standards.

As we have learned, significance is a tough concept to deal with, because in the end it means that something will have to be discarded (Thompson 1982). Thompson is correct that sites are significant relative to sites that are not. He is absolutely correct in emphasizing the point that our problems in cultural resource management persist because we have failed to develop means to identify insignificant sites satisfactorily. Our significance-determining methods should first be geared toward establishing the relevance of resources to research by defining the context in which they occur. The new Department of the Interior (1983) standards and guidelines for archaeology and historic preservation discuss this process. However, the process defined in the standards and guidelines is based on the thinking that is appropriate for historic buildings, with the illustration being 'Coal mining in northeastern Pennsylvania between 1860 and 1930'. From this perspective the process is to identify those few properties that illustrate the theme or 'historic context', and then to ignore the rest. The rest are presumably all *in*significant once the process has been completed.

In marked contrast the significance-determining methods appropriate for archaeological materials important for their potential contribution to scientific analysis should provide procedures which state *why* various archaeological resources should be discarded. In many ways it is the mirror-image of the process that is appropriate for historic buildings.

Under the National Historic Preservation Act as amended (P.L. 96–515) it is the function of state plans to develop the historic context in which the significance (relevance) of a resource is to be established. Many state programmes are now well under way along the lines that were spelled out in 36–CFR–61 and other regulations. The state plan is the legally defined vehicle for organizing the guiding research questions which help to determine research relevance and therefore legal significance. The GAO study devoted a chapter to this point (GAO 1981, pp. 23–34). Nevertheless, I do not think that any of the state plans are adequate to the task at hand, nor do any of them begin with the premise that determining *irrelevance* is part of the process. How many of you would feel confident in using the existing 'state plans' in your area to decide which archaeological sites to throw away? For one thing, any state plan that is worth its salt must have ways to integrate and make constructive use of the results of all archaeologists working in a state. It cannot be written by a single person or a select clique and expect to have the respect and co-operation that is needed. It also has to be able to keep track of and sensibly utilize research and planning efforts in adjacent states – so 'significance' does not change when one crosses a state line . . . .

Some people think that the process is to provide a method for justifying the expenditure of public money. That is part of it. From the point of view of conservation archaeology the process also has to provide a justification for throwing away some of the scarce non-renewable resources that are in our charge. In short, the process should be able to justify irrelevancy and redundancy, and therefore insignificance.

References

Aldrich, A. 1982. Changing times. *American Society for Conservation Archaeology Report* **9**(2), 1–5.

Cantwell, A.-M., J. B. Griffin & N. A. Rothschild 1981. The research potential of anthropological museum collections. *Annals of the New York Academy of Sciences* **376**.

Department of the Interior 1983. Archeology and historic preservation: Secretary of the Interior's standards and guidelines. *Federal Register* **48**, No. 190, Thursday, 29 September 1983, 44 716–42.

Flannery, K. V. 1982. The Golden Marshalltown: a parable for the archeology of the 1980s. *American Anthropologist* **84**(2), 265–78.

General Accounting Office 1981. *Are agencies doing enough or too much for archeological preservation?* Guidance needed. Report to the Chairman, Committee on Interior and Insular Affairs, House of Representatives, by the Comptroller General of the United States. Report CED–81–61, 22 April 1981. Washington, DC: General Accounting Office.

Heisenberg, W. 1958. *Physics and philosophy: the revolution in modern science.* New York: Harper & Row.

Heisenberg, W. 1972. *Physics and beyond: encounters and conversations.* Harper Torchbooks. New York: Harper & Row.

Hempel, C. G. 1966. *Philosophy of natural science.* Foundations of Philosophy Series. Englewood Cliffs, New Jersey: Prentice-Hall.

Hill, J. N. 1970. Prehistoric social organization in the American Southwest: theory and method. In *Reconstructing prehistoric Pueblo societies*, W. A. Longacre (ed.). Albuquerque: University of New Mexico Press.

Kidder, A. V. 1932. *The artifacts of Pecos.* New Haven, Connecticut: Yale University Press.

Kidder, A. V. 1958. Pecos, New Mexico: archaeological notes. *Papers of the Robert S. Peabody Foundation for Archaeology*, Vol. 5. Andover, Massachusetts: Phillips Academy.

King, T. F. 1971. A conflict of values in American archaeology. *American Antiquity* **36**, 255–62.

King, T. F. 1981. Archaeology for scholars or squirrels? A view of archaeological data recovery from the Advisory Council. *American Society for Conservation Archaeology Proceedings*, 48–55.

Leone, M. P. (ed.) 1972. *Contemporary archaeology: a guide to theory and contributions.* Carbondale & Edwardsville: Southern Illinois University Press.

Lipe, W. D. 1970. Anasazi communities in the Red Rock Plateau, Southeastern Utah. In *Reconstructing prehistoric Pueblo societies*, W. Longacre (ed.). Albuquerque: University of New Mexico Press.

Lipe, W. D. 1974. A conservation model for American archaeology. *The Kiva* **39**(3–4), 213–45.

Lipe, W. D. 1984. Conservation for what? In *Proceedings of the American Society for Conservation Archaeology*, W. J. Mayer-Oakes & A. W. Portnoy (eds).

Martin, P. S. 1971. The revolution in archaeology. *American Antiquity* **36**(1), 1–8.

Mayer-Oakes, W. J. & A. W. Portnoy (eds) 1984. *Proceedings of the American Society for Conservation Archaeology*.

McGimsey, C. R. III 1972. *Public archaeology*. New York: Seminar Press.

Northrop, F. S. C. 1958. Introduction. In *Physics and philosophy: the revolution in modern science*, by W. Heisenberg. New York: Harper & Row.

Rohrlich, F. 1983. Facing quantum mechanical reality. *Science* **221**(4617), 1251–5.

Schaafsma, C. F. 1979. *The Cerrito Site (AR–4): a Piedra Lumbre phase settlement at Abiquiu Reservoir*. Sante Fe: School of American Research.

Schaafsma, C. F. 1984. Significant until proven otherwise: ASCA President's Message. In *Proceedings of the American Society for Conservation Archaeology*, W. J. Mayer-Oakes & A. W. Portnoy (eds), 65–76.

Tainter, J. A. & G. J. Lucas 1983. Epistemology of the significance concept. *American Antiquity* **48**(4), 707–19.

Thompson, R. H. 1982. Archeological triage: determining the significance of cultural properties. In *Rescue archeology*, R. L. Wilson & G. Loyola (eds), 40–6. Washington, DC: The Preservation Press.

4 Science, service and stewardship – a basis for the ideal archaeology of the future

WILLIAM J. MAYER-OAKES

The philosophy: broadened responsibilities

In the USA in the mid-1970s the term 'conservation archaeology' became popular about the same time as the phrase 'cultural resource management' (CRM) first came into use. The Airlie House report contained a glossary, and defined 'conservation' as follows (McGimsey & Davis 1977, pp. 109–10):

> An approach to archeology based on a philosophy stressing the protection, preservation and/or managed use of the cultural resource base for future generations. Protection of representative sites and preservation of data through scientific study are major aspects of this approach. It differs from salvage archeology which stressed the immediate recovery of material from threatened sites.

Throughout the middle to late 1970s the concurrent and complementary development of the conservation ethic and of CRM in the USA brought forth a new awareness of potentially conflicting responsibilities of archaeology which had always been present, but never so evident. Several archaeologists recognized these responsibilities and described and defined them in various ways: they may be most generally described as responsibilities to resources, to research and to sponsors. Fitting (1978) described resource, problem and client orientations. His 'client orientation' referred quite narrowly to the needs of the business or whoever else was paying directly for archaeological services; his comments provoked much discussion. Client orientation is, however, only a small, if essential, part of sponsor responsibility. Dickens & Hill (1978, p. 3) formulated the idea regarding the responsibilities of CRM as follows: 'We must preserve the resource if we are to benefit from it, we must study it if we are to understand what the benefits can be, and we must translate the knowledge we gain to the public at large. After all, it is with the public that the process begins, and it is with them that it all must ultimately be fulfilled'. Here we have resource, research and sponsor responsibilities spelled out, with the public as the ultimate 'client'.

Although Fitting and Dickens & Hill were applying this idea specifically to CRM activities, it can be applied more generally to *all archaeological activities*. They all depend on and utilize the same non-renewable resources, engage in some type of research and have some sort of sponsor, be it the private patron of times past, museum or foundation, or the public through a government agency or a business complying with public laws. These three responsibilities characterize all archaeology.

Stewardship

My first use of this term comes from a small volume (McGimsey *et al.* 1970) in which an attempt was made to get the message of broad responsibilities in archaeology to the lay audience. A major response to modernization, especially rapid development, has been a movement for the conservation of resources, mostly natural resources. In the USA this movement began almost 100 years ago, and it became institutionalized about 50 years ago, as reflected by the formation of several national conservation societies. Gifford Pinchot, the first Chief (and founder, with President Theodore Roosevelt) of the US Forest Service, defined conservation as (Tombaugh 1986):

> Conservation means the wise use of the earth and its resources for the lasting good of men. Conservation is the foresighted utilization, preservation, and/or renewal of forests, waters, lands, and minerals, for the greatest good of the greatest number for the longest time.

An important concept in the US conservation movement is 'stewardship'. It has been defined as 'the conservation and wise use of resources for public benefit' (Fowler 1984, p. 116). It also implies the recognition of and provision for *future* needs. In an interview with an official of the Wilderness Society, the current Chief of the US Forest Service, R. Max Peterson, stated (Wilderness Society 1986):

> I think we're trying to become better stewards of the land for this and future generations . . . you must maintain and nurture the productivity of the land . . . . I would feel constrained to defend [in the budget] some reasonable balance between research and management of the national forests . . . this long-term stewardship.

The basic rôle of 'research' in agencies like the Forest Service is to gain the knowledge to decide what is the wisest treatment of resources and the best means of providing it. This is, of course, 'applied science'.

Implicit in Fowler's statement, quoted above, is that 'conservation' and 'wise use' are two different things. Most archaeologists have more or less equated the two terms, but the need for a broader, all-encompassing term that denotes all choices, not just various 'uses', had led to the adoption of the term 'treatment' of resources. Mayer-Oakes & Portnoy (in press) define 'conservation' as 'wisest treatment of resources'. This recognizes that resources, both natural and cultural, may be avoided, destroyed, preserved or utilized (e.g. excavated). The greatest need is for *wisdom* in making choices.

US experience in a nutshell

By the early 1970s in the USA archaeological sites and materials had come to be seen as 'resources' – 'cultural resources', analogous to 'natural resources'. They are the resources upon which archaeologists depend for their livelihoods and upon which the public depend for increased knowledge about their heritage. As resources they can be used, overused, misused, abused and used up. As resources they can also be wisely utilized, planned for and 'managed'.

Consciousness of these characteristics of the 'archaeological record' developed among some North American archaeologists in the late 1960s, a few years before the concepts of 'cultural resources' and their 'management' became explicit. By 1970 several regional expressions of concern for 'the archaeological record' and the various threats to it had emerged. A useful non-technical pamphlet for landowners and businessmen whose activities might affect archaeological sites is *Stewards of the past* (McGimsey *et al*. 1970).

The present author and his colleague, Alice Portnoy, have actively participated in much of the development of US public archaeology, and have come to see both US and all other public archaeology as being strongly shaped by the broad processes of 'modernization'. In all likelihood the primary causes of CRM and public archaeology can be found in responses to aspects of modernization, everywhere.

The forces of modernization have required most archaeologists – in the USA, at any rate – to become more pragmatic, more involved with the 'real world'. However, even if some of them feel that they must put most of their energies into strengthening the legal protection of cultural resources or dealing with other practical problems, they must remember *why* these resources deserve protection. Most of the reasons are to be found in the realm of ideas, ideals and ethics. A battle without a cause is not worth fighting. For the USA, Mayer-Oakes & Portnoy (in press) have examined the cause – the archaeological contribution to the knowledge and understanding of human heritage – described the battle – the coming together of various archaeological interests and the development of a working conservation ethic – and tried to show that the fight for the preservation and development of human heritage will be well served by an archaeology which, while healthily diverse, is becoming unified in its insistence on the wisest treatment of its resources.

Archaeology helps fulfil universal human needs, especially during increasing modernization. Mayer-Oakes & Portnoy (in press) show how archaeology, a major contributor to knowledge of human heritage, is responding and changing. Society is growing more aware of the importance and fragility of heritage values and resources. My colleague and I describe philosophical and practical responses by archaeologists working in a variety of US contexts. Diverse archaeological interests are converging as they recognize needs for conservation and wise utilization of heritage resources. Our book suggests in detail how a universal archaeology can be based on a framework of conservation and a concept of stewardship.

In any case, many people are interested in human origins and development. They want to know *what* happened, *how* it happened and *why* it happened. These questions are congruent with the three broad goals of contemporary archaeology, whether or not they are stated in the theoretical jargon of lifeway reconstruction, cultural history and culture process. When archaeology satisfies popular interest in these topics with accessible and understandable information, it deserves and is likely to receive strong public support.

These trends in archaeology may be seen as specific examples of general trends of modernization. It can be said of contemporary archaeology in the USA and in several other countries that:

(a) it is represented by a formalized and diversified 'profession';
(b) as a discipline it has achieved a level of technical sophistication and methodological competence that suggests calling it 'mature';
(c) it has a distinctive and massive 'applied' branch, especially in the areas of contract archaeology, public archaeology or CRM; and
(d) it has achieved wide appeal and recognition as a phenomenon of mass interest and participation.

Basis for a universal or holistic archaeology

There are two principles which have become widely accepted through the recent development of public, CRM or conservation archaeology. These constitute the essential basis for similarities, congruencies and, in fact, unity among the bewildering variety of archaeological special interests. Although this diversity can be a strength, in the face of continuing modernization of the surface of the Earth, greater effective strength is more likely to derive from our similarities and agreements.

The first principle has been well and widely stated and accepted, if often only tacitly. It is the principle which describes the archaeological record as finite and non-renewable. The record is, in fact, disappearing, and rapidly so under the onrush of modernization.

The second principle has not been so well stated, but it seems increasingly widely acceptable. This is the principle that describes human heritage information gained from archaeological work as worthwhile. The inexorable logic that flows from acceptance and understanding of these two principles is the basis for uniting all archaeology, everywhere, in both a profession and a discipline that subscribes to a conservation ethic supported by faithful performance in three major areas of responsibility: the resource base, the research effort and the sponsor (namely, the human race, whose heritage is the subject of archaeology and whose financing supports it). Should such an ideal as this ever be achieved, it would be justifiable to refer to a universal, world or holistic archaeology, in which all could participate, together and unified in motivation and broad philosophy, but separable and specialized in our working topics and geographic regions.

A recommendation

The study of the process of professionalization suggests that formal codes of ethics are drawn up and adopted when more personal ways of ensuring high standards begin to weaken. Such codes often accompany attempts to convince regulatory agencies that the public welfare is increased by restricting certain activities to members of guild-like organizations, such as the Society of Professional Archaeologists (SOPA). Another approach to ensuring high standards and increasing public welfare is to form a 'conscience society' within a profession. These societies concern themselves with the fundamental activities of the profession, its use of resources and its effects on society. These societies continually bring basic issues in these areas to the attention of all members of the profession: this is how they act as a 'conscience' of a profession.

For example, electrical engineering in the USA has the Society on Social Implications of Technology (SSIT) which publishes *Technology and Society* magazine. The SSIT is a society within the Institute of Electrical and Electronics Engineers (IEEE). The 'scope of the society' covers 'health and safety implications of technology; engineering ethics and professional responsibility; engineering and public education in social implications of technology; history of electrotechnology; technical expertise and public policy; social issues related to energy, information technology, and telecommunications; systems analysis in public policy decisions; economic issues related to technology; peace technology'. The magazine 'serves as a forum of free, informed discussion of all aspects of social implications of technology' (SSIT 1986). The society also sponsors various symposia which attempt to focus the attention of the entire profession on social issues. Both the magazine and the symposia welcome contributions from non-engineers.

World archaeology has a similar regional 'conscience society' – the American Society for Conservation Archaeology (ASCA). The ASCA performs similar functions in similar ways: it usually sponsors a symposium at the Annual Meeting of the Society for American Archaeology, which focuses attention on fundamental issues; it publishes its *Report* as a forum for discussion of these issues. Both SSIT and ASCA consist of a small group of individuals dedicated to the recognition and realization of the broader implications and responsibilities of their professions. The conservation (i.e. wisest treatment) of cultural resources, the fulfilment of responsibilities to resource, research and sponsor, the satisfaction of public needs to understand human heritage – all are activities that affect society. The practitioners of these activities, including archaeologists, therefore have social responsibilities which can be emphasized by a 'conscience society' such as ASCA.

There is scope for the establishment of an international organization of this kind, to continue the development of a universal, worldwide discipline of archaeology. Basing such an organization on the two most broadly accepted principles of the archaeological record should help to ensure its viability and successful development.

Conclusion

Responsible popular archaeology, based on solid research and thorough dissemination of results, is a major contributor to the development of a general interest in *human* heritage, beyond national and ethnic heritage. This interest can lead to greater respect for other (in both time and space) societies, to greater willingness to share with members of other societies, and to greater concern for the future of all humankind.

As cultural resources *in situ* dwindle, conservation will become even more important both to archaeologists and to society as a whole. Cultural resources previously collected or recorded will be more responsibly curated and better utilized. These factors will have to be recognized and dealt with in general archaeological education and in the training of archaeologists.

The public, faced with increased leisure time and perhaps a somewhat 'dehumanized' modern world, may make new demands on archaeology. Archaeology can not only help to fill those leisure hours profitably and pleasurably, it can also remind and reassure people of their humanity. Knowledge and understanding of our long, continuous and ever-changing human development – our heritage – is one of our most precious assets. It will become even more precious as the forces of modernization continue to accelerate. Archaeologists will have to assume even greater social responsibilities as stewards of the human heritage and of the cultural resources on which it is based.

References

Dickens, R. S. & C. E. Hill (eds) 1978. *Cultural resources: planning and management.* Boulder, Colorado: Westview Press.

Fitting, J. E. 1978. Client oriented archeology: a comment on Kinsey's dilemma. *Pennsylvania Archaeologist* **48**, 12–25.

Fowler, D. D. 1984. Ethics in contract archaeology. In *Ethics and values in archaeology*, E. L. Green (ed.), 108–16. New York: Free Press.

McGimsey, C. R. III & H. A. Davis (eds) 1977. *The management of archaeological resources*. Special Publication of the Society for American Archaeology.

McGimsey, C. R. III, H. A. Davis & C. Chapman 1970. *Stewards of the past*. Mississippi Aluvial Valley Archeological Program, University of Missouri, Columbia.

Mayer-Oakes, W. J. & A. W. Portnoy (eds) (in press). *Scholars as stewards: archeology and modernization*.

Society on Social Implications of Technology 1986. *Technology and society*.

Tombaugh, L. W. 1986. Is conservation outmoded? *American Forests* **92**(4), 58–61.

Wilderness Society 1986. A few minutes with the Chief on New Year's Eve. *Wilderness* **49**(172), 44–9.

5 The 'cultural dimension of development' – an archaeological approach

GUSTAF TROTZIG

This chapter deals with problems concerning development activities in the Third World from the archaeological point of view. The problems of archaeological resource management in developing countries may seem extremely unlike those in the 'developed' parts of the world. However, there are areas where lack of legislation, intensive land use and shortage of funds outbalance whatever advantages there may be in access to experts and technical facilities. 'Archaeological underdevelopment' is therefore to be found in countries which one would hesitate to call underdeveloped in any other sense. This means that most of the issues should be well known to everyone in the trade.

During recent decades the hope of a rapid change for the better in the developing countries from a solid input of foreign aid has changed to a more pessimistic or realistic view. The negative side-effects of developing projects have become increasingly evident. The economic progress is mostly not encouraging; even where the efforts may have been successful they also have created or stimulated the growth of economic inequality. There also have been, in many cases, unexpected and undesired effects on the local society where the projects have been planted. As a consequence of observations of the latter, the Centre International de Développement, under the auspices of the International Fund for Protection of Culture, has carried out a study which appeared in a report published in 1980. The work was entrusted to six eminent researchers in the fields of economics, philosophy, agronomy, microbiology and geography from different parts of the world. The concept of culture was redefined in an anthropological way as 'the collection of values, aspirations, beliefs, patterns of behaviour and interpersonal relations, established or predominating, within a given social group or society'.

Having penetrated the problems and discussed the matters from their professional points of view, they sum up their results in conclusions and recommendations, which as always in the international context are very temperate and cautious. The following types of projects are considered to be of special interest for the discussion:

(a)   large infrastructure works (ports, roads, canals and dams) not involving shifts of population and benefiting all of the inhabitants of a region or a country;

(b)   the case of infrastructure works requiring the displacement of large population groups;

(c)   'rural development' projects, of any kind;

(d)   programmes and projects linked to education, training, community life or health;

(e)   industrial development projects; and

(f)   tourism development projects.

The study establishes the fact that in almost all of these cases there are major cultural consequences for the 'beneficiary' populations. It also identifies the non-participatory character and exogenous nature of development in the Third World as one of the reasons why the cultural side often is neglected. Others are the economic aspect generally associated with the idea of development, the difficulty in quantifying cultural effects and, finally, a lack of consideration among decision makers for the sciences linked to the cultural dimension (sociology, social psychology, anthropology and ethnology). The last of these is assumed to be caused partly by less awareness of them by comparison with other sciences that are closer to the economic view of development, such as engineering, and partly to the tendency among social scientists to question the 'development'.

What might be called the historical element of the 'cultural dimension' is no doubt included in this study, although never emphasized. However, it is doubtful whether any account has been taken of the archaeological component. There are many ways of redefining archaeology. In this case a rather simple definition of archaeological remains is sufficient: 'the abandoned physical remains of past human activities'. For many countries in the Third World archaeological remains constitute the only objective source material for the study of their precolonial history. This makes the archaeological remains more valuable in these parts of the world than elsewhere. Except for what may be called National Monuments, these are often relatively inconspicuous. They are also extremely vulnerable in dry tropical climates, where dense surface-covering vegetation is lacking.

Looking back on the types of development projects listed above, it is easy to realize the impact that they may have on archaeological remains. That 'large infrastructure works' can result in irreparable damage is a well known fact (see Fig. 5.1). On some occasions the world conscience has been stimulated to considerable efforts when well-known objects such as the monuments of the Nile valley have been threatened. 'Rural development' projects, such as, for example, changes in ploughing methods of the kind now being used in Europe, erode tombs and cultural layers very quickly. Of course, the same will happen when changing from hoe and slash-and-burn agriculture to ploughing and intensive farming. 'Industrial development' too, will lead to changes in land use in many respects from the building of factories and expansion of infrastructure and energy supply. 'Tourism

Figure 5.1 An illustration from the ILO publication on road construction which should alarm every archaeologist: the stone construction being attacked by 'activities for site clearance' may well be the remains of a prehistoric site. The first stage includes activities for site clearance such as bush-clearing, tree and stump removal, grubbing, boulder removal and rock excavation.

development' may be disastrous when hotels are built in the immediate vicinity of archaeological sites. Tourism, however, is also one of the few development activities which could be used in a positive way for the archaeological heritage.

As for the final conclusions of the study, its main purpose has been to point out the problems and put forward some ideas about cause and effect. The recommendations are addressed to a number of international bodies and institutions, and the main points in the message may be summarized as follows: to improve knowledge of cultural implications in developing projects among decision-makers and organizers, to incorporate the notion of the cultural dimension in plans and to engage experts in the social sciences in the projects and include a certain percentage (10 per cent) in the budget of the projects to ensure that the cultural dimension is taken into account, and, last but not least, to allow the so-called 'target population' to participate in the drafting of the projects.

It may seem rather impertinent to regard archaeology as being equal in merit to other, more-socially and economically relevant, disciplines when the well-being and even survival of whole populations are at stake. Archaeology may, however, in some cases contribute to practical solutions on an everyday level where high technology has failed and may also provide some optimism in situations where mere rational thinking based on the present situation can offer no solution. The main thing, though, is the belief that every nation has a right to its history, and that archaeology offers methods of regaining lost history where few other sources are available. 'Prehistoric times' can be very recent in those parts of the world where foreign influence has prohibited or delayed the growth of an indigenous historical consciousness and feeling of identity.

So far so good. It is not difficult to draw up a list of the ideal demands from an archaeological point of view:

    general awareness of the value of the archaeological heritage;
    protective legislation, including funding of rescue activities;
    general survey of archaeological resources;
    planning to avoid damage to archaeological remains;
    rescue operations where damage cannot be avoided;
    communication, information and publication; and
    secure storage of finds and documents.

However, there is probably a wide gap between what is desirable and what is feasible.

In most countries there is a general awareness of the archaeological heritage but very little is known about its extent. Apart from a few national monuments, only parts of the country may have been surveyed. In many countries there also is some form of legislation, but this is usually insufficient in many ways. Owing to a lack of information it is difficult to use planning as a means of protecting the archaeological heritage. There is also a risk that questions relating to development schemes may be handled in different governmental agencies from those dealing with the cultural heritage. Rescue operations can only be promoted when it is known where archaeological remains are to be found and if exports and funds are available. Sometimes foreign 'expeditions' may be a solution, but the risk is then that the results are published and the finds exhibited far away from those whose ancestors had produced the archaeological remains. Finally, it may be difficult to find suitable localities for storing the less glamorous finds and the excavation archives.

There are no quick or easy solutions to these problems, but there are ways of handling them. For example, interest in archaeology can be stimulated at the governmental level when development projects are first being discussed: there is a high-status, glamorous side of archaeology which might be exploited quite unashamedly. Programmes of action can be adopted to regulate the handling of archaeological remains affected by the project. Provisional surveys may be carried out with the help of the local population and 'barefoot' archaeologists (in Sweden, for example, school teachers have been an invaluable help for the general survey). Planners can be briefed and encouraged to take archaeological remains into account; many technicians have a strong interest in history and archaeology which simply needs to be applied to the actual situation. On-site exhibitions involving local and central authorities can create interest for the future. Good site information in solid mountings, documents lodged in official archives, and publications constitute the best guarantees for the preservation of the material.

There is a change in progress in development policies. Large-scale projects have proven to be expensive and ineffective. The new direction is based on the Schumacher axiom of 'small is beautiful': this means that a number of small projects are taking the place of single large ones. This change of emphasis will probably call for small-scale archaeological solutions. The impact on archaeological remains may create just as many problems, but funding may become more difficult, which presents a new challenge.

Finally, a few words on what needs to be done next. The archaeological heritage must constantly be presented and promoted as a natural component of the 'cultural dimension'. Domestic archaeological institutions in the Third World should receive support in every possible way from their colleagues in better-favoured countries – by the exchange of personnel, for example – to their mutual benefit. Finally, the moral responsibility within the 'developed' (sometimes overdeveloped) countries must continuously be stressed.

References

Centre International de Développement 1980. *The cultural dimension of development*. Paris.
Clarke, R. 1985. *Science and technology in world development*. Oxford & New York.
Odak, O. 1985. The roots of the future. *Unesco Courier* (Swedish edition) September.
Road construction and maintenance in the Third World: choice of technology in developing countries. Geneva 1985.

6 *Cultural resource management and environmental education in Venezuela*

MARIO SANOJA and IRAIDA VARGAS

(translated by Henry Cleere)

Cultural property and natural resources

The study and organization of cultural resources are concerned with materials resulting from human activity in the past and in the present – artefacts, monuments, structures, customs, ideas, works of art, etc. – with the object of preserving their integrity and survival. This act of preservation of cultural property and resources must also take account of those processes by means of which a culture transforms its material and spiritual products over the centuries and at the same time preserves those which encapsulate the essential nature of the people that gives rise to them – the cultural heritage.

The creation of the cultural heritage is the phenomenon that is essential for all peoples. It acquires special characteristics when, in the course of history, the quality of life manifested by a given cultural form becomes identified with a territory which is at the same time geographical and natural, historical and political: a nation. In this way the expression of a culture emerges as a political concept: cultural identity – that national culture which comprises and reproduces all the diversity of the historical experience of the people which makes up the nation.

It will be seen that the definition of cultural heritage and national identity demands the recognition and legitimization of a landscape or of a certain collection of landscapes which constitute the physical background against which the historical processes leading to the formation of a society can take place.

Just like human beings, socially organized communities interact with the landscape in order to change and adapt it to conform with the requirements of the development of its productive resources, and so past and present cultural and natural landscapes must also be considered as cultural property and resources.

The natural environment, organized in a series of ecosystems, enters history proper with the appearance of socially organized human societies. When its natural components begin to be utilized as decisive factors in the survival of the species, they are transformed into natural resources. In this way, as we have seen, the man-made environment within which human social groups live comes to constitute the material basis and condition for its existence, made up of the natural elements and those created or acquired by man. A natural environment may or may not have been modified by human activity but, whatever the case, it is used and conceived according to the values of the culture for which it forms a material base (Childe 1981, pp. 239–63).

The survival of all or part of past natural or cultural environments acts as a guide to the preservation of the tangible nodes which are considered by individuals to represent their cultural heritage. Bearing in mind that neither can be renewed in terms of their historical significance for a social group, it is imperative that both forms of resource should be considered as forming part of the cultural heritage which confers their individuality and national character on different peoples. If the cultural heritage is to be managed on behalf of the nation, it is essential that it should be accessible to every member of the community by means of an adequate selection of the natural and cultural resources or values, and their promotion and interpretation through education and the mass media, as in the case of educational museums.

Neglect of this important educational resource has had profound implications for Venezuelan society. The schoolchildren of today are the voters and administrators of the future; if their awareness of the need to preserve natural and cultural resources and values is confined to the appreciation of national symbols, such as the flag, the national coat-of-arms or the national anthem, and is not based on a deep understanding of the totality of those components which make up the natural environment within which they live, such as their historic past, then they will be unable to adopt a conservationist attitude towards nature and the historic past as a whole.

One of the solutions to the problems posed by the preservation of the culture and the geographical and historical territory of the Venezuelan nation would be the development of popular facilities such as educational museums, which relate environmental, historical and geographical education closely to formal education in primary and secondary schools.

The conservation ethic for natural and cultural property and resources cannot be imposed by law, it must arise naturally from the community itself. If conservation attitudes and activities are to be assimilated deeply into the consciousness of the general public, then this must be as a result of a deliberate act of education in its broadest sense. In Venezuela, unfortunately, the educational potential of museums has generally been completely ignored.

The rôle of the ecological museum

Man and nature are the twin agents of a continuous revolution which is, at one time or another, changing the face of the Earth and modifying nature through the activities of social groups. The dialectic relationship between these two forces, and between men themselves, shapes the potential of human energies behind a process of creative activity – advances, promises and destructions.

This synoptic vision of dynamic relationships confined in space and time can assume a tangible didactic expression through the medium of the ecological museum, thereby permitting an appreciation of the transformations that man has set in train on the Earth as part of a continuous revolution and to understand its dynamic unity as a whole. By converting this human experience into reality in the form of a museum, it will become possible to understand properly the processes of social and cultural change which are taking place before our eyes, and the need to preserve that which constitutes the material basis of organized social life.

Man's technological development has highlighted the fact that unity between the scale of the individual and the totality of the environment has been superseded. The new perception depends on our degree of awareness of the relationships between the individual and the social group, between functional and personal life, between the cultural landscape and the natural landscape, and between every part of the immediate natural environment and the social world that surrounds us.

Human communities have always been compelled to evaluate the economic potential of the area in which they live, and to organize their lives within the natural environment in terms of their own skills and values. This exploitation of the environment and of natural ecosystems constitutes the deformation of the original, prehuman landscape by the appropriation of the habitat resulting from the dispersion of separate cultures over the *oikumene*.

The aims of the ecological museum

Through the medium of the ecological museum, designed as the pivot of environmental education related to the total ecosystem – ecology–society–culture – it becomes possible to:

- understand how man has intervened in and disturbed the organic world, converting its natural elements into resources for his own survival;
- understand and analyse how social activities have altered the surface of the Earth, its soils, its water resources, its plants and animals, and how minerals have been extracted from it; and
- understand and analyse how the activities of urban life changed the original ecosystems, creating new social relationships between man, space, and the biological and natural elements that surround them.

In an ecological museum, environmental education would provide a teaching tool in order to promote an awareness of the dependence of man upon his natural environment, and favouring the teaching of the principles of ecosystems in primary schools and at various levels, including the adult population, which is not involved in the processes of formal education.

The main objective of ecological museums, finally, would be to ensure that the process of social growth and expansion would proceed within the framework needed for harmony between socio-economic development and the preservation or improvement of the quality of life.

The ecological museum and environmental education in Venezuela

The ecological museum, by virtue of its character as an educational or thematic museum, is a response to the socio-economic and cultural conditions which have caused a decline in the quality of life in Venezuela, in so far as environmental deterioration has grown considerably.

This process has been due essentially, we maintain, to the fact that most, if not all, conservationist policies have tended to consider society as something which exists outside and separate from nature. Following this line of argument, there has been a tendency to consider that there are certain laws which relate solely to nature, and others designed specifically for the government of human society.

When the natural world is conceived of as separate from the world of man and governed according to different principles, men think of the environment within which they live their lives as though it is an inexhaustible reservoir of raw materials and of resources which can and should be used without any heed for their importance for the community. The facts show, however, that in general man and society constitute the most important part of nature, since it is they who, by their interventions, have caused rapid changes and destruction in the natural world.

As a result of this philosophy, which separates the social world from the natural world, men have, since the beginning of the technological and industrial development of their respective societies, seen the natural environment as an open ecosystem from which limitless supplies of energy and raw materials might be extracted and into which the by-products of this development could be injected, in the form of an immense quantity of refuse and pollutants. Although it has seen the environment as an open ecosystem, society has behaved as though it were a closed ecosystem, independent of the natural one. Thus, all those constituents of the environment that have been used – air, water, soil, collective resources, etc. – could be renewed.

In recent years the growth in human populations and of their material and spiritual needs which have had to be accommodated by governments or the economic groups which control them have been forced to give serious consideration to the fact that natural resources are finite and that, through regulating the development of society, it is necessary to understand and to work within the natural laws which, in one way or another, have affected (and continue to affect) their socio-economic development.

In Venezuela the response to this problem that has been adopted in recent decades has centred almost entirely on education in order to protect nature or to mitigate the consequences of socio-economic development – water and air pollution, destruction of hydrographic basins, forests and wildlife. This means that environmental education has been planned from the standpoint of the philosophy enunciated above, which separates the natural world from the social and cultural world, making the problem of conservation essentially a biological one. This must be changed, and we believe that an improvement is in progress.

As Childe pointed out, the environment is not an object of contemplation, but a field for social activity. It is not merely the natural environment of biologists and ecologists, but a world of ideas and collective representations which every society finds surrounding that in which it lives. Environmental education must therefore transcend this formal separation between subject and object, and ensure, through its actions, that it is the cultural structure of society which determines the form of intervention, whether positive or negative, in the environment. As a result, this should operate through the collective view that a society has of its environment, using the vehicle which allows it to visualize that environment objectively – the ecological museum.

Against this background, environmental education should be organized so as to teach those individuals that make up society that they are living within a dynamic complex of interrelated systems, of which they are an integral part. This means that there must be a focusing on the ecosystem for the management of natural and cultural resources based on:

(a)   a physical relationship between society and its surroundings; and
(b)   the levels of political decision-making; the quality and quantity of socio-economic development, and the cultural heritage which determine this relationship.

Everything that has gone before implies that men must be able to live in harmony, not only with natural ecosystems, but also with the cultural ecosystems that they have themselves created – towns, irrigation systems, cultivated lands, industrial areas, etc. If they are to be capable of understanding this concept of the ecosystem, however, man and society in general must learn to understand and respect the potential which the concept of the ecosystem represents.

Living within such a concept implies the substitution of a consumer economy by one that is orientated towards the maintenance and preservation of the physical base, of capital goods and the recycling of materials, which means a more austere society that is heedful of the need for rational utilization of natural, historical, cultural and social resources. This need is becoming increasingly apparent in Venezuela, in that the decrease in the financial power of the state, as a result of the world oil crisis, is forcing us to redefine social goals and criteria relative to the preservation and improvement of the quality of life.

The ecological museum and social aims

A network of ecological museums in Venezuela needs to be considered as something much more than a simple problem of the preservation of the natural environment; it should take account of the fact that the human eco-system also includes the social, political, economic and educational systems – in short, the cultural heritage – and the effect that Venezuelan society has in this way on its surroundings.

An ecological museum would make it possible for the student community, young people and the public at large to contemplate in all its diversity the totality and the infinite variety of ecosystem models, at the same time appreci-ating dynamic relationships defined by space and time, from the earliest or most primitive to the most recent interventions on the part of man in the natural environment. It would range from isolated and unconsidered small-scale activities to those planned programmes of change which society has set in train to change the environment in various parts of the country. Without this synoptic view of the historical and cultural process of relations between man and his environment in Venezuela, we shall not be able – we have not been able – to make the Venezuelan people understand why it is necessary to preserve the physical and material basis for the survival and continuance of organized social life – the natural and cultural ecosystems which make up man's habitat.

This form of environmental education should depend on the work of teach-ers and educators who provide the diffusion element for conservationist prin-ciples. At the same time the formal education process should be complemen-ted by visual and participatory demonstration of the overall concept of the ecosystem, which the ecological museum will supply, combining in a single message the preservation of the cultural and the environmental heritage.

Neglect of this intimate relationship between those processes which synthe-size the achievements and experiences of different generations of Venezuelans in the diverse fields of human activity has had profound negative implications for our society. If we do not inculcate, by means of an integrated environ-mental education policy, a deep appreciation of all of the components that go to make up the overall historical ecosystem – natural, social and cultural – the Venezuelans of today and tomorrow will be incapable of adopting a soundly based conservationist attitude towards nature, culture and history. They will simply not know how, why or for whom to preserve the future of their country.

Reference

Childe, V. G. 1981. Los mundos sociales del conocimiento. In *Presencia de Vere Gordon Childe*, J. Pérez (ed.). México: Instituto Nacional de Antropología e Historia.

7 The ICOMOS International Committee on Archaeological Heritage Management (ICAHM)

MARGARETA BIÖRNSTAD

The immense process of reconstruction following World War II confronted architects and building conservators with tasks that necessitated collaboration between various experts. Until then relatively few people had concerned themselves with historic buildings, but immense efforts were now called for in order to rescue and recreate an important cultural heritage. The problems were frequently identical, so the need arose for an interchange of experience and the establishment of co-operation across national boundaries in support of building conservation. This led to the formation, at a meeting in Venice, of The International Council on Monuments and Sites (ICOMOS), which is defined in its statutes as an international forum for the conservation, protection, rehabilitation and enhancement of monuments, groups of buildings and sites.

The work of ICOMOS embraces a wide field of activities, including both the urban and rural cultural heritage, major international monuments and also more modest settlements, and environments of significant local and regional characteristics. For obvious reasons the main preoccupation has been with the conservation of buildings, but archaeological remains were also included in ICOMOS's sphere of interest from the very beginning. This applies particularly to large monuments and buildings. In recent years, however, a growing threat to the archaeological heritage – and a widespread growth of interest in that heritage – have prompted a discussion within ICOMOS of the organization's rôle in the archaeological field. This discussion led, in 1985, to the decision to appoint a special International Committee on Archaeological Heritage Management (ICAHM).

ICOMOS established ICAHM in order to provide an international forum for the exchange of experience and expertise between those concerned with archaeological heritage management, to promote international co-operation and to advise on the development of ICOMOS policies and programmes in this field. To those archaeologists who were instrumental in bringing about ICAHM, the main objective, at least initially, was to create a meeting point where those who are actively involved in archaeological heritage management could compare notes and obtain new ideas for their own work. The situation regarding conservation of the archaeological heritage has a great deal in common with the scene confronting the building conservators at the end of World War II. More and more archaeologists (and experts in other fields) are now becoming involved in archaeological heritage management. The threat to the archaeological heritage is growing, and we find that different countries and continents have problems which are similar in nature or whose solution demands roughly identical inputs.

The main threats to the archaeological heritage are the accelerating pace of change in society, large-scale exploitation, new technical systems and changes in land use, but also a lack of knowledge and awareness concerning the values inherent in the archaeological heritage. Lack of awareness and, in certain cases, deliberate lack of consideration means at the same time that the solution to many of the problems facing those of us whose work, in various capacities, is related to the archaeological heritage lies, not in improvements to our own working methods, but in the mobilization of opinion at all levels – among politicians, urban and regional planners, landowners and the public. Widespread destruction of archaeological monuments and sites is in progress in various parts of the world. Here, as with building conservation, an international forum is needed in which to discuss ways of influencing attitudes to the archaeological heritage and creating better conditions for the preservation, not only of the big monuments, but also of less-spectacular remains, as well as adequate methods of rescue archaeology.

For my own part I was fairly late in realizing the absence of a forum of this kind and the actual need for one. By a happy coincidence I was able, in 1978 and 1981, to take part in symposia organized by French colleagues in Paris. The subject was 'Archaeological policy in Europe', and the symposia turned into a general review of the archaeological heritage management situation in the countries represented, as regards organization, legislation, activities, and the structure and emphasis of archaeological training. Not unexpectedly, the account given on those occasions confirmed not only that there were great differences from one country to another as regards administrative structure and legislation, but also that the points at issue and the problems to be faced as regards the handling of archaeological remains in urban and regional planning, rescue archaeology and conservation and information are astonishingly similar.

When the UK National Committee of ICOMOS later recommended that ICOMOS respond to the desire for an international platform for archaeological heritage management, and that ICOMOS extend its commitments in this field, a positive response was forthcoming. Of course, this would make ICOMOS a common organization for the various specialists concerned with cultural resource management, and would enable them to draw on the experience accumulated by ICOMOS in the 20 years of its existence. In many countries, especially outside Europe, the ICOMOS National

Committees were, in fact, already acting as a joint forum for architectural and archaeological heritage management.

The International Committees of ICOMOS operate very independently, drawing up their own programmes of action. In ICAHM's case specific demands have been made concerning the actual programme work. This is because the Committee differs from the other International Committees of the organization in that, as far as the archaeological heritage is concerned, it will be covering the full range of ICOMOS activities. This has made it necessary to attempt a definition of ICAHM's work within ICOMOS and in relation to other international organizations, especially ICOM (the International Council of Museums) and ICCROM (the International Centre for the Study of the Preservation and Restoration of Cultural Property). We have done this partly by defining the terms 'archaeological heritage' and 'archaeological heritage management'. We have based our definition of the archaeological heritage on archaeological methods, in saying that 'the archaeological heritage includes all sites, remains and objects which bear witness to human existence in epochs and civilisations for which excavation and field survey are the main sources of scientific information'. This means that there is no reference to a specific period or periods, but that standing historic buildings are not included in the term 'archaeological heritage' except in so far as archaeological methods may be used in such activities.

We have defined archaeological heritage management as 'the protection and administration of archaeological heritage in its original environment and in its relationship to history and contemporary society'. These activities can be viewed as a process which includes survey, inventorization, excavation, research, protection, presentation, education, etc. Archaeological heritage management thus defined includes rescue archaeology, which plays an important rôle in the protection and interpretation of archaeological heritage.

Given these definitions, ICAHM's field of operations supplements the archaeological work of ICOM in the museum sector. However, at the same time there is bound to be close co-operation between ICOMOS and ICOM, e.g. as regards the transmission to museums of information and finds from rescue excavations. Similarly, there are natural interfaces between ICOMOS and ICCROM as regards the conservation of archaeological objects and sites.

The actual programme for ICAHM's work follows two main lines, and thus it includes measures aimed at creating understanding and awareness of the importance of the archaeological heritage among the general public, politicians and government institutions, thereby improving the general starting position for our activities and, secondly, questions of particular interest to those who are professionaly active in the field. The promotion of a systematic inventory of the world archaeological heritage and the development of efficient sympathetic strategies of management are important tasks which can form part of a long-term policy-making process and play an important part in lending added weight to our activities. Programme points addressed specifically to professionals are concerned with such concrete subjects as methods and standards of documentation, sampling procedures, recording, publication, etc., and with questions of minimum standards for the training and qualifications of those engaged in archaeological heritage management, as well as the more general task of encouraging an exchange of experience and expertise.

The ICAHM programme also includes a point referring to the encouragement of a multidisciplinary approach to the cultural heritage. This can be taken as an appeal to promote a holistic view of the cultural heritage and better collaboration between architectural and archaeological heritage management. It can also be taken as a reminder of the important interconnection and interdependence of archaeological heritage management and archaeological research.

Writing a programme is one thing, proceeding to concrete action is another. Many people are doubtless wondering what initiatives ICAHM can really be expected to take. ICOMOS is an association of individuals, and the efforts made are based primarily on members' contributions. Thus, where the International Committees are concerned, it is the members of the Committees' managing group who are expected to be active. ICOMOS does not command any vast resources in the form of money or especially employed personnel, but there are nevertheless good opportunities for generating activity.

In 66 countries all over the world there are ICOMOS National Committees which can be mobilized and, under their own auspices or in association with national authorities or with ICAHM and ICOMOS at central level, can organize seminars and symposia for discussions and the interchange of experience. ICOMOS's close co-operation, for example, with Unesco, ICOM and ICCROM also provides certain opportunities for joint action, such as projects to elucidate particular problem fields or meetings to discuss assignments or problems of common concern.

ICOMOS also has a membership journal, *ICOMOS Information*, which is published quarterly and can become a useful forum of information for those involved in archaeological heritage management. This journal has space for presentations, case studies and analyses of general problems. It also includes a diary of current seminars, symposia and other meetings, both national and international, which makes it easy to keep up with events in different parts of the world and to establish personal contacts in fields of particular interest.

However, what exactly is ICAHM doing here and now, apart from trying to market itself and ICOMOS? The first thing we did when our programme had been approved by ICOMOS was to write to the 66 National Committees, appealing to them to include archaeological heritage management in their programmes or to redouble their efforts in this field. Another task we have undertaken is the very banal one of constructing an address list of authorities and organizations that are actively involved in archaeological heritage management in different countries. This is because of the difficulties we have ourselves experienced in obtaining correct data when trying to establish contacts and publicize our plans. We have also printed a short presentation brochure describing ICAHM and its programme.

We like to think of the next task that we have begun to tackle as part of the business of establishing understanding for and interest in the archaeological heritage and its importance. There are, of course, many different ways of approaching this. We have chosen to create an opinion-mobilization document which can be used by a large number of people, in the form of an ICOMOS Charter for Archaeological Heritage Management. We have been partly influenced here by the encouraging results of the Venice Charter, which has been ICOMOS's guiding star for archaeological heritage management, and which has played an important part in strengthening the position of care of the archaeological heritage.

Of course, a fair amount of policy documentation already exists in the form of international recommendations and conventions, above all those of Unesco, but also regional ones such as those adopted by the Council of Europe. However, there is no comprehensive document on archaeological heritage management as we understand it. Archaeological investigations, for example, are dealt with in one document and preservation questions in another. An ICOMOS Charter could state a holistic view. Work on a charter, naturally involving the ICOMOS National Committees and, I hope, the entire archaeological community, should itself form part of a process of opinion mobilization. A charter should effectively support and supplement existing conventions and recommendations in discussions with politicians and national authorities, and in the formation of public opinion. This applies both in countries where reasonable instruments of archaeological heritage management already exist and in countries where work is in progress on building up activities, or where work of this kind has not yet begun.

The last point of the working programme for ICAHM's first period of activity is a symposium, which we hope will herald an entire series of symposia and seminars on various subjects. As the subject of our first symposium we have chosen 'Archaeology and society – large-scale rescue operations – possibilities and problems'. Our choice of large-scale rescue operations is, of course, connected with the relevance that they have acquired in connection with such large-scale development undertakings as gas pipelines, major road construction projects, extensive land-development projects of various kinds, and so on.

Investigations of this kind have, however, sometimes very sharply highlighted the way in which planning deficiencies and uncertain or limited finances, primitive scientific objectives and inadequate follow-up of investigations can impair or completely frustrate the results otherwise attainable. A discussion of large-scale investigations ought therefore to provide an excellent foundation on which to compare notes concerning archaeological strategies vis-à-vis politicians, national authorities, developers and the public, theoretical premises and rescue archaeology methods, and – by no means the least important – the influence of large-scale rescue operations on the development of archaeological models and explanations. In this way the symposium could provide an excellent opportunity for elucidating the interaction of archaeological heritage management with development interests and archaeological research.

These questions are constantly arising and always in need of discussion, especially, of course, in countries now in the very process of building up their cultural heritage management. The same goes for countries in which we have already been able to establish a firm structure of archaeological heritage management but in which the progress of research, as well as changes in society and in the relationship between different sectors of society, changes in our own organization, or changing ideas concerning the apportionment of responsibilities between different public agencies and organizations, make it necessary for us to be perpetually prepared to develop new ideas and reconsider established ones.

So much for the tasks which we expect ICAHM to accomplish during the period between 1986 and 1988 – and by 'we' I mean the ICAHM Managing Group and the Secretariat jointly organized by the Nordic countries. The real constraints on ICAHM's activities at the moment are the resources at our disposal in the Secretariat; that is, the amount of time we are able to set aside privately and in the course of our regular duties at our various institutions. Will this be enough in order for ICAHM to measure up to expectations in the long run? Yes and no: it may be enough for the archaeological heritage to be highlighted more distinctly than hitherto within ICOMOS, thus strengthening the position of archaeological heritage management in the dialogue conducted by ICOMOS at international level (with Unesco, for example) and also with its committees in the individual countries.

However, whether ICAHM will become the forum of discussion and experience interchange which was our main motive for committing ourselves during an introductory phase will depend on the archaeologists themselves, and on those who, in their various capacities, are actively involved in archaeological heritage management. After all, the work of ICOMOS and ICAHM at international level and the work of the National Committees in the individual countries are completely dependent on the active participation of archaeologists. In some countries the establishment of ICAHM will not come as any great novelty, because archaeologists there are already committed at national level to the work of ICOMOS and are influencing the course that it takes. In other countries, archaeologists have been completely excluded.

One can also view the matter from another angle, namely in terms of the responsibilities of archaeologists in connection with international efforts to protect archaeological monuments and sites and to ensure that knowledge of the archaeological heritage is not destroyed. Archaeologists are needed in this work, to mobilize public opinion and to provide politicians with support and arguments.

REGIONAL AND COUNTRY STUDIES

8 'Tread softly for you tread on my bones': the development of cultural resource management in Australia

JOSEPHINE FLOOD

The development of heritage protection

The first historic site in Australia to be declared as such by law was Captain Cook's landing place at Kurnell, south of Sydney in 1899, and two years later the Royal Australian Historical Society was founded. However, it was not until after World War II that public interest in heritage conservation quickened both in Europe and in Australia. The impetus came from the community rather than government, and the National Trust movement (a voluntary non-governmental organization) commenced in 1945. There is now a National Trust in every state, with a total membership of some 85 000 (out of a national population of 15 million).

During the 1970s the efforts of the National Trust to preserve Australia's cultural heritage were joined by what is probably the first unique feature of the conservation movement in Australia: the development of 'green bans' by the trade unions. The first green bans were placed by the Builders Labourers Federation, who refused to work on a site if to do so would mean destroying a place of heritage value. The green bans movement spread from union to union and from state to state, arousing public concern over heritage issues and leading eventually to both State and Federal Government reviews and legislation (Mundy 1981).

The Australian Heritage Commission was established in 1975 to compile a Register of the National Estate, which was defined as 'Those places, being components of the natural environment of Australia, or the cultural environment of Australia, that have aesthetic, historic, scientific or social significance or other special value for future generations as well as the present community' (Australian Heritage Commission Act 1975: Section 4(1)).

The National Estate therefore includes places of natural environmental significance, such as forests, wetlands, geological formations and habitats of rare plants or animals, as well as historic sites, structures, buildings and gardens, shipwrecks, Aboriginal sites and places of archaeological value, both Aboriginal and historic. The Register of the National Estate is a public, fully computerized database, easily accessible to planners, developers, conservationists, researchers, educationalists and the community at large (Australian Heritage Commission 1981, 1985a). The computer information system contains information (at 30 June 1987) on 16 400 data entries, of which 7990 are actually on the Register of the National Estate. The compilation of a comprehensive, accurate and up-to-date register will clearly, by its nature, be a continuing process over many years.

Particular current concerns of the Commission are the formulation of detailed criteria and guidelines for assessing the significance of sites (cf. Sullivan & Bowdler 1984) and the institution of financial incentives as a means of conserving the national heritage (Australian Heritage Commission 1985b). Some other issues in cultural resource management have been tackled by Australia ICOMOS (the Australian National Committee of the International Council on Monuments and Sites). These include the development of a set of objectives for legislation to protect the National Estate (see Appendix 1), a Charter for the Conservation of Places of Cultural Significance (the Burra Charter) and for regulation of archaeological work (Appendix 2) and guidelines for the establishment of cultural significance (Appendix 3).

Aboriginal sites legislation

Since the 1960s Australia has developed reasonably comprehensive legislation to protect both the Aboriginal and the European heritage. The resolution of conflicts between development and conservation interests has involved the governments of Australia and a large number of voluntary and private organizations. The powers of the Federal Government are limited by a constitution which gives most of the responsibility for heritage, environment and planning to the State Governments, except for those actions carried out by the Federal Government in transacting its own business (this includes the power to legislate with regard to Aboriginal affairs). This Federal/State division of authority has led to a proliferation of different state laws governing heritage matters, overlain by five Federal Acts.

Legislation to protect Aboriginal sites came before that aimed at conserving the European heritage. During the late 1960s and early 1970s all Australian states introduced some legislative measures to protect Aboriginal 'relics', which were basically archaeologically visible sites and archaeological artefacts. This archaeological bias was not surprising, in view of the strong lobbying and input into the legislation by archaeologists concerned at the threat of damage or loss of sites from amateur unscientific research, private collectors and development pressures.

Characteristic of the legislation of this period was the focus on archaeological sites and neglect of sites which contain no material evidence of Aboriginal occupation, but which are sacred or significant to Aborigines as part of their religious beliefs in accordance with Aboriginal tradition. Other common features of this legislation (quoted in full in Edwards 1975) were the control of archaeological research, particularly of excavation, the establishment of State Government advisory committees dominated by non-Aborigines and with strong archaeological input, and the 'blanket protection' of Aboriginal sites and artefacts.

The system of overall statutory protection for Aboriginal artefacts and all sites containing material traces of Aboriginal culture means that artefacts cannot be collected, nor can sites be damaged or destroyed except with written permission of the State Government agency after the appropriate salvage archaeology has been done. Ownership of sites remains with the landowner, but landowners, like the public, are subject to the provisions of the legislation. Artefacts discovered or collected after the introduction of the relevant State Act became the property of the Crown. This system has advantages over that operating in the USA, where the rights of private property owners seem to be given more weight than the need to conserve the national heritage.

All of these Aboriginal heritage Acts designate a State Government authority such as the State national parks service or museum to administer the legislation and manage the sites, and an official repository for artefacts is also usually specified. These Acts have generally worked well, but legislation that is suitable for the urbanized southern half of Australia may not be appropriate for the tropical north, where the traditional Aboriginal life-style is still strong.

The Western Australian legislation of 1972 partially recognized these differences, by including special provisions for Aboriginal custodians and traditional use of sites and artefacts, and for the protection of sacred sites, including those lacking visible traces of Aboriginal culture. These were defined as 'any place, including any sacred, ritual or ceremonial site, which is of importance or of special significance to persons of Aboriginal descent' (Western Australia Aboriginal Heritage Act 1972: Section 5(b)).

The recognition given in the Western Australian Act that sacred sites exist was a step forward, and was followed in 1978 by the Aboriginal Sacred Sites Act of the Northern Territory. The principal functions of the Aboriginal Sacred Sites Protection Authority set up under this Act are (Aboriginal Sacred Sites Act 1978: Section 13):

(a)   to establish and maintain a register of sacred sites;
(b)   to examine and evaluate all claims for sacred sites made to it by Aboriginals;
(c)   to record sacred sites, with full details of significance to the traditional Aboriginals, including any story, of each sacred site and any relevant factors including custodianship of the sacred site.

It should be noted that 'evaluate' in (b), above, is not defined in the Act, and the process of evaluation has not yet been formalized in any Australian legislation, regulations or guidelines. This remains a task to be tackled by cultural resource managers, anthropologists and archaeologists.

Another piece of legislation (Native and Historical Objects and Areas Preservation Act 1955–60) administered by the Northern Territory Museum relates to protection of Aboriginal and historic archaeological sites and artefacts in the Northern Territory, dealing with 'relics' rather than sacred sites. This division of Aboriginal cultural resources into two types – sacred and non-sacred – has worked remarkably well, although inevitably there is some overlap, as when a rock-painting site containing an occupation deposit is also a site of great traditional significance to contemporary Aborigines. The advantage of such a distinction between archaeological and sacred sites is that without it all sites tend to be termed significant or sacred. As Sullivan (1985, p. 149) stated in a recent book on the question of 'Who owns the past?':

> For Aborigines, sites have strong symbolic or religious value. Some sites are specifically sacred or significant, but all sites are, to many Aborigines, tangible proof of their ancestors' life in Australia from what is, to them, literally time immemorial. The Aboriginal community regards all Aboriginal sites as 'sacred' sites in this sense, and uses this term increasingly in southeastern Australia to describe all Aboriginal sites.
>
> Sites provide evidence of prior occupation of the whole of Australia by Aborigines, and are a basis for land rights claims. There has never been any agreement or treaty with Aborigines to acknowledge this prior ownership, and from the Aboriginal point of view this occupation is illegal. The issue of custodianship of sites is, for this reason, inextricably bound up with the issue of land rights. Assertion of custodianship of sites is for Aborigines at least a symbolic assertion of their ownership of Australia.

The most recent piece of legislation relating to Aboriginal sites is the federal Aboriginal and Torres Strait Islanders Heritage Protection Act of 1986. The aim of this Act is to protect places and artefacts of particular significance to Aborigines and Torres Strait Islanders in accordance with their traditions. It was designed to enable direct and effective action to be taken by the Federal Government to deal with situations where significant Aboriginal sites or artefacts are under threat and where State or Territory laws are lacking or not enforced.

An interesting feature of the Act is the very broad definition of a significant Aboriginal area, which can embrace a newly discovered archaeological site such as Kutikina Cave in south-west Tasmania, a cave whose significance and even existence was unknown to contemporary local Aborigines until it was discovered by archaeologists, but which can now be claimed as a significant Aboriginal place under the terms of this Act. Other points of interest are the extremely heavy penalties for contravention of a provision of a declaration, such as knowingly setting foot on a declared significant site. The penalty involved is a fine of up to $A10 000 or a period of imprisonment not exceeding five years, or both, for an individual, or a fine of up to $A50 000 for a body corporate.

No site has yet been declared under the Act, but the auction sale of one collection of artefacts has been prevented by declaration. It is in relation to significant artefacts that the Act may well prove to be most useful, since there are glaring inadequacies in existing State legislation governing the sale of Aboriginal traditional artefacts. It should also be mentioned that Australia has recently become a party to the 1970 Unesco Convention on the Means of Prohibiting and Preventing the Illicit Import, Export and Transfer of Ownership of Cultural Property, by the passing of the Protection of Movable Cultural Heritage Bill 1985.

The Federal Government is wisely keeping the issue of protection of significant sites and artefacts separate from the far more contentious issue of land rights. However, the land rights issue inevitably affects both cultural resource managers and archaeologists. Many landowners are reluctant to give permission for archaeological research to be carried out on their property in case it leads to discovery of significant Aboriginal sites, and hence to the fear of an Aboriginal land claim, although the Federal Government has made it very clear that only unalienated Crown land and *not* private property will be subject to land claims. Sites have even been deliberately destroyed by landowners in the course of this white backlash. It is a difficult situation, and the sooner the land rights issue is resolved satisfactorily, the better.

Consultation and involvement

The 1970s revealed an additional skill needed by Australian prehistorians: the ability to communicate effectively with Aborigines. Gone are the days when archaeologists could dig away and pose their theoretical problems without dealing with living people or concerning themselves with social or ethical problems. The need both to consult and to involve Aborigines in archaeology is very clear, and the ethical, philosophical, legal, social and political arguments in favour are overwhelming. In addition, archaeological research has much to gain from consultation, and most archaeologists should see the benefits and relevance of consultation from the point of view of self-interest, if nothing else.

The desirability of consultation with Aboriginal people regarding all aspects of research and management of their sites has been accepted by the Australian Archaeological Association (the archaeologists' professional body), which accepted a motion proposed by the Tasmanian Aboriginal Centre at its 1982 Annual General Meeting in Hobart that (Allen 1983):

This conference acknowledges Aboriginal ownership of their heritage. Accordingly, this conference calls on all archaeologists to obtain permission from the Aboriginal owners prior to any research or excavation of Aboriginal sites.

Likewise, in recognition of the rights of Aboriginal people in decisions regarding the disposition of their cultural heritage, Government Sites Authorities have, through the National Aboriginal Sites Authorities Committee, expressed the view that adequate consultation with Aborigines on all aspects of work affecting their heritage should be a basic principle of Aboriginal cultural resource management.

Aboriginal people are very concerned about custodianship and who shall be the guardians of knowledge of the past (Willmot 1985). They want to have a greater say in archaeological work and to be involved in decision-making about any activities which might adversely affect sites, and about the kind of research that is done into Aboriginal culture, in order to ensure that it is not offensive and is of relevance to Aboriginal people.

These are very reasonable aspirations, but they still seem threatening to some archaeologists, who fear exclusion from research opportunities, a downgrading in the importance of prehistoric archaeological sites relative to sacred sites, and possibly censorship of unacceptable theories about the Aboriginal past. Although these fears are understandable, they are probably groundless for several reasons.

Since the acknowledgement by the Australian Archaeological Association and by the National Aboriginal Sites Authorities Committee of the need for consultation and involvement of Aboriginal people in cultural resource management, there has been no slackening in the pace of archaeological research, nor has there been censorship of archaeological publications, but only some mild protests over terminology or over presentation of scientific theories as the only possible interpretations. For example, Aborigines do not regard themselves as the first migrants to Australia, but as indigenous people, since they have no other race history except from the place where they live. (This definition of Aborigines as an indigenous nation was proposed by the first Aboriginal Senator, Neville Bonner, at a lecture at Macquarie University in 1982, and has been adopted by leading educationist, Eric Willmot (1985, p. 45).)

Prehistoric sites, even burials, are still being excavated by archaeologists, but now usually after consultation with the relevant Aboriginal group participating (cf. Jones 1985). This situation is likely to continue. What has changed is that the archaeology of Aboriginal sites now tends to be more of a co-operative venture between archaeologists and Aborigines. Aborigines continue to be concerned about prehistoric sites, and occasionally they request archaeologists to carry out research into such sites. The results of such research often prove useful in supporting the Aboriginal struggle for recognition of their prior ownership of Australia and their consequent land rights or compensation claims, and in saving significant sites from development proposals.

There are at present only two professionally qualified Aboriginal archaeologists in Australia; archaeology is not given a high priority among Aboriginal tertiary students, who tend to be more interested in law, health, education or history, particularly their own history over the past two centuries. There will therefore be a need for non-Aboriginal archaeologists and cultural resource managers for a very long time. What is changing is the relationship between Aborigines and archaeologists, which is becoming more like that found in the field of anthropology, where the professional anthropologist works for, at the request of, or at least in close co-operation with, local Aboriginal people. A model for this type of co-operative approach in the archaeological field is a recent project on a burial site in Victoria (Sullivan 1985, p. 154):

> Recently, on the initiative of the local Aboriginal community, the Victoria Archaeological Survey provided a consultant, Sandra Bowdler, to excavate and remove prehistoric burials near the Murray River which were threatened by water erosion. The excavation was carried out with Aboriginal assistance and its extent and conduct was the result of close and continuous consultation with the Aboriginal community, which was, to all intent and purposes, the employer. The excavation generated a great deal of Aboriginal interest; there was considerable debate about the extent of the excavation, the nature of the evidence revealed, and the correct final resolution of the problem. The investigation showed that the site was an extensive burial ground; that it had been used over a long period, and that earlier burials had been disturbed to make way for later ones. This was interpreted by the Aboriginal community as evidence of a massacre by Europeans and their subsequent burial of the victims, since it was said that Aborigines would not disturb the earlier dead in this way. There was a lot of debate with the archaeologist on this point. When it became apparent that the site was a major burial ground, the community called a halt to the work, and requested that soil conservation experts attempt to save the whole site. This was done and a stabilization and monitoring pro-gramme has now been carried out by the community. The skeletal material was excavated and documented in the field prior to reburial. Archaeology, carried out at the request of the community, established the significance of the site and supplied information and a time scale for the local people; within this context debates about interpretation and decisions about future management were possible. Since neither was imposed by the archaeologist her own interpretation of the site was not offensive or objectionable. Considerable scientific information was derived from the site, and it was conserved as part of the Aboriginal heritage, and available for future research, should the community wish.

There are as yet in Australia no specific legislative provisions for consultation between archaeologists and Aborigines, although the Northern Territory Sacred Sites Act does have general provisions which cover this area. This problem has been receiving attention from the National Aboriginal Site Authorities Committee, and the following principles for consultation have been circulated for consideration of appropriate legislative and administrative procedures (Buchan 1985).

1. Provision should be made for direct access between researchers and Aboriginal communities. Appropriate Aboriginal bodies or State Sites Authorities should make personnel available to provide assistance in the consultation process, and whenever possible, monitor the activities of archaeologists to ensure that consultation takes place.
2. Archaeologists should visit Aboriginal communities before the project begins to explain it and to solicit Aboriginal views on it. Initial contact should be sufficiently in advance of the project starting time to allow for any necessary modification of the project as a result of Aboriginal input.
3. Abandonment of a project in view of Aboriginal wishes should always be an option.
4. Permits for archaeological work at Aboriginal sites should not be considered unless the applicant supplies evidence that relevant Aborigines have been consulted, and gives details of Aboriginal views of the project. Any Aboriginal wishes on a particular project should always be given a high priority for consideration when decisions about granting permits are being made.
5. If a permit for archaeological work is granted, the archaeologist should be required to seek and facilitate Aboriginal involvement in the project at all stages, including providing advice and visiting, and participating in the project. This should be reflected in any contractual arrangement between the archaeologist and the State Sites Authority.
6. Payment should be made to Aboriginal informants, and the employment of Aboriginal people on the project or work associated with it should be given a high priority.
7. Archaeologists should be required to detail in any report to the Sites Authority on their project, all consultation with Aboriginal people.
8. Reports of archaeological projects should be circulated to relevant Aboriginal communities for comment, prior to their being submitted to the Sites Authority.
9. State Sites Authorities should facilitate this process by themselves establishing contact with Aboriginal communities throughout their State and as a result, compiling lists of contact individuals, bodies or communities for use in the consultation process.

The above principles apply to situations in which an archaeologist has applied to a State Sites Authority for permission to undertake a specific project. There is, however, scope for encouraging archaeologists to think in terms of consulting Aborigines regarding the nature of the archaeological research being carried out and to design projects accordingly.

Even more than any procedures, it is essential to know how to go about consulting Aboriginal people (Creamer 1983, Lewis & Rose 1985, von Sturmer 1982).

An example of a recent successful archaeological project has been the research carried out in Kakadu National Park, east of Darwin, by Rhys Jones, Betty Meehan, Ian Johnson, George Chaloupka, and others (Jones 1985). This was pure research, not salvage or rescue archaeology, carried out with the blessing, co-operation and participation of some of the most traditional Aboriginal people in Australia. It also involved excavation, which is always likely to be more problematic than analysis of surface campsites, and in the event human burials. The success of the project is due in great part to the protracted consultation carried out by Jones and his precursors, archaeologist Harry Allen and rock-art specialist George Chaloupka (Jones 1985, pp. 17–24).

The Kakadu National Park has also been a success story as an exercise in cultural resource management (ANPWS 1980, Flood 1983, 1985). The land was granted to Aboriginal people under the Aboriginal Land Rights (Northern Territory) Act of 1976, but in an unprecedented gesture was leased back to the Australian National Parks and Wildlife Service in 1978 to be managed as a national park on behalf of all Australians. Management has had its problems. Kakadu contains not only Australia's richest treasury of rock art, but also Australia's richest uranium deposits. There are also problems in reconciling the interests of the traditional Aboriginal owners of the park with those of tourists who believe that parks are for people, and that access to all sites should be unrestricted. The park managers are treading a tightrope, with commendable success, between these competing interests. Certain Aboriginal outstations are out of bounds to the public, and only two major complexes of Aboriginal rock-art sites have been developed as tourist destinations.

In 1983 a meeting of Aborigines and archaeologists was held in Kakadu National Park to discuss the issues of visitors to Aboriginal sites, access, control and management (Sullivan 1984). Visitor management at sites is also the subject of a recent book by Gale & Jacobs (1987). It is at Kakadu also that the employment of Aboriginal rangers has been pioneered, and visitors can enjoy the memorable experience of having rock paintings explained by those who have traditional knowledge of their meaning.

Human skeletal remains

Finally, there is the difficult question of the Aboriginal wish to dispose, according to Aboriginal tradition, of human remains held in museums, universities and other institutions. In most of Australia this means re-interment, but in Tasmania it means cremation.

During the 1980s the issue of disposal of human remains has come to the forefront of Aboriginal concerns, with frequent headlines such as 'Skeletons rattle down under', 'Extinction threatens Australian anthropology' or 'Aborigines: now it is bone rights'. It began in Tasmania with the Crowther collection, a collection of human remains culled at the end of the 19th century from the dying Tasmanian Aborigines by Crowther in an appalling piece of grave-robbing. Aboriginal demands for return and cremation of the Crowther collection were supported by the Australian Archaeological Association, which considered that 'ethical considerations of the manner in which the collection was obtained far outweigh any potential scientific value' (Meehan 1984: 125). The Australian Archaeological Association subsequently developed a position paper on the heritage and scientific importance of Australian Aboriginal skeletal remains (ibid., pp. 128–33). The Association's general policy may be summarized as follows (ibid., p. 127):

1   The AAA supports the disposal of Aboriginal skeletal remains of known individuals according to the wishes of the deceased, where known, and if not, by being transferred to the appropriate Aboriginal community to dispose of as they see fit.

2   The AAA believes that all other Aboriginal skeletal remains are of scientific importance and should not be destroyed by being reburied or cremated.

3   The AAA believes that the Aboriginal community and the archaeological profession share a common concern to protect and preserve prehistoric sites and material of significance.

4   The AAA believes that it is possible for Aborigines and archaeologists to reach a compromise about what should happen to Aboriginal skeletal remains. The employment and training of Aborigines as museum curators, the construction of Aboriginal Keeping Places and joint projects carried out by Aborigines and archaeologists are examples of such compromises.

This policy was developed as the result of the Aboriginal threat in the State of Victoria to reclaim and perhaps destroy all of the prehistoric human material held in museums and university collections. At risk is the University of Melbourne's Murray Black collection of Aboriginal skeletal remains, comprising 804 skeletons excavated by Murray Black from the River Murray valley in the 1940s, including 126 skeletons from Coobool Creek, dated to about 11 000 years ago. This is one of the most important sample human populations in the world from the late Pleistocene, providing invaluable evidence concerning the range of human variation at that time and the ancestry of Australian Aborigines.

The threat developed as a result of amendments to archaeological relics legislation with wider than intended effect, but has now extended to the 40 burials excavated from Kow Swamp, which are dated at between 9000 and 13 000 years old, and to the 13 000-year-old Keilor cranium (for their significance, see Flood 1983, pp. 33, 56, 58–68, 72–4, 94, 102, 152, 252).

A moratorium of 12 months has been placed on any action concerning the

Victorian Aboriginal remains to allow further discussion and detailed examination of the relative scientific importance of each specimen, but meanwhile the Tasmanian Government announced that it was preparing to transfer *all* Aboriginal remains held in its museums to the Tasmanian Aboriginal community to dispose of as they saw fit (probably by cremation). So far only the Crowther collection has been handed over, but the threat remains, and Tasmanians of Aboriginal descent have also travelled to Europe to request the return of skeletal material held in European museums and universities. Such destruction would be an inestimable loss to the international scientific community, as well as to generations of Australians to come, both black and white, who may wish to learn more about our biological past than is known at present.

In New South Wales there is the question of the fate of the human remains from Lake Mungo, an area which is on the World Heritage List for its archaeological and geomorphological significance (Flood 1983, pp. 40–52). More than 50 hominids have been found in the area, including Mungo I, a 26 000-year-old cremation which is believed to be the oldest example of cremation yet known in the world, and Mungo III, a 30 000-year-old interment showing evidence of burial ritual. There has been discussion among local Aborigines, the State Parks Service, and the Australian Museum as to whether a simple underground structure should be built at Lake Mungo as a 'Keeping Place'. A lockable chamber has been suggested to house the human remains, and another to provide working space for scholars to examine the skeletal material, if Aboriginal custodians have given their permission (Meehan 1984, p. 126).

If this compromise is successful, it will bring a ray of hope into what is a very worrying situation, and it is to be hoped that satisfactory solutions will be worked out elsewhere. There are many scientific and other reasons why Australian archaeologists believe that these prehistoric skeletal remains from Australia should be preserved, not only for study by present scholars, but as the heritage of present and future generations.

References

Allen, J. 1983. Aborigines and archaeologists in Tasmania. *Australian Archaeology* **16**, 7–10.

Australian Heritage Commission 1981. *The heritage of Australia: the illustrated register of the National Estate*. Melbourne: Macmillan.

Australian Heritage Commission 1985a. *Australia's National Estate: the role of the Commonwealth*. Canberra: Australian Government Publishing Service.

Australian Heritage Commission 1985b. Financial incentives for conserving the built environment. Unpublished report.

Australian National Parks and Wildlife Service 1980. *Kakadu National Park plan of management*. Canberra: ANPWS.

Buchan, R. 1985. Position Paper – Provisions by State Aboriginal Sites Authorities for consultation between archaeologists and Aborigines. *Australian Association of Consulting Archaeologists Newsletter* **25**, Appendix 3, 1–6.

Creamer, H. 1983. Contacting aboriginal communities. In *Australian field archaeology: a guide to techniques*, G. Connah (ed.), 10–7. Canberra: Australian Institute of Aboriginal Studies.

Edwards, R. (ed.) 1975. *The preservation of Australia's Aboriginal heritage*. Canberra: Australian Institute of Aboriginal Studies.

Flood, J. 1983. *Archaeology of the dreamtime*. Sydney & London: Collins.

Flood, J. 1985. Archaeology of Kakadu. *Heritage Australia* 4(2), 6–11.

Gale, F. & J. Jacobs 1987. *Tourists and the National Estate: procedures to protect Australia's heritage*. Canberra: Australian Heritage Commission.

Jones, R. (ed.) 1985. *Archaeological research in Kakadu National Park*. Canberra: Australian National Parks and Wildlife Service.

Lewis, D. & D. B. Rose 1985. Some ethical issues in archaeology: a methodology of consultation in northern Australia. *Australian Aboriginal Studies* 1, 37–44.

Meehan, B. 1984. Aboriginal skeletal remains. *Australian Archaeology* 19, 122–42.

Mundy, J. 1981. *Green bans and beyond*. Sydney: Angus & Robertson.

Sullivan, H. (ed.) 1984. *Visitors to Aboriginal sites: access, control and management*. Canberra: Australian National Parks and Wildlife Service.

Sullivan, S. 1985. The custodianship of Aboriginal sites in southeastern Australia. In *Who owns the past?* I. McBryde (ed.), 139–56. Melbourne, Oxford & New York: Oxford University Press.

Sullivan, S. & S. Bowdler (eds) 1984. *Site surveys and significance assessment in Australian archaeology*. Canberra: Australian National University.

von Sturmer, J. 1982. Talking with Aborigines. *Australian Institute of Aboriginal Studies Newsletter* 15, 13–30.

Willmot, E. 1985. The dragon principle. In *Who owns the past?* I. McBryde (ed.), 41–8. Melbourne, Oxford & New York: Oxford University Press.

Appendix 1. Australia ICOMOS: Objectives for Legislation to Protect the National Estate and Guidelines for Discussions with State Governments

This is a statement by Australia ICOMOS on the need to enact in each State and/or Territory appropriate legislation to protect the National Estate. At present such legislation exists only in New South Wales, South Australia, Victoria and in the Commonwealth Territories so far as the Australian Heritage Commission Act is applicable. Even where there is presently legislation it is not necessarily the best that could be achieved. It is appreciated that different State and Territory Governments have different priorities and views on the conservation of the National Estate. However, ICOMOS believes that in each State and Territory of the Commonwealth there should be effective legislation to protect the National Estate.

Set out below are seven objectives which are considered essential to any such legislation. There are other matters of detail which would have to be considered before legislation could be prepared in those States which do not so far have appropriate legislation, but these may vary from State to State.

Australia ICOMOS believes that it is the duty of each State and Territory Government to consider without further delay the introduction of new legislation or amendments to existing legislation which will in that State or Territory achieve the objectives listed below.

The objectives are:

I A REPRESENTATIVE COUNCIL OF INFORMED MEMBERS WITH APPROPRIATE CONSERVATION SKILLS:

There must be a majority of members with skills in historic conservation, historians, restoration architects, archaeologists, planners etc. It is essential for the Minister responsible for the administration of the Act to receive the best advice. The Council must have on it those people most knowledgeable in the conservation field. Representatives of other interests and disciplines may be included but not so as to increase the size of the Council beyond a workable one.

II It is important that the Council is able to provide a wide range of service and functions to advise the Government and to assist in the conservation of the National Estate. The exercise of legislative powers to ensure compliance by private property owners should only be a small part of its duties. The Council should be able to give general advice on all matters related to the National Estate. It should be able to engage in research, professional training, the provision of information and the promotion of the National Estate. It should also have responsibility for recommending assistance for privately-owned buildings. It should have a responsibility for all kinds of places (including those parts of the natural environment of National Estate value which are not protected by National Parks or other similar legislation) and with all kinds of ownership which form part of the National Estate. It should not, however, have a responsibility for administration of property. Existing Acts may, however, already protect Aboriginal Places.

III ADEQUATE POWERS TO LIST AND PROTECT THE NATIONAL ESTATE:

This is the area where there may be the greatest variation between States. It is, however, essential that the Act should require that all State Government Instrumentalities take account of the effect of all their actions on National Estate places and should be required to consult the Council before taking any such action.

There must be power to provide an adequate early warning system. That is to say, there must be a system whereby demolition and alteration control can be effectively imposed so that places are not damaged or destroyed without notice being given to the Council. The degree to which the Council makes use of this power will vary but the power must be there. There must be adequate sanctions. There must be penalties severe enough to ensure compliance with the requirements of the Council. These penalties can vary from direct financial ones to controls implemented under the planning system. Wherever possible conservation provisions should be treated as part of the normal planning system albeit administered by a specialist branch.

IV AN ACT WHICH IS SIMPLE TO OPERATE AND SIMPLE TO UNDERSTAND:

It is absolutely essential that the operative provisions of the Act are simple and that they do not place an impossible burden on the administration staff so that places are lost through inability to complete procedures within a given time. There is no 'second opportunity' where the question of demolition or destruction of buildings is concerned. There must be a simple and efficient system of dealing with matters coming before the Council. Failure by the Council to act must result in the property owner's request being treated as rejected and not allowed.

V ADEQUATE STAFFING AND ADMINISTRATION:

It is essential that there is an adequate and competent staff. The administrative structure should be such that the Council is responsible through its Chairman to the Minister under whose jurisdiction the Act comes. The Council should have a Director and staff responsible through its Director to the Council. An acceptable alternative would be to provide in the Act that professional staff are seconded from the relevant Department to the Council to work at the direction of the Council through its Chairman.

VI NEGOTIATING DEVICES:

There should be provision for 'Heritage' Agreements which are binding on places in perpetuity. The Minister should be empowered to waive rates and land tax on the advice of the Council.

26 May 1980

Appendix 2. The Australia ICOMOS Charter for the Conservation of Places of Cultural Significance (The Burra Charter) [Recent minor amendments were ratified in April 1988.]

Preamble

Having regard to the International Charter for the Conservation and Restoration of Monuments and Sites (Venice 1966), and the Resolutions of

5th General Assembly of ICOMOS (Moscow 1978), the following Charter has been adopted by Australia ICOMOS.

Definitions

Article 1. For the purpose of this Charter:

1.1 *Place* means site, area, building or other work, group of buildings or other works together with pertinent contents and surroundings.

1.2 *Cultural significance* means aesthetic, historic, scientific or social value for past, present or future generations.

1.3 *Fabric* means all the physical material of the *place*.

1.4 *Conservation* means all the processes of looking after a *place* so as to retain its *cultural significance*. It includes *maintenance* and may according to circumstances include *preservation, restoration, reconstruction and adaptation* and will be commonly a combination of more than one of these.

1.5 *Maintenance* means the continuous protective care of the *fabric*, contents and setting of a *place*, and is to be distinguished from repair. Repair involves *restoration or reconstruction* and it should be treated accordingly.

1.6 *Preservation* means maintaining the *fabric* of a *place* in its existing state and retarding deterioration.

1.7 *Restoration* means returning the EXISTING *fabric* of a *place* to a known earlier state by removing accretions or by reassembling existing components without the introduction of a new material.

1.8 *Reconstruction* means returning a *place* as nearly as possible to a known earlier state and is distinguished by the introduction of materials (new or old) into the *fabric*. This is not to be confused with either recreation or conjectural reconstruction which are outside the scope of this Charter.

1.9 *Adaptation* means modifying a *place* to suit proposed compatible uses.

1.10 *Compatible use* means a use which involves no change to the culturally significant fabric, changes which are substantially reversible, or changes which require a minimal impact.

Conservation principles

Article 2. The aim of *conservation* is to retain or recover the *cultural significance* of a *place* and must include provision for its security, its *maintenance* and its future.

Article 3. *Conservation* is based on a respect for the existing *fabric* and should involve the least possible physical intervention. It should not distort the evidence provided by the *fabric*.

Article 4. *Conservation* should make use of all the disciplines which can contribute to the study and safeguarding of a *place*. Techniques employed should be traditional but in some circumstances they may be modern ones for which a firm scientific basis exists and which have been supported by a body of experience.

Article 5. *Conservation* of a *place* should take into consideration all aspects of its *cultural significance* without an unwarranted emphasis on any one at the expense of others.

Article 6. The conservation policy appropriate to a *place* must first be determined by an understanding of its *cultural significance* and its physical condition.

Article 7. The conservation policy will determine which uses are compatible.

Article 8. *Conservation* requires the maintenance of an appropriate visual setting, e.g. form, scale, colour, texture and materials. No new construction, demolition or modification which would adversely affect the settings should be allowed. Environmental intrusions which adversely affect appreciation or enjoyment of the *place* should be excluded.

Article 9. A building or work should remain in its historical location. The moving of all or part of a building or work is unacceptable unless this is the sole means of ensuring its survival.

Article 10. The removal of contents which form part of the *cultural significance* of the *place* is unacceptable unless it is the sole means of ensuring their security and *preservation*. Such contents must be returned should changed circumstances make this practicable.

Conservation processes

Preservation

Article 11. *Preservation* is appropriate where the existing state of the *fabric* itself constitutes evidence of specific *cultural significance*, or where insufficient evidence is available to allow other conservation processes to be carried out.

Article 12. *Preservation* is limited to the protection, *maintenance* and where necessary, the stabilisation of the existing *fabric* but without the distortion of its *cultural significance*.

Restoration

Article 13. *Restoration* is appropriate only if there is sufficient evidence of an earlier state of the *fabric* and only if returning the *fabric* to that state recovers the *cultural significance* of the *place*.

Article 14. *Restoration* should reveal a new culturally significant aspect of the *place*. It is based on respect for all the physical, documentary and other evidence and stops at the point where conjecture begins.

Article 15. *Restoration* is limited to the reassembling of displaced components or removal of accretions in accordance with Article 16.

Article 16. The contributions of all periods to the *place* must be respected. If a *place* includes the *fabric* of different periods, revealing the *fabric* of one period at the expense of another can only be justified when what is removed is of slight *cultural significance* and the *fabric* which is to be revealed is of much greater *cultural significance*.

Reconstruction

Article 17. *Reconstruction* is appropriate where a *place* is incomplete through damage or alteration and where it is necessary for its survival, or where it recovers the *cultural significance* of the *place* as a whole.

Article 18. *Reconstruction* is limited to the completion of a depleted entity and should not constitute the majority of the *fabric* of a *place*.

Article 19. *Reconstruction* is limited to the reproduction of *fabric* the form of which is known from physical and/or documentary evidence. It should be identifiable on close inspection as being new work.

Adaptation

Article 20. *Adaptation* is acceptable where the *conservation* of the *place* cannot otherwise be achieved, and where the *adaptation* does not substantially detract from its *cultural significance*.

Article 21. *Adaptation* must be limited to that which is essential to a use for the *place* determined in accordance with Articles 6 and 7.

Article 22. *Fabric of cultural significance* unavoidably removed in the process of *adaptation* must be kept safely to enable its future reinstatement.

Conservation practice

Article 23. Work on a *place* must be preceded by professionally prepared studies of the physical, documentary and other evidence, and the existing *fabric* recorded before any disturbance of the *place*.

Article 24. Study of a *place* by any disturbance of the *fabric* or by archaeological excavation should be undertaken where necessary to provide data essential for decisions on the *conservation* of the *place* and/or to secure evidence about to be lost or made inaccessible through necessary *conservation* or other unavoidable action. Investigation of a *place* for any other reason which requires physical disturbance and which adds substantially to a scientific body of knowledge may be permitted, provided that it is consistent with the conservation policy for that *place*.

Article 25. A written statement of conservation policy must be professionally prepared setting out the *cultural significance*, physical condition and proposed *conservation* process together with justification and supporting evidence, including photographs, drawings and all appropriate samples.

Article 26. The organisation and individuals responsible for policy decisions must be named and specific responsibility taken for each such decision.

Article 27. Appropriate professional direction and supervision must be maintained at all stages of the work and a log kept of new evidence and additional decisions recorded as in Article 25 above.

Article 28. The records required by Articles 23, 25, 26 and 27 should be placed in a permanent archive and made publicly available.

Article 29. The items referred to in Article 10 and Article 22 should be professionally catalogued and protected.

Appendix 3. Guidelines to the Burra Charter

Cultural Significance

1.0 PREFACE

1.1 **Intention of Guidelines**
These Guidelines are intended to clarify the nature of professional work done within the terms of the Burra Charter. They recommend a methodical procedure for assessing the cultural significance of a place, preparing a statement of cultural significance and for making such information publicly available. The Guidelines refer to Articles 6, 23, 25 and 28 but do not cover all the matters referred to in those articles.

1.2 **Applicability**
The Guidelines apply to any place likely to be of cultural significance regardless of its type or size.

1.3 **Need to establish cultural significance**
The assessment of cultural significance and the preparation of a statement of cultural significance, embodied in a report, are essential pre-requisites to making decisions about the future of a place.

1.4 **Skills required**
In accordance with Article 4 of the Burra Charter, the study of a place should make use of all relevant disciplines. The professional skills required for such study are not common. It cannot, for example, be assumed that any one practitioner will have the full range of skills required to assess cultural significance and prepare a statement. Sometimes in the course of the task it will be necessary to engage additional practitioners with special expertise.

1.5 **Issues not considered**
The assessment of cultural significance and the preparation of a state-

ment does not involve or take account of such issues as the necessity for conservation action, legal constraints, possible uses, structural stability or costs and returns. These issues will be considered in the development of conservation proposals. Guidelines for the development of conservation proposals are the subject of another document.

2.0 THE CONCEPT OF CULTURAL SIGNIFICANCE

2.1 **Introduction**

In the Burra Charter Cultural Significance means 'aesthetic, historic, scientific or social value for past, present or future generations'.

Cultural significance is a concept which helps in estimating the value of places. The places that are likely to be of significance are those which help an understanding of the past or enrich the present, and which we believe will be of value to future generations.

Although there are a variety of adjectives used in definitions of cultural significance in Australia, the adjectives 'aesthetic', 'historic', 'scientific' and 'social', given alphabetically in the Burra Charter, can encompass all other values.

The meanings of these terms in the context of cultural significance are discussed below. It should be noted that they are not mutually exclusive, for example architectural style has both historic and aesthetic aspects.

2.2 **Aesthetic value**

Aesthetic value includes aspects of sensory perception for which criteria can and should be stated. Such criteria may include consideration of the form, scale, colour, texture and material of the fabric: the smells and sounds associated with the place and its use; and also the aesthetic values commonly assessed in the analysis of landscape and townscape.

2.3 **Historic value**

Historic value encompasses the history of aesthetics, science and society and therefore to a large extent underlies all of the terms set out in this section.

A place may have historic value because it has influenced, or has been influenced by, an historic figure, event, phase or activity. It may also have historic value as the site of an important event. Places in which evidence of the association or event survives in situ, or in which the settings are substantially intact, are of greater significance than those which are much changed or in which evidence does not survive. However some events or associations may be so important that the place retains its significance regardless of subsequent treatment.

2.4 **Scientific value**

The scientific or research value of a place will depend upon the importance of the data involved, on its rarity, quality or representativeness, and on the degree to which the place may contribute further substantial information.

2.5 **Social value**
Social value embraces the qualities for which a place has become a focus of spiritual, political, national or other cultural sentiment to a majority or minority group.

2.6 **Other approaches**
The categorisation into aesthetic, historic, scientific and social values is one approach to understanding the concept of cultural significance. However, more precise categories may be developed as understanding of a particular place increases.

3.0 THE ESTABLISHMENT OF CULTURAL SIGNIFICANCE

3.1 **Introduction**
In establishing the cultural significance of a place it is necessary to assess all the information relevant to an understanding of the place and its fabric. The task includes a report comprising written material and graphic material. The contents of the report should be arranged to suit the place and the limitations on the task, but it will generally be in two sections: first, the assessment of cultural significance (see 3.2 and 3.3) and second, the statement of cultural significance (see 3.4).

3.2 **Collection of information**
Information relevant to the assessment of cultural significance should be collected. Such information concerns:
(a) the developmental sequence of the place and its relationship to the surviving fabric;
(b) the existence and nature of lost or obliterated fabric;
(c) the rarity or technical interest of all or any part of the place;
(d) the functions of the place and its parts;
(e) the relationship of the place and its parts with its setting;
(f) the cultural influences which have affected the form and fabric of the place;
(g) the significance of the place to people who use or have used the place, or descendants of such people;
(h) the historical content of the place with particular reference to the ways in which its fabric has been influenced by historical forces or has itself influenced the course of history;
(i) the scientific or research potential of the place;
(j) the relationship of the place to other places, for example in respect of design, technology, use, locality or origin;
(k) any other factor relevant to an understanding of the particular place.

3.3 **The assessment of cultural significance**
The assessment of cultural significance follows the collection of information.
The validity of the judgements will depend upon the care with which the data is collected and the reasoning applied to it.

In assessing cultural significance the practitioner should state conclusions. Unresolved aspects should be identified.

Whatever may be considered the principal significance of a place, all other aspects of significance should be given consideration.

3.3.1 Extent of recording

In assessing these matters a practitioner should record the place sufficiently to provide a basis for the necessary discussion of the facts. During such recording any obviously urgent problems endangering the place, such as stability and security, should be reported to the client.

3.3.2 Disturbance of the fabric

Disturbance of the fabric at this stage should be strictly within the terms of Article 24 of the Burra Charter, which is explained in separate Guidelines.

3.3.3 Hypotheses

Hypotheses, however expert or informed, should not be presented as established fact. Feasible or possible hypotheses should be set out, with the evidence for and against them, and the line of reasoning which has been followed. Any attempt which has been made to check a hypothesis should be recorded, so as to avoid repeating fruitless research.

3.4 Statement of cultural significance

The practitioner should prepare a succinct statement of cultural significance, supported by, or cross referenced to, sufficient graphic material to help identify the fabric or cultural significance.

It is essential that the statement be clear and pithy, expressing simply why the place is of value but not restating the physical or documentary evidence.

3.5 The report

3.5.1 Content

The report will comprise written material and graphic material and will present an assessment of cultural significance and a statement of cultural significance.

In order to avoid unnecessary bulk, only material directly relevant to the process of assessing cultural significance and to making a statement of cultural significance should be included.

3.5.2 Written material

The text should be clearly set out and easy to follow. In addition to the assessment and statement of cultural significance as set out in 3.2 and 3.3. it should include:

(a) name of client;
(b) names of all the practitioners engaged in the task;
(c) authorship of the report;
(d) date;
(e) brief or outline of brief;

(f) constraints on the task, for example: time, money, expertise;
(g) sources; refer to 3.5.4.

3.5.3 Graphic material

Graphic material may include maps, plans, drawings, diagrams, sketches, photographs and tables, and should be reproduced with sufficient quality for the purposes of interpretation.

All components discussed in the report should be identified in the graphic material. Such components should be identified and described in a schedule.

Detailed drawings may not be necessary. A diagram may best assist the purpose of the report.

Graphic material which does not serve a specific purpose should not be included.

3.5.4 Sources

All sources used in the task must be cited with sufficient precision to enable others to locate them.

It is necessary for all sources consulted to be listed, even if not cited.

All major sources or collections not consulted but believed to have potential usefulness in establishing cultural significance should be listed.

In respect of source material privately held the name and address of the owner should be given, but only with the owner's consent.

4.0 PROCEDURES FOR UNDERTAKING THE TASK

4.1 **Brief**

Before undertaking the task, the client and the practitioner should agree upon:

(a) the extent of the place and any aspect which requires intensive investigation;
(b) the dates for the commencement of the task, submission of the draft report and submission of the final report;
(c) the fee or the basis upon which fees will be paid;
(d) the use of any joint consultant, sub-consultant or other practitioner with special expertise;
(e) the basis for any further investigation which may be required within the terms of section 4.5 of these Guidelines;
(f) the representative of the client to whom the practitioner will be responsible in the course of the task;
(g) the sources, material or services to be supplied by the client;
(h) any requirements for the format or reproduction of the report;
(i) the number of copies of the report to be supplied at each stage;
(j) copyright and confidentiality;
(k) the conditions under which the report may be published by the client, the practitioner or others;

(l) the procedure for any required exhibition of the report and consideration of comment upon it.

4.2 Responsibility for content of report
The content of the report is the responsibility of the practitioner. The report may not be amended without the agreement of the practitioner.

4.3 Draft report
It is useful for the report to be presented to the client in draft form to ensure that it is understood and so that the practitioner may receive the client's comments.

4.4 Urgent action
Where it becomes clear that urgent action is necessary to avert a threat to the fabric involving, for example, stability or security, the client should be notified immediately.

4.5 Additional expenditure
Where it becomes clear that some aspect of the task will incur additional expenditure by requiring more investigation or more expertise than has been allowed, the client should be informed immediately.

4.6 Recommendations for further investigation
In respect of major unresolved aspects of cultural significance recommendations for further investigation should be made only where:

(a) the client has been informed of the need for such investigation at the appropriate stage and it has been impossible to have it undertaken within the budget and time constraints of the task;

(b) further information is anticipated as a result of disturbance of the fabric which would not be proper at this stage, but which will become appropriate in the future (see Guidelines for Article 24 of the Burra Charter).

Such recommendations should indicate what aspects of significance might be established by such study.

4.7 Exhibition and comment
The report for any project of public interest should be exhibited in order that interested bodies and the public may comment and reasonable time should be allowed for the receipt and consideration of comment.

4.8 Further evidence
If after the completion of the report further evidence is revealed, for example by disturbance of the fabric or as a result of further investigation or public comment, it is desirable for such evidence to be referred to the original practitioner so that the report may be amended if necessary.

4.9 Permanent archive
A copy of the report should be placed in a permanent archive and made publicly available.

9   *The administration of China's archaeological heritage*

ZHUANG MIN

China, with its area of 9.6 million km^2 and its population of 1000 million, has a continuous history as a nation that stretches back to Peking Man. Written history began some 4000 years ago, and written records form an important part of China's rich archaeological heritage.

Foreigners have been attracted to China's archaeological remains for many years, some bent on legitimate archaeological studies, but many with more-reprehensible motives, and as a result there was undisguised pillaging of archaeological sites to meet the demands of an international collecting market. There was no heritage protection legislation in China until 1930 when, in response to the immense export trade in antiquities, the Chinese Republic promulgated its Regulations on the Preservation of Ancient Relics. These were progressively expanded and added to in the subsequent five years.

The People's Republic of China was founded on 1 October 1949. On 24 May 1950 the State Council of the Central People's Government promulgated rules to protect historical sites, rare relics and books, and endangered animals. In addition, Provisional Measures on Prohibition of Export of Precious Cultural Relics and Books and Provisional Measures on Investigation and Excavation of Ancient Cultural Ruins and Ancient Tombs were also published. This has brought to an end the situation in which large quantities of cultural relics were stolen and exported to foreign countries. The Provisional Measures on Excavation are aimed at protecting the research into China's archaeological heritage. It encourages planned investigation and excavation of cultural ruins and ancient tombs. Its main provisions are the following.

(a)   All ancient relics buried in the ground or excavated belong to the state.
(b)   Discoveries of cultural ruins, ancient tombs and relics during river dredging, road building and other constructional work shall be immediately reported to the local People's Government, which shall protect the site and in turn report the case to the Ministry of Culture under the Central People's Government; no excavation shall be conducted without permission from the Ministry.
(c)   Foreigners and foreign organizations are not allowed to conduct or take part in excavation work without the permission or invitation of the Central People's Government.

(d) Confirmation of qualifications and other conditions of the excavating organization, application and approval procedure of the excavation project, and requirements on quality of excavation.

In the early years following the foundation of the People's Republic of China the Administrative Bureau of Cultural Relics of the Ministry of Culture was in charge of the supervision of cultural relics. The Institute of Archaeology of the Chinese Academy of Sciences was in charge of investigation and excavation. Cultural relics protection and administration committees were set up in each of the provinces, autonomous regions and independent municipalities to supervise archaeological investigation and excavation and the management of historical sites and structures.

In 1952 China entered the first five-year period of planned economic construction. Leaders in the cultural and educational fields and prominent archaeologists considered that modern construction on the land of an ancient civilization constituted a great threat to the preservation and protection of cultural relics. As capital construction proceeded, buried monuments were revealed one after another. A little carelessness would have caused irremediable losses and so, in order to save as many treasures as possible, these celebrated scholars appealed to the state to co-ordinate archaeological investigation and excavation with capital construction. A letter from the Cultural and Educational Committee asked the Finance and Economics Committee to inform the Ministries of Water Conservancy, Railway and Communications, as well as the financial committees of East China, Central South China, North-West China and South-West China and their subordinate institutions of the historical value of cultural relics so as to protect them from damage during canal and road construction. Any discovery of cultural ruins or ancient tombs had to be reported immediately to the Ministry of Culture for further investigation and excavation.

To save cultural relics from the construction projects that spread all over the country, the Institute of Archaeology of the Chinese Academy of Sciences, the Administrative Bureau of Social and Cultural Affairs of the Ministry of Culture and Beijing University jointly ran an archaeological personnel training course in 1952. This was attended by young archaeological workers from the provinces, autonomous regions and independent municipalities. In six months it trained 72 field archaeological workers, who are the seeds of New China's archaeological work. Similar training courses were held in the subsequent three years, each lasting for one year.

The protection of historical relics from the impact of capital construction became a major development in New China's archaeology. Further regulations issued by the State Council included the Notice on Protecting Relics from Capital Construction (1953) and the Notice on Protecting Relics from Agricultural Production and Construction (1956). In addition, Xi'an, Xianyang, Luoyang, Longmen, Anyang, Datong and Yungang were declared major reserves of cultural remains. In co-ordination with the construction of large reservoirs, such as the Sanmenxia and the Liujiaxia, archaeological teams from the central authorities carried out investigation over the entire areas that would be submerged.

In 1961 the State Council promulgated the Provisional Regulations on Protection and Administration of Cultural Relics. Its main provisions are the following.

(a)   Definition of the scope of cultural relics that fall under state protection. A special organ shall be established by the provinces, autonomous regions and independent municipalities, as well as by prefectures and counties where cultural relics abound, to be in charge of protection and administration, investigation and study, popularization, collection and excavation of cultural relics in their respective areas.

(b)   The cultural administration at different levels shall conduct the routine investigation of cultural relics and make a list of important revolutionary ruins, memorials, ancient structures, cave temples, stone carvings, ancient cultural relics and ancient tombs determined as coming under the protection of the county (city) or the province (autonomous region, independent municipality) according to their historical, artistic and scientific value. The list shall then be approved by the government at the same level and reported to the next higher government for the record. The Ministry of Culture shall select from among the lists relics of great historical, artistic and scientific value, and report them in groups to the State Council to be designated as relics under national protection.

(c)   Before the start of large-scale industrial agricultural, water conservancy, communications, defence and urban construction, the building departments, together with the cultural administration of the province, autonomous region and independent municipality, shall conduct cultural relics investigations within the limits of the project. Methods for protection or handling of any relics found during the investigation shall be discussed by the units concerned. The funds and labour needed for prospecting, excavation, dismantling and removal of cultural relics related to construction projects shall be included in the budget and labour plan of the construction department concerned.

(d)   Excavations of cultural relics by relics administration, scientific institutes and colleges that are not related to construction shall submit their excavation plans to the Ministry of Culture and the Chinese Academy of Sciences for approval.

(e)   The export of all important cultural relics of historical, artistic and scientific value is prohibited, apart from those approved by the State Council for exhibition in foreign countries and for exchange. This regulation is the prototype of the Law on Protection of Cultural Relics of the People's Republic of China.

During the ten-year 'Cultural Revolution', which started in 1966, large numbers of cultural relics were destroyed. However, a few rare objects and nationally protected relics were well-preserved by the army. In 1973 the State Administrative Bureau of Cultural Relics and Archaeological Data was established directly under the State Council. It is responsible for the preservation, maintenance and popularization of archaeological heritage, ancient structures and museums. At the same time the Institute of Archaeology resumed its activity under the Chinese Academy of Social Sciences.

On 19 November 1982 the 25th Session of the Fifth National People's Congress Standing Committee approved the Law on Protection of Cultural Relics of the People's Republic of China. It comprises eight chapters and 33 articles. The major points are the following.

(a) The general principles in formulating this law are to strengthen the state's protection of cultural relics in order to promote scientific research, inherit the splendid historical and cultural heritage, facilitate education in patriotism and revolutionary tradition, and build up a socialist culture.

(b) The chapter on protected relic units (monuments) is broadly similar to the Regulations, apart from those clauses which define a buffer belt round the units for environmental protection and designate the famous historical–cultural cities.

(c) The six articles on archaeological excavation are similar to those stipulated in the Provisional Measures on Investigation and Excavation, issued in 1950. However, they stress that all archaeological excavation projects must obtain the approval of the departments concerned; otherwise, no excavations by units or individuals are allowed. Excavation conducted in co-ordination with construction projects shall be under the control of provinces, autonomous regions and municipalities, which are responsible for conducting survey and prospecting work and reporting the excavation plan to the state cultural administration departments and the Chinese Academy of Social Sciences, to be approved by the former. If the period of construction is pressing or if the cultural ruins and ancient tombs are endangered by the elements, then the cultural administrations of the provinces, autonomous regions and independent municipalities can take emergency measures to organize excavations and at the same time go through the necessary procedures.

Based on these regulations, the Ministry of Culture provided that a prior application for permission must be made by the head of the excavation group; only after an archaeological excavation licence of the People's Republic of China has been granted can an archaeological excavation be conducted. When the excavation comes to an end, an excavation report form must be filled out. Since archaeological excavation licences were first issued in 1983, the archaeological sites excavated up to the end of 1986 have totalled some 2000. In order to train qualified leading personnel for excavation groups, training courses have been run by the Ministry of Culture. After four months of training, qualifications are granted to those who pass examinations set by competent archaeologists and experts.

This describes the development of archaeological heritage management legislation in China. At present there are some tens of decrees and provisions relating to their enforcement in respect of the protection and administration of the cultural heritage in China, including Regulations on Archaeological Field Work, Provisions on the Work of Administrative Department in Provinces, Autonomous Regions and Independent Municipalities of Cultural Relics and Archaeology, On the Reinforcement of Underwater Archaeological Work in China, etc.

In implementing these regulations, the most important thing is to train personnel qualified in archaeological investigation, excavation, research and administration. In addition to the training courses mentioned above, which have operated continuously since 1952 with more than 300 trainees, a Speciality of Archaeology (initially four years, changed to five years in 1958, then back to four years in 1976) has been run in the Department of History of Beijing University since 1953, and a Department of Archaeology was later established at the University. At present, specialities of archaeology and teaching and research sections have been established in 15 universities throughout the country. These specialities and teaching and research sections produce more than 100 graduates annually. In Beijing, Jiling and Fudan universities, postgraduate courses have been run to train experts in cave art, palaeolithic archaeology, neolithic archaeology and science and technology for the preservation of cultural relics. At the same time many short-term training classes have been set up by departments of central authorities as well as local governments, at different levels.

The State Administrative Bureau of Cultural Relics and Archaeological Data of the Ministry of Culture is now the central authority in charge of archaeological heritage management. The Institute of Archaeology of the Chinese Academy of Social Sciences is the central research department of archaeology. The Institute of Palaeovertebrate Studies and Anthropology of the Chinese Academy of Sciences is in charge of palaeolithic archaeology. This institute created individual appointments and research sections at important archaeological sites all over the country. The local authorities for archaeological heritage management are the administrations of cultural relics or cultural affairs of all provinces, autonomous regions and independent municipalities. Cultural and educational departments of country governments and lower-tier governments are in charge of archaeological heritage management. Altogether, there are 58 local cultural relics and archaeological departments and archaeological sections in museums in the country in charge of investigations, excavations and research. The Archaeological Institute of China and 14 local archaeological institutes have set up links with one another across the country in selecting fields of study. The Chinese Academy of Social Sciences draws up plans for subject studying.

In order to designate the important archaeological heritage and ancient structures that need to be protected and made known to the public, two general investigations have been carried out throughout the country. In the 1958 study, about 8000 sites were recorded. The more recent one, started in 1981, has concentrated on recording types of immovable cultural relics, including those that are still buried. It is estimated that at the conclusion of the investigation about 100 000 sites will have been recorded. The Ministry of Culture in collaboration with the Map Press will produce an atlas showing the distribution of these sites in considerable detail.

As a result of the general investigations of cultural relics, the State Council has recorded and made known to the public 500 important cultural sites which are protected by the state. More than 3000 sites are protected by provincial, regional and municipal governments, and approximately 10 000 sites by county (city) governments. In addition, the State Council has designated 62 famous historical–cultural cities.

The People's Republic of China has made remarkable progress in the protection and administration of its archaeological heritage over the past 30 years. Successive new archaeological discoveries have been recorded in *Archaeological Discoveries and Research Work in New China*, compiled by the Chinese Academy of Social Sciences, and in the 'Archaeology' volume of China's new *Encyclopaedia*; the latter volume is a very rich one, and it includes as an annexe a chronological table of 'important events in China's archaeology from 1898 to 1984'.

Recent discoveries of China's archaeological heritage have been spread widely over the country in space and time, from 'Ape Man' fossils onwards. Systematic excavations and investigations have been conducted in the ancient capitals of Changan, Luoyang and Beijing. All new archaeological results have been published in books or journals for a wide audience. Newly discovered cultural relics have been displayed in exhibitions, both at home and in foreign countries. Scientific and technical results have been disseminated in specific articles or books. Important historical relics have been lodged in museums and are put on display periodically. Important excavation sites, such as the Peking Man site at Zhoukoudian, near Beijing, the Yangshao Culture site at Banpo, in Shaanxi Province, and the terracotta figures of soldiers and horses near the Qin Shi Huang mausoleum, have been housed in site museums which are open to the public so as to popularize archaeological knowledge.

During the national modern construction programme and the implementation of reform and open policies in recent years, the scale of construction has been ever-expanding. As China is a country with a long history and a large population who inhabited a vast land with a complicated topography, archaeological remains are very often revealed during the construction of large reservoirs, factories, railways and highways, and in urban and township construction, land reclamation or the building of brick-kilns. As a result the impact on the protection and administration of the archaeological heritage becomes ever greater. As a result of the continuing demands of the international antiquities market, grave-robbing, looting of ancient kiln sites and smuggling of antiquities has plagued many parts of the country, and many archaeological sites have been damaged. To check such criminal activities the State Council recently issued an urgent circular publicizing the prohibition and calling for enforcement of the law on the protection of relics. Dealing with theft and robbery of this kind is one of the difficult administrative tasks; detailed provisions covering every aspect of the enforcement of the law are needed.

Archaeologists in China have been concerned about whether archaeological excavations carried out in co-ordination with capital construction works will be affected in terms of their academic quality. However, the facts have shown that most of the important discoveries which have supplied vital missing links in archaeology have, in fact, been made in the course of capital construction and mass projects. Rare treasures have come from these excavations, and this is why many archaeologists have been attracted by rescue excavation. Nevertheless, the number of archaeological workers is limited, and they have barely been able to meet the enormous demands of excavation, conservation, research and publication in respect of cultural remains, relics, specimens and materials. It is difficult to conserve excavated artefacts such as bamboo, wood, lacquer, silk and tapestries scientifically. Because of the sudden change of environment on excavation, conservation requirements are very diverse and complex. Unless preparations are properly made, the excavated artefacts may be damaged or even destroyed.

To carry out a general investigation of the archaeological heritage over large areas, the resources of modern science and technology, such as remote sensing, surveying and geophysical prospecting, are needed. Since the number of excavation sites is increasing greatly in the country, it is necessary to draw up overall plans, to establish better administrative arrangements and to improve technology, so to facilitate management, planning, execution, control, conservation and the application of computers in this work. In addition there is the problem of securing funds and monitoring expenditure.

The enormous scale of development in world modernization and industrialization makes the investigation, protection, excavation, management, research and popularization of the archaeological heritage a problem of world importance. The greater impact will be on those countries with old civilizations, and these countries in particular should exchange experiences and co-operate and support one another in training competent personnel and improving the administration of the archaeological heritage.

10 Historical development and attendant problems of cultural resource management in the Philippines

FLORANTE G. HENSON

Introduction

The Philippines is an archipelago of several thousand islands lying on the eastern fringes of Asia, in the Pacific Ocean. Its rich prehistoric and historic national heritage is reflected in the wide variety of culturally significant sites that have been discovered in the islands, ranging from the Middle Pleistocene kill sites in northern Luzon to the Upper Pleistocene blade and flake-blade assemblages in the Tabon Cave complex, to the Neolithic burial sites in Palawan Island, to the contact period burial sites containing Chinese and South-East Asian tradewares in Batangas and Laguna Lake, down to the historic Spanish fortresses and churches found in major population centres of the country. The sites mentioned in this chapter are shown on the map in Figure 10.1.

The thoughtless destruction of archaeological sites in the Philippines has been going on for several centuries. As early as the 15th century, Spanish settlers had been reported to have unwittingly disturbed contact period sites in the process of constructing houses and other edifices (Beyer 1949). In 1868 Marche, a French archaeologist who conducted an archaeological exploration in Marinduque Island, found several disturbed burial sites, mostly located in caves (Beyer 1949). Guthe, an American who conducted archaeological work in the islands in central Philippines from 1922 to 1926, also reported finding several disturbed sites (Guthe 1929). Beyer, an American archaeologist who had continuously conducted research in the Philippines for approximately 40 years, similarly listed several disturbed sites (Beyer 1949).

Before the 1960s the destruction of archaeological sites generally occurred randomly and accidentally, often resulting from building construction and land-modification activities, e.g. ploughing and road building. After this period, however, the market for Chinese and South-East Asian ceramics grew, and dealers found themselves buying and selling these antiquities at a

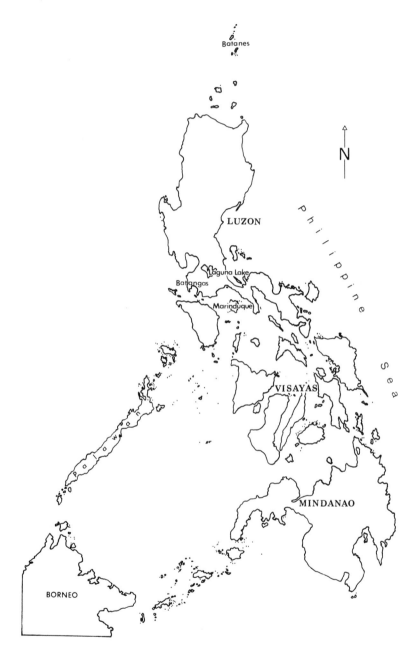

Figure 10.1 Map of the Philippines, showing sites and areas mentioned in the chapter.

brisk pace. Ironically, it was the systematic excavation of burial sites by Fox (1959) in the Batangas peninsula that brought to the collectors' and dealers' attention the existence of large quantities of valuable prehistoric ceramics in the country, and gave them the idea of financing well-organized groups to undertake pot-hunting activities in the different islands of the Philippines.

Laws pertinent to cultural resource management

Recognizing the need to conserve and preserve its gradually eroding, non-renewable cultural resources, the Philippine Government enacted a number of laws, the first and most important of which was Republic Act No. 4846, otherwise known as The Cultural Properties Protection and Preservation Act. This Act, passed by the defunct Congress in 1966, declared it to be the policy of the state to preserve and protect the cultural properties of the nation and to safeguard their intrinsic value. It similarly provided

(a)　the bases for classifying cultural materials into cultural properties, cultural treasures, antiques, relics, artefacts and natural history specimens;
(b)　the procedure to be followed in the designation of a particular cultural property as 'cultural treasure' as well as the conditions governing the change of ownership and exportation of these cultural treasures;
(c)　the requisite conditions for the excavation and exploration of archaeological sites;
(d)　the conditions under which the purchase of cultural properties can be deductible from the income tax returns of purchasing individuals or institutions;
(e)　the designation of the National Museum as the agency of the government which shall implement the provisions of this Act; and
(f)　the penalties for violation of the provisions of this Act.

In 1974 President F. Marcos of the Philippines issued Presidential Decree No. 374 which amended certain sections of Republic Act No. 4846. Presidential Decree No. 374 added the following features:

(a)　definitions of critical terms such as anthropological area, historical site, archaeological site, collector, dealer and exporter of cultural properties;
(b)　additional conditions and restrictions in the exportation of cultural properties; and
(c)　provision for the creation of a Division of Cultural Properties in the National Museum.

In addition to Presidential Decree No. 374, President Marcos issued Proclamations Nos 996 and 1743 and Presidential Decrees Nos 260, 356, 373, 375, 1109, 1683 and 1492 which

(a) declared certain sites and edifices as national landmarks, national monuments, national shrines, national cultural treasures or national reservations;
(b) identified the implementing agencies (National Museum, National Historical Institute and Ministry of Tourism); and
(c) appropriated the necessary funds for carrying out the intents of these laws.

He further issued Proclamation No. 913, which declared the period from 1 to 7 October of every year as National Museum Week.

Major problems

These legal measures taken by the state to preserve and protect its cultural resources have been rather ineffective because of some inherent limitations of the laws and major problems encountered in the implementation of the provisions of these laws.

Difficulties in interpreting legal provisions

Many specific elements of the cultural resource conservation or protection laws are still subject to various interpretations. A number of concepts are defined loosely. For example, Section 3 of Presidential Decree No. 374 defines the terms 'cultural properties', 'important cultural properties' and 'national cultural treasure' as follows:

> *Cultural properties* are old buildings, monuments, shrines, documents, and objects which may be classified as antiques, relics, or artefacts, landmarks, anthropological and historical sites, and specimens of natural history which are of cultural, historical, anthropological or scientific value and significance to the nation.
>
> Cultural properties which have been singled out from among the innumerable cultural properties as having exceptional historical and cultural significance to the Philippines, but are not sufficiently outstanding to merit the classification of 'National Cultural Treasures' are *important cultural properties.*
>
> A *national cultural treasure* is a unique object found locally, possessing outstanding historical, cultural, artistic and/or scientific value which is significant and important to this country and nation.

The definition of the term 'cultural properties' is so general and broad that practically anything that has even the remotest chance of being culturally, historically, anthropologically or scientifically valuable or relevant can be subsumed under the term 'cultural properties'. The definitions of 'important cultural properties' and 'national cultural treasures' are extremely vague.

Furthermore, the law does not provide specific guidelines or criteria for evaluating the relative 'value', 'significance' or 'uniqueness' of objects, thus making the task of classifying them (according to whether they are 'cultural properties', 'important cultural properties' or 'national cultural treasures') extremely difficult and highly subjective.

Inadequate preventive measures

The current conservation and preservation legislation programme in the Philippines consists more of curative rather than preventive measures. Measures (e.g. salvage archaeology and apprehension of violators of the legal provisions of pertinent laws) are often taken only after a site has already been partially destroyed (e.g. accidentally by road construction workers, or intentionally by illegal diggers). Minimal preventive measures are taken to safeguard the country's cultural resources. The legislative programme can be improved by requiring all private and government agencies and organizations involved in massive land modification projects (e.g. construction of roads, dams or buildings) to set a certain percentage of their budget to fund archaeological surveys adequate to identify the impact of their projects on cultural resources.

The biggest factor that can account for why the Cultural Properties and Preservation Act has been ineffective in curtailing or minimizing the destruction of archaeological sites is the National Museum's practice of registering artefacts from illegal excavations. This practice 'legalizes' the acquisition, buying and selling of artefacts from dubious sources. Every year, 5000–6000 pieces or artefacts are registered as antiquities with the National Museum. Most of the antiquities registered have doubtful provenances or none at all. Records of registered artefacts from the Cultural Properties Division of the National Museum show that large numbers of antiquities are registered by only a few people or dealers. This suggests that these artefacts were not randomly found, but were systematically looted. This fact is known to some key administrators of the National Museum, but they apparently turn a blind eye to it.

Another self-defeating practice of the National Museum is that of giving permits and exclusive rights to both local and foreign underwater explorers and excavators, who are generally commercially motivated rather than academically oriented. These permits entitle them to explore and excavate large bodies of underwater areas in the Philippines. In most cases 70–75 per cent of the finds go to these 'treasure hunters' whereas only 25–30 per cent go to the National Museum. This practice places the National Museum at a great disadvantage. It is therefore imperative that the National Museum should leave underwater sites untouched until it is capable of undertaking and financing its own underwater archaeology projects. In addition, the activity of foreign and local underwater companies should be closely monitored by the Coast Guard, Bureau of Customs, and the Bureau of Immigration and Deportation, so that the flow of antiquities out of the country could be controlled.

Minimal opportunity for problem-oriented research

During the past 20 years the country's archaeological resource base has been continuously plundered by commercially motivated illegal diggers. When reports of illegal excavations reach the National Museum, it usually sends a team of researchers to the site to stop the illegal activities and conduct salvage archaeology. Faced with the grim prospect of imminent destruction of sites, the National Museum researchers dig the reported sites and try to retrieve as many artefacts as possible without much regard to the salvaging and recording of other relevant contextual data. This leaves the researchers minimal opportunity to conduct problem-oriented research during excavation. Consequently, reports based on salvaging activities have been limited to descriptive accounts of the specimens recovered.

The implementing agencies should veer away from the position that salvage is the only solution to the potential destruction of archaeological sites. Instead, these agencies should consider other alternatives with respect to conservation and protection of cultural resources, such as avoidance of destruction of cultural resources, by redesigning and relocating land modification projects and researchers' involvement in the planning stage of such projects to ensure that they are given sufficient opportunity to gather archaeological data systematically for future scientific analysis.

Weak linkages among implementing agencies

In accordance with Section 4 of Presidential Decree No. 374, the National Museum has been designated as the main agency of the government to implement the provisions of this decree. Following Section 21 of the same decree, the Cultural Properties Division, with adequate police powers to prosecute violators of this decree, has been created in the National Museum. In addition to the National Museum, other government agencies, such as the Ministry of Tourism and the National Historical Institute, have been asked to supervise and control the preservation, restoration and reconstruction of national shrines, monuments and landmarks.

At present the linkages among these implementing agencies are not well established or well defined. Areas of responsibility and guidelines for collaboration are not clearly specified. More-extensive cross-sharing and cross-enrichment of resources and expertise are recommended in order to improve programmes, minimize duplication of activities and reduce operational costs.

Lack of highly qualified professional staff

To date there are very few formally trained archaeologists in the agencies mandated to protect the nation's cultural resources. Only a few professionals in these agencies can render specialist services, both in assessing the archaeological value of a resource and in determining the cultural value of a resource that transcends the boundaries of archaeology. Most of the personnel in these agencies, who hold undergraduate degrees in social and physical sciences as well as in humanities, undergo archaeological training while on the job. Only four members of the staff have obtained formal graduate training in archaeology, because there are very few local educational institutions that offer graduate training in anthropology, and none that enables a student to specialize in archaeology.

To remedy this situation, the National Museum, through the South-East Asian Ministers of Education Organization Special Project in Archaeology and Fine Arts, holds periodic training programmes in archaeology which lead to certification of technicians. These programmes enable trainees to develop some of the necessary skills in archaeological excavation and documentation. However, these training programmes generally focus only on field techniques. What the National Museum needs now are professional archaeologists with advanced academic training who can design viable programmes for cultural resource management. The National Museum should develop a more responsive staff development programme and a more attractive reward system in order to upgrade the quality of its professional services.

Lack of public appreciation of the value of cultural resources and awareness of pertinent legal provisions

Several archaeological sites have already been destroyed and a lot of valuable information on the country's cultural heritage has been lost owing to the people's lack of appreciation of the value of cultural resources and general lack of awareness of pertinent legal provisions. To encourage the Filipino public to comply with existing laws, the National Museum, the National Historical Institute and the Ministry of Tourism should undertake an active campaign to disseminate information on the legal provisions regarding the conservation, protection and management of the nation's cultural resources. Efforts should similarly be made to maximize the utilization of the educational system and the media to institutionalize, on a national level, a deeper appreciation of the importance and value of the nation's cultural resources and a heightened awareness of the need to conserve and manage this finite set of resources.

Inadequate funding

At present the operations of the agencies mandated to preserve and protect the nation's cultural heritage are crippled by inadequate funding. This seriously hampers the operations of the implementing agencies. Because of insufficient funding, these agencies lack adequate facilities for systematic storage and record keeping, adequate safety and security measures to protect specimens and records, basic field equipment and vehicles, and highly qualified professional staff.

Conclusions

The cultural resource management programme of the Philippines is still in its early stage of development. The fledgeling programme is beset by a host of major problems. Some critically important provisions of pertinent laws are not clearly drafted and are therefore subject to various interpretations. Most of the measures taken to conserve and protect the nation's cultural resources are generally curative rather than preventive. Because of the limitations of salvage archaeology, which is resorted to when sites are in imminent danger of being destroyed as a result of illegal diggings, researchers are often left with little opportunity to conduct problem-oriented research. The existing linkages among the implementing agencies are relatively weak, with poorly defined areas of responsibility and unclear guidelines for collaboration. There are only a few qualified professional staff to carry on the tasks of cultural resource management. The public does not fully appreciate the value of cultural resources, and possesses only minimal awareness of pertinent legal provisions. The operations of the agencies mandated to preserve and protect the nation's cultural heritage are crippled by inadequate funding.

In order to evolve a more effective cultural resource management programme, the Philippines still has to undertake several steps, among which are the following:

(a)   to review and amend certain pertinent legal provisions;
(b)   to institute more preventive than curative measures;
(c)   to consider alternative solutions to the potential destruction of archaeological sites rather than relying solely on salvage;
(d)   to firm-up linkages among implementing agencies and encourage more-extensive cross-sharing of resources and expertise;
(e)   to upgrade qualifications of professional staff through more-responsive and relevant staff development programmes and more-attractive pay and incentive schemes;
(f)   to undertake a massive information dissemination campaign, through the educational system and the media, to heighten the public's appreciation of the value of cultural resources and awareness of pertinent legal provision; and
(g)   to generate additional funds for cultural resource management in order to enable the implementing agencies to carry on their mandate successfully.

References

Beyer, H. O. 1949. Outline review of archaeology by islands and provinces. *Philippine Journal of Science Philippines* **77** (July).

Fox, R. B. 1959. The Calatagan excavations. *Philippine Studies* **7**, 321–90.

Guthe, C. 1929. The University of Michigan Philippine expedition. *American Anthropologist* **29**, 69–76.

Philippine Government 1966. *Republic Act No. 4846*: An Act to Repeal Act Numbered Thirty-Eight Hundred Seventy-Four, and to Provide for the Protection and Preservation of Philippine Cultural Properties, Sixth Congress of the Republic of the Philippines, First Session, 18 June.

Philippine Government 1971. *Proclamation No. 913*: Declaring the Period from October 1 to 7 of every year as National Museum Week.

Philippine Government 1973. *Presidential Decree No. 260*: Declaring the Santa Ana Site Museum in Manila, the Roman Catholic Churches of Panay and Bacarra in Ilocos Norte, the San Agustin Church and Liturgical Objects therein in Intramuros, Manila, Fort Pilar in Zamboanga City, the Petroglyphs of the Rockshelter in Angono, Rizal, the Petroglyphs of Alab, Bontoc, the Stone Agricultural Calendars of Dap-ay Guiday in Besao, Bontoc, the Mummy Caves of Kabayan, Benguet and of Sagada and Alab, Bontoc, the Ifugao Rice Terraces of Banaue as National Cultural Treasures; and the Barasoain Church in Malolos, Bulacan, Tirad Pass in Cervantes, Ilocos Sur, the Miagao Church in Miagao, Iloilo, the site of the Battle of Mactan on Mactan Island, Cebu, the San Sebastian Church in Quiapo, Manila, and the church and convent of Santo Nino in Cebu City as National Shrines, Monuments, and/or Landmarks, Defining the Implementing Agencies and Providing Funds Therefore.

Philippine Government 1974. *Presidential Decree No. 373*: Exempting from taxation all Donations to the National Museum, the National Library, and the Archives of the National Historical Institute.

Philippine Government 1974. *Presidential Decree No. 374*: Amending Certain Sections of Republic Act No. 4846, Otherwise Known as The Cultural Properties Preservation and Protection Act.

Philippine Government 1974. *Presidential Decree No. 375*: Amending Presidential Decree No. 260 by including the Two Hundred Year Old Basilica of Taal, Batangas and the Church of Santa Maria, Ilocos Sur, among the National Landmarks and Monuments Declared as National Shrines.

Philippine Government 1975. *Presidential Decree No. 756*: Amending Presidential Decree No. 260 to Include the Mestizo Section, the Houses of Padre Jose Burgos and Leona Florentino in its Scope.

Philippine Government 1977. *Presidential Decree No. 1109*: Declaring the Archaeological Areas in Cagayan Valley and Kalinga-Apayao as an Archaeological Reservation.

Philippine Government 1977. *Proclamation No. 1683*: Declaring the Burial Caves at Sitio Alabok, Barangay Cambali, Bugulin, La Union, as a National Cultural Treasure.

Philippine Government 1978. *Proclamation No. 1743*: Reserving for Anthropological and Archaeological Research Purposes a Certain Portion of the Public Domain Situated in the Municipality of Quezon, Province of Palawan.

Philippine Government 1978. *Presidential Decree No. 1492*: Amending Presidential Decree No. 260 to Include the Petroglyphs in the Cave at the Tau't Batu Area in Barangay Ransang, Quezon, Palawan.

11 *Cultural resource management in sub-Saharan Africa: Nigeria, Togo and Ghana*

KWASI MYLES

Introduction

This chapter surveys the legislative and administrative provision for recording, investigating, protecting, conserving and presenting to the public ancient monuments in three countries of West Africa – Nigeria, Ghana, and Togo. Some of the problems involved are common to all three countries.

First there is the problem of conservation: although efforts are being made to conserve monuments, this concept is a new one and runs counter to current practice. A considerable number of examples of indigenous forms of architecture continue to be destroyed and their technology lost. This is partly because the building industry does not spare sufficient time to examine indigenous forms of architecture. As a result some sections of the community see monuments preservation as the opposite of progress.

Secondly, in Nigeria and Ghana, where there has been legislation for over two decades the legislative and administrative provisions are adequate for the protection and presentation of monuments. The problem is the ability to employ sufficient staff and to provide them with adequate financial resources to conserve the monuments. The training and retention of staff for monuments preservation face the problem of competition with the building industry, which offers more-lucrative remuneration than the monuments service, a non-profit-making organization. Furthermore, the acute demand on the limited financial resources of government for various socio-economic projects makes it difficult for monuments services, which are government-sponsored, to be able to carry out their functions. This is particularly the case with maintenance works, which are a recurrent expenditure. In the present period of economic stress, if other forms of assistance are not sought it will be very difficult to continue to protect the monuments that have been restored.

In the case of Togo, where no antiquities law has yet been passed, there does not appear to be any interference with the activities of the Monuments

Division and the other departments that are collaborating with it in protecting and presenting monuments and sites to the public. These services have sufficient authority to carry out their duties. However, as has already been mentioned, their problem is lack of adequate financial resources and trained personnel.

It has been realized that the tourist industry can offer some assistance in the protection and promotion of monuments. As tourism makes use of the monuments and sites, it can publicize them by contributing financially towards the preparation of publications. In these three countries tourism does not yet contribute significantly to the economy, and there are not many private tourist agencies. There is still a pressing need to examine other means of finding financial resources to preserve and present monuments.

Nigeria

The National Commission for Museums and Monuments

The Commission was set up in 1979, charged with the responsibility of conservation in Nigeria, and was placed under the general administrative supervision of the Federal Ministry of Information, Youth, Culture and Sports.

Before 1979 the Federal Department of Antiquities had been responsible for conservation; it came under the Federal Ministry of Information. The Commission, which replaced the Federal Department of Antiquities, was created by the Federal authority, and it therefore operates on a national basis. Its creation is derived from item 57(b) of Article 233 of Nigeria's constitution (Enactment Decree No. 25 of 1978) which states: 'The establishment and regulation of authorities for the Federation or any part thereof to identify, collect, preserve or generally to look after ancient and historic monuments and records, and archaeological sites and remains, declared by the National Assembly to be of national significance or national importance'.

Decree No. 77 of 1979 established the National Commission for Museums and Monuments, with the conservation, restoration and preservation of architectural monuments and sites in the country as its sole responsibility.

THE CONSTITUTION OF THE COMMISSION

According to the Decree, the Commission is a corporate body with perpetual succession and common seal; it may sue or be sued in its corporate name.

The chairman of the Commission is appointed by the Federal Executive Council. The Commission is made up of five persons, on the recommendation of the Commissioner, who should be persons with knowledge or experience in education, culture, natural history, science and technology, and the sciences, and capable of making a useful contribution to the work of the Commission; nine representatives of the state, who are appointed in rotation, so that no state shall have more than one representative at any time, and the Director.

FUNCTIONS OF THE COMMISSION

(a)   To administer national museums, antiquities and monuments.
(b)   To establish and maintain national museums and other outlets for, or in connection with, but not restricted to, the following: antiquities, science and technology, warfare, African black and other antiquities, arts and crafts, architecture, national history and educational services.
(c)   To make recommendations to any State Government or other person or authority concerning the establishment and management of museums or antiquities and monuments not being those declared to be national antiquities or monuments.

APPOINTMENTS WITHIN THE COMMISSION

The Commission appoints the following officers: (a) an Administrative Secretary; (b) a Director of Research and Training; and (c) a Director of Museums and Monuments. The Director of Museums and Monuments is responsible to the Director General for the upkeep and general maintenance of museums and monuments under the management of the Commission, the collection of material for such museums, and the identification of antiquities to be declared as monuments.

ADMINISTRATIVE PROCEDURE FOR SCHEDULING MONUMENTS

The Commission may, if it considers that any antiquity is in need of protection or preservation and ought in the national interest to be protected or preserved, publish notices to that effect in the *Federal Gazette*. The Commission also sends a copy of the notice to the owner of the antiquity concerned.

Every notice shall:

(a)   specify the antiquity and place where it is, or is supposed to be;
(b)   state that it is intended to make an application to the Head of the Federal Government to declare the antiquity to be a national monument; and
(c)   state that any objection to such a declaration shall be lodged with the Commission within two months from the date of publication of such a notice.

Furthermore, the Commission shall, in any case in which it is reasonably practicable to do so, cause a copy of any notice published to be posted in a conspicuous place on or near the antiquity to which it relates.

Additional copies of the notice should be sent to the Local Government in which the antiquity is located, and the Secretary to such a Local Government concerned must post a copy of the notice in a conspicuous place in the principal office of such Local Government.

SANCTIONS

From the date of publication of this notice until the publication of an order by the Head of the Federal Government or, if no such order is made, until the expiry of three months thereafter, it shall be an offence to destroy, deface, alter, remove or transfer the possession of the antiquity to which the notice relates, except with the written permission of the Commission. Anybody who contravenes this shall be guilty of an offence, and would be liable on conviction to a fine of ₦200 or imprisonment for six months, or both.

The Commission may, with the consent of the owner of a monument, if it appears that the monument is in danger of decay, destruction, removal or damage from neglect or injudicious treatment, maintain such monument.

When an antiquity has been declared a monument, the owner shall be entitled to a compensation for the value at the date of such declaration, and thereafter any title, right, estate and interest in such an antiquity shall be nullified.

In case of dispute as to the amount of compensation payable, such dispute shall be referred to a court of competent jurisdiction in the area concerned.

Where an antiquity has been declared a monument, any person who wilfully destroys, defaces, alters or removes the structure shall be guilty of an offence, and shall be liable on conviction to a fine of ₦1000 or twice the value of such monument (whichever is higher), or to an imprisonment of twelve months, or both.

Any person who without lawful authority destroys, defaces or removes any notice, mark or sign denoting any monument or any fence, covering or other things erected or provided for the maintenance of a monument shall be guilty of an offence and liable on conviction to a fine of ₦500, or to imprisonment for six months, or both.

The old Antiquities Act and these provisions of decree No. 77 of 1979 have enabled the Commission to list monuments and sites of national significance. The declaration of monuments in Nigeria dates to 1956.

OTHER RESPONSIBILITIES OF THE COMMISSION

The Commission may accept gifts of any antiquity, monument, museum or land, money, loan, building, work of art or other property connected with its functions under or pursuant of the decree upon such trusts and conditions if any, as may be specified by the person or organization making the gift.

It may, with the consent of the Commissioner or in accordance with any general authority given on behalf of the Federal Government, borrow by way of loan or overdraft from any source any sums required for meeting its obligations and discharging its functions under the decree. Subject to the provisions of this decree and the conditions of any trust created in respect of any property, the Commission may invest all or any of its funds with the consent of the authority.

FUNDING

At the end of every financial year the Commission submits an estimate of its income and expenditure during the next succeeding year to the Commissioner for approval. This is followed by the allocation of votes to the various units of the Commission.

Problems connected with conservation

These are many, for the idea of conservation is new, and not many people appreciate the need for it. Conservation works on monuments are seasonal, since repairs and construction can be carried out only during the dry season. Moreover, the geographical distribution of monuments over such a large country makes inspection and supervision very difficult. The political complexity of the country does not favour having only nine states out of the 19 represented annually on the Board of the Commission. National priorities constitute another problem when estimates are discussed at that level. Furthermore, even when estimates are duly approved, priorities within the Commission also affect the allocation of funds for conservation of monuments and sites. Although the decree authorizes loans, only a few of the monuments can be restored or acquired for revenue-generating purposes. The importance of traditional architecture in Nigeria has not been firmly established, and it is therefore difficult to ask visitors to monuments to pay substantial entrance fees. The practice of foreign architecture has replaced traditional craftsmanship as far as the younger generation is concerned. Besides, traditional building materials are sometimes difficult or expensive to obtain.

Monuments in Nigeria

Legislation to preserve monuments was passed in 1953 when it was discovered that many old traditional buildings were being demolished and replaced with modern structures.

Decree No. 77 of 1979 empowers the Commission to designate as a monument any site, building or other immovable property in need of preservation, that ought in the public interest to be protected or preserved. The Commission has the duty of undertaking any restoration work, making the monument accessible to the public and carrying out maintenance as and when needed. Altogether about 500 examples of various traditional buildings have been recorded, and about 60 monuments have been designated in various parts of the country. These monuments include rock paintings, ancient earthworks and causeways, sites of settlements, statues, memorials and trees.

The architectural monuments may be divided into two groups: traditional buildings and early colonial buildings. The colonial buildings are easier to look after, even though they fit less conveniently into a national demand for cultural heritage.

Several structures and sites have so far been declared monuments in 17 out of the 19 states of the country. Gongola and Ogun states still have to be fully explored. Although there are hints of possible monuments in the other states, these have not yet been recorded. Archaeological work has been and is still being done in Gongola State.

It should be noted that most of these monuments were recorded and declared before the creation of new states in the country, and consequently some of the states do not yet have any recorded monuments.

Togo

The Monuments and Sites of Togo come under the Division of Monuments and Sites of the National Museum. The National Museum, founded in November 1975, is still in its developmental stages. This is the first museum, and is located in the Maison du RPT (Rassemblement du Peuple Togolais), the headquarters of the only political party in Lomé, the capital city. Another important Division of the National Museum is the Village Artisanal de Lomé, a crafts centre, where many handicrafts, including woodworking and textiles, are made and sold to the public. The Division of Monuments and Sites has its office located in this crafts centre.

Like the National Museum itself, the Division of Monuments and Sites is also in the process of development. There is no legislation yet on the scheduling and protection of monuments and sites, though efforts are being made to get such legislation prepared and promulgated. Nevertheless, the Division is working on a project which is listing all of the monuments and sites in the country. The main categories of monuments listed so far are the following.

(a) Political monuments, of which there are three in the capital city, Lomé:
      (i)   The Monument of Independence, inaugurated on 27 April 1960;
      (ii)   Monument to commemorate the Dead, inaugurated in 1958 in memory of those who fought for political independence; and
      (iii) The Old Presidency, which is being renovated as a Presidential Guest House for visiting Heads of State to Togo. It should be added that there are other political monuments in other cities of the country.
(b) Another significant category of monuments are buildings constructed during the period of German rule: 1884–1914. Many of these buildings have been demolished, because not many people realized their importance. Of the remaining buildings of this period the cathedral of Lomé, built in 1902, may be cited as a significant example. However, to commemorate the 100th anniversary of German rule, two monuments were built, at Baguida and Togoville in June 1984. These monuments recall the Treaty of Protectorate signed between Mlapa II of Togoville and Dr Gustav Nachtigal.

      Colonial monuments include some historical sites which are villages or towns by themselves. One such historical town is Agbodrafo, which the Portuguese named Porto Seguro, as this coastal town was their point of entry into the country. Aneho (formerly known as Little Popo), a fishing village, later became the capital city before Lomé. An old building of the German period located in a beautiful setting in Aneho is being developed as a local museum. These examples represent monuments along the coast, and are all historical sites.

Inland in the Atakpame area is Kamina, another historical site. This is the site where the German Colonial Government had installed a communication system by which it communicated directly with Berlin. The Germans were heavily defeated here during World War I, and the remains of these installations mark the site.

Kpalime is another historical town, and also a site of natural beauty. Here Chateau Viale was built on the top of the Avatime Hill by François Rémond Viale. On the way to this castle, which is a historical monument, there is a waterfall. Farther inland in the Akposso area there is another waterfall, Akrowa, 9 km from Badou.

At Notse there is an important archaeological site, a settlement, and at Ahlo there are archaeological sites with interesting collections which have not been published. At Bassar there is a historical site where iron was worked, and there are remains of the structures for smelting iron. About 64 km from Bassar there is a river with crocodiles which have connections with a shrine, which is a tourist attraction. In this neighbourhood there is a historical site called Camp-Massu, a European residence.

(c) Forest reserves form another group of sites; there are reserves at Malfakassa, Fazao, Kouve, Keran and Dapaong. Keran is a national park, and hunting and the cutting of wood is prohibited in all of these reserves.

Traditional architecture has not been left out of the work, and at Tamberma one traditional form of architecture called Tata has been preserved. This type, built for defensive purposes, is used by a group of families. When the project is completed photographs and slides will be prepared of all the monuments and sites.

Supervision of monuments and sites

Monuments and sites come under the administrative supervision of the Division of Monuments and Sites of the National Museum, and the Forest Reserves come under the Ministry of Rural Development. The Ministry of Tourism also provides guides who organize visits to these monuments and sites. These three organizations have worked out a method of co-ordinating their various activities.

Problems

The problems being experienced by the project are basically financial. For example, there is the need to obtain sufficient vehicles to be able to visit the sites regularly and start detailed studies on them. Another problem is that of staff; the Division requires more staff, and these are to be given more-intensive training to equip them for work in the field.

Ghana

The monuments and sites of Ghana come under the Monuments Division of the Ghana Museums and Monuments Board. The activities of the Board are currently regulated by National Museum Decree 1969 (also referred to as National Liberation Council Decree 387). The work of the Monuments Division may be traced to the Monuments and Relics Commission, created in 1948 to initiate the preservation of antiquities and the restoration of architectural monuments.

In 1950 a National Museum was founded as a research centre, and was temporarily housed in the University Department of Archaeology. By 1957 the Monuments and Relics Commission and the National Museum had done an appreciable work; they were merged to form the Ghana Museum and Monuments Board, and were given legal standing by the creation of the Ghana Museum and Monuments Board Ordinance 1957 (also referred to as Ordinance No. 20).

The provisions of Ordinance No. 20 were strengthened by those of NLCD 387. Paragraph 11 of this Decree provides adequate legislative and administrative measures on the declaration of national monuments. The procedure is as follows. On the recommendation of the Ghana Museums and Monuments Board, the Government may proclaim any monument to be a national monument. Before the Board makes this recommendation, it gives two months' written notice to the owner of the monument. If the owner has any objections, these are brought to the attention of the Board, which has to submit them, together with its recommendations, to the Government.

The main duties of the Board include to equip, maintain and manage the National Museum, to preserve, repair or restore any antiquity that it considers to be of national importance, and to keep a register of all antiquities it acquires or are brought to its notice.

The Board is empowered to undertake the excavation of any site of any antiquity with the prior written permission of the owner of the site. It is also empowered (with the written consent of the owner of a property) to erect notices or tablets to provide information about historic events occurring at the site. It is also empowered to make general regulations for carrying out the principles and purpose of the Decree, provided these regulations are approved by the government.

Forts and castles

These post-medieval European forts and castles were constructed by various trading companies as trading posts during the period from the late 15th century to the end of the 18th century. Numbering about 25, they were the first to be declared national monuments. Most have been thoroughly investigated, restored and conserved. Some are being used as prisons, offices for central and local government, a few have been left as ruins, and others provide rest-house accommodation for tourists. These monuments are so significant that they have been listed as a group in the World Heritage List.

Mosques

Seventeen mosques have been recorded, all located in the savannah territory up-country. Restoration work has been done on most of them. It was arranged that local worshippers should assist in maintenance; in the initial stages this method achieved a measure of success, but as time went on there were problems.

Places of indigenous buildings

Thirteen buildings which form a distinctive group of indigenous buildings have been scheduled as national monuments. The complete examples consist of a compound house with a courtyard enclosed. The characteristic features of the buildings include mural decorations and thatched roofs. Most of these buildings housed shrines, though a few of them were residences of traditional rulers. Complete restoration work was carried out on several of them and, in order to keep them in good condition, the owners were allowed to live in them.

Historical buildings

There are a large number of historical buildings which show European architecture. Thirteen of these have been selected in Accra in order to initiate a project of negotiating with their owners to get them declared as national monuments. As a first stage of the project these buildings are being drawn.

Archaeological Sites

These include three rock-shelters, outcrops of rock with grooves resulting from the grinding of stone cells, and two late Iron Age sites.

Fortifications

There are remains of two town walls: Nalerigu and Gwolu in the savannah area.

Protection and conservation

The conservation and presentation of these monuments present many problems. Some of these monuments are situated in remote parts of country which cannot be visited regularly. The cost involved in maintenance is quite heavy, considering the cost of building materials and the movement of trained monuments staff from one monument to another. Very often modern building materials have to be used and these are expensive; even when indigenous materials are used, they are often not easy to procure, and indigenous technology is gradually being lost. Nevertheless, there is a continuous search for effective means of protecting monuments. For example, the method of getting the users of the monument to assist in its maintenance has not proved very successful. There have been discussions aimed at getting local people in the area where the monument is located to become more aware of it, so that they may become involved in its maintenance. It is certainly too burdensome for central government alone to bear the financial cost.

Acknowledgements

Information for preparing the section on Togo was provided by the Division of Monuments and Sites of the National Museum of Togo. The section on protection and conservation in Ghana was prepared from material obtained from the Monuments Division of the Ghana Museums and Monuments Board.

12 Problems in the conservation and restoration of ruined buildings in Madagascar

DAVID RASAMUEL

The problems associated with the protection of the cultural heritage of Madagascar depend on the interest shown in that heritage, on the legislation currently in force and on the application of that legislation. Despite passing allusions to the past in political speeches, the safeguarding of the monuments that bear witness to that past cannot yet be regarded as having become a national priority. Nevertheless, in the face of the growing threat which is undermining certain monuments and sites that are too famous not to attract the attention of the authorities (and also that of the public), it has been decided to reactivate the official regulations relating to the conservation of these cultural treasures.

However, the new law overlooks certain fundamental points, if it is to be effective, such as the training of personnel and research into methods of intervention appropriate to the original building techniques and the specific material used. The rôle assigned to scientists, researchers, teachers and experts in the history of culture, archaeology and museology in this operation is minimal, even non-existent. It is left exclusively to administrators to plan and carry out measures to protect the national heritage. It is therefore hardly surprising that control measures and sanctions should concentrate on technical studies, and that the intervention effected is sometimes subject to grave weaknesses. It would be too much to hope, in the current situation, that any efforts will be undertaken to conserve and restore the sites and buildings that have been the subject of research and archaeological investigation, and that require rescue work to be carried out on them. Many of them are already in a dangerous condition.

Legislation relating to the cultural heritage

There is no shortage of legislative measures relating to the protection of the national heritage in Madagascar. As early as 1937 the French colonial government brought out a decree regarding natural monuments and sites of historic interest (Edict of 25 August 1937, Article 2). Two years later, G. G.

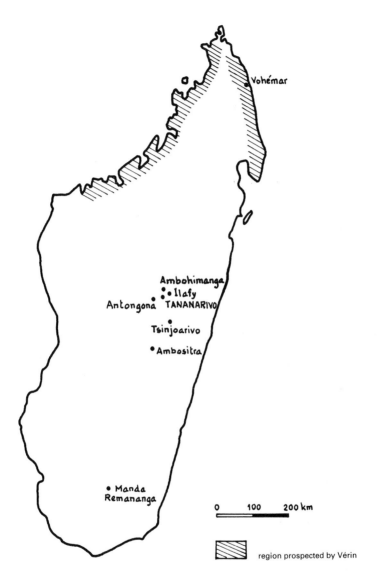

Figure 12.1 Map of Madagascar, showing sites mentioned in the chapter.

Léon Cayla, Governor General of Madagascar and the Dependencies, made public in the *Journal Officiel* (No. 2770 of 11 February 1939) a decree relating to the natural monuments and historic sites within the Colony (Decree of 8 February 1939). A list drawn up on that occasion included monuments and sites that are currently being maintained by the Ministry of Culture, namely the Queen's Palace at Tananarive and the *rova* (a wooden palisade surrounding the residence of a king or prince) at Ambohimanga, Ilafy, Antongona, Tsinjoarivo and Ambositra. (These and other sites mentioned in this chapter are shown in Fig. 12.1.) Another law (No. 56–106) was passed on 3 November 1956. Later, a French writer, Louis Molet, published in the *Bulletin de Madagascar* (No. 138, 1957, pp. 996–8) a text for the regulation of archaeological excavations in Madagascar.

Soon after Independence other laws saw the light of day, the first of which was that of 1961 (No. 61–031) regarding historic monuments and art objects. It was passed by the President of the Republic, Philibert Tsiranana, after having been adopted by the National Assembly and the Senate. It was concerned principally with the buildings that needed to be classified as historic monuments (the 1st Article of the present law). In the case of public institutions the designations were made public by edict or by decree of the President of the Republic after consultation with the Historic Monuments and Art Objects Department (Articles 1, 3 and 4). That law provided for the protection and maintenance of the monuments designated as historic and included in the general list drawn up in 1939, publication of which is required to take place only once every ten years (Articles 2 and 25). Designated monuments may not be altered in any way, but the state can provide financial aid or materials required for their conservation.

A commission can be set up to examine the measures that need to be taken in order to ensure the protection of a monument. It is presided over by the Secretary of State delegated for this work, and consists of representatives of the President of the Republic, the Malagasy Academy, the local authorities and the Service des domaines et de techniciens. Article 28 of this Law established regulations for excavations and discoveries. Penal measures in cases of their infringement were also specified. A Commission for Sites and Historic Monuments, with an advisory function, was set up in order to supervise the application of these legislative measures.

Statute No. 73 050, dated 7 September 1953 and adopted by the Head of the Government, General Gabriel Ramanantsoa, is also concerned with the preservation of cultural property. The World Heritage Convention adopted by Unesco in 1972 was not to be ratified so as to come into force in Madagascar for another ten years (Statute No. 82 030, of 6 November 1982). This Convention draws attention to the need to provide international aid to those countries which cannot fund work for the conservation and restoration of monuments or sites that may be of world importance. It also provides each member state with advice for the implementation of an effective programme for the protection and development of its heritage, initially on a national scale.

On the same day that the State of Madagascar ratified the Convention, 6 November 1982, it adopted a statute regarding the protection of the national heritage, which is currently in force and which abrogates all other previous laws (No. 82 029, of 6 November 1982). This statute, having been first submitted to the High Court for Constitutional Matters and subsequently ratified by the National Popular Assembly, was then adopted by the President of the Republic, Didier Ratsiraka, together with the Supreme Revolutionary Council, the two highest authorities in the land. It goes some way towards meeting the Unesco recommendations, though only certain provisions of the Convention have been retained, in particular the institution of legislation and an administrative structure designed to protect the national heritage. The registration and designation of the monuments and the sites, their maintenance or possible repair, safeguards against cultural treasures being exported, control over research work – in particular excavations and the finds resulting from them – and sanctions against infringements of such regulations are all included in the law.

On the other hand, no provision has been made for the training at either secondary or tertiary level of 'appropriate personnel', i.e. staff and technicians with specialized training in conservation and restoration. The same is true with regard to scientific research, of which there is no mention, not even that necessary for improving methods of intervention, at a time when ancient buildings in Madagascar present a specific technical challenge that needs to be investigated in detail, including laboratory analysis. Local communities are required to take responsibility for the protection and control of the national heritage. This responsibility is entrusted to communities, usually of a rural nature, whose members do not have even the most rudimentary knowledge concerning matters of conservation.

Moreover, this new legislation risks creating an overloaded administrative system to deal with the formalities of registering cultural property, which in every case has to be reviewed by the National Classification Commission, made the subject of a decree drawn up by the Minister of Culture responsible for the protection of the national heritage (the Ministry of Revolutionary Culture and Art). This means that only those sites and monuments that have already been registered and designated will continue to be maintained, preserved and repaired. Action at sites newly registered as a result of archaeological surveys and in respect of objects discovered during recent excavations is not something that can be hoped for in the short term, at the very time when their condition calls for urgent action.

Conservation work undertaken at state expense, as provided for in Article 9 of the Statute, is something that usually applies to sites and monuments that have been registered or that are sufficiently well known by virtue of the political rôle they have played. Other items of cultural property, above all those that have been the object of recent research and whose historical and cultural importance has been demonstrated in the course of archaeological investigations, have little chance of benefiting from state funding in the immediate future, even if they are under serious threat. The maintenance of a large number of items already registered is, moreover, left to decentralized groups or to private individuals who have at their disposal only very limited funds for this work. It is not difficult to foresee the disastrous results that will stem from such practice.

One somewhat astonishing fact is the absence of the institutions engaged in historical or archaeological research from the list of the organizations which can submit proposals for the registration of cultural property, as laid down by Article 11 of State No. 82 029, even though the researchers and experts who are best placed to appreciate, on the basis of scientific knowledge, the importance of the sites and monuments which need preservation and restoration work, as well as their current state, are included. Collaboration between the ministry responsible for the protection of the national heritage and the other ministries who might be involved is mentioned in Article 3.

The decree implementing Statute No. 82 029, which appeared in 1983, confirmed the fears raised by the 1982 Statute with regard to the composition of the commissions to be set up in order to protect the national heritage: the National Designation Commission, the National Commission for the Control of the Export of Items from the National Heritage and the Commission for Excavations and Research. None of these commissions contains researchers or teachers in history, archaeology, ethnology, museology, conservation or restoration! It would have seemed normal for trained archaeologists with adequate experience of excavations, along with research historians who had proved themselves through their publications and other work and who were thus closely acquainted with the history and civilization of Madagascar, to have been appointed to these commissions.

Councils made up of specialized scientific personnel are indispensable to examine requests for authorization of excavation and research work. The surveillance and assessment of the quality of the work undertaken at such sites, so as to limit as far as possible the damage resulting from excavation, depend on the competence of such specialists. The same applies to control over exports of archaeological objects and specimens: the opinions of specialists such as metallurgists, ceramics experts, zoologists and botanists with archaeological knowledge is greatly to be desired, since these are the only people capable of judging whether the export licence should be granted. Who can have a better knowledge of the ancient sites and monuments that need preserving and protecting than historians and archaeologists? However, they are not asked for their opinions, nor is their advice sought. This does not in any way exclude the presence (which is very desirable) of planners, lawyers, technicians and administrators, who make their own specialised contributions to the work of these commissions.

Conservation and restoration practices

The gaps in the legislation noted above cannot fail to have repercussions on its implementation. Current practices in the conservation and restoration of sites and monuments provide examples of mistakes that have sometimes proved irremediable. As mentioned above, there is a lack of training for the personnel charged with protecting the cultural heritage on the one hand, and a failure to take the advice of researchers, historians and archaeologists on the other.

First of all, the systematic inventory of sites and monuments of historical interest, with a view to protection, appears to have been neglected. This explains why there is a readiness merely to continue maintaining the main *rova*, to which there is fairly easy access, which were registered as far back as 1939 and which only require simple and routine maintenance work. Archaeological research and publishing activities have been going on for a long time, but little account is taken of them. The first major excavations at the *rasikajy* necropolis in Vohemar (Gaudebout 1941) were carried out in 1941 and 1942. Pierre Vérin (1975) recorded, described and studied the mosques, ruined houses and *analotse* necropolises on the northern shores of the island. Adrien Mille (1970) recorded and classified 16 421 archaeological sites on the high central plateaux of Madagascar. No-one in authority paid any serious attention to this work.

A serious problem arises with regard to monuments and sites that are currently protected and which have been selected for intervention. It concerns the repair of ancient buildings which do not conform with the rules laid down for restoration work. It is not enough to consolidate an archaeological structure (a tomb, a dry-stone wall or a cult site); what is also required is that its original character should be preserved. This fundamental, albeit elementary, precaution is not being taken. The rapid and easy solution that is currently being adopted consists of the abundant use of cement to hold the original stone elements of the structure in place, even if this entails covering them up. This is neither a method of conservation nor a process that should be used for restoring remains. It is rather a technique of 'modernization', a transformation of ancient structures that robs them of all their authenticity and their cultural, historical or archaeological value.

Large cement walls are being erected round certain sites, allegedly to 'protect' them. No consideration is given to the original appearance of the places concerned. These walls are structures that are artificial and arbitrary, and that dominate the ancient landscape. The authentic structures which would normally constitute the focus of interest for visitors are no longer prominent, having been relegated to the background. It is no exaggeration to assert that our 'restorers' are more than generous with their mortar.

Meanwhile, other ancient structures are continuing to fall in ruins without any hope of intervention, even though some of these are rare or even unique specimens. How many Islamized warehouses in the north of the island have been left to the mercy of the elements? How many forts of the *merina* of central Madagascar or of the Europeans have been abandoned to nature and invaded by vegetation? How many *manda* (stone enclosures often found in south and central Madagascar) and *tamboho* (earthworks enclosing 19th century estates) crumble to nothing each year? How many neglected *hadivory*

Figure 12.2   The Raininboay tomb (photograph A. Ravasiloa).

(ancient ditches enclosing hilltop villages) result in an acceleration in hillside erosion?

As an example, consider an estate situated in the heart of the capital. The Raininboay estate, in the Ankadifotsy district, consists of a main building and an enormous tomb (Fig. 12.2) surrounded by a *tamboho*. The large house, of traditional type, is in the original 19th century style; it has thick mud walls, supported by stone pillars with decorated capitals, and has a tiled roof that is at present in a clearly dilapidated state. The owners do not have the necessary means to maintain and repair the building. The same goes for the tomb, a fine stone structure which has partly collapsed. Elements of the buildings which fall down are re-used for less-dignified purposes by the current occupants of the property.

The other problem is the voluntary demolition of components of the cultural heritage which are not the subject of protection orders. How many *tamboho* (see Fig. 12.3) have been dismantled round Tananarivo to supply immediate needs? They have simply been sacrificed in the interests of the modern buildings that are being erected or to make way for new roads. Sometimes they have simply been replaced by enclosures of brick and cement. Most of the *vavahady* (gates of stone discs which closed off ancient ramparted villages: see Fig. 12.4) have disappeared in recent times because the present inhabitants of the surrounding area have removed, sawn up and

Figure 12.3 A ruined *tamboho* (photograph Michel Richard).

Figure 12.4   An example of a *vavahady vato* (drawing based on a Teissonnière photograph in the Musée de l'Homme, Paris).

re-used the granite. It is not uncommon in the south to come across parts of *manda* (see Fig. 12.5) that have been used to construct modern tombs. There is an urgent need to bring the destruction of cultural property in these ways to an end.

Faced with a situation such as this, the archaeologist cannot remain passive. He or she feels obliged to hasten to investigate the surviving ancient structures before it is too late. Excavations are undertaken in order to rediscover the traces of the past, to exhibit them to the public and to pass on this knowledge to future generations. This mission will not, however, be accomplished if conservation measures are not put in hand for the excavated sites and the structures which have been brought to light. By the same token, archaeological material will continue to be scattered throughout research institutions, or even in private hands, if a National Museum is not set up in Madagascar in order to house it.

Policies for training and research

The policy for protecting the cultural heritage suffers from the lack of interest shown in the specialized training of personnel for conservation and

Figure 12.5 A ruined *manda* (photograph B. Manjakahery).

restoration with regard both to scientific research and to the related technical studies. Nevertheless, the University of Madagascar does provide facilities for teaching and research into cultural history, the history of art, archaeology and museology. The teaching and research are shared out among and provided by specialists from the Unité d'Enseignement et de Recherche for History and the Centre for Art and Archaeology of the Faculty of Letters in Tananarivo (the present title of this institution is the Etablissement d'Enseignement Supérieur et de la Recherche des Lettres (EESRL)). This teaching usually does not include more than one or two subjects, on a complementary or optional basis, according to the level of study. The courses are followed by history or geography students because there are not yet sufficient courses available specifically for the study of museology, archaeology or cultural history.

In the second year of their university course students have the chance to study courses in Material Cultures of the Malagasy People. The third year offers them an optional module entitled Methods in Archaeology, another on Inititiation into Museology and another on Traditional Art and Malagasy Art. An optional subject that can be taken up in the fourth year is the Archaeology of Madagascar and another is Problems of Cultural History. The teaching sessions listed above do not consist merely of theoretical lessons in the classroom, they also include guided projects, practical work in laboratories, and even field trips. Each year, during vacations, the Centre for Art and Archaeology organizes courses in excavation and restoration that are open to university teachers, schoolchildren and anyone else interested in this practical training.

As mentioned above, none of these courses, which are very limited in variety, is obligatory. It is not possible to envisage any expansion of these facilities at present, nor the setting up a course for specialized training in these fields, since there would be no career opportunities for students to continue in this line of work. There is always the possibility in individual cases for rare individual students to acquire their training abroad, as has already been done at the Institute of Art and Archaeology and the Musée de l'Homme in Paris.

Yet even this handful of courageous and motivated students, once their training is over and they return home, find themselves confronted by employment difficulties that are in some cases insurmountable.

The Ministry of Culture, through its Department for the Protection of the National Heritage, occasionally organizes mini-courses of a theoretical nature, the maximum duration of which is one month; these are restricted to staff who are already responsible for the protection of the cultural heritage. In 1986 an instructor from France, specializing in conservation and restoration, led a training seminar of this type in Tananarivo.

These efforts to provide in-service training are wholly inadequate, and can in no way be seen as substitutes for long-term in-depth training for competent experts and proficient technicians. The establishment at national level of a training programme for conservation and restoration personnel remains to be planned or implemented. In the programme for the reorganization of the University, the Faculty of Arts at Tananarivo is proposing to arrange specialized training for conservation–restoration personnel which will be sponsored jointly by the UER for History and the Centre for Art and Archaeology. It will include theoretical, supervised work on the one hand, and practical sessions, both in the laboratory and in the field, on the other.

For certain specialities it will be possible to turn to foreign teachers who will come to Madagascar to help with particular projects. Some advanced students will also be able to go abroad to enhance their qualifications. This is current practice in other academic disciplines. Whatever happens, this project will be of real interest only if an overall policy for training personnel responsible for the protection of the cultural heritage is introduced.

It is essential to provide, alongside the training for specialized staff, technical study facilities and in-depth research aimed at resolving the specific problems of deterioration that face the national heritage of Madagascar, and this necessitates the specification of effective methods of intervention. The materials most commonly used are vegetable in origin, or wooden. Hard construction materials are rare; this adds to their value and makes the need for their preservation even more urgent. In addition, such structures were often built using the most rudimentary of techniques – albeit original ones – but which are nevertheless difficult to preserve. The materials used are vulnerable in nature – as, for example, the red-laterite mud used for building house walls or *tamboho*.

Drystone structures, such as the *manda* and the walls supporting terraces of dwellings, have no binding materials. The granite blocks of which they are composed are simply piled up, so that any work to strengthen or repair them will necessitate a special study of the techniques involved. Why should we not proceed like the prehistorians, who, in order to reconstitute prehistoric techniques, attempt to reproduce the actions made by early men? This is the only way to obtain satisfactory results.

Structures that involve digging are even more frequent than built constructions: this applies in particular to the *hadivory*. Among ancient fortifications the *hadivory* which surrounded the hilltop villages pose a major preservation problem. They were usually constructed on slopes and created enormous *lavaka*, a kind of ravine or gulf shaped by the waters of the rainy season. As a result many fortified villages are under threat because their moats are causing accelerated erosion, which is destroying hills already stripped bare of vegetation. In the past the bottoms of the moats were protected by thick vegetation, but this has recently been disappearing because of repeated bush fires. No preventive steps in this sphere have been undertaken to date.

Article 3 of Statute No. 82 029, dated 6 November 1982, stipulates that 'the ministry responsible for the Protection of the National Heritage is to take general measures appropriate for ensuring the conservation and protection of the cultural property and items listed in this statute in collaboration with the various ministries concerned and local communities'. This close

Figure 12.6   The Palace of the Prime Minister Rainilaiarivony at Andafiavaratra
(built in 1872).

collaboration must be implemented by the ministries involved with the problems of conservation of the cultural heritage. It constitutes a *sine qua non* condition for the success of the operation. The government bodies concerned are the Ministry of Culture (MCAR), responsible for the protection of the national heritage, the Ministry for Scientific and Technological Research for Development (MRSTD), and the two ministries in charge of primary and secondary education and higher education, respectively (MINESEB and MINESUP).

In addition, it is important that discussion should not be restricted to the level of politicians and civil servants, since teachers and researchers working in the fields of history, archaeology and museology also have contributions to make. It is upon them that depends the training of scientific personnel and technicians who are going to draw up the plans for the conservation of monuments and sites and to implement those plans. It is from them that will come the initiatives for research into the remains of the past and the results of archaeological discoveries which contribute to our knowledge of the cultural heritage. Specialized institutions exist for this work, which until now have only rarely been consulted by those who are directly responsible for the protection of the national heritage.

How can an interest be created in those ancient objects which are difficult to find, analyse and preserve, and which date from before the 19th century or 'which are more than 150 years old', if little or no attention is paid to the still-visible traces of a more recent past and the protection of which is less difficult to ensure? These remains are thought to testify to the presence of

Figure 12.7   The town hall of Tananarivo (built in 1936).

rulers of old – either that of royalty and the *merina* oligarchy of the 19th century, or that of the French colonizers during the first half of the present century. This lack of interest is the most likely explanation of the total destruction by fire of the 19th century prime minister's palace at Andafiava-ratra, Tananarivo (see Fig. 12.6), which was no doubt the result of negligence, without any attempt being made to stop the fire. What kind of authenticity will it still possess after it has been dismantled piece by piece, despite all the efforts of those working on its reconstruction? The same can be said of the fire at the *Hôtel de Ville* of Tananarivo (Fig. 12.7) at the time of the popular demonstrations in May 1972. This building, incidentally, recently disappeared forever, since the area has been completely cleared. Should historians and those responsible for the protection of the cultural heritage, whose task it is to inform and involve the public in these matters, adopt a partial stance, and can they disregard the real situation to this extent?

References

Gaudebout, V. 1941. *Bulletin de l'Académie Malgache*, **24**, 100–14.
Mille, A. 1970. *Contribution à l'étude des villages fortifiés de l'Imerina ancien.*
Vérin, P. 1975. *Les échelles anciennes du commerce sur les côtes nord de Madagascar.*

13 *Archaeological rescue and conservation in the North Andean Area*

PRESLEY NORTON

Background

The North Andean Area, as defined at the Paracas Conference of 1979 by Luis Lumbreras, consists of the present territory of Ecuador, plus the bordering areas of southern Colombia and Northern Peru, or roughly what the Republic of Ecuador possessed in the early 19th century.

The earliest known instance of archaeological looting in the Western Hemisphere was recorded in this area by Cabello de Balboa in the 17th century; he mentioned that as early as the 16th century the local indigenes dug for gold, silver and platinum trinkets on La Tolita Island, at the mouth of the Santiago River. Digging for Indian treasure was vigorously pursued throughout the Spanish Colonial Period and right on up to the present day. Pot-hunting, as opposed to searching for gold, did not become a lucrative occupation until the mid-20th century. Before the 1860s a few old antiquarians practised what sometimes then passed for archaeology, but the name of the game was essentially gold and, unfortunately, just enough gold hoards turned up from time to time, especially in the southern highlands, to keep legends alive and to fuel the fever.

There is no way of estimating the percentage of pre-Hispanic cemeteries, mounds and settlement sites that have fallen prey to demographic expansion, public works and the ubiquitous *huaqueros*, the Andean catch-all name for pot-hunters and antiquities smugglers. In an area that has seen sedentalism and intensive occupation for more than 5000 years, certainly more than half of the original sites have been obliterated, and more partially despoiled.

In the 1950s the Central Bank of Ecuador started buying pre-Colombian artefacts for a museum that it planned to set up in Quito. In so doing, the central bankers considered that they were rescuing the 'national patrimony' by preventing the sale of the objects abroad. Although this may have initially been achieved to a certain degree, as purchases were stepped up over the years and prices climbed, in reality these well-meaning bankers unwittingly came to subsidize a growing pot-hunter subculture, amassing an amorphous collection of over a quarter of a million objects in their ever-expanding storage vaults.

It was not until 1979 that a National Patrimony Law was enacted, though a relatively ineffectual National Institute for the Cultural Patrimony had already been in existence for 15 years. In 1983 the law was codified, establishing mild-to-stiff fines and prison terms of up to four years for infractions. A major defect in the law, however, is that although it makes unauthorized excavation and export of antiquities illegal, it allows the buying and selling within Ecuador of illegally excavated objects.

Thus, though Ecuador has antiquities legislation, established sanctions and a government bureau charged with enforcing the law, to date there has not been a single attempt on the part of the National Institute for the Cultural Patrimony to do anything about it. Although Colombia and Peru also have their own laws and agencies, again there is little concern for controlling looting and trafficking in the areas bordering with Ecuador.

So, who cares?

Certain recent developments have shed a faint ray of hope for the future. Increasingly, the news media and a few public officials are pointing out the need for rescue and conservation. Unfortunately, this message does not filter out beyond the principal cities, whereas the unchecked looting goes on almost exclusively in the rural areas. However, this does represent the first faltering steps toward creating public awareness of the problem. My own contribution in this area is a weekly column on the editorial page of *El Comercio*, Quito's leading daily newspaper, largely devoted to this subject.

The recent proliferation of museums, not only in the capital but also in provincial cities, should contribute considerably to building public support for archaeological conservation. The Central Bank now maintains major archaeological museums in the country's three principal cities – Quito, Guayaquil and Cuenca – plus half a dozen small ones already functioning or building in other towns. The Banco del Pacífico, the country's largest private bank, maintains museums in Quito and Guayaquil.

The Casa de la Cultura, a relatively somnolent government-supported institution, and also a few municipalities, devote some space to the display of archaeological artefacts. A few educational institutions have also followed suit. Site museums have been established at Salango, Santa Elena, Real Alto, Rumicucho, Cotocollao, Cochasquí and Ingapirca.

In the face of traditional apathy and indifference, all this is to the good. It forms part of the infrastructure that is indispensable for building up public awareness and, hopefully, public support, without which all our efforts toward rescue and preservation are doomed to failure. This may smack of preaching to the faithful, but certain things should be restated from time to time, if only to keep us vigilant.

The Italian caper

In the early 1970s an enterprising gentleman from Milan made a considerable investment in Ecuadorean antiquities, which he shipped without any apparent difficulty to his homeland. Then he made a mistake. He printed a very handsome sales catalogue, a copy of which fell into the hands of the Director of the Central Bank Museum.

The Government of Ecuador started legal proceedings in Milan, on the basis that the approximately 10 000 pieces that Signore Damusso possessed had been illegally removed from Ecuador, that they were part of the National Patrimony, and that they should be returned. Breaking what surely must be a record for Italian litigation, Ecuador won its case after only four years of legal sparring, and the objects were returned.

Although this did not do anything for the hundreds of archaeological sites that were trashed in the process of amassing the Milan hoard, Ecuador's victory is of almost incalculable importance as a precedent for recovering smuggled antiquities. Having been, along with Greece, Egypt and Turkey, a victim of constant sacking and removal of its antiquities, Italy was undoubtedly more sensitive to the issues involved than most other industrialized countries. It is interesting to observe in passing, though, that although public indignation can be stirred up over one's antiquities being spirited abroad, no-one is really concerned about how they were extracted from the ground.

It really does matter

So, the question arises: in areas of the Third World, such as the North Andean Area, can anything effective really be done in the way of rescue and conservation? After all, where there is not enough of anything, where the poorest segment of the population goes hungry and is inadequately clothed and housed, and education and health care are rudimentary, are we right to insist that resources be diverted to preserve an archaeological heritage?

It is no longer necessary to apologize for archaeology *per se*. The legitimacy of our craft, albeit a luxury craft, has been firmly established, and in the UK well-behaved archaeologists even get knighted for it. As for Third World priorities, I venture to propose that the rescue and conservation of a country's archaeological heritage is of far greater importance than it is in the developed nations.

A sense of national identity, ethnic pride and cultural continuity are intangible but vitally important potential assets for any country. Upper Volta does not have its Drakes and Wellingtons, Pitts, Newtons and Shakespeares on which to fall back. Poor countries, often of relatively recent coinage, with decidedly unglorious presents and not much of a recent past to speak of, desperately need something to which they can point with pride and say: 'Look at us! While you were running around naked and painted blue, we were making these lovely bronzes, building great pyramids, working jade and turquoise. Our great sailing rafts plied the seas. Our head people wore richly worked garments, read the secrets of the firmament, and administered their realms with justice and mercy'. A good archaeological rescue and conservation programme can help to provide this. The effort and expense are more than justified in terms of national objectives.

Conclusion

The main reason why the National Institute of the Cultural Patrimony of Ecuador makes no effort to enforce the patrimony laws is that, apart from the necessary infrastructure, they do not have the competent trained personnel with which to do it. The first step in a Third World country toward establishing an effective rescue and conservation programme is training the archaeologists, technicians and administrators that will run it, plus a cadre of personnel to patrol the countryside and enforce the pertinent laws. Without enough trained people, site destruction cannot be throttled off or a meaningful conservation programme launched.

In this respect there is now certain cause for optimism in Ecuador. Two institutions, the Polytechnical University of Guayaquíl and a private foundation, Programa de Antropología, have undertaken programmes for training archaeologists in Ecuador. Through the creation of a Centre for Anthropological and Archaeological Studies, ESPOL (Guayaquíl Polytechnical) awards a four-year degree in archaeology and encourages its graduates to go on to PhD programmes in the USA. The Programa de Antropología, at its research centre in Salango, conducts three-month intensive field-school courses in the techniques of rescue and conservation. It is hoped that the combination of both of these programmes will produce the personnel required to implement a viable national programme.

Once we have the people, the next challenge will be to obtain adequate funding and logistical infrastructure from the Government of Ecuador and other sources to support such an effort. The rewards involved in establishing an effective programme of rescue and conservation in the North Andean Area will more than compensate the joint effort involved.

14 Cultural resource management at the federal, provincial, municipal and corporate levels in southern Ontario, Canada

ROBERT J. PEARCE

Introduction

Cultural resource management (CRM) studies in southern Ontario, Canada, may arise from projects at the federal, provincial, municipal or corporate level. Various pieces of legislation and guidelines, which make CRM studies mandatory or regulate the way in which they are carried out, are discussed, with examples taken from work completed by the Museum of Indian Archaeology (MIA).[1]

Federal

At the Federal level, CRM contracts arise primarily from two agencies: Parks Canada and the Archaeological Survey of Canada.

Parks Canada is a Federal Crown Corporation responsible for administering all aspects of Canada's 29 National Parks and more than 100 monuments and forts. They have commissioned external contracts to complete such work as an inventory of heritage resources to provide data for park interpretation and management (MIA 1980), an assessment of heritage resources potentially impacted by the proposed construction of park facilities (MIA 1985a), and the expert analysis of specific artefact classes from archaeological and historic sites under their jurisdiction (Fecteau 1978).

The Archaeological Survey of Canada (ASC), a branch of the National Museum of Man, National Museums of Canada, operates an Archaeological Salvage Program to minimize the loss of archaeological resources and information resulting from federal construction projects such as international harbours and airports. It has a limited budget, and most of its salvage programme has been financed by the federal department responsible for the proposed construction.

The largest archaeological survey and salvage project so far undertaken in Canada has involved a series of contracts to the Museum of Indian Archaeology, arranged through ASC, for lands expropriated by Transport Canada for the New Toronto International Airport in southern Ontario. This initially involved a survey of 7487 ha expropriated for the airport and the salvage excavation of a large Iroquoian village (*c.* AD 1500) situated under one of the proposed runways. The survey documented 113 previously unknown archaeological sites, the salvage excavation grew into a ten-year project, and additional sites have been test excavated or salvaged (Finlayson & Poulton 1979, Finlayson 1985). Including funds from Transport Canada, the Canada Council and the Social Sciences and Humanities Research Council, more than $C1 million dollars were expended on this project between 1975 and 1985.

Provincial

Archaeological resource assessments in the Province of Ontario are regulated by a variety of legislative acts and guidelines.

The main legal implication of the Ontario Heritage Act[2] concerns a Stop Work Order, which authorizes the Minister of Citizenship and Culture to shut down a construction project for up to 180 days if a significant archaeological or historic site will be impacted. To avoid this, it is obviously desirable to have qualified archaeologists assess a property before construction to determine whether heritage resources are present. Resource assessments are required for all projects that must be reviewed by a hearing board under the terms of the Environmental Assessment Act, or guidelines and policies of the Ontario Energy Board, the National Energy Board or the Ontario Ministry of the Environment.

The Environmental Assessment Act[3] includes in its definition of environment 'any building, structure, machine or other device or thing made by man'. As a result such man-made items are subject to all of the regulations of that Act; they require assessment before any major construction undertaking. Projects falling under the jurisdiction of this Act include any 'undertaking' by a 'public body', with public body defined as provincial ministries, development corporations, colleges and universities, Conservation Authorities, Ontario Hydro, and others. Archaeological resource assessments carried out under this legislation must demonstrate that no significant heritage sites will be impacted. If significant heritage sites are discovered, then the proponent of the undertaking must, under the Environmental Assessment Act or the Ontario Heritage Act, provide for the mitigation of that site through avoidance or excavation.

Examples of projects that have required an environmental assessment, incorporating an archaeological resource assessment, include highways and rapid-transit railways to be constructed by the Ministry of Transportation and Communications (MIA 1981a, 1983), transmission corridors and other facilities to be constructed by Ontario Hydro (MIA 1981b, 1984a), major residential or industrial subdivisions to be constructed by development corporations (MIA 1984b, 1985b) and the development of lands controlled by Conservation Authorities (MIA 1981c). Other projects regulated by this Act, but also governed by separate policies and guidelines, include hydrocarbon pipelines and municipal waste-management facilities.

The Ontario Energy Board guidelines[4] state that 'potential and existing archaeological sites within the study area must be identified' before the construction of any hydrocarbon pipeline. The Ministry of the Environment has guidelines[5] which set forth the manner in which environmental assessments for municipal waste-management facilities must be prepared; these go beyond the requirements of the Environmental Assessment Act. This is in part because such facilities are also regulated by the Environmental Protection Act and may require a hearing before the Consolidated Hearings Board, which incorporates the Environmental Assessment Act, the Environmental Protection Act, the Expropriations Act, the Planning Act, the Municipal Act, and others.

Municipal

Projects at the municipal level are also regulated by the Planning Act.[6] This Act stipulates that the Minister of Municipal Affairs and Housing 'will have regard to, among other matters, matters of provincial interest such as . . . the protection of features of significant natural, architectural, historic or archaeological interest'.

Municipalities must have Official Plans to be approved by the Minister. Developments such as industrial, commercial or residential subdivisions must first be based on a Draft Plan of Subdivision to be reviewed by and approved by the Minister. Under the provisions of the Planning Act, any individual may review the appropriate documentation and petition the Minister to consider matters of 'provincial interest'. Theoretically, any individual could initiate an appeal to have significant archaeological sites considered as being 'of provincial interest' and cause the excavation or preservation of such sites before approval of the plan. Under the Ontario Heritage Act, municipalities may designate properties as being of historical or archaeological significance, and ensure that they are preserved or mitigated.

A wide variety of projects covered under these pieces of legislation are subject to review by a number of provincial ministries, including the Regional Archaeologist, Archaeology Unit, Ministry of Citizenship and Culture. As part of the review procedure within certain municipalities, the Regional Archaeologist is submitted Draft Plans of Subdivisions and maps or documentation relating to the proposed construction of pipelines, hydro corridors, roads, road widenings, and other types of construction or development. The Regional Archaeologist has the authority to request that the proponent undertake an archaeological survey of the area to be developed, to ensure that no archaeological sites are impacted.[7] He provides the proponent of the undertaking with a list of CRM consultants, from whom the proponent may solicit proposals to undertake a CRM study.

Corporate level

The Ontario Environmental Assessment Act and Planning Act do not necessarily apply to all developments, and in numerous instances commercial–industrial–residential developments have been exempted from such legislation. In southern Ontario a number of archaeological resource assessments have been arranged between developers and CRM consultants exclusive of these Acts. One reason for this is that CRM consultants can present the argument to a developer that, if significant archaeological sites are uncovered during construction, the development can be shut down by the Stop Work Order of the Ontario Heritage Act. However, more often the corporate heads of development companies recognize (or can be persuaded to appreciate) the potential danger construction might have on our native heritage, and have voluntarily agreed to fund both the initial resource assessment and the resulting mitigation (MIA 1981d, Pearce 1983).

Conclusion

An increase in public and governmental awareness for native heritage over the past ten years had had several ramifications:

(a) introduction of new government legislation, and revisions to existing legislation, to deal with native heritage;
(b) creation of the Archaeology and Heritage Units within the Ontario Ministry of Citizenship and Culture, to deal with heritage matters at the Provincial level;
(c) creation of private CRM firms;
(d) expansion of the Museum of Indian Archaeology's facilities and staff, arising in part from external CRM contracts and large mitigation projects;
(e) creation of full-time jobs for two archaeologists within the Ministry of Transportation and Communications and one heritage planner within Ontario Hydro;
(f) inclusion of archaeological sites as sensitive areas in municipal plans and on lands controlled by the Niagara Escarpment Commission; and
(g) appointment of a provincial ministry archaeologist to the Ontario Energy Board's Pipeline Coordinating Committee.

Since 1976 the Museum of Indian Archaeology, serving as a CRM consultant, has completed over 100 CRM projects involving over 13 830 ha of land and more than 630 km of linear corridors. This has led to the documentation of 552 archaeological and historic sites and the mitigative excavation of 15 sites. Funding for resource assessments has been provided primarily by the proponent of the undertaking, whereas mitigation projects have received diverse funds which include federal and provincial summer-job creation programmes and local municipalities.

Although there has been some criticism of the complex legislation and a reluctance by some developers to fund mandatory CRM, there has also been considerable support. In fact, all of the 15 sites mitigated by MIA have received financial support from the proponent of the undertaking, ranging from Transport Canada, Parks Canada and Ontario Hydro to private developers. The result has seen significant contributions to research and knowledge, without which CRM is useless (Wright 1983, p. 263).

Notes

1   The Museum of Indian Archaeology was founded at the University of Western Ontario in 1933. In 1978 it was reorganized and established as a corporation without share capital, a registered charitable organization, and an affiliate of the University devoted to the interpretation of and research on the archaeology of southern Ontario. Today the Museum has six full-time staff and a fluctuating support staff, with two cross-appointments to the University (one a part-time academic teaching position, the other an endowed research chair). The Museum occupies a 1350 m² custom-designed building with research facilities, a display gallery, and public interpretive facilities and programmes, including the excavation and authentic reconstruction of a 15th century Iroquoian village site. The structure of the Museum and its University affiliation make it eligible for certain external funds (i.e. government-funded job creation programmes and grants) not available to other institutions or private CRM firms to support research and to minimize costs to proponents on mitigation projects.

2   Ontario Heritage Act, 1974: Statutes of Ontario, 1974, Chapter 122; Revised Statutes of Ontario, 1980, Chapter 337.

3   Environmental Assessment Act, 1975: Statutes of Canada, Chapter 69; Revised Statutes of Ontario, 1980, Chapter 140.

4   Environmental Guidelines for the Construction and Operation of Hydrocarbon Pipelines in Ontario: Ontario Energy Board, 1984.

5   Guidelines for the Preparation of Environmental Assessments for Municipal Waste Management Activities: Ontario Ministry of Environment, 1983.

6   Bill 159, An Act to Revise the Planning Act, 1983: Revised Statutes of Ontario, 1983, Chapter 1.

7   Guidelines on the man-made Heritage Component of Environmental Assessments, 1980: Historical Planning and Research Branch, Heritage Branch, Ministry of Culture and Recreation (now Archaeology Unit, Heritage Branch, Ministry of Citizenship and Culture) (Supplement to General Guidelines for the Preparation of Environmental Assessments, Ministry of Environment, 1978.)

References

Fecteau, R. 1978. *Analysis of archaeobotanical remains from Fort St Joseph, Ontario.* Report submitted to Parks Canada, Ottawa.

Finlayson, W. D. 1985. The 1975 and 1978 rescue excavations of the Draper Site: introduction and settlement patterns. *Archaeological Survey of Canada Mercury Series Paper* **130**. Ottawa: National Museum of Man, National Museums of Canada.

Finlayson, W. D. & D. Poulton 1979. *A preliminary report of investigations at the New Toronto International Airport.* Agency Report prepared by the Museum of Indian Archaeology to the Ministry of Transport and The National Museums of Canada, Ottawa.

Museum of Indian Archaeology 1980. *A metal detector survey of interior portions of Grenadier Island Centre, St Lawrence Islands National Park.* Report submitted to Parks Canada, Cornwall.

Museum of Indian Archaeology 1981a. *Final report on the phase I and II archaeological resource assessment of the Highway 403 Project from Highway 5 to Oakville Link.* Report submitted to the Ministry of Transportation and Communications, Toronto.

Museum of Indian Archaeology 1981b. *Final report on the archaeological resource assessment of land to be affected by the proposed construction of a microwave repeater tower, Lot 16, Concession 3, Maryborough Township, Wellington County.* Report submitted to Ontario Hydro, Toronto.

Museum of Indian Archaeology 1981c. *Report on an archaeological resource assessment of areas of Cooksville Creek Bottomlands to be affected by channel improvements.* Report submitted to M. M. Dillon Ltd, Toronto, and The Credit Valley Conservation Authority, Meadowvale.

Museum of Indian Archaeology 1981d. *Report on the archaeological resource assessment of the proposed Windermere subdivision.* Report submitted to Enod Holdings Ltd, London, and the Ronto Development Corporation, Toronto.

Museum of Indian Archaeology 1983. *Report on the phase II archaeological investigation of selected areas on the GO ALRT extension: Whitby to Oshawa (Government of Ontario Rapid Transit System).* Report submitted to M. M. Dillon Ltd and the Ministry of Transportation and Communications, Toronto.

Museum of Indian Archaeology 1984a. *Report on an archaeological resource assessment of the proposed 230/115 kilovolt transmission line from Holland Road Junction to Louth Junction, St Catharines, Ontario.* Report submitted to Ontario Hydro, Toronto.

Museum of Indian Archaeology 1984b. *Report on an archaeological resource assessment of the proposed Westport Extension subdivision in Port Dalhousie.* Report submitted to Kerry T. Howe Ltd and Fairview Land Developments Ltd, St Catharines.

Museum of Indian Archaeology 1985a. *Report on an archaeological investigation of two selected areas on the tip of Point Pelee National Park, Essex County, Ontario.* Report submitted to the Landplan Collaborative Ltd, Guelph, and Parks Canada, Cornwall.

Museum of Indian Archaeology 1985b. *Final report on an archaeological resource assessment of a proposed industrial subdivision (30T–85009) in the City of Waterloo.* Report submitted to Magna International Inc., Markham.

Pearce, R. J. 1983. The Windermere, Ronto, and Smallman sites: salvage excavations of prehistoric Iroquoian hamlets. *Museum of Indian Archaeology Research Report* **13**.

Wright, J. V. 1983. Archaeological cultural resource management – preserving the past for what purpose. In *Directions in archaeology: a question of goals*, P. D. Francis & E. C. Poplin (eds), 263–7. Proceedings of the Fourteenth Annual Chacmool Conference, The Archaeological Association of the University of Calgary, Alberta, Canada.

15 *Heritage management and training in England*

ANDREW SAUNDERS

Definitions

The phrase 'cultural resource management' first registered on British ears at the Conference of the Society for American Archaeology at Dallas in 1975. Although in use, the phrase still does not come easily to English-speaking archaeologists on this side of the Atlantic, and certainly not to the ordinary person. Here the equivalent jargon expression is the 'heritage'.

We distinguish between the natural and the man-made heritage. By the latter we mean the built environment (sites, monuments and historic areas); that is, the surviving patterns of successive land use and settlement, whether domestic, ceremonial, funerary, economic or defensive, from prehistoric times onwards to include the recent past. With these archaeological survivals we include buildings of architectural and historic importance, and the townscape and street pattern of our historic towns. However, in Great Britain we also distinguish between the built environment and portable antiquities and works of art. These are administered separately in legislative and practical terms. They belong to the province of our national and local museums, public and private. These objects and their safekeeping lie mainly outside the scope of this chapter, although it will be seen that museum management is not irrelevant to our subject. The separation, however, of sites (buried archaeological remains, historic sites and earthworks) and monuments (standing structures, whether roofed, inhabited or ruined) from museums and the objects that they contain is a distinction which is also maintained internationally by Unesco. The International Council on Monuments and Sites (ICOMOS), whose parent body is Unesco, has its counterpart in the International Council for Museums (ICOM).

Legislation

Continuing with the British model it is necessary to look at the legal background in some detail. The legislative framework which lies behind the management of the British cultural heritage or man-made environment is embodied in the Ancient Monuments and Archaeological Areas Act 1979 and, for historic buildings, mainly in the Town and Country Planning Act

1971. The reason for the two codes is historical. The first Ancient Monuments Protection Act was passed in 1882. An ancient monument can be any structure or the remains of one, provided that it is not in residential or ecclesiastical use. Powers for the protection of inhabited buildings and an extremely wide range of buildings of special architectural and historic interest first came into being in 1947. The Town and Country Planning Act 1971 also stated that 'every local planning authority shall from time to time determine which parts of their area are areas of special architectural or historic interest, the character or appearance of which it is desirable to preserve or enhance, and shall designate such areas as Conservation Areas'. This legislation therefore goes further than individual buildings, and seeks to preserve those parts of our cities, towns and villages which are part of the fabric of our architectural and social culture. The Secretary of State for the Environment is the Minister concerned. He has direct responsibilities for the protection of ancient monuments. The local planning authorities have the primary responsibility for the operation of the historic buildings and conservation area legislation. The identification of historic buildings of sufficient importance to be so listed is governed by a set of ministerially approved criteria and working from these, it can be estimated that nearly 500 000 buildings will eventually be so protected in England. However, the protection of ancient monuments is much more selective. Monuments must be judged to be of 'national importance'. Although protection (known in Great Britain as scheduling) has been in progress for more than 100 years, less than 13 000 monuments are protected, but it is estimated that perhaps as many as 40 000 more sites in England will qualify for protection (see Wainwright, ch. 16, this volume).

Heritage management

Before considering the question of heritage management training, it is necessary to go over what the subject covers in some detail. To begin with, there are several obvious reasons for seeking to preserve elements of one's cultural heritage. As archaeologists we seek to retain a sample of sites and monuments as a long-term research tool from which we can improve our knowledge of the past. A wider objective is to maintain buildings, sites and landscapes as an educational resource for the public, which can then provide a physical and often visible background for the understanding of history. Monuments of the past may also be a source of pleasure, as well as providing fixed points in the landscape which help to establish roots and a sense of place in space and time.

By the National Heritage Act 1983, the government transferred many of its heritage management functions in England to a new agency called the Historic Buildings and Monuments Commission, or English Heritage, for short. Among the objectives behind the setting up of this agency were the creation of a dedicated body which could be a powerful voice for heritage management, a body which could apply an imaginative approach to the presentation and commercial management of that part of the heritage in its direct care. The general duties of English Heritage are, so far as is practicable:

(a)   to secure the preservation of ancient monuments and historic buildings situated in England;
(b)   to promote the preservation and enhancement of the character and appearance of conservation areas in England; and
(c)   to promote the public's enjoyment of, and their knowledge of, ancient monuments and historic buildings situated in England, and their preservation, in exercising the various functions conferred upon it.

These functions include:

(a)   making grants to individuals and bodies in respect of historic buildings, conservation areas, town schemes and ancient monuments, and for archaeological investigation and recording of sites threatened with damage or destruction (rescue archaeology);
(b)   acquiring or becoming guardians of ancient monuments and historic buildings;
(c)   advising the Secretary of State on the selection of buildings for inclusion in the list of buildings of special architectural or historic interest, on the monuments to be added to the schedule of monuments of national importance, and on the designation of areas of archaeo-logical importance;
(d)   advising the Secretary of State on applications for permission to carry out works to listed buildings and to scheduled monuments;
(e)   carrying out, or contributing towards the cost of, research in relation to ancient monuments, historic buildings and conservation areas in England;
(f)   undertaking archaeological investigation, and publishing the results;
(g)   providing educational facilities and services, instruction and infor-mation to the public in relation to ancient monuments, historic buildings and conservation areas in England;
(h)   making and maintaining records in relation to ancient monuments and historic buildings in England; and
(i)   advising any person in relation to ancient monuments, historic build-ings and conservation areas in England.

In summary, English Heritage's duties can be grouped under two main headings:

(a)   the management of some 400 monuments in the care of the Secretary of State for the Environment; and
(b)   the general responsibility to help to preserve ancient monuments, historic buildings and conservation areas throughout England.

The Welsh Office has created a similar agency, Cadw to take on its similar responsibilities in Wales. The Scottish Development Department, part of central government, retains and operates these powers itself, and so does Northern Ireland, whose heritage legislation is similar to, yet distinct from, that of the other countries in the UK (see Hamlin, ch. 17, this volume).

Other official bodies and agencies have heritage management responsibilities. These principally lie with local government. Many of the powers of central government are also in the hands of county and district councils. They can take monuments and buildings into their care, they can make grants, with their planning powers they can control works affecting the majority of listed buildings, and they can initiate the designation of conservation areas. Many councils maintain or make use of county sites and monuments records which provide a local database of the cultural heritage, often for planning constraints. Local government has a crucial rôle in heritage management.

The Royal Commissions on Ancient and Historical Monuments of England, Scotland and Wales have, since 1980, had the duty to record and compile inventories of sites and monuments. Their productions are of a high scholarly standard. They also maintain their respective National Monuments Records, which provide an essential central database for the study of the historic environment, past and present. Recently the Royal Commissions have assumed responsibility for the archaeological surveying for and representation on the official Ordnance Survey maps.

The Redundant Churches Fund, as its name implies, maintains a large number of historic churches which might otherwise have been demolished and lost. The National Heritage Memorial Fund administers a substantial fund which it uses to help preservation programmes and, more particularly, to aid the purchase of works of art or objects and buildings of historic importance.

Outside the state and public agencies is a very wide spectrum of organizations concerned with the protection and maintenance of cultural resources. The most extensive and most famous is the National Trust. Founded in 1894, it is the biggest private landowner in the country, owning and preserving many thousands of hectares of natural landscape, including lakes, rivers and hills, woods and moorland, and nearly 300 miles (500 km) of coastline. As a substantial landowner, the National Trust is inevitably responsible for many archaeological sites and monuments, as well as about 200 historic buildings, from small vernacular structures to palatial country houses. Through its membership policy, over a million individuals feel involved with the Trust's work.

There are many other, often small, preservation trusts and organizations frequently concerned with a single object, such as a windmill or an obsolete industrial pumping engine. Many voluntary societies, particularly the long-established county archaeological societies, own sites and monuments for their better protection.

Then there is the form of cultural resource management provided by the surveying, investigation and recording of archaeological sites and monuments before their damage or destruction. Most of this work is now carried out by professional archaeological teams, known as 'units', operating within a particular town or across a county. These units draw their financial backing from a variety of sources: central and local government, and contributions from the site developers in some circumstances. The funds available are inadequate for the investigation and recording of all threatened sites, and therefore much careful selection is needed in order to apply resources towards the most significant academic research objectives. Although the archaeological units play the major rôle because of their full-time capacity, a good deal of 'rescue' activity is also carried out by amateur groups and the archaeological societies.

To summarize, heritage management in the UK operates from a very limited legislative base. The basic legal elements are protective rather than prohibitive. The scheduling or listing of an ancient monument or historic building does not deny the owner the opportunity to do with the property as he or she thinks fit, but it does mean that official consent must first be obtained. This provides a means for giving time for second thoughts, and time for central or local government to determine the conflict of interests by means of a public enquiry, where the wishes of the owner can be set against the arguments for preservation. In the last resort the Secretary of State is the final arbiter. In certain instances preservation has to be achieved by compensating the owners or developers against the frustration of their wishes for their property. The traditional rights of private property are most obviously brought home to the archaeologist in respect of objects found in the soil. With the exception of discoveries of gold and silver which, under certain circumstances, may belong to the Crown as Treasure Trove, all material found in the ground belongs to the landowner, and he or she is entitled to sell or dispose of it as he or she wishes. The state has no rights, and if portable objects are wanted for a museum they must be paid for, unless the owner can be persuaded to give or lend them.

Here we come to an important element in British heritage management. Success in achieving the preservation of our historic fabric rests very much on consent. Time and again this success depends on collaboration between private interests and those responsible for managing the cultural heritage. It can sometimes be achieved by persuasion alone. It may be done by making financial grants, often proportionally quite small, but enough to encourage an owner that the site or monument really is important, and that the little bit of monetary pump-priming involved is sufficient for the owner to put in a larger sum for restoration or to modify the intended land use. Likewise, with rescue archaeology, developers are frequently persuaded to contribute towards the costs of excavation, although they are not obliged to do so. The strong position of the landowner calls for education, persuasion and collaboration with owners and developers. Not surprisingly, it influences our whole approach to heritage management in the British Isles. It requires a form of management that develops partnership.

Heritage managers

Who are the heritage managers? With such a range of organizations summarized above, both professional and amateur, public and private, a very large number of individuals are involved. Indeed, it would be a great mistake to underestimate the influence of public opinion in support of the conservation movement. However, in the context of this chapter we need to look at those whose employment is directly related to heritage management. We must look first at English Heritage, the agency empowered to advise and carry out some of the responsibilities of the Secretary of State for the Environment in this field.

English Heritage is staffed by a widely qualified team of administrators, architects, architect–planners, archaeologists, and architectural and garden historians (Inspectors), archaeological scientists and conservators, quantity surveyors, civil engineers, artists and craftsmen of many kinds. Since this chapter is primarily concerned with archaeologists in CRM, I shall concentrate on the Inspectorate of Ancient Monuments and Historic Buildings, but it must be kept in mind that they are part of a multidisciplinary team, and much of their work relates to and depends on the contributions of other professions. However, there are some areas of work where the Inspector takes the lead.

The first task of an Inspector is to select those sites and monuments which meet the criteria for protection. He or she has to make value judgements on the rarity, age, degree of survival, state of completeness, and physical condition and relative importance of the site or building. Upon his or her judgement and ability to defend his or her decision, if necessary at public enquiry, may depend the success or failure of the effort to secure long-term preservation. Although some types of site or monument may be so rare, and of such age, that every example that survives in a reasonable state of completeness must be protected, there are classes of monument where examples are numerous, and these are treated with a varying degree of selectivity. Therefore, prehistoric ceremonial sites may be protected in their entirety as a class, whereas only a small sample of the defensive structures of World War II will be so identified. Among the industrial monuments surviving from the 18th or 19th centuries, perhaps only those which represent a particular technological development may be selected as 'historic firsts'. Selectivity of a similar order applies to buildings of special architectural or historic importance. A policy of inclusiveness is followed among those buildings built before 1700 which survive in anything like their original condition, but the number of buildings of high quality designed between 1914 and 1939 is limited to a few hundred protected examples.

Having identified those sites and monuments which merit protection according to the criteria accepted by the Secretary of State, the Inspector's next task is to advise on the way in which the protective legislation is operated. As I stated above, the scheduling of an ancient monument or the listing of an historic building does not guarantee its future survival.

Sometimes survival has to be fought for. There will often be times when consent to alter or demolish will be refused. Such decisions may be difficult politically, and will require much argument and justification. Sometimes the decisions may involve paying financial compensation. Consent applications to demolish or alter buildings and to carry out any works to a monument, even works of repair, have to be commented on and, where necessary, opposed. Often it is possible to allow an owner to make alterations which cause no significant archaeological damage, or it is possible to persuade the owner to modify his or her plans and, if these modifications will cause some archaeological loss, ensure that such losses are recorded before they occur.

Where sites and monuments cannot be preserved and when they are threatened by unavoidable destruction, it is the Inspector who either develops or regulates the process of rescue archaeology. Indeed, the Inspector is frequently closely involved with the balance between preservation *in situ* and preservation by record. With limited financial resources the choice of those excavations and recording exercises to support is difficult. As far as possible the excavation programme is based on widely agreed research priorities which Inspectors have established with their statutory advisory committee and with their academic colleagues. Monitoring the programme, checking on value for money and ensuring that the post-excavation work and the publication of the results is done without excessive delay is all part of the Inspector's job.

For those sites and monuments scheduled by the Secretary of State (and at the moment there are only 13 000 of them), management goes further than simply applying legal sanctions. The practice of positive management has developed in recent years. Regular inspection, contact with owners and occupiers, and reports on the site's condition are provided by about 25 'field monument wardens' who work from their homes across the country on a part-time basis. Their reports often serve to stimulate the negotiation of management agreements with occupiers in order to achieve, by means of financial grants, changes in agricultural practices which will assist in the preservation of a site or monument. This type of monument management brings the archaeologist–inspector face to face with the owner and farmer. He or she has to explain the archaeological value and importance of a site which may have little or no visible surviving surface features. He or she has to be reasonably knowledgeable about farming practices in order to command the respect of the farmer, and has to put to best use the very limited funds that may be available for this form of positive management.

Where the objective is to encourage the repair and maintenance of sites and monuments, more-substantial grant-aid may be available to assist the owner. The Inspector's job is to select and evaluate both the importance of the site or building for grant-aid, and whether the works proposed will be harmful to the structure and its archaeological evidence. Often well-meaning schemes of repair can be destructive to the historic fabric, and expert archaeological advice as well as recording is necessary. Often, where the monument is a ruin and of no beneficial use to the owner, the inducement of grant-aid may be the only effective way of achieving its preservation for the long-term future. With buildings that are in use or lived in, grants can be the only way in which dilapidation and decay can be avoided if the owner is too impoverished to carry out proper repairs. Grants may also encourage the re-use of a building which would otherwise have been allowed to fall into ruin. The saving and conservation of individual historic buildings by financial grants has also come to be applied to groups of buildings whose importance lies in the sum of their parts rather than to individual merit, and thence to the core of historic towns generally. In sum, taking monuments, historic buildings and towns together, roughly one-third of English Heritage's annual budget goes towards grant-aid for these purposes to individuals and institutions.

Part of heritage management means taking a direct rôle in preserving important national sites and monuments, and not just relying on grant-aid. This was among the first functions for which the state became responsible when government acknowledged its duty to maintain the monuments of the past. There are now about 400 monuments, great and small, which are in the care of English Heritage. This historic estate involves management and presentation of the most direct kind. Again the archaeologist has an important part to play, helping to devise the preservation regime and, most importantly, in their collaboration with those responsible for the practical methods of repair, ensuring that the archaeological integrity of the monument is maintained. All forms of intervention to delay the processes of decay do, in themselves, alter the monument. It is the duty of the heritage manager to ensure that such intervention is kept to a minimum and is well documented.

There are other fields of activity which fall to the Inspector. He or she may be personally concerned with excavation and the investigation of standing bulidings, as well as organizing others to carry out this work, either at threatened sites or where this is part of a repair programme at a grant-aided monument belonging to someone else. Most frequently he or she will be closely involved with the archaeological recording at the monuments in the care of English Heritage. Because Inspectors are likely to be the people most knowledgeable about the archaeology and history of the monuments they look after, they take the lead in providing material for the presentation of these monuments to the visiting public, preparing site museums, advising on education material for teachers, and writing guidebooks and academic reports.

I have dealt at length with those archaeological heritage managers employed at the behest of central government. Many county councils in local government employ one or more archaeologists, mainly in their planning departments, to advise on applications for developments which might adversely affect the local historic environment. One of their most frequent jobs is to maintain county sites and monuments records, which can be linked with planning constraint maps. Sometimes a local authority will support an archaeological unit to provide an archaeological service for the area, particularly to record threatened sites. A county- or district-based unit may also be associated with the local museum. These local archaeological units can provide wider services than simply excavations; they can set up information centres and make a contribution to local education. In parallel with the archaeologists in local government are the conservation officers, mostly employed by district councils, who are responsible for local planning. The rôle of conservation officers is primarily to advise on listed building consent applications and on the management of the conservation areas within their local authority. It is their task to help to operate the historic buildings legislation in the first instance.

Qualifications for heritage managers

It goes without saying that all those engaged on heritage management should have the broadest possible archaeological and historical knowledge and a practical background. It is not enough to be an expert on a particular period or type of material. Indeed, it is often better for him or her to have limited detailed specializations in order to have a broader grasp of the whole range of the man-made environment. For Inspectors the basic academic requirement is a good first degree. History and archaeology are, understandably, the most common subjects, but any subject is sufficient, provided that the applicant can demonstrate experience in and enthusiasm for archaeology or architectural history. Experience of archaeological fieldwork and of the techniques of excavation is essential for those Inspectors primarily concerned with sites and monuments, together with some acquaintance with the principles of building construction and with the development of architectural styles. For historic buildings Inspectors a thorough knowledge of architectural history is required, and often the possession of particular expertise is the basis of recruitment, such as a knowledge of church architecture, industrial monuments, or post-Renaissance furniture and interior decoration. Although Inspectors are primarily archaeologists, they should also have an appreciation of historical sources, and should be able to study intelligently medieval and later records.

As well as these extensive academic qualifications the Inspector has to have something of the gifts of an administrator. He or she needs to have the ability to make the best use of the available resources, and has to establish priorities and take hard decisions. Usually he or she will be expected to take on staff-management at some point in his or her career. The ability to work effectively with those in other disciplines is needed. He or she has to be an educator and, as I stressed above, must be able to persuade and interest those whose first reactions are unsympathetic to the concept of conservation, especially when it is likely to cost them money.

Training

It is not the practice in the UK to train people specifically for heritage management. This is a skill that is learnt on the job. It is also a job which has to appeal to a particular type of person. For the academically trained archaeologist it is essentially 'applied archaeology'. Someone who imagines that it is an easy means for furthering an academic career is quickly disillusioned, although the opportunity for working with a very wide range of material can produce important contributions to scholarship. The number of people now involved in heritage management in all of its disciplines is enormous. In English Heritage alone there is a total staff of about 2000 people of various skills, crafts and disciplines. It is diffcult to estimate those in local government, in other government-supported agencies or in the private sector. However, because heritage management is a career to which many people become devoted, it is perhaps odd that more attention has not been given to formal training.

One aspect of heritage management training which is catered for is that element related to the conservation of historic buildings and townscape. This is the part of the heritage to which the personal and financial interests of the average person are most closely involved. It is, after all, the most visible and accessible. Furthermore, the legislation may be restricting the way in which he or she may wish to treat his or her house, or the way in which he or she is carrying out his or her livelihood if it involves historic buildings and historic areas. He or she is also concerned with the development, for good or ill, of his or her own environment. Heritage management can be a highly political area. It is not therefore surprising that among planners and architects there has been a demand for discussion and shared experience in the management of this part of the built environment. Courses, both long and short, have become established at the Institute of Advanced Architectural Studies at York University, at the Architectural Association in London, and at a large number of universities and polytechnics across the country.

For the archaeologist in heritage management there are no similar opportunities, apart from an annual week-long seminar at Oxford on 'Planning and the Historic Environment'. Yet the variety and complexity of the work, and the wide range of skills required cry out for some kind of postgraduate training once the academic foundation has been acquired. It is time that 'learning on the job' ceased to be the sole option in Britain; more opportunities must be provided for developing the philosophical concepts behind cultural resource management and improving its practical applications.

British universities are notorious for their lack of attention to the practical side of archaeology. Few do more than require students to undertake two or three weeks' experience at an excavation each year. There are some recent exceptions which develop the course around fieldwork of various kinds, of which excavation is just one, and instruct the students in the construction, writing and use of excavation reports. Heritage management is also only lightly touched upon, despite the fact that most of the students who will get jobs in archaeology will be in the applied fields rather than the academic. Perhaps just one lecture will be devoted to the legislative background.

It is impossible to generalize on the training requirements for heritage or cultural resource management. The needs will vary from country to country and with the changing legislative background. However, there are some obvious starting points.

(a)   Knowledge of the law and how it may be applied and adapted is crucial.
(b)   The creation of the best-possible database and retrieval system which identifies and locates the known archaeological resource and can then permit the establishment of informed choices and the setting of priorities.
(c)   The most effective deployment of the limited physical and financial resources that are available for the preservation and understanding of our sites and monuments.
(d)   Land management abilities as well as general management skills.
(e)   The ability to communicate and explain to the general public the importance of the archaeological resource and to instill an appreciation and understanding of people's history and material culture.

Heritage managers must decide among their objectives in the same way that they preserve monuments. For example, what should the attitude be towards the restoration of missing elements and to conjectural reconstructions? It is also important to integrate the whole range of material culture, and not to limit attention to a particular period of the past, nor to a particular class of site and monument. Too often archaeology is seen to be equated solely with prehistory, and with sites and monuments which have deteriorated to such an extent that they survive as ruins, earthworks or, more commonly, as buried sites. Yet, if archaeology is the study of man's material past, and is an adjunct to the fuller understanding of history, then all material change and technological advance at any point in time is grist to our mill.

Postgraduate training has for some time been seen to be appropriate to that other field of CRM, the museum profession and, as we have seen, has begun to appear in the field of historic building conservation. If it is sensible to train museum staff in the matters of object conservation, climatic controls, display techniques and presentation of the material in an informative way along with many other aspects of museum work, then it is surely sensible to train the heritage manager in what is a vastly more difficult and varied responsibility. Perhaps what is needed is something much wider than separate museum or CRM training – a Diploma in Applied Archaeology which could integrate all of these facets and include with them the practical application of all aspects of archaeological fieldwork and its publication.

It is a cliché, but no less true for all that, that the archaeological resource, although growing from recent material changes, is declining rapidly in terms of the remains of more-distant societies. Much of Britain's heritage is disappearing unrecognized and unevaluated under more-intensive agriculture, commercial and public developments of all kinds, and the robbing of sites for financial gain. It is essential to make the public more aware of this fragile and disappearing cultural past, and this can be done only by better management. Instead of muddling through as in the past, this side of archaeology must be recognized for what it can provide, with managers being trained to operate more productively and more professionally.

References

Hamlin, A. 1989. Government archaeology in Northern Ireland. In *Archaeological heritage management in the modern world*, H. F. Cleere (ed.), ch. 17. London: Unwin Hyman

Wainwright, G. J. 1989. The management of the English landscape. In *Archaeological heritage management in the modern world*, H. F. Cleere (ed.), ch. 16. London: Unwin Hyman.

16 *The management of the English landscape*

G. J. WAINWRIGHT

Objectives

The English landscape is almost entirely the result of human activity. Since the time of his first arrival in these islands during the last Ice Age, some 500 000 years ago, man has influenced the development of the natural environment to the extent that, from wild moorland to heavily cultivated fen, all owe their present appearances to millennia of human activity. Viewed in this broad sense, the entire English landscape has an historic value, and an understanding of its past is essential to an appreciation of its fauna, flora and natural beauty, for all are the outcome of exploitation by man. There is as a result a strong community of interest between the organizations which care for the historic, scenic and natural environments (The Historic Buildings and Monuments Commission (English Heritage), the Country-side Commission and the Nature Conservancy Council, respectively). Although this chapter is concerned with the historic landscape, this commu-nity of interest should be acknowledged as a constant theme, although it is not enshrined in legislation. This landscape is constantly changing through both natural and man-made processes, and archaeology provides the basis for documenting the trajectory of these changes through the past and into the future. The archaeological heritage is therefore not only a component of a much admired landscape but also a national resource with very considerable scientific, educational, economic and amenity value. The primary objective of managing this resource is to ensure that the national heritage of sites, monuments, townscapes and ancient buildings remains as large and diverse as possible, so that society as a whole may use and appreciate their value to the full. The purpose of this chapter is to describe how this is achieved for the countryside.

The protection of monuments

The legislative and organizational background is described in Chapter 15. The choice of monuments to be given statutory protection ('scheduling') has always been subjective. Over the years it has been widely accepted that the rarer examples of monuments are almost automatically candidates for inclusion in the schedule. Despite the term 'ancient monument', the legislation does not prescribe that a monument should be of any particular age to qualify for scheduling. As defined in the 1979 Act a monument means 'any building, structure or work, whether above or below the surface of the land, and any cave or excavation; any site comprising the remains of any vehicle, vessel, aircraft or other movable structure or part thereof which neither constitutes nor forms part of any work which is a monument'. Excluded from these provisions are buildings in residential occupation other than by a resident caretaker, buildings in ecclesiastical use and historic wrecks protected by the Protection of Wrecks Act 1973. The only statutory criterion laid down in the Act is that a monument must appear to the Secretary of State to be of national importance. Using these criteria, the most recent structures to have been scheduled are some defence works dating from World War II. In 1983 criteria for the selection of ancient monuments were reviewed and set down in a more formal way than hitherto. The Secretary of State circulated these non-statutory criteria which are as follows.

(a) *Survival/condition*: the survival of the monument's archaeological potential both above and below ground is a crucial consideration and needs to be assessed in relation to its present condition and surviving features.

(b) *Period*: It is important to consider for preservation all types of monuments that characterize a category or period.

(c) *Rarity*: there are some monument categories which in some periods are so scarce that all of them which still retain any archaeological potential should be preserved. In general, however, a selection must be made which portrays the typical and commonplace as well as the rare. For this, account should be taken of all aspects of the distribution of a particular class of monument, not only in the broad national context but also in its region.

(d) *Fragility/vulnerability*: highly important archaeological evidence from some field monuments can be destroyed by a single ploughing or unsympathetic treatment; these monuments would particularly benefit from the statutory protection which scheduling confers. There are also standing structures of particular form or complexity where again their value could be severely reduced by neglect or careless treatment and which are well-suited to protection by this legislation even though they may also be listed Historic Buildings.

(e) *Diversity*: some monuments have a combination of high-quality features, others are chosen for a single important attribute.

(f) *Documentation*: the significance of a monument may be given greater weight by the existence of records of previous investigation or, in the case of more-recent monuments, by the support of contemporary written records.

(g) *Group value*: the value of a single monument (such as a field system) is greatly enhanced by association with a group of related contemporary monuments (such as a settlement and cemetery) or with monuments of other periods. In the case of some groups it is preferable to protect the whole rather than isolated monuments within it.

(h) *Potential*: on occasion the nature of the evidence cannot be precisely specified but it is possible to document reasons for anticipating its probable existence and importance and so demonstrate the justification for scheduling. This is usually confined to sites rather than upstanding monuments.

It is open to anyone, whether a local authority, private citizen or conservation body, to propose a monument for scheduling. Since 1 April 1984 the Secretary of State has been advised in all matters concerning his responsibilities under the 1979 Act by the Historic Buildings and Monuments Commission for England. The Commission's specific functions include giving advice to the Secretary of State in respect of additions to the Schedule and in relation to applications for scheduled monument consent under Section 2 of the 1979 Act. These matters continue to be determined by the Secretary of State, who is obliged to consult English Heritage before arriving at a decision.

The fact that a monument is scheduled does not mean that it will be preserved intact in all circumstances, but it does ensure that the case for its preservation is fully considered through the procedure for obtaining scheduled monument consent. Section 2 of the 1979 Act makes it an offence to carry out certain works without the prior written consent of the Secretary of State. This is known as scheduled monument consent (SMC), and nearly 600 applications were made to the Secretary of State during 1986. The consent may be granted unconditionally or subject to conditions or refused. Specific provisions about the types of conditions that can be imposed are in Subsections 2(4) and (5) of the Act. They permit conditions to relate to the manner in which, or the person by whom, the works are to be executed, and allow the Secretary of State to require that he, or a person authorized by him, be allowed to inspect the site and to carry out investigations if necessary. Unlike Historic Buildings Legislation, which is administered in the first instance by Local Planning Authorities, the Secretary of State has direct responsibility for Ancient Monuments. Local Authorities have no power to handle SMC applications. Failure to obtain scheduled monument consent is an offence, the penalty for which may be a fine which, according to the circumstances of the conviction, may be of an unlimited amount. Before determining an application the Secretary of State is required either to hold a public inquiry or to offer the same to the applicant and any other person or organization (including English Heritage) who has strong objections to a proposed decision. The Secretary of State will then finally decide the application, taking into account the various representations.

It should be noted that scheduling does not require prior notice to owners and occupiers: it is effective as soon as notice is served upon them, there is no appeal mechanism, and it carries no compensation provision. Compensation for the refusal of consent or for conditional consent to work to scheduled monuments is payable only for the frustration of a planning permission granted *before* the monument was scheduled and still effective at the time of the application for scheduled monument consent. Compensation is also payable for refusal of consent for works in connection with agriculture or forestry, even though the works may result in the destruction of the monument. If scheduled monument consent is given subject to conditions, compensation is payable if those conditions make it impossible to use the monument for the purposes for which it is currently being used.

At present there are some 12 800 scheduled monuments in England. Scheduling has proceeded slowly and somewhat erratically over the past 100 years, and since 1945 extensive aerial and ground surveys have increased the number of known sites and monuments in England from about 50 000 to about 635 000. In 1984 the then Department of the Environment issued a paper which attempted to assess the extent to which the schedule of ancient monuments is a representative sample of the national archaeological resource in England by reference to both numbers and quality based on the non-statutory criteria. The assessment was made using county-based Sites and Monuments Records (SMRs). These are largely housed in County Planning Departments, and their major use is as an aid in planning and land-management decisions. In recent years English Heritage has invested in the development and enhancement of SMRs but, despite this support, their contents remain an uneven and inadequate representation of the surviving remains of England's archaeological past. Nevertheless, county SMRs are currently the best national archaeological database. The assessment indicated that the rate of scheduling had not kept up with the rate of discovery of previously unrecognized sites. Of the approximately 635 000 known archaeological sites and monuments in England only 2 per cent are scheduled. At the same time it was clear that the schedule had slowly become structurally imbalanced. The overall distributions of scheduled sites by county, by chronological period and by monument type all bear little relation to the distribution of the national archaeological resource. In short, the existing schedule is not a representative sample.

On the basis of the non-statutory criteria it was estimated that out of the 635 000 identified sites, about 60 000 qualify for protection as being of national importance. This figure implies a fourfold increase in the schedule of ancient monuments to approximately 10 per cent of the known site population. However, given the inadequate state of our knowledge of the national archaeological resource and the continuing rate of new discoveries, the figure of 60 000 monuments of national importance should not be regarded as a final estimate. Since much of the archaeological heritage of England is fragile and vulnerable to the pressures of modern land use, English Heritage intend to find the resources to initiate a scheduling enhancement programme to quadruple the present number of scheduled monuments over the next 7–10 years.

The management of monuments

There will, of course, be important longer-term costs and implications arising from a substantial increase in the number of scheduled monuments. It is a common fallacy that scheduling alone is sufficient to protect a monument. For that positive step to be realized, each monument requires a proper management plan and a management agreement with the owner.

In the countryside planning is accomplished by offering to pay developers for not making changes that they would otherwise like to make. Such payments are called 'management agreements', and Section 17 of the 1979 Act provides for a wide range of such agreements with owners and occupiers of land. All scheduled (field) monuments (and those which are not scheduled) are potentially eligible for management agreements. In return for an agreement to keep the monument in good condition, occupiers or any other interested parties are paid a tax-free sum, which is normally calculated on the area of the monument. Wherever possible, agreements are registered as a local land charge and run with the land, a single capitalized payment being made. Agreements are devised to meet problems special to a monument, and can include land necessary for the setting of a monument and its interpretation as well as pest control, scrub clearance and the employment of minimal cultivation techniques. They are not intended to compensate for loss of profits or capital values arising from the scheduling of a monument or refusal of scheduled monument consent.

Archaeological resource management therefore applies to all sites, and it aims to reconcile conflict and competition for land-use. There may be several aims to the management of a single site, and these aims can often be linked with those of other countryside interests – providing suitable habitats for wildlife, creating recreational and leisure facilities, and accommodating legitimate farming needs. In practical terms the management of archaeological sites can only be undertaken efficiently with commitment on the part of the landowner and land-user, and the integration of management needs with all other demands placed on the land.

Preservation by record

The archaeological heritage is a fragile and irreplaceable resource. An individual monument or landscape must not only have physically survived to the present day, but also it needs to have been recognized by historians or archaeologists. Subsequently, if the monument is of national importance it must be protected, managed and preserved from the many legitimate pressures in modern society which lead towards the destruction of the historic environment. Those monuments and landscapes which cannot be protected and managed should be recorded before their destruction. By virtue of Section 45 of the Ancient Monuments and Archaeological Areas Act 1979, 'English Heritage may undertake or assist in, or defray or contribute towards the cost of an archaeological investigation of any land which they consider may contain an ancient monument or anything else of archaeological or historical interest'. This power is used to finance archaeological investigations and the publication of the results before a site is destroyed. The term 'rescue archaeology' is in popular use, though possibly 'preservation by record' would be a better description, since the objective is an archive of what was found as well as more-widespread publication.

Rescue grants are demand-led and the budget (£5.3 million in 1986/7) is invariably under considerable pressure. The great increase in the number and variety of sites and landscapes which are now recognized as being of archaeological or historic importance means that numerous highly desirable projects can be identified. It is therefore necessary to pursue a selective funding policy, and grants for rescue archaeology are allocated for projects that can be justified within a framework of academic priorities. The criteria which provide the framework for funding rescue projects are the same as those which define a monument as being of national importance for the purposes of scheduling.

English Heritage allocates the funds at its disposal for recording those archaeological sites (whether scheduled or not) which cannot be preserved and whose destruction is taking place beyond the control of agencies with the powers and resources to deal with the problem. In all cases of rescue archaeology the need for excavation is a response to a threat of destruction of a site by some form of development or change, and it has been argued that those to whom development permission is given should invariably finance rescue archaeology – or at least a substantial part of it. In practice many private developers make a site available for archaeological exploration and help to finance the work. The Commission welcomes participation by developers and other bodies in the funding of rescue programmes, for its resources are inadequate to carry the burden alone. In particular, Local Planning Authorities have a clear rôle to play in ensuring that the archaeological implications of their planning decisions are properly assessed, and that, where destruction of important archaeological sites is unavoidable, due provision for essential archaeological recording is agreed and made before permission for a particular development scheme is given.

Conclusion

The ancient monuments and historic landscapes of the English countryside represent the surviving remains of 500 000 years of human endeavour, achievement and failure. The primary objectives of archaeological resource management are to secure the preservation of that resource and to promote the public's knowledge and enjoyment of it. The first provides for academic needs which lie largely in the future, and both objectives cater for the present needs of modern society on whose sympathy and interest the survival of the historic environment depends.

References

Gosling, P. F. 1985. Archaeological conservation in practice. In *Archaeology and nature conservation*, G. Lambrick (ed.), 45–9. Oxford: Department of External Studies.

Historic Buildings and Monuments Commission for England 1986. *Rescue archaeology funding: a policy statement*. London: HBMC.

HMSO 1983. Ancient Monuments and Archaeological Areas Act 1979 (revised to 1 June 1983).

Lambrick, G. (ed.) 1985. *Archaeology and nature conservation*. Oxford: Department of External Studies.

Morgan-Evans, D. 1985. The management of historic landscapes. In *Archaeology and nature conservation*, G. Lambrick (ed.), 89–94. Oxford: Department of External Studies.

Wainwright, G. J. 1984. The pressure of the past. *Proceedings of the Prehistoric Society* **50**, 1–22.

Wainwright, G. J. 1985. The preservation of ancient monuments. In *Archaeology and nature conservation*, G. Lambrick (ed.), 23–7. Oxford: Department of External Studies.

17 Government archaeology in Northern Ireland

ANN HAMLIN

Government archaeology in Northern Ireland has developed quite differently from elsewhere in the UK, and this has led to a very tightly integrated operation in which all government archaeological functions, except museums, are concentrated within the Department of the Environment for Northern Ireland. Before describing this work I outline the nature of the cultural resource which survives, and sketch briefly the historical development which led to the present organization.

Ireland enjoys a high rate of survival of field monuments compared with many other countries and, despite the various agencies of destruction (to which I shall return), the countryside is still rich in certain types of site. In the north there are many fine megalithic tombs, many standing stones and, in mid-Ulster, impressive groups of stone circles, cairns and alignments. Upland marginal areas are still rich in traces of prehistoric activity, sometimes sealed below peat. From the Early Christian period are the enclosed earthen and stone 'forts', raths and cashels, our most common field monument and, in Ireland as a whole, numbering at least 30 000–40 000. From the same period are the many ecclesiastical sites, some with churches, cells, round towers and crosses. With the Anglo-Norman invasion of the late 12th century came earthwork and stone castles, and new monastic houses, with small secure tower-houses in the late Middle Ages and Plantation castles and bawns and planned towns in the early 17th century.

There is, however, another side of the picture. Ireland on the whole is not rich in good building stone, and it has generally lacked the wealthy patronage necessary for ambitious projects. The architectural heritage before the 18th century is therefore modest, and a combination of a troubled history and a tendency to build anew rather than alter, add and mend has resulted in a very poor survival rate of early buildings. There are few medieval churches still in use in Ireland, and only three in Northern Ireland. Few medieval or 17th century castles are still roofed, and there are few houses of any size roofed and in use from earlier than the 18th century in the north. This lack of living examples of early structures with their fittings and furnishings means that the public imagination has little chance to develop and much guidance is needed to help clothe the 'bare bones'.

Official care of the monumental heritage in Ireland goes back to the disestablishment of the Church of Ireland in 1869. It was realized that many

Figure 17.1 Devenish, County Fermanagh: Early Christian and medieval monastery in state care since the disestablishment of the Church of Ireland in 1869. The 12th century round tower was the monastic belfry and safe storage place. (Crown copyright.)

important ruins were in the Church of Ireland's care, and provision would have to be made for their future upkeep. Under the terms of the 1869 Irish Church Act 137 ruined churches and crosses were vested in the Commissioners for Public Works to be 'maintained as national monuments'. Seventeen of the sites in our care in Northern Ireland came by this route (see Fig. 17.1).

This Irish precedent was quoted in debates on what became Sir John Lubbock's 1882 Ancient Monuments Protection Act. This Act applied to both Britain and Ireland, but the Irish legislation soon diverged from the British. A new Ancient Monuments Act in 1892 widened the scope for protection beyond the sites in the 1882 schedule (only 18 in Ireland, three in what is now Northern Ireland) to any ancient or medieval structure whose preservation the Commissioners thought was a matter of public interest.

For the 40 years following 1882 state involvement was confined to the care of a few outstanding monuments, but after partition the care of the 22 sites in the six northern counties passed to the Ministry of Finance for Northern Ireland (in 1922). Through the 1926 Ancient Monuments (NI) Act the state

Figure 17.2 Beaghmore stone circles, cairns and alignments, County Tyrone: discovered in the 1940s, excavated in the 1960s and now in state care. The peat-covered area at the bottom of this air view was acquired recently to save it from reclamation. (Crown copyright.)

accepted a greatly enlarged responsibility for monumental care. The new Act provided for protection by scheduling and preservation orders and for the reporting of all archaeological finds, not just gold and silver. A further Act in 1937 included the licensing of all archaeological excavations, adopting a provision found in the Republic of Ireland's 1930 Ancient Monuments Act. In these two important areas – reporting finds and licensing excavations – legislation in Ireland, both north and south, still differs from in Great Britain. The Department of the Environment is the licensing body for Northern Ireland, and it is responsible for administering the law relating to finds and for dealing with Treasure Trove cases.

During the 1930s and 1940s the number of sites in care (see Fig. 17.2) increased, from 27 in 1928 to 50 in 1947, and some 340 monuments were scheduled, but the most important archaeological work of those years was done by amateurs, who were involved in excavation and survey. When the Royal Commissions on Ancient and Historical Monuments were set up in Scotland, Wales and England in 1908, no provision was made for Ireland, despite protests. Robert Cochrane, for example, argued forcefully that for the state to protect, it had to know the range of surviving material. This failure to set up a government-financed recording agency in Ireland left field survey largely in amateur hands for more than a generation. During the

1930s a dedicated group collected the information from which the 1940 *Preliminary survey of the ancient monuments of Northern Ireland* was published, but it was not until 1950 that a government survey was established, with the appointment of Dudley Waterman and Pat Collins. Their task was to carry out a county-by-county survey on similar lines to the Royal Commissions in Great Britain, but without the Royal Warrant. Their rôle was also seen as 'to provide the Ministry with complete records of monuments in order that it can direct its policy of protection and presentation into the most necessary and desirable channels'. So, in 1950, survey was accepted as a function within government, with a practical as well as an academic aim, and the body still known as the Archaeological Survey of Northern Ireland came into being.

During the 1950s the two-man survey was active in County Down and small-scale research excavations were an integral part of the work, to set the field monuments in their chronological and cultural context. Staff numbers grew slowly in the 1960s, more quickly in the 1970s, and now the group of eight archaeologists, one architectural historian and four support staff who make up the Archaeological Survey covers the wide range of activities carried out in Great Britain by the Inspectorates, the Royal Commissions, the many county and area units and trusts, the county archaeologists and sites and monuments records, and doubtless by other bodies. The legislative basis is the Historic Monuments Act (NI) 1971, a fairly short piece of legislation which emphasizes the protection of monuments, an aim which can be said to underlie all the Department's archaeological work.

The database is the Northern Ireland Sites and Monuments Record (the NISMR), built up over the past ten years. It holds information about all known sites to the early 17th century, numbering at present about 12 000, but the total is increasing all the time as a result of research on maps and documentary sources, continuing survey, work on air photographs, and information from the public and from colleagues in the public service, like agricultural and forestry officers. Maps and lists showing all known sites were distributed in 1979/80 to all land-using agencies, including planning, quarries, roads, drainage, agriculture and forestry, to museums, universities and colleges, and on a local basis to historical societies. It is planned to distribute updated, revised material in 1986/87. In return we seek information about monuments and 'early warning' of any work which may affect a site. Although this request carries no statutory weight, the response has generally been good, and communications are fostered by visits to regional offices, lectures at agricultural colleges, and similar contacts.

Between 1982 and 1985 a basic record of industrial monuments (the IAR) was built up, on similar lines to the SMR, map-based, with accompanying cards and lists. However, there is no full-time industrial specialist on the staff of the Archaeological Survey, and the work goes little further than the holding of this record and some rescue recording. There is an embryo Historic Building Record already in existence, but Northern Ireland does not have the equivalent of the National Monuments Records which exist for England, Scotland and Wales. There are hopes of establishing a properly

Figure 17.3 Creggandevesky Court Tomb, County Tyrone: before excavation this tomb was covered by bog; it was excavated under threat of total removal for argricultural reclamation, taken into state care and put on public display. (Crown copyright.)

housed and staffed Monuments and Buildings Record, but in a time of tight resources and competing demands the way ahead is not yet clear.

The Sites and Monuments Record both forms the basis of and is supplemented by the survey work. We have not abandoned the county survey pattern, but planned county survey has to be combined with reactive rescue survey, and the publication of the county survey has fallen badly behind. The first of three projected volumes on County Armagh is nearing completion, for publication in 1987/88, and a first Fermanagh volume is well advanced. As part of the Fermanagh work we undertook the first extensive survey of crannogs in recent times in Ireland, investigating about 100 in the county. During recent work in County Antrim there has been an attempt to adopt a broader 'landscape' approach than in the past, and this, together with the use of air photographs, has led to the recognition of extensive remains of upland field systems, enclosures and houses, extending from prehistoric to post-medieval times and largely, though not wholly, escaping the notice of earlier workers. The one architectural historian on the Survey's staff also combines county survey with rescue recording of threatened historic buildings all over the province.

Rescue survey is inevitably largely reactive. The three Inspectors involved with archaeological survey, each covering two counties, respond to all threats which come to our notice. There is a wide range of possible reactions. The owner may be dissuaded from carrying out damage when the interest of the site is made clear; he or she may change his or her plans to avoid impinging on a site; constraints may be built into a development. The Department may give practical help in making a monument more 'acceptable', with fencing, clearing growth, and draining or infilling a dangerous wet ditch, though we have increasingly tended to encourage the keeping of growth when it provides a good natural habitat. It is also empowered to make recognition payments to an owner for leaving a site unharmed in agricultural land. If no other course can be agreed, an excavation may be mounted, or for a site of very high quality the option of state care may be pursued.

Some special surveys are done to investigate areas of particular concern, such as bog in the course of reclamation (see Fig. 17.3), land designated for forest, or areas where quarrying is planned. We have issued a poster pointing out the possibility of finding archaeological remains during peat cutting, booklets on farming and conservation (with the Department of Agriculture for Northern Ireland), and articles in farming journals, as well as mounting a display at the annual agricultural show in Belfast.

Northern Ireland forms a manageable unit in which to respond to emergencies, and each year the Department's workforce caps several newly discovered souterrains. Dug-out boats, dating from the Bronze Age through to medieval times, are recorded and, when possible, salvaged for display. Unexpected finds arising from quarrying, reclamation, erosion, and other agencies are followed up. In the past three years, for example, there has been a particularly rich 'crop' of Bronze Age burials from cists, superficially unmarked but disturbed during sand and gravel quarrying and agricultural reclamation.

One Inspector with particular urban and post-medieval interests scrutinizes all planning applications for historic 'towns', numbering 40–50 places. Many of these are now quite small villages, creations of the early 17th century Plantation of Ulster, but for larger urban centres like Armagh, Carrickfergus, Coleraine, Downpatrick and Londonderry there are strategy plans to pinpoint the potentially important areas for investigation. There have been excavations in all of these towns over the past decade, and the 1980s have seen the first modern excavations in central Belfast. These urban projects, very much in the public eye, have attracted a good deal of interest, but with the capacity to do at most three or four urban excavations a year, our scope for following up all potentially promising sites is limited, and there has to be stringent selection year by year.

Each year 20–25 excavations are licensed by the Department in Northern Ireland, rural and urban, a few directed by individuals as research projects, but mostly done by or for the Department. Excavation is normally done to test the potential of a threatened site, to investigate a monument before unavoidable destruction, or to elucidate a site before conservation. Much

Figure 17.4 Deer Park Farms, County Antrim: excavation in progress on a threatened raised rath. (Crown copyright.)

effort goes into avoiding excavation, which is regarded very much as a last resort, done only when all other ways of saving a site are exhausted. Excavation is no longer the 'automatic' reaction to a threat which it tended to be early in the 1970s. We have tried to develop criteria for choosing sites for excavation, in terms of area, type and period, though inevitably choices tend to be influenced by practical considerations as well as theoretical criteria. In recent years the Department has not carried out any purely 'research' excavations, but we would maintain that within a 'rescue' framework our excavations have made important 'research' contributions, and I would agree with those who maintain that an over-rigid distinction between rescue and research is unhelpful.

Work is in progress at present on a book describing the results of a selection of excavations done between 1970 and 1986, and I will here mention just a few examples of areas of important progress. The excavation of four threatened raised raths (motte-like mounds) has built up a valuable body of information about the mechanics and chronology of mound growth in the Early Christian period, and about the types of structures buried and preserved during the process of growth (see Fig. 17.4). A programme of testing any proposal for disturbance close to any known early ecclesiastical site (graveyard extensions, roads, parish halls or other buildings) has confirmed beyond doubt that the early nucleus of activity is normally more extensive than any visible features, and excavation has revealed burials, enclosures, buildings and areas of technological activity. Urban archaeology was late to develop in Ireland, but excavation in towns is gradually building up a fuller picture of urban growth, for example in Armagh and Downpatrick in Early Christian and medieval times, in Carrickfergus and Coleraine in the medieval and Plantation periods, and in Londonderry from the Plantation onwards.

Most of the Department's excavations are published in the *Ulster Journal of Archaeology*, but there is an occasional HMSO monograph series for major projects. Volumes have appeared on Carrickfergus Castle (1981) and the excavations at Mount Sandel (1985), and others in preparation include three posthumous projects: Gerhard Bersu's work at Lissue rath, Dudley Waterman's at Navan Fort and Tom Delaney's in Carrickfergus town.

Excavated materials are treated in the Conservation Laboratory at the Archaeological Survey's headquarters. Over the past ten years the conservator has also undertaken a major programme of cleaning carved-stone monuments, including not only those in state care, but also, by agreement, many in private ownership. This has been valuable in removing disfiguring and damaging algae and lichen, and revealing details of carving, but it has also shown up the state of the weathered stone surface in more detail than was visible before, sometimes disclosing disturbing cracks and fissures. The state of exposed carved-stone monuments is a cause of serious concern, but the question of moving stones indoors for protection is a sensitive one, and it has not yet been addressed very seriously in Ireland. The Board of Works in the Republic has, however, recently moved the cross at Cashel inside, replacing it outside with a cast, and in Northern Ireland we are developing several indoor stone stores for smaller carved stones and architectural fragments. These are sorted, recorded and indexed as part of the county survey activity.

Statutory protection of monuments takes two main forms: scheduling and state care. Scheduling is under the terms of the Historic Monuments Act (NI 1971), not the 1979 Ancient Monuments and Archaeological Areas Act which applies in Great Britain, and Northern Ireland does not yet have the scheduled monument consent procedure or field monument wardens. Owners of scheduled sites must give six months' notice of any work which will affect a monument. Although during the 1930s some 340 sites were protected under the 1926 Act, there was little further progress with scheduling until the passing of the 1971 Act. During the 1970s some sites were scheduled when threatened, to give a breathing space for action, but scheduling is now directed towards a careful selection of 'quality' monuments, though threat is still sometimes a factor. The present total of scheduled sites is nearing 700, almost 6 per cent of the monuments listed in the SMR, but considerably more than 6 per cent of visible upstanding sites. The state of protection at present is uneven, partly resulting from the pattern established in the 1930s. The most common type, raths and cashels, is under-represented, partly because earlier workers were deterred by the sheer numbers. Sadly, this has meant that many have been destroyed since the 1930s without coming to notice, but now, with the information from continuing survey and the SMR, we have a better basis for selection, although still only about half of our area has been covered by systematic survey.

During 1986/87 it is planned to visit all scheduled sites and to produce a statement, similar to the 1984 English *Resource* document, analysing the present state of protection and looking to the future. We do not foresee being able to put in hand a scheduling enhancement programme on the scale planned in England, but we do intend to raise the number of protected sites to at least 1000 by 1990, and to ensure that protection covers the surviving sites more evenly than is presently the case.

However, the protection offered by scheduling is limited, especially in the face of an unsympathetic owner. There is little hope of saving a site after the six months' notice period, as the present procedures for protection orders and vesting (compulsory purchase) are lengthy. Fortunately the problem cases are few, but we do hope to move before long towards a scheduled monument consent procedure and more regular surveillance of protected sites.

Although I emphasized at the start that Ireland enjoys a high rate of survival of monuments – and I would add that there is fairly widespread interest in and goodwill towards monuments – there is, nevertheless, an urgent need for more protection. The intensified survey of recent years has demonstrated the high rate of destruction in the past, sometimes the recent past. Of the 423 recorded raths and cashels in County Armagh, for example, 42 per cent have disappeared entirely, and many of the surviving sites are damaged. In recent years the scale and pace of agricultural improvement have increased enormously, especially in marginal, often upland, areas, and often aided by EEC grants. Among the factors furthering the survival of field monuments in the past were the emphasis on pasture, the frequently small scale of operations, leading to small fields, and the cutting of peat by hand. There has been no major move to arable cultivation, but in the drive for improved pasture and more silage there have been rapid changes. Peat is cut mechanically, bogs are drained, rivers are rerouted, hills are pushed into adjoining hollows, 'obstructions' to large machines are removed, and walls and hedges are taken away to form bigger fields. It has been impossible to monitor all this activity, and it is clear that, despite our best efforts and help from officials of the Department of Agriculture, many sites have been lost, but the levels of grant-aid have recently been reduced and it seems that the pendulum is swinging towards more interest in conservation.

The other main form of protection, besides scheduling, is state care, whether by ownership, lease or deed of guardianship. The Department of the Environment for Northern Ireland now has 164 monuments in care, looked after by a direct labour force of 105, divided between a central workshop and four regions. The crafts represented include stonemasons, smiths, joiners, a plasterer, painters and mechanics. We operate a small sandstone quarry and burn our own lime to meet needs which can no longer be met locally.

The range of monuments in care is wide, including megalithic tombs, stone circles, a hillfort, raths and cashels, crosses, round towers, churches and abbeys, castles of earth and stone, artillery forts, a Martello tower, a wind-mill, an 18th century market house, fine wrought- and cast-iron gates of the 18th and 19th centuries, and a vernacular structure of uncertain date, a sweat house. For historical reasons there is some emphasis on masonry buildings, and a considerable concentration of sites in County Down, but in recent years more earthworks have been taken into care, and with improved grass-cutting machinery we have been able to tackle larger areas, including the large monastic precinct at Inch Abbey, County Down, the 16 acres (6.5 ha) at Navan Fort, County Armagh, and an upland tract of 11 acres (4.5 ha) at Bally-groll, County Londonderry, which includes several megalithic tombs and field walls. In considering new acquisitions we try to apply sound criteria of choice, including geographical and chronological factors, and rarity and group value, although more pragmatic considerations can come into play, like threat or an offer. The approach is less élitist than in earlier years: the fact that a good example of a certain type is in care will not prevent consideration of another good example, even if it initially has to be on a 'first-aid' basis.

It is through the state care monuments that the most active public contacts arise. Though the Northern Ireland efforts may now pale before recent English Heritage and Cadw initiatives, the scale and variety of presentation activity have increased greatly over the past decade. Publications include a general guide (1983), guide-cards, postcards, leaflets, slide packs, a children's guide and badges. Our new generation of site information notices, done by screen-printing, are colourful and attractive, and in the summer months guides are provided at the most popular sites to help visitors. We do not have the resources to go as far or as fast as we would like in improving presentation, but we plan to open one new visitor centre each year, to improve other site facilities, to extend the range of popular publications and to encourage appropriate events and activities at monuments. Although the range of sites in care is wide, they are not generally spectacular or very large, and the potential visiting public is modest: the population of Northern Ireland is about 1.5 million and nearly 1 million people visited the country in 1985. The most-visited monument at present is Carrickfergus Castle, with just under 50 000 in 1985.

The presentation efforts are directed as much (or more) towards local people and schoolchildren as towards tourists. Over the past three years the Department of Education has seconded a school teacher for a year to work with the Archaeological Survey on the use of monuments in school work, and we have co-operated with teachers' centres and groups in developing projects based on monuments. We firmly believe that time and effort spent with schoolchildren now will prove to be well invested in terms of future appreciation and protection.

Having outlined the wide range of work carried out by the government's archaeological service in Northern Ireland, I now comment further on the organization. In 1976 the monuments work was moved from the Department of Finance to the Department of the Environment for Northern Ireland, and was combined with Historic Buildings functions within the present Historic Monuments and Buildings Branch. Protection and grant-aiding for historic buildings started later in Northern Ireland than in Great Britain, through the Planning (NI) Order of 1972. Late in 1985 a Conservation Service was established within DOENI under a Director, embracing Countryside and Wildlife as well as Monuments and Buildings, thus combining different but related conservation interests, again a different pattern from that applying in Great Britain.

The centralized integrated operation works well, in an area of only six counties, 80 per cent of the land being agricultural. No site is more than two hours' drive from Belfast, and most are much closer. The present structure of government in Northern Ireland is highly centralized. The 27 district councils have limited functions; there is no middle (county) tier of administration, and all of the main functions are carried out by central government. This highly centralized structure aids the process of consultation and helps in the maintenance of good communications. I do not want to sound complacent: our manpower and resources are small, and we cannot do all that we would like to do, but I believe that the integrated centralized government archaeological service based in Belfast works well for the six-county area.

It is at best optimistic, at worst foolhardy, to express hopes for the future at a time of contraction, but I shall conclude by expressing some all the same! I hope to see the establishment of a Northern Ireland Monuments and Buildings Record, equivalent to the National Monuments Records in Great Britain. I hope that the publication of survey volumes will become a regular feature of our output. I look towards continuing advances in presentation and education, growing visitor numbers, better facilities, more publications, and ever-increasing public awareness and enjoyment of monuments. Also, closely connected with education, I look for stronger protection for those monuments which have survived to this day. The resource of historic monuments which we do our best to record, protect and present, though largely in private ownership, is a *shared* heritage. The philosophy underlying government archaeology in Northern Ireland is well expressed in Ruskin's words: 'What we ourselves built, we are at liberty to throw down, but what other men gave their strength and wealth and life to accomplish, their right over it does not pass away with their death, still less is the right to the use of what they have left vested in us only. It belongs to all their successors'.

18 *The new Spanish archaeological heritage legislation*

JAVIER GARCÍA FERNÁNDEZ

(translated by Cecilio Mar Molinero
and Henry Cleere)

Legislation before 1985

The approval by the Spanish Parliament (*Cortes Generales*) of Law
No. 16/1985 and the extension of that law through Decree No. 111/86 has
meant that it is now possible to speak of a new legislative framework for
archaeology in Spain. In order to appreciate the transformation that this
represents, it is necessary first to refer to earlier legislation.

Many historians and lawyers (Fernández 1978, García de Enterría 1983)
have stressed the systematic disregard for the protection of the historic
heritage in the Spanish legislation of the 18th and 19th centuries. Until the
enactment of the Law of Archaeological Excavations of 7 July 1911 and its
regulations (Tramoyeres 1919), approved in the Royal Decree of 1 March
1912, the only legislation in operation was the Law of the Enlightenment,
dating from the 18th century.[1] These two statutes were in force until 1985
and 1986, respectively. They were complemented later by legislation
introduced during the dictatorship of General Primo de Rivera, the Second
Republic and the dictatorship of General Franco:

*Royal Decree-Law of 9 August 1926 on the protection and preservation of
the artistic heritage.* This was a very innovative statute (Fernández 1978,
pp. 16–19), and introduced the concept of national artistic and archaeological treasure (*Tesoro artístico/arqueológico nacional*), defined by reason of
its being protected by the state and covering sites and objects of palaeontological and archaeological interest.
*Law of 10 December 1931 on the sale or disposal of artistic, archaeological,
and historical material more than 100 years old.* Legislation to regulate
trade in cultural property.
*Law of 13 May 1933 on the defence, preservation and expansion of the
national historic and archaeological heritage* (and the relevant regulations
approved by the Decree of 16 April 1936). The most important statutes
relating to the historical heritage, the importance for which for archaeology

residing in the fact that they directed finds from excavations to museum collections, an aspect insufficiently developed by the 1911 Law and 1912 Regulations (Benitez de Lugo 1983, Roca Roca 1976, Fernández 1978).
Law of 22 December 1955 on the preservation of the historical and artistic heritage. Designed to complement the 1933 Law.

These statutes created the framework for archaeological excavations. The following criteria had also to be applied:

Material extent. Defined by two fundamental concepts relating to state intervention – excavations (systematic and deliberate movements of soil in areas which might contain archaeological remains) and antiquities (all artefacts belonging to any historical period).[2]

Procedures for administrative action. The state reserved the right to undertake excavations, even on private property. Subject to the state's reserved rights, authorization to excavate was based on concessions granted to official institutions, private individuals and scientific bodies, both Spanish and foreign. Regulations governing casual finds modified the way in which they were treated in the Civil Code of 1889. An inventory of monuments and antiquities incorporated in more-recent buildings was instituted.

Protection of archaeological materials. Awards (monetary or honorific) were instituted for those who made major finds. Authorization was needed for any work that might endanger legally protected objects; legal penalties were prescribed in cases of infraction.

Legislation on property. The 1911 Law and the 1912 Regulations established strict limitations on certain property rights, such as the use of ruins as sources of building materials and the right of the state to excavate on private properties. Casual finds became state property. Less severe constraints were imposed on alterations to buildings of archaeological interest, especially those on the national inventory.

Administrative organization. State activity was structured at three levels: the Ministry of Public Instruction and Fine Arts, the Higher Council for Excavations and Antiquities, and the General Inspectorate of Fine Arts; the second of these was rendered largely ineffective by being an honorific body (Fernández 1978, pp. 590–1).[3]

On the one hand the 1911 Law and the 1912 Regulations created for the first time a reasonably effective legal framework for archaeological excavations (though without a strong administrative back-up). On the other hand however rights of private property clearly prevailed over public interest, and the largely honorific supervisory structure led to inefficiency and lack of professional commitment (Fernández 1978, pp. 27–9, García de Enterria 1983, pp. 588–90).

The importance of the 1978 Constitution for the archaeological heritage

The 1978 Constitution was radically transformed Spanish legislation. Without this framework it would have been impossible to enact the 1985 Historical Heritage law. The following innovations in the Constitution are relevant in this context:

> *Public commitment to the conservation and promotion of the artistic, cultural and historical heritage of the whole Spanish people, regardless of ownership or legal status.* This extends to the prosecution of any offence against the heritage (Article 46), which has precedents in the 1931 Constitution and similar provisions in Italy, Portugal and Greece (Perez-Luño 1984, García-Escudero & Pendas 1986). The state is committed not only to the protection of archaeological materials, but also to their promotion (Perez-Luño 1984, pp. 298–301).
>
> *Regional decentralization.* Regional governments (*Comunidades Autónomas*) can now take charge of museums and monuments within the provisions of their Statutes of Autonomy, but the state reserves the right of action over exports and vandalism and in certain museums (García de Enterria 1983, pp. 585–8, García-Escudero & Pendas 1986, Muñoz Machado 1982, pp. 574–600).
>
> *Subordination of private property to public interest (Article 128.1).* This expressly relates to the cultural heritage. Archaeological material in public ownership is especially well protected.

These principles help to understand the scope of Law No. 16 of 25 June 1985 as well as the regulations promulgated by the regional governments which, with Royal Decrees Nos 585 of 24 April 1985 and 111 of 10 January 1986, constitute the present legislative regulation of Spanish archaeology.

Archaeological aspects of Law No. 16/1985

Basic legal concepts

The new Law has an all-embracing definition of the historical heritage (Article 1.2):

> any buildings, and fixed or movable objects of artistic, historic, palaeontological, archaeological, ethnographic, scientific, or technical interest. Archaeological deposits and areas and the documentary and bibliographic heritage are also a part of it, as well as any natural sites, gardens, and parks of artistic, historical, or anthropological value.

This wide definition is consistent with the Granada Convention of October 1985 (García-Escudero & Pendas 1986), but the draft Law was published

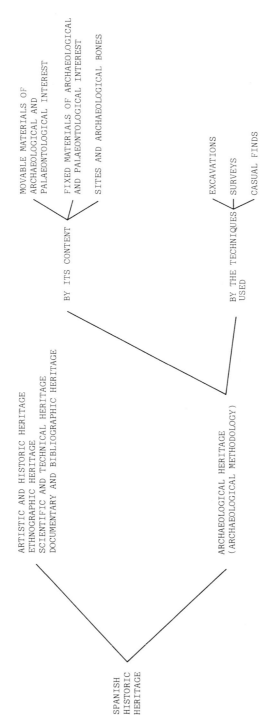

Figure 18.1 Basic legal concepts underlying the Spanish Historical Heritage Law No. 16/1985.

earlier. Its legal value is defined by its objects, since this inventory of historical and artistic values is introduced into the legal code to define those objects worthy of protection, promotion and transmission to future generations. Article 1 of the Law establishes a public legal relationship (of protection, promotion and transmission) with two subjects (public bodies and individuals upon whom duties of an equally public legal nature are laid) and an object (all of the items covered by Article 1.2). The reason for this specific relationship is the subjective right to collective enjoyment of certain cultural property: the aim of the Law is to provide 'access to all the property that constitutes our historical heritage' (Perez-Luño, p. 14, García de Enterria 1983, pp. 581–5).[4]

The second important legal concept is that of the archaeological heritage, which has three interrelated aspects – instrumental, material and functional–descriptive. The legal definition is based on the application of scientific methods and on chronological criteria (see Fig. 18.1). Once these criteria have been applied, descriptive criteria can then be used.

The Law adds descriptive and functional elements in defining excavations, surveys and casual finds (Article 41):

> *Archaeological excavations.* Movement of soil on the surface, below ground or under water, carried out to discover and investigate all types of historical or palaeontological remains and geological elements associated with them. This definition incorporates both the will to discover and investigate and a material aspect.
> *Archaeological surveys.* Surface or underwater exploration which does not require the movement of soil.
> *Casual finds.* Discoveries of objects or remains by chance or as a consequence of non-archaeological earth-moving, demolition or other cause. The precedent for this concept in the Civil Code contains only a material element (Diez-Picazo & Gullon 1981, Espin 1968).

The Law goes into greater detail in enlarging the concept of the archaeological heritage. In Section II, which relates to fixed materials, Articles 14 and 15 include archaeological areas, defined as places on the surface, below ground or in Spanish territorial waters that contain fixed or movable materials, whether excavated or not, which are amenable to study by archaeological methods. This definition links up with the previous three in such a way that excavations, surveys and casual finds may all qualify a site as an archaeological area.

The Law of the Spanish Historical Heritage has thus created the legal concept of archaeological heritage, which provides for: (a) the inclusion of the archaeological heritage within the historical heritage, from which it follows that public bodies have a legal duty to look after it and that citizens acquire certain rights in it; (b) the descriptive characterization of the materials that constitute the historical heritage as being amenable to study by archaeological methods; and (c) a distinction between fixed and movable

PROTECTION TECHNIQUES					PROMOTION TECHNIQUES	
TECHNIQUES THAT ARE SPECIFIC TO ARCHAEOLOGICAL HERITAGE	TECHNIQUES THAT ARE COMMON TO ALL HISTORIC HERITAGE					
	IN THE CASE OF MOVABLE MATERIAL		IN THE CASE OF FIXED MATERIAL "ARCHAEOLOGICAL AREAS"	IN THE CASE OF FIXED AND MOVABLE MATERIAL	Public funding of excavations and surveys	Tax benefits
	MATERIAL OF CULTURAL INTEREST 1st category	GENERAL INVENTORY OF CULTURAL MATERIAL 2nd category				
Administrative authorization for excavations and surveys	Administrative inspection	To allow visits two months per year		Conservation duty		
Guarantees needed to give the authorization	To allow scientific study	Requires authorization before being exported		Possibility of use without loss of archaeological values		
- coherent programme	It is forbidden to dispose of them					
- objects to be deposited				(Duty to carry out preservation work if the owner fails to do so)		
Powers to order the carrying out of excavations and surveys				Prosecution in case of damage		

Figure 18.2 The administration of the archaeological heritage.

material, with different legal procedures for each (but unified later within the general concept of the archaeological area).

To this complex legal concept are appended all of the legal mechanisms that permit the archaeological heritage to be enjoyed by society – characterization of the materials that constitute it, classification into fixed and movable components, administrative action for protection and promotion, and the definition of subjective rights which affect its use in respect of enjoyment, research or ownership. This approach deliberately eschews subjectivity, since both public bodies and citizens are the subjects of legal public relationships.

Administration of the archaeological heritage

The Law places a duty on public bodies to implement protection and promotion activities; the way in which this obligation is made effective depends on the nature of the archaeological materials involved. The ways in which these actions take place in the field of archaeology are shown in Figure 18.2.

SPECIFIC ACTIONS

Specific administrative actions including policing of archaeological areas, to prevent their being looted and to ensure the rational and scientific use of the archaeological heritage. Public bodies use traditional policing methods. They impose a compulsory legal framework upon the individual: any specific activity within this framework must be approved by the state administration (Article 42.1):

> Any archaeological excavation or survey must be approved by the competent authority who, using appropriate methods of inspection and control, will verify that the work has been planned and carried out according to a detailed and coherent programme. This programme must satisfy conditions relative to convenience, professionalism, and scientific interest.

Administrative authorization operates through a licensing system that is superior to that laid down in the 1911 Law and 1912 Regulations. Those undertaking surveys or excavations are also better protected, since the conditions are more stringently prescribed, and these conditions in turn ensure a higher quality of work. Archaeologists are obliged to deposit any materials found with a predetermined local institution, together with a report.

Article 43 allows the administration to order excavations and surveys to be carried out on any publicly or privately owned site where the existence of archaeological remains may be presumed, and can, if necessary, use powers of compulsory purchase.

THE PROTECTION OF FIXED MATERIALS

Archaeological areas are protected by a new device of declaring them to be 'Materials of Cultural Interest' (*Bienes de Interes Cultural*). This is done by Royal Decree, which provides for the inscription of such sites on a special register. This procedure is set out in Royal Decree No. 111 of 10 January 1986 (Estella Izquierdo 1975, García-Escudero & Pendas 1986). Such a declaration has the following effects. All municipal consent for division into plots, demolition or building are suspended; no earth-moving may take place; any work that may affect the area requires authorization, as does the erection of advertisements or signs of any kind; and the municipal authority must prepare a Special Protection Plan for approval.

THE PROTECTION OF MOVABLE MATERIALS

The way in which movable archaeological materials are protected under the 1986 Law is somewhat complex and unsystematic. Section III provides protection linked with the General Register and the General Inventory of Movable Material (*Inventario General de Bienes Muebles*); the procedures are set out in Royal Decree No. 111/1986:

Movable material declared to be of cultural interest. Owners must permit inspection by the administration, study by researchers and viewing by the public; it may not be transferred to anyone other than the state or other public bodies, who may not sell or dispose of it in any way.

Movable material on the General Inventory. The administration must be informed if it is proposed to sell or transfer ownership, it must be available for inspection or research, there is an obligation to lend it for temporary exhibitions, it may not be exported without a licence and any application for an export licence carries an implicit offer to sell it to the state.

Techniques appropriate to both fixed and movable materials. The owners or custodians of any component of the historical heritage must preserve it, maintain it in good condition and keep it secure. They may make use of it, provided that its preservation is not endangered. Dereliction constitutes a criminal offence and the state has powers that extend to expropriation in cases of infraction.

Administrative action for the protection of the archaeological heritage has two characteristic features:

Levels of protection are graduated to create concentric circles of protection, the inner relating to the archaeological heritage and the outer to more-general levels of protection. Archaeological material is the best-protected category, documentary and bibliographic materials receiving less-detailed treatment.

The use of traditional supervisory and policing methods which impose limitations on the freedom of the individual, who must obtain administrative authorization to surmount them.

The administrative action of promotion of the archaeological heritage is dealt with in a more diffuse way in the Law. Section VIII is divided into two economic–financial levels of relevance to the archaeological heritage: the state is given a general mandate to ensure the financing of, *inter alia*, archaeological excavations and surveys through preferential official credit sources, and certain fiscal benefits in respect of income taxes, corporation tax and death duties are available in such cases.

The organization of archaeological heritage management in Spain

One of the characteristics of the new Spanish legislation is its regional pluralism. Article 6 defines public bodies at central and regional government level as being competent authorities for the purposes of the Law.

Specific techniques for protecting the archaeological heritage

The relevant authority for policing excavations is the regional government; only if there is a risk of illicit export or looting does competence pass to the state.

Certain statutory advisory bodies are set up at state level, such as the Higher Council for Rock Art (*Junta Superior de Arte Rupestre*) and the Higher Council for Archaeological Exploration and Excavation (*Junta Superior de Exploraciones y Excavaciones Arqueológicas*). These bodies have special responsibilities within their respective fields for advising the state administration.[5,6]

Administrative management operates at two levels, the state and the autonomous region:

> *State level.* Royal Decree No. 565 of 25 April 1985, which established the new structure for the Ministry of Culture, created the Institute for the Conservation and Restoration of Cultural Property (*Instituto de Conservación y Restauración de Bienes Culturales, ICRBC*), which includes the Department of Archaeology. This Department is statutorily responsible for looking after the state's interests in the archaeological heritage by guaranteeing its conservation, promoting its enrichment, providing public access, promoting its scientific investigaton, protecting it against illicit export and looting, and promoting knowledge of it internationally.
>
> *Regional level.* The *Comunidades Autónomas* may be involved at various levels with the archaeological heritage: through a *Consejería* (Advisory Body), a General Directorate of the Historical and Archaeological Heritage, an Archaeological Sub-directorate or Service, an Area Service or Delegation, or honorary Archaeological Councils or Advisory Commissions.

PROTECTION TECHNIQUES COMMON TO THE ENTIRE HISTORICAL HERITAGE

The common techniques discussed here are the duty, in descending order, of the state administration, the regional governments and municipal administrations:

State administration. To designate fixed and movable material to be Material of Cultural Interest (through Royal Decree), and to manage the General Register; to include movable material on the General Inventory and to manage the Inventory; to take action against looting when the regional government declines to do so; to exercise the right of first refusal when owners wish to dispose of such material; to authorize export licences for certain classes of material.

Regional governments. To initiate requests to designate Material of Cultural Interest (except where this has been assigned to a public body or forms part of the National Heritage); to initiate requests to include movable material on the General Inventory.

Municipal administrations. To co-operate in the preservation and care of the heritage; to protect designated archaeological areas (see above).

TECHNIQUES FOR THE PROMOTION OF THE ARCHAEOLOGICAL HERITAGE

These are the duty of the state and the regional governments. The former can grant fiscal benefits and give allowances when movable material is imported. Both can give rewards to those who discover objects or other remains, and to the owners of the sites on which these are found, and both can finance excavations.

Ownership of the archaeological heritage

Earlier legislation failed to solve the problem of ownership of archaeological material, since it did not guarantee its ultimate destination or public availability. The new Law has established clearer criteria to ensure its enjoyment by the public.

The specific principles involved may be summarized as follows.

Material found as a result of authorized excavations or surveys. This must be deposited with the institution nominated by the administration; the finder has no right of property or reward. Owners of private properties where the administration has ordered excavations or surveys to be carried out will be indemnified in accordance with compulsory purchase legislation.

Material found by chance. This is declared to be in the public domain, irrespective of the ownership of the site on which it was found. Both the finder and the landowner receive a monetary reward equivalent to half the official valuation. The new Law unequivocally establishes the principle of automatic acquisition by the state by stating that Article 351 of the Civil Code does not apply.

Other obligations placed on the owner or custodian of archaeological material were discussed earlier in this chapter.

Conclusions

From the conceptual and ideological points of view the new legislation represents a number of innovations in the principles that have previously governed Spanish law on this subject. With the definition of the independent concept of the archaeological heritage, within the wider context of the historic heritage, it becomes possible to take account of the most innovative techniques of modern archaeology. It might be argued that the law has taken a partisan view of a special trend in archaeology,[7] but it nevertheless reflects the concern that the legislature has felt for the creation of a legal system that relates to the scientific needs of those who must apply it. The notion of protection has been clarified, despite the sharing of responsibility for it between central and regional government. The new legislation on property rights has solved the old problem of private initiatives, and at the same time strengthened public ownership of archaeological material.

Legislation in the *Comunidades Autónomas*

Eight regional governments (Cataluña, Galicia, Andalucía, Cantabria, Aragón, the Balearic Islands, Madrid and Castilla y León) have enacted legislation relating to archaeology, all relating to the administration of the licensing system.[8] The other aspects of archaeology – fieldwork programming, promotion, protection of archaeological material through urban regulations, etc. – are covered sketchily, if at all. The *Comunidades Autónomas* have concentrated on the policing of excavations to the exclusion of all else. There is considerable variation in the machinery established and the definitions adopted by the different regions. As a result the special archaeological characteristics of the regions are not being taken into account, and they are failing to keep pace with modern developments in archaeological techniques. In general no provision is made for co-operative arrangements with other *Comunidades Autónomas*, and only in Cataluña, Galicia and Andalucía is grant-aid available for archaeological work.

Although the present regional legislation is limited in scope, there is reason to believe that, when they have consolidated their control over archaeological work, the *Comunidades Autónomas* will begin to promulgate more-comprehensive legislative measures.

Notes

1   The only statute worthy of mention coming between the Novísima Recopilación of 1805 and the Law of Excavations of 1911 is the Royal Order of 1844, which

created the provincial commissions for monuments, the Law of Public Instruction of 9 September 1857, which gave the Real Academia de San Fernando control over the provincial commissions, and, finally, the Royal Decree of 24 November 1865, which approved the regulations of the provincial commissions. The only concern of this legislation was with administrative organization, and not the supervision of excavations.

2   The 1912 Regulations made the timescale even more precise when it specified the beginning of the reign of Carlos I in 1516 as the chronological limit for the recognition of antiquities.

3   Martin Mateo (1966) gives a detailed picture of the administrative organization relating to the historical heritage up to 1966.

4   García de Enterria (1983) appears to take Massimo Severo Giannini as the starting point. It should be noticed that the concept of judicial relation is used here without the anti-liberal connotations that it acquired with Savigny. The intention is to extract a conceptual definition that may contribute to the understanding of the convergent positions of the state and the individual on the subject of the cultural heritage, without denying the subjective rights that the latter has acquired.

5   The *Junta Superior de Excavaciones y Exploraciones Arqueológicas* consists of 11 academic members who specialize in history or fine arts, are university professors and members of the *Cuerpo Facultativo de Museos*, or are people of well-established reputation in the world of archaeology.

6   The *Junta Superior de Arte Rupestre* consists of a Chairman and between eight and 12 ordinary members. Its secretary is the Director of the Museum and Research Centre of Altamira. Nominations are made by the Ministry of Culture on the basis of proposals from the General Director of Fine Arts and Archives.

7   The influence of the so-called New Archaeology is clear, especially as it has been represented in Spain through papers published in *Revista de Arqueología* (Brothwell & Higgs 1982).

8   Archaeological survey on the surface; archaeological survey with stratigraphic survey; archaeological survey under water; reproduction and direct study of rock art; systematic archaeological excavation under water; systematic archaeological excavation; archaeological consolidation; archaeological restoration; archaeological restitution; archaeological works involving enclosure, fencing and covering; archaeological work involving graphic documentation (planimetric, photographic and other audio-visual means); and the study of archaeological materials deposited in museums belonging to the *Comunidad Autónoma*.

References

Benitez de Lugo, F. 1983. Las excavaciones arqueológicas y los museos en la Ley del Patrimonio artístico nacional de 1933. *Boletin del ANABAD* **2**.

Brothwell, D. & E. Higgs (eds) 1982. *Ciencia en Arqueología*. México: Fondo de Cultura Economica.

Diez-Picazo, L. & A. Gullon 1981. *Sistema de Derecho Civil*, 2nd edn, vol. III, 221–3. Madrid: Tecnos.

Espin, D. 1968. *Manual de Derecho Civil Español*, 3rd edn, Vol. II, 111–4. Madrid: Revista de Derecho Privado.

Estella Izquierdo, V. 1975. El Patrimonio Histórico-Artístico en la jurisprudencia. *Revista de Administración Pública* **76**, 135–9.

Fernández, T. R. 1978. La legislación española sobre el patrimonio histórico-artístico. Balance de la situación de cara a su reforma. *Revista de Derecho Urbanístico* **60**, 13–36.

García de Enterria, E. 1983. Consideraciones sobre una nueva legislación del patrimonio artístico, histórico, y cultural. *Civitas: Revista de Derecho Administrativo* **39**, 575–91.

García-Escudero, P. & B. Pendas 1986. *Régimen jurídico del Patrimonio Histórico Español (Análisis sistemático de la Ley 16/1985, de 25 de Junio)*. Madrid: Ministerio de Cultura.

Martin Mateo, R. 1966. La propiedad monumental. *Revista de Administración Pública* **49**, 49–100.

Muñoz Machado, S. 1982. *Derecho Público de las Comunidades Autónomas*, Vol. I, 574–600. Madrid: Civitas.

Perez-Luño, A. E. 1984. Articulo 46. In *Comentarios a las leyes políticas. Constitución española de 1978*, O. Alzaga (ed.), Vol. IV, 285–9. Madrid: Edersa.

Roca Roca, E. 1976. *El patrimonio artístico y cultural*. Madrid: Instituto de Estudios de la Administración Local.

Tramoyeres, L. 1919. *Legislación vigente en España sobre antigüedades monumentales*. Archivo de Arte Valenciano.

19 *Archaeological heritage management in the USSR*

V. M. MASSON

The organization of archaeology in the USSR, in scientific and administrative terms, is complex, with a number of separate branches associated with different sectors of administration (Fig. 19.1). A planned approach to the concentration and co-ordination of research efforts has resulted in a considerable degree of effectiveness, but the system nevertheless needs constant review and revision in order to take account of new problems that arise and of acquired experience. The present period of restructuring (*perestroika*) and openness (*glasnost*) has provided the opportunity for these problems to be discussed openly by the scientific community; considerable attention is also being paid to problems of heritage and monuments protection, which are intimately linked with archaeology.

Until the 1917 October Revolution, the main archaeological institution in Russia was the Imperial Archaeological Commission, founded in 1859; this became the Russian State Archaeological Commission in 1917. In 1919 the Russian (later the State) Academy for Material Culture was established, in accordance with a decree signed by V. I. Lenin; this institution was renamed the Institute for the History of Material Culture in 1939, and has operated under its present title, the Institute of Archaeology, since 1959, as part of the Academy of Sciences of the USSR.

From the late 1920s young scholars have been developing new methodologies for archaeology, which is considered to form an integral part of the historical sciences, in conformity with Marxist–Leninist philosophy. The initial theoretical bases of Soviet archaeology (Masson 1980, Guening 1982), although being continuously modified and expanded to take account of scientific developments, have nevertheless retained their primary orientation towards the study of economic and social patterns in prehistoric societies.

It is not by chance that many of these principles can be detected in the systematic and structuralist terminology of the so-called 'New Archaeology', which began in the USA and is often looked upon as a 'revolution' in archaeology. Starting with the premise that archaeology is a branch of history, the first Soviet Marxist archaeologists sought to study the total archaeological record, not merely the luxury goods that had hitherto been the object of archaeological study, in order to understand their functions as well as their typologies; at the same time they undertook multidisciplinary field investigations of archaeological sites. Another basic premise of Soviet

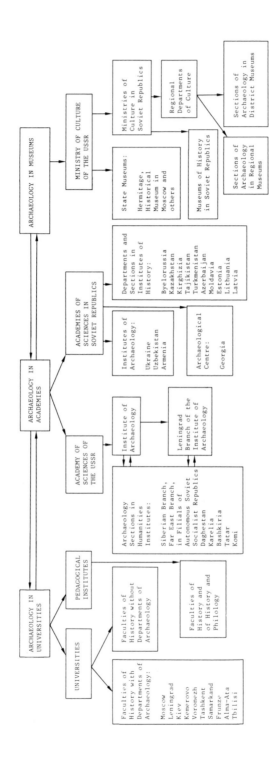

Figure 19.1 The organization of archaeology in the USSR.

archaeology was that of the fundamentally progressive character of history and of the associated causal relationship between culture and its roots, its social structure and the productive forces that motivated it. In this way it has been possible since the 1930s to open up broad perspectives in historical reconstruction on the basis of the archaeological record. The recognition of the rôle of productive forces and relationships as being fundamental mechanisms in the historical process has resulted in particular attention being paid to the socio-economic aspects of ancient societies, and especially to technology, and to tools and implements. This latter consideration has formed the basis for the technique of microwear analysis created by S. A. Semenov. The same principle underlay the large-scale excavations of habitation sites and settlements, which are seen as providing the best reflection of the social and economic structures of prehistoric societies.

From the organizational point of view, archaeology as a science in the USSR has followed three distinct lines of development, each connected with a separate administrative structure. Thus, academic research archaeology ('academy archaeology') is the province of the Academy of Sciences of the USSR (AS USSR) and of the Academies of Sciences in the Soviet Socialist Republics. Archaeological teaching and research at the tertiary level ('university archaeology') has been developed by the universities and specialized institutes, and in particular by the pedagogical institutes that come under the aegis of the Ministry of Higher Education of the USSR and the equivalent Ministries of the Soviet Republics. Finally, there are the archaeological bodies attached to museums, which come under the Ministry of Culture ('museum archaeology').

In respect of scientific research potential, personnel and output (including publication), academy archaeology is in the premier place, employing no fewer than 1500 scientific and technical workers. The main institution is the Institute of Archaeology of the AS USSR (60th Anniversary of the Institute of Archaeology 1980), which has been based in Moscow since 1945, when the archaeological departments in Leningrad were absorbed into the Institute's Leningrad Branch. The AS USSR has a number of regional branches, situated in the Russian Soviet Federative Socialist Republics (RSFSR) of Tatar, Bashkiria, Dagestan and Komi. All the institutes devoted to the humanities have archaeological sections or departments, and there are archaeological laboratories in some of these, such as the Siberian Branch at Novosibirsk.

Institutes of Archaeology have been established by the Academies of Sciences in three Soviet Republics – Uzbekhistan, the Ukraine and Armenia. The Georgian Academy of Sciences has a large archaeological centre which functions independently, though without the status of an institute. In other Republics archaeological departments or sections operate as components of the Institutes of History of the Academies; in some cases there are separate sections for prehistoric and medieval archaeology. The Institute of History of the Kazakh Academy has an archaeological museum within its structure.

The AS USSR is designated the headquarters of the sciences for the whole country by government decree; its main task is the co-ordination of all of the scientific institutions in the USSR. University archaeology occupies the second tier in this system. Archaeological work is carried out both by the universities and by the institutes of the Ministry of Higher Education of the USSR and the corresponding Ministries in the Soviet Republics. Certain universities also have special departments of archaeology where the training of students is accompanied by research and fieldwork; there are departments of this type in the Universities of Moscow and Leningrad, and in those situated in the capitals of the Soviet Republics. In certain regional universities Departments of Archaeology have been set up as a result of the initiative and enthusiasm of teaching staffs – at Voronezh and Kemerovo, for example. Archaeological research is also conducted at universities and institutes which do not possess special Departments of Archaeology; in such cases this work is usually carried out within Departments of the History of the USSR or in archaeological laboratories. The obligatory participation of all history students in archaeological fieldwork for a three-week period is an essential element in all of these courses.

A great deal of archaeological research is carried out in the museums administered by the Ministry of Culture. The major state museums, such as the Hermitage in Leningrad and the State Museum of History in Moscow, offer the greatest potential for work of this kind, and they have long traditions of archaeological research. Only limited archaeological research can be carried out by the smaller museums, and this is usually with the object of enlarging their collections. They often make use of other sources of funding, however, such as the New Project Area design foundations.

This complex and devolved structure of archaeological research is, on the whole, a stable and traditional one, covering a broad range of archaeological studies based on a constant increase in data yield. Its success can be judged by the fact that in the early 1970s some 3000 archaeological publications appeared annually in the USSR, according to the records of the library of the Leningrad Branch of the Institute of Archaeology AS USSR. If this is taken together with the number of permits to excavate ('open lists') issued for work in the RSFSR, which grew from 116 in 1951 to 595 in 1978, it will be seen that there is a marked trend towards decentralization in Soviet archaeology. In the late 1950s nearly half of these permits were granted to scientific workers of the Institute of Archaeology (including the Leningrad Branch), but in the 1970s they received only one-quarter of them. It should also be borne in mind that permits to excavate in the Soviet Republics are issued by regional official bodies.

Short reports on recent archaeological discoveries in the USSR are concentrated in the annual publication *Archaeological discoveries*, which has been published since 1966 by the Institute of Archaeological AS USSR. Similar annual reports are also published in a number of the Soviet Republics, under various titles. *Archaeological work in Tadjikistan* is published in Dyushanbe, and eight surveys of recent discoveries under the title *Kara-Kum antiquities* have appeared in Ashkhabad. *Archaeology*, published by

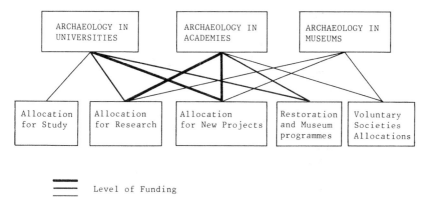

| ARCHAEOLOGY IN UNIVERSITIES | ARCHAEOLOGY IN ACADEMIES | ARCHAEOLOGY IN MUSEUMS |

| Allocation for Study | Allocation for Research | Allocation for New Projects | Restoration and Museum programmes | Voluntary Societies Allocations |

Level of Funding

Figure 19.2   The funding of archaeology in the USSR.

the Ukrainian Institute of Archaeology, is a quarterly magazine, but the main periodical is *Soviet Archaeology*, issued by the Institute of Archaeology AS USSR.

Standardization and the introduction of new materials have created substantial difficulties. In the late 1950s the Institute of Archaeology AS USSR began the publication of a multi-volume series, the *Code of archaeological resources*. It was originally intended that this should consist of some 400 volumes; however, with the publication of some tens of volumes the realization of the overall project has been seen to be more complicated than was first thought. The 20-volume *Archaeology of the USSR* is currently being published as a synthetic survey, which will form the high-quality basis for the ancient and medieval history of all of the peoples of the multinational USSR. The three-volume *Archaeology of the Ukraine SSR*, published in Kiev, is now on its second edition. Similar single-volume publications have appeared in the Pre-Baltic Republics, but preparatory work is still in progress for a companion volume dealing with the archaeology of Central Asia.

Soviet archaeology and its management are financed from a variety of sources (see Fig. 19.2). Both the Academy of Sciences and the Ministries of Higher Education are responsible for the financial planning of scientific research in academies and universities. The financial system is a rigid one which has tended to increase over the past decade; it corresponds with the approved five-year plan of any given institution. Within the AS USSR the Institute of Archaeology forms part of the History Section, in which the main research themes for the current five-year plan relate to primitive society, the evolution of slavery, and the medieval period. Considerable attention is being paid to the preparation of basic synthetic works in the Soviet Republics, in the form of multivolume academic histories of the Republics. The first two volumes of the *History of the Moldavian SSR* and the *History of the Kirghizian SSR* have recently been published, containing many contributions by archaeologists. It is regrettable that programmes of fieldwork have not been related to these themes, with the result that substantial financial resources have been dissipated on minor projects.

In the past 20 years archaeological field investigations in the New Project Areas have constituted the second most important source of funding. To meet the increasing demands of the construction organizations, museum archaeologists have been recruited and institutes and universities have organized special project teams and laboratories, employing additional staff at the expense of the construction organizations.

Another source of funding for archaeology has been the restoration programmes at ancient monuments and in historic urban buildings and complexes, where these are being converted into museums in order to increase their appeal for tourists. Although there has been a considerable increase in such projects, which come under the Ministry of Culture, over the past decade, the way in which they have been carried out has in some cases been found unacceptable in terms of scientific validity and quality of implementation, and as a result they have attracted criticism in public and academic circles. Archaeologists are taking part in projects of this kind in order to improve their authenticity and their validity in terms of the information about ancient culture and history that they can yield. Successful work of this nature that can be cited includes excavations by the Institute of Archaeology of the Academy of Sciences of the Ukrainian SSR in Kiev, and that by the Leningrad Branch of the Institute of Archaeology AS USSR in Vyborg and Ivangorod. An extensive programme of archaeological participation in projects in Moscow has been prepared under the guidance of the Institute of Archaeology AS USSR.

Since fieldwork forms part of the educational process, it is possible to make use of university funds for student projects. It should also be noted that voluntary associations for the protection of historical and cultural monuments often subsidize archaeological programmes. These are primarily concerned with the recording of monuments and the compilation of archaeological maps. A vast project aimed at compiling an archaeological map that will cover all districts in the Republic was carried out by the local voluntary association in Uzbekhistan, and the archaeological map of the Tashkent region has already been published.

Archaeological work in the New Project Areas is very typical of Soviet archaeology (Masson 1983). Planning and carrying out projects of this kind is only possible in a Socialist country implementing an integrated policy which includes concern for the cultural heritage. The legislative basis of this archaeological structure and policy is the clauses in the Constitution of the USSR which relate to state ownership of all land, and the corresponding obligation laid upon the state to protect and make proper use of the land and the mineral wealth that it contains. Soviet archaeology, which forms part of the sciences in this Socialist country, is responsible for performing this function so far as cultural monuments of the past are concerned. Direct threats are often created to the cultural heritage, and in particular to archaeological sites and monuments, as a result of expansion in national economic activity. In such cases the law requires that these monuments should be investigated by specialists, the finds assigned to the appropriate museums, and in special cases the most important monuments to be reconstructed elsewhere, and all this at the expense of the construction organization concerned. State legislation is continually being revised and improved, in the same way that research techniques are kept under constant review.

In 1923 urban development in Samarkand resulted in the first study being made of the archaeological deposits in the ancient centre of Central Asia. The first field project directly linked with a construction project, the Volga-Don expedition, was organized in 1929 by the State Academy for the History of Material Culture. Archaeologists supervised the construction of the Dnieper hydroelectric power station and the Moscow Metro. Since the State Decree on 'The protection of archaeological monuments' was promulgated on 10 February 1934, New Project Areas have acquired particular significance. The Decree provided for the obligatory scientific investigation of those archaeological monuments where destruction was inevitable. In the 1930s extensive archaeological investigations were carried out on all main state constructions works, from the Belomor–Baltic Canal to the Fergana Valley in Central Asia (Meshchaninov 1934). Special instructions were issued in respect of these works, and a series of reports on the results were published. Archaeological work in the New Project Areas is currently governed by the law on 'The protection and use of cultural and historical monuments', adopted by the Supreme Soviet of the USSR on 29 October 1976. This law lays down that construction, land reclamation and other projects must be carried out in co-ordination with the state organizations for the protection of monuments.

The archaeological institutes have set up special sections to carry out this work. In this way archaeological fieldwork by the academic institutes is integrated into economic planning, which imposes special demands with regard to organization and to completion dates. At the same time the concentration of archaeological fieldwork in areas of extensive construction permits the database to be enlarged, providing opportunities for fundamental research in connection with planned or current projects. Investigations in the New Project Areas are characterized by a reciprocal relationship between national economic development and scientific research, a new rôle for Soviet archaeology. A cycle of fundamental research–detailed study–fieldwork has been evolved which reverses the traditional process: this is one of the unusual features of present-day science, where production furnishes an extended experimental framework.

An example of how this works is the archaeological investigations in the construction zone of the Krasnoyarsk hydroelectric power station, carried out over 15 years by the Leningrad Branch of the Institute of Archaeology AS USSR. This constituted a major advance in both qualitative and quantitative terms in the understanding of the prehistory of this region. The local variants of the Upper Palaeolithic culture, the remarkable Okounev sites of the early 2nd millennium BC, were discovered, the latest of them producing the expressive reliefs on stone slabs, the subjects of which have been compared by specialists with subjects in Indo-European mythology. An enormous amount of material was found relating to the early nomadic culture of the 6th to the 3rd centuries BC, vividly depicting the mounted warriors of that period.

Extensive archaeological investigations in areas of land reclamation have thrown light on the dynamics of land-use in specific ecological contexts (*Archaeological Investigations, Leningrad* 1985). The present vast cultivated areas were originally exploited by man in very different cultural and economic conditions; for example, in the steppe zone of the Eurasian region of the USSR the current level of scientific and technological achievement permits enormous areas to be included in a single agricultural cycle, lands which were occupied by discrete hunter–fisher communities in the Stone Age and were widely settled by cattle breeders in the Palaeometal Age. Archaeologists were first able to study the funerary sites of these cultures in the region between Moldavia and the Volga thanks to fieldwork in the New Project Areas. Data obtained in this way by Ukrainian archaeologists have shown that the density of population in the lower Dnieper regions reached its maximum in the second half of the 2nd millennium BC.

In the Asian part of the USSR population optima in the steppe zone have been demonstrated to correspond with the early and late nomadic periods, as a result of long-term investigations carried out by Leningrad archaeologists in the Krasnoyarsk region, and especially in Khakasii. In most of the regions of southern Kazakhstan and in Central Asia the situation was different. Land previously known to have been under cultivation in prehistory is now being farmed intensively. Of particular importance here is the complex study of archaeological sites, with the object not only of excavating protected sites, but also of making a comprehensive survey of them in order to be able to reconstruct the ancient land-use systems and to determine the reasons for their decay. This kind of investigation results in the formulation of specific recommendations related to the future use of these lands.

The study of archaeological sites is closely related with their protection and subsequent use (Bader 1969). The basic strategy for the study of such monuments is a tripartite progression: conserve–study–use. Soviet archaeology plays an important rôle in this process, although the work of protection and presentation is the responsibility of departments of the Ministries of Culture of the USSR and of the Soviet Republics. These Ministries have specialist departments of protection and restoration that are engaged in the evaluation of monuments and in conservation and restoration projects. Associations for the Protection of Historical and Cultural Monuments have played a leading part over the past 15 years in the process of compiling inventories of such monuments. It has become a regular practice for the 'commitment to protection' entered into by organizations with monuments on their land to be registered in this way. In spite of this it is not uncommon for monuments to be destroyed; this results from inadequate guidance combined with technocratic overzealousness related to bogus economic targets. The scientific body which oversees this work in the Ministry of Culture of the USSR is the Scientific and Methodological Council for the Protection of Historic and Cultural Monuments, which is made up of eminent scientists, architects and public figures. The Council is responsible for the development of scientific and methodological aspects of monuments protection, conservation and restoration; it also controls all work of this kind over the whole of the USSR. Its rôle is an especially important one, since restoration organizations are sometime under financial pressures which lead them to neglect quality in their work and to ignore scientifically based recommendations, which in turn results in severe criticism from public opinion and the mass media.

The state protection bodies hold conferences and meetings and publish articles and proceedings. A special conference was held in 1982 at Yerevan on the protection of archaeological deposits in large towns, which is an important problem for urban centres that have been occupied continuously for many centuries, and where hasty building operations may cause irremediable damage to archaeological monuments. After the 1966 earthquake in Tashkent extensive control was exercised over the archaeological layers that were to be destroyed in the course of reconstruction; however, this was an exceptional situation where there was full support for the construction organizations involved. Similar measures, though on a more systematic basis, are in operation in the Soviet Pre-Baltic Republics; they are administered by urban councils and their architectural departments. The Scientific and Methodological Council recommends that, where development takes place in historic town centres, archaeological investigations must take place in order to evaluate the archaeological potential and the extent of necessary supporting studies. This work is being carried out in the historic town centre of Vyborg by the Leningrad Branch of the Institute of Archaeology AS USSR.

Archaeological parks in the USSR are open-air museums, which combine opportunities for protection, study and presentation. They are usually based on sites that have been thoroughly excavated and studied, and where archaeological research has not yet been completed. The land is reserved from agriculture or other forms of land use by means of a state order and is transferred to Ministries of Culture or, more rarely, the Academies of Sciences in the Soviet Republics, to ensure that the sites are not damaged further. The work of restoration and conservation required is carried out by special organizations of the appropriate Ministry of Culture. Visitors can see the work of conservation in progress. There are a large number of such national parks in the USSR, some purely based on prehistoric sites and others on sites of the historic period. They form part of a larger unit, the general directorate of museums in the relevant region – in the Krasnodar Territory, for example. The national parks based on monuments and sites from the classical period on the northern shores of the Black Sea, such as Olbia, Tanais, Khersonese and others, are well known. In the southern Urals a national park has been established at Shul'gan-Tash around a cave with Palaeolithic wall paintings, though it is still only protected, without public access.

The conservation of ruined buildings and the degree of reconstruction laid down by those organizations responsible for their protection is a complex problem from the scientific and methodological points of view: the scientific community is unanimous in its opposition to over-reconstruction. Extensive and ill-considered restoration work of this kind has been carried out at the Urartu settlement of Yerebuni, near Yerevan, the scientific and artistic value of which has been justifiably called into question by specialists. Another Urartu settlement, Kamir-Blur, was investigated and the upper parts of the stone walls of the excavated structure were reconstructed by traditional methods but using cement, which was clearly differentiated from the original elements; this is an excellent example of this technique. Conservators working in Central Asia encounter many technical problems in dealing with mud-brick structures. They are still using techniques such as coating with synthetic resins in their work. The most acceptable method is to heighten the ancient walls using modern unbaked bricks, as was done at Kamir-Blur, a method still in use in Central Asia. At Pendjikent, near Samarkand, modern-style unbaked brick is used, which again allows the ancient fabric to be distinguished immediately from the modern. Conservators working on the Parthian settlement of Old Nisa, near Ashkhabad, are making mud-bricks in the ancient form.

Another method currently being used involves the erection of a modern building over archaeological sites; the most noteworthy example is probably the building over the Upper Palaeolithic settlement of Kostenki, which was put up by the district authorities. A similar conservation experiment that is worthy of note is at the Upper Palaeolithic settlement of Avdeevo, in the Briansk District; the wooden building, which is not perhaps outstanding in design but is very serviceable, was erected over the archaeological site using the funds of the local *kolkhoz* (collective farm).

It will be seen that archaeology and its related scientific and resource management services in the USSR constitute a complex system with a tradition all of its own. It may not function perfectly in every respect, but it is a vital and continuing activity which requires constant expansion and improvement.

The administrative fragmentation of archaeology between academies, universities and museums may result in unnecessary duplication and hinder the exchange of information and the concentration of effort on the most fruitful sites and research objectives. There is the further problem of duplication of activities by the Academies of Sciences of the Soviet Republics. In this regard the hope for the future lies in the co-ordination of archaeological research in three successive stages: exchange of information, co-operation (especially in field projects) and mutual solution of problems, using programmed targets as the superior vehicle for co-ordination. A planned experiment is in progress in the Central Asia–Kazakhstan region, where the Scientific Council on Problems in the Field of Archaeology in Central Asia and Kazakhstan was set up by the History Section of the AS USSR in 1970 (Zadneprovskii 1982). The Council organizes regular problem- and theme-orientated meetings, and these have led to the organization of similar symposia within the framework of international co-operation – three Soviet–American (Boston 1981, Samarkand 1983, Washington 1986), three Soviet-French (Dushanbe 1982, Paris 1985, Samarkand 1986) and two Soviet–Indian (Allahabad 1982, Ashkhabad 1984). In certain cases fieldwork expeditions are organized jointly by several institutions: thus, the Pedjikent expedition is run by the Leningrad Branch of the Institute of Archaeology AS USSR, the State Hermitage Museum and the History Institute of the AS of the Tadjiki SSR. In principle many forms of co-ordination exist in an embryonic form. It is however, impossible to ignore the inadequate level of exchange of basic information between some of the Caucasus Republics: this results in unsatisfactory investigation of the ancient cultures of the region, which in some cases span the modern administrative boundaries.

Large-scale investigations in the New Project Areas have brought considerable problems to light. The academic institutions designated to carry out the basic work are understaffed for dealing with these huge projects. It has been proposed that a special organization to carry out this work should be set up within the Ministry of Culture, but it is doubtful whether a complicated administrative system of this kind would be the correct solution. A better approach would be to use individual laboratories set up by the different institutions in order to achieve specific goals over a predetermined period. There are also difficulties associated with the storage of archaeological material, especially in the Academy and in the universities. One very important area is the improvement of methods of field investigation, recording and documentation. There is little harmonization between these as a result of the ever-increasing number of excavations being carried out, especially in the New Project Areas, where restrictions are imposed on the archaeologists by the construction schedules.

In scientific research, with its three essential components of experiment, description and interpretation, field excavation provides a basic database which supplies the foundations for research. Unlike historians, who study documents, archaeologists destroy the raw material of their research as they investigate it, and in doing so sever the links between artefacts in the process of transforming the true ancient culture into the 'museum' culture that is studied by archaeologists. If the methodology and the documentation on an excavation are not prepared with care, the eventual researcher has at his disposal for study an artefact that might just as well have been brought to light by an agricultural worker or a bulldozer driver. In recent years the Institute of Archaeology AS USSR has done a great deal to improve the quality of fieldwork. New instructions and guidelines have been produced which contain detailed recommendations for different aspects of the conduct of excavations in varying field conditions, such as the use of mechanical excavators and bulldozers with wide tracks.

Finally, it is necessary to emphasize the problems relating to scientific and technical progress in archaeology. Interpretations and syntheses dating back to the 1950s, when special laboratories were established in Moscow and Leningrad, are no longer adequate or acceptable. Archaeology continues to pose many problems in theory and methodology. The main objective must be to combine the creative Marxist–Leninist philosophy with modern methods of scientific analysis, and this must include consideration of the technical reliability of the latter. Archaeologists must react positively to the modern world, which has seen the growth of the ideological, political and educational functions of the social sciences. The long traditions of Soviet archaeology, its wealth of accumulated experience and its human potential provide all the necessary prerequisites for the solution of these and many other problems that continue to arise in the ever-evolving process of archaeology.

References

Arkheologicheskie issledovanie v zonakh melioratsi [Archaeological investigations in reclamation zones]. In *Itogi izouchenia i perspektivy ikh intensificatsii*. 1985, Leningrad.

Bader, O. N. 1969. Okhrana i propaganda arkheologicheskikh pamiatnikov v SSSR i aktualnye voprosy [Protection and presentation of archaeological monuments in the USSR and current problems]. In *Tezisy dokladov na sessii Otdelenia Istorii AN SSSR, posviashchennoi 50-letiu leninskogo dekreta o sozdanii RAIMK*. Leningrad: Institute of Archaeology.

Guenning, V. F. 1982. *Ocherki po istorii sovetskoi arkheologii [Essays on the history of Soviet archaeology]*. Kiev.

Institutu Arkheologii 60 let [The 60th anniversary of the Institute of Archaeology], *Kratkie soobshchenie Instituta Arkheologii AN SSSR*. **163**, 1980.

Masson, V. M. 1980. U istokov teoreticheskoi mysli teoretichesko arkheologii [The sources of the theoretical concepts of theoretical archaeology], *Kratkie soobshcheniia Instituta Arkheologii AN SSSR*. **163**.

Masson, V. M. 1983. Arkheologicheskie raboty na novostroikakh i izuchenie drevnikh kultur [Archaeological investigations in the New Project Areas and the study of ancient cultures]. In *Drevnie kultury evraziyskikh stepei. Po materialam arkheologicheskikh rabot na novostroikakh*. Moscow.

Meshchaninov, N. N. 1934. Arkheologicheskie raboty na novostroikakh [Archaeological investigations in the New Project Areas], *Problemy istorii dokapitalisticheskikh obshchestv*. **5**.

Zadneprovskii, J. A. 1982. Desiat let raboty Soveta po problemam arkheologii Srednei Azii i Kazakhstana [Ten years of the Council on Archaeological Problems in Central Asia and Kazakhstan]. In *Narody Azii i Afriki*.

20 A review of the South African cultural heritage legislation, 1987

GABEBAH ABRAHAMS

Historical development

A movement towards the preservation of the South African cultural heritage was initiated with the founding of the South African National Society in 1905. The Society soon gained ground, forming branches in Grahamstown, Durban and Pietermaritzburg. The main aims were to foster an appreciation of the country's heritage, and to make the public aware of the vandalism occurring on certain sites and of the need to rectify the situation through effective legislation. The first protective law was the Bushmen Relics Protection Act No. 22 of 1911, introduced largely in response to the rapid increase in the export of prehistoric rock paintings and engravings. As the interest of local and overseas scientists grew in the wealth of prehistoric rock paintings and engravings in the country, expeditions were sent to collect examples, resulting in much damage, destruction, and the removal and loss of many specimens. The 1911 Act deemed damage or disturbance to these sites a punishable offence. Although an important precedent, the Act was rather inadequate, and confined only to the protection of rock art and the contents of caves, rock shelters, graves and shell middens.

In 1923 the Natural Historical and Monuments Act No. 6 was introduced. This Act provided for the appointment of an Historical Monuments Commission. This Commission, however, was not supported with funding for conservation, nor was it given the powers to proclaim National Monuments. In 1934 these deficiencies were partly remedied by the introduction of the Natural and Historical Monuments, Relics and Antiques Act No. 4 and repeal of the previous two Acts of 1911 and 1923. The 1934 Act empowered the Commission to recommend the proclamation of any monument, relic or antique to the Minister. Furthermore, the destruction or alteration of a proclaimed monument without a permit was prohibited. This legislation also embodied the first attempt to protect antiques from export without a permit. At the time, however, the Commission consisted of only two members of staff, and control over the export of antiques was only exercised in 1946 when a few export permits were issued (Rudner 1982, p. 75). The 1934 Act also empowered the Commission to control access to proclaimed areas and to issue permits with subclauses for excavations of archaeological and palaeontological sites.

The 1934 Act was subsequently amended by Act No. 9 of 1937 and that of Act No. 13 of 1967, mainly to increase the powers of the Commission. It was finally replaced by the War Graves and National Monuments Act No. 28 of 1969, which brought about several changes, particularly with regard to the establishment, administration, duties and responsibilities of a new National Monuments Council which replaced the Historical Monuments Commission (Oberholster 1980). More supporting staff was made available, the Council was given the legal power and funds to purchase properties for preservation, to supply some financial aid to owners of National Monuments for restoration work, and to recommend the declaration of property, with or without the owner's agreement, but subject to a final decision by the Minister of National Education. Further amendments to the Act were introduced through No. 22 of 1970, No. 30 of 1971, No. 63 of 1975 and No. 35 of 1979. These changes include details on the objectives and functions of the Council, the concept of marking the monuments with bronze badges, and the preservation, repair and restoration of both declared and provisionally declared monuments. Further amendments have followed through No. 21 of 1980, No. 13 of 1981 and, most recently, the War Graves and National Monuments Amendment Act No. 11 of 1986.

Current legislation

Organization and administration of the National Monuments Council

The current War Graves and National Monuments Amendment Act mainly provides for the establishment of a National Monuments Council directly under the authority of the Minister of National Education in the central government. The Council is responsible for the declaration of national monuments and cultural objects and for the repair, maintenance and protection of the country's cultural heritage, subject to the decision of the Minister.

The main objective of the Council outlined in the 1986 Act (Section 2) is to co-ordinate activities related to the preservation of the cultural heritage. This involves a number of different duties (Oberholster 1980). Preservation is primarily achieved through proclamation. The procedure involved is described below. In order to ensure the protection and preservation of important monuments, the Council has the power to purchase or to apply for a state subsidy to assist with their restoration or maintenance. The Council has been granted the right to establish committees, for particular purposes, to assist with their many and varied functions (Section 4). Committees have been appointed, such as those to deal with finance, publicity, permits and wording of plaques. The Council may delegate its powers to members, committees or officers. Along these lines the Council has developed liaison with other conservation bodies, such as the Simon van der Stel Foundation, the Architectural Heritage Committee, the Robertson Trust, Captrust, The SA Town Planning Institute, and local historical societies (National Monuments Council 1981, 1985). Decisions made by its delegates and not approved of by the Council may be amended or withdrawn at any time (Section 7). In addition, the Council has introduced a system of Honorary Curators, many of whom are also attached to the archaeological discipline and who, through their experience and activities, provide a direct input into the Council policies. The Council or any person authorized by them may, at any reasonable time, inspect a property in order to investigate or carry out their objectives (Section 14).

An important aspect of the Council's work is to encourage and promote the preservation of monuments through the media (Section 5). This is presently attempted through publication, workshops and congresses on conservation (Oberholster 1980). The Council's achievements in this sphere can clearly be seen in its annual reports. These reports are also specifically requested by the Minister with an annual financial analysis open to auditing by the Auditor-General (Section 9). As a statutory body, the Council receives funds for its administration from the state, and it may receive monies from other sources (Section 9). The Council is exempt from paying duties, taxes and fees in respect of documents required for any of its transactions (Section 15).

General proclamation procedure

A Council member first investigates the historical, architectural and aesthetic importance of a building or site brought to their attention (Oberholster 1980). A report on the findings is submitted to a regional committee. The committee comments in support of or against proclamation to the full Council. If the Council approves, then consent is sought from the owner for provisional proclamation. Final approval rests with the Minister of National Education. Declarations are then published in the *Government Gazette* and essentially lodged with the Registrar of Deeds to be noted in the relevant registers (Section 13). It is obligatory to inform the Council of the sale, exchange or letting of any monument (Section 12). The Council has the right to loan any monument under its control to a museum or other public institution (Section 5).

If the owners of a property do not consent to proclamation, then the Council is obliged to serve a written notice on them, advising them of the proposed declaration and calling for objections to be lodged with the Council within one month of the date of service of the notice (Section 10). The case is then finally referred to the Minister. The Minister has the right to override all objections, especially in warranted cases of important buildings or features. On the other hand, the Minister is also capable of withdrawing any provisional declarations noted in the *Government Gazette* (Section 5).

A proclaimed monument remains the property of the owner, who is not obliged to allow entry to visitors, except to Council representatives on official business at reasonable hours. By agreement with the owner, an access road to the monument may be constructed. The Council should ensure that the surroundings of a monument do not obstruct a view of the monument (Section 5).

Prehistoric remains, fossils and meteorites

The present legal boundary between prehistory and history is taken to be 1652, the year of the Dutch settlement at the Cape, even though it is known that earlier historic records, predating 1652, of voyages of discovery do exist and that the history of areas further north, such as in the Transvaal, is only noted much later (Rudner 1982a, p. 5).

Prior to 1652, however, the Act covers the prohibition of damage, destruction, excavation, alteration, removal from its original site, or the export in respect of prehistoric artefacts or sites (Section 12). Meteorites, fossils, rock paintings, engravings, implements, ornaments, structures and anthropological or archaeological contents of graves, caves, rock shelters, middens, shell mounds or other sites used by indigenous or visiting people before 1652 are specifically noted. This part of the Act still ties in strongly with the 1969 legislation, which in turn is related to the original 1911 legislation that came about mainly as a result of the vandalism and export of many of the local rock paintings and engravings in the late 19th century.

The wealth of meteorites, fossils, rock paintings and engravings in South Africa provides the research data of many international scientists. The areas covered by rock paintings, engravings, meteorites and fossils are vast, and are often in very isolated locations. Under these circumstances the protective legislation has little or no effect, and the importance of conservation education manifests itself as a priority. Twenty thousand painted images were recorded from sites in the Natal Drakensberg by Mazel. He emphasized (Mazel 1982, p. 7) the vital importance and present neglect of public education:

> convincing the general public of the importance of archaeological sites and need for their conservation would indeed represent a major breakthrough in the conservation of archaeological resources and considerably reduce management requirements in the field. Thus it is not stricter laws that are desired but rather the understanding and support of the general public.

The Karoo formations, which extend across most of the country, have provided many important specimens of Permo-Triassic fish, reptiles, mammal-like reptiles and amphibians. In the northern Cape and Transvaal fossils have supplied evidence of some of the earliest Australopithecine hominid remains. Stone artefacts ranging from the crudest chipped cobbles dating back some 1.7 million years to relics of the Later Stone Age and of the first Portuguese explorers lie scattered over the vast fields of South Africa (Rudner 1982a, p. 6).

Under the present legislation these sites are automatically protected. However, the Council may issue permits for scientific research work involving the excavation and removal of artefacts. High standards are ensured by the issue of permits with conditions such as specifications for adequate supervision of excavations, recovery of deposits, recording methods, final reports and the lodging of excavated collections with authorized institutions. These by-laws have been effectively used in the archaeological discipline in South Africa for legal supervision and control, 'a situation which would seem to be unique to our profession' (Hall 1977, p. 272).

Apart from working under permit conditions, another exception to the rule is the effects of mining, engineering and agricultural activities. Under these circumstances a report must be lodged with an authorized cultural institution in order that the removal and safe custody of objects under legislative protection may be discussed (Section 12). In the past farmers often removed cave deposits including bat guano for use as fertilizers (Rudner 1982a, p. 5). Many important sites, such as those at Montagu Cave and at Plettenberg Bay, were subject to this stripping, often including archaeo-logical deposits. In the case of the Plettenberg Bay site, deposits were carted away by ox-wagon and some of the stones were thrown out by the farmers. These stones were later found to bear prehistoric paintings. The legislation exempting the destruction of or damage to archaeological sites through mining engineering or agricultural activities now excludes cave or midden deposits. This is presently prohibited under any circumstances without a permit (Section 12). Unfortunately, most shell middens were depleted along the Cape coastal regions as early as the 17th and 18th centuries, when they were used in the manufacture of lime mortar. During that time the entire Table Bay coast was stripped, and boats were sent as far afield as Saldanha Bay along the west coast to collect shell (Rudner 1982a).

Similarly, many of the relics of the first Portuguese explorers have been lost, whereas only a few of their stone crosses (Padroes) used as markers of their voyages of discovery and inscribed postal stones (under which mail was deposited and collected by passing ships) have been recovered (Abrahams 1985, p. 39). However, most of the areas in which these were found have already been developed, and records of those found since the early 19th century are vague and can never be regained.

Historical sites and antiques

The Act now makes provision for the protection of historical sites. Antiques specified are paintings, prints, documents, deeds, seals, stamps or other objects made of paper that are generally accepted to have been in the country for more than 50 years. Objects of any substance other than paper are also protected if they have been in the country for more than 100 years (Section

12). Furthermore, any movable object may be declared a cultural treasure. As in the case of declared monuments, the Minister may, however, at the request of the owner and after consultation with the Council, withdraw a provisional declaration on cultural treasures noted in the *Gazette* (Section 5).

Although the new Act is a tremendous improvement in legislation, the main drawback experienced by the Council relates to the definition of historical sites which refers to 'any identifiable building or part thereof, marker, milestone, gravestone, landmark or tell older than 50 years' (Section I). For all intents and purposes it is practically impossible for the Council with its present staff to control demolition and alteration to all buildings older than 50 years spread over the entire country. The delegation of power to local authorities has been suggested as a possible solution (Rudner 1986b).

As part of its duties the Council has to compile and maintain a register of immovable property and a national list of cultural treasures. The practical solution to the implementation of this legislation proposed by Rudner & Pistorius (1987) involves closer collaboration between the Council, local authorities and appointed architects in the preparation of lists of buildings worthy of conservation. A book such as that on the architectural and historical background of buildings in central Cape Town (Cape Provincial Institute of Architects 1978) and that on the archaeological potential of listed sites in central Cape Town (Abrahams 1985) could obviously be of use in this respect.

The implications of the legislation related to cultural treasures pose a number of problems (Rudner 1986b). First of all, the criteria used to define cultural treasures require elaboration. Definition in the Act (Section I) describes cultural treasure to mean '. . . any movable property declared under this Act to be a cultural treasure'. This raises the question of whether most of the cultural treasures found in museums should be registered. Private collections must be registered, but many collectors are unwilling, for the sake of security, to allow access to their collections. The registration and description of the many important collections of South African antiques is a major specialized task which cannot be accommodated by the present staff of the Council. Rudner (1982b) has therefore suggested delegation of the duty of compiling a cultural treasure register to art galleries and cultural museums before consultation with the Council. Prior to this, however, the definition will have to be made more explicit.

Graves and memorials

The 1986 War Graves and National Monuments Amendment Act now in operation also provides for the establishment of two committees, the *Burgergraftekomitee* and the British War Graves Committee (Section 3). Their main function is to report to the Council on the desirability of declaring any burial ground or grave a national monument. The Council is bound to declare, maintain, and restore proclaimed burial grounds, graves and gardens of remembrance established and memorials erected by them

(Section 5). A register of information related to graves must be compiled, maintained and published periodically by the Council. The Council may exhume or re-inter the remains of declared graves unless the owner of the land, if a descendant of the buried person, objects to it (Section 5). The War Graves Trust Fund established by the War Graves Act of 1967 continues to exist and to be used under the control of the Council (Section 9).

Whenever possible, archaeologists are now involved in exhumations and re-interment while the remains of graves are accurately recorded. This was the case recently for 18 British soldier burials saved from flooding on the Crocodile River (National Monuments Council 1985, p. 20).

Conservation areas

The proclamation of conservation areas is a very important extention to the legislation which now allows the conservation of public squares, battlefields, landmarks, geological or scientifically important areas and areas of the built-up environment such as streets, villages, mission stations and sur-roundings of monuments. This may be carried out on the grounds of historic, aesthetic or scientific merits, after consultation with the relevant authorities (Section 5). Guidelines may be drawn up to retain the character of an area intact (Section 18), and controls may even include specifications of the scale, design and colour of additional houses on empty plots (Rudner 1986b, p. 2).

Shipwrecks

The South African coastline is an area along which shipwrecks ranging from the mid-16th century to the present are concentrated (Kennedy 1955). It is small wonder that Cape Town was once nicknamed the Cape of Storms, a nightmare to circumnavigating sailors. During the first Dutch occupation of the Cape in the 17th and 18th centuries, many salvage attempts were staged to save both human lives and precious cargo and species on board sinking vessels (Burman 1968). The traumatic and hazardous experiences are ade-quately described in existing references (Kennedy 1955, pp. 1–25). However, it was only with the invention and use of the SCUBA diving apparatus during this century that the salvage of turbulent and previously depth-protected wreck sites has been made possible. This poses a serious threat to the conservation and protection of shipwrecks. These invaluable and relatively unexplored cultural resources are of international importance as a result of the vast trade network which existed during the periods of exploration and colonization.

The plundering of shipwrecks has become increasingly conspicuous with the fast-developing hobby of sports diving and the active formation of local salvage companies which often indulge in indiscriminate exploitation of irreplaceable early wreck sites. It started with a surge of publicity in the 1960s accompanying the discovery of the wreck of the *Fame* (1822) and the excitement aroused by the public auctioning of quantities of gold jewellery and coins from the wreck. Soon to follow were artefacts on sale from the *Het Huis te Crayenstein* (1698), the *Catwyk aan Rhyn* (1786) and large quantities of intact porcelain and other artefacts from the *Middelburg* (1781) and the *Meeressteijn* (1702). Some 20–30 wrecks are known to have been actively exploited from the 1970s to the 1980s. These range from 16th to 20th century sites, including English, French, Portuguese and Dutch vessels (Rudner 1981).

Sad stories of the melting down of bronze cannon and coins, the destructive use of explosives on wreck sites, and the wholesale export and dispersal of salvaged goods are not uncommon (Rudner 1982a, p. 6, 1982b, p. 76). The first legislation proclaiming wreck sites more than 100 years old was introduced in 1981. In an attempt to bring some order into the chaotic situation of shipwreck salvage, the Council issued permits to divers under certain conditions. Permits could only be obtained for scattered wrecks without identifiable structure or stratification, accurate recording techniques of a professional archaeological standard were to be maintained, and half of the artefacts had to be lodged with an authorized museum with whom the salvors were to collaborate.

The situation was, however, fraught with controversy (Rudner 1986d). The commercial divers resisted attempts at conservation of wrecks, since this posed a denial to their financially motivated salvage. The Council and other conservation-oriented bodies were seen to be unable to enforce the legislation and by-laws introduced by them. Lack of communication existed between the Council, commercial divers and archaeologists. None of these groups had the practical experience of having worked together and, in so doing, resolving their differences.

In 1986 the Council placed a moratorium on all salvage. Three shipwreck symposia have been held up to date to encourage communication between divers and archaeologists, and the South African Historical Wreck Society has been formed as a result of divers' interest in maritime archaeology (Rudner 1986a). In accordance with the new Act, the Council may proclaim any wreck older than 50 years. Any abandoned wreck may be placed at the disposal of the Council or a declared institution such as a museum (Section 10). The destruction, damage, alteration to or export of any wreck-related object which has been in territorial waters for more than 50 years is forbidden. Applicants for permits to salvage shipwrecks must first be in possession of a salvage licence, obtained from the Department of Customs and Excise, and a letter confirming collaboration with an authorized museum. All applications must be advertised in the *Government Gazette* to enable counter-claims or objections to be lodged. The Council stipulates that the salvage procedure should be undertaken according to archaeological standards and that the artefacts should be equally divided between the salvor and the collaborating institution (Rudner 1986a, p. 3, 1986c, p. 1).

If a wreck has not been salvaged after a 50-year period and no ownership claims have been received after advertisement in the *Government Gazette*, then the assumption is made that it has been abandoned and is therefore ownerless. Van Meurs (1985, p. 81) suggests that the possibility of ownership claims has not been included as a clear, definite statement in the Act, and should perhaps be specifically included in the legislation. In the case of the British warship HMS *Birkenhead* (1852), the British Government claimed ownership since warships are never abandoned. The right to ownership was denied because the wreck had been sold at auction after the accident. No claims have to date been received for salvage from the British wreck of the *Arniston* (1815) or *Colebrook* (1778), nor for Dutch wrecks such as the *Rygersdal* (1747), the *Meresteyn* (1702), or the *Haerlem* (1747).

Punitive measures

The Council has the right to sue or be sued (Section 2). Contraventions by way of damage, destruction, removal or export of monuments, the prescribed prehistoric and historical artefacts and shipwreck sites and related artefacts, are liable to penalties not exceeding 10 000 South African Rands or to imprisonment for two years, or both. In the case of similar offences related to graves, memorials, gardens of remembrance or failure to comply with permit conditions, fines of 1000 Rands or imprisonment for a period not exceeding 12 months can be imposed on conviction (Section 16).

Discussion

From the historical development of conservation legislation, it is obvious that numerous alterations and extensions have been introduced over time. The legislation has been constantly updated to cope with new problems. Since the establishment of the National Monuments Council, impressive results have been achieved (National Monuments Council 1985). The total number of declared monuments since 1934 now stands at 1281. About 3000 buildings are safeguarded under group conservation. Bronze plaques and badges have been affixed to most of these monuments, including movable objects. The Council has also extended closer ties with numerous organizations covering a wide field. Six regional committees of the Council have now been established, diversifying and simplifying the tasks of the Council.

The future of shipwreck archaeology is an issue currently receiving priority status. A Maritime Museum Advisory Committee has been formed, combining the forces of research scientists and institutions concerned about the state of the discipline. As a result, numerous representations have been forwarded to the central government. A building for the existing maritime collection has been hired, one post for a qualified maritime archaeologist (the first in the country) and four subsidiary posts have been granted, and agreement has been reached with the central government for the establishment of a maritime museum attached to the existing South African Cultural History Museum. During 1988 a concerted effort will be made to draw public support during the 500th anniversary of Bartholomeu Dias's circumnavigation of the Cape (Axelson 1973).

The Maritime Committee has also discussed issues pertaining to the recruitment of suitably qualified staff possibly through importing specialized consultants, encouraging South African postgraduate students studying overseas to return with their expertise, preparing local university departments to initiate training programmes for marine archaeology, the necessary conservation facilities, the survey of shipwreck areas (Deacon 1985) and the compilation of a national register of historic shipwrecks.

Although the new legislation generally promises to be a considerable improvement, four fundamental problems require attention – the lack of staff, implementation of the law, the prevalence of ignorance and apathy, and further legislation. The tasks of the Council have been greatly increased as a result of additional provisions in the new legislation. In particular, the need to compile catalogues of conservation-worthy areas, sites and artefacts is great. In 1986 20 new posts were granted to the Council, but as a result of the present climate of economic recession, ten of these were subsequently withdrawn and the other ten were frozen indefinitely. Under these constraints, assistance and expertise may be gained by delegation of duties to other specialized professionals. More reliance will need to be placed on related bodies and institutions, necessitating much closer liaison and communication with them. Preparatory work such as the detailed and useful catalogue of buildings in central Cape Town (Cape Provincial Institute of Architects 1978, 1986) should be encouraged at research institutions. The provision of sufficient experts and permanent staff at the Council is, however, still essential in order to co-ordinate a number of these projects and to implement the law.

Apart from the dire lack of staff, it appears that conservation legislation is also considered 'an empty threat' (Hall 1977, p. 275, Humphries 1977, p. 284). Court schedules are often tight, and infringements against conservation are considered less important than certain others such as routine criminal actions (Hall 1977, p. 274). Without the facility to police the remains entrusted to the Council, they are seen as, 'being protected virtually in name only' (Sachs & Smith 1981, p. 321). Reported cases are rare. Relevant and useful case histories are even scarcer, and therefore cannot serve as precedents to guide the preparation of a prosecution. However, notorious instances demonstrating the ineffectiveness of the legislation are well circulated. The legal prosecution of offenders to the Act is an unpleasant and undesirable course of action, but setting a precedent is a necessary deterrent which, in the end, may be seen to justify the means.

In addition to the legal course of action, a great deal may be achieved through conservation education, which is at present a grossly neglected aspect of the local education system. Quite simply, there is no formal training-ground for attitudes towards cultural conservation anywhere in South Africa. 'Firstly then, as part of an ongoing programme we need to educate the educators and the politicians, in addition to our children' (Stewart

1984, p. 145). When this has been attained, a far greater proportion of the public will become the built-in custodians of their heritage. Without this support the limited number of conservation scientists face a daunting task.

Even though archaeological sites are mentioned in legislation, there is no specific provision for the opportunity for archaeological investigation during or before industrial development. In the exempted cases, when archaeological sites are exposed in the course of mining, engineering or agricultural activities, a cultural institution should be informed. However, there is no legislative provision allowing the time for an archaeological investigation. There is, furthermore, no provision for the ownership rights of the excavated material, and there is no recognition of the fact that the very activities which are exempted from the Act often present a major threat to the conservation of archaeological and other sites. The basis of the problem which gave birth to the concept of rescue archaeology overseas is the devastating pace of development assisted by highly sophisticated machinery capable of destroying entire landscapes within a matter of a few hours. It is critically important for local conservation legislation to incorporate protection against this worldwide phenomenon of archaeological destruction.

Acknowledgements

My sincere appreciation goes to G. Avery of the South African Museum, J. Rudner of the National Monuments Council, and A. P. Roux of the South African Cultural History Museum for their useful comments on the script. J. Rudner checked the legislative aspects contained in the chapter, T. Zieve executed the typing meticulously, and my husband bore through the pains of the legislation with me.

References

Abrahams, G. 1985. The archaeological potential of central Cape Town. *Munger Africana Library Notes*. California.
Axelson, E. 1973. *Congo to Cape: early Portuguese explorers*. London: Faber & Faber.
Burman, J. 1968. *Strange shipwrecks of the Southern Seas*. Cape Town: Struik.
Cape Provincial Institute of Architects 1978. *Buildings of central Cape Town 1978*, Vols I and II. Cape Town: Provincial Institute of Architects.
Deacon, H. J. 1985. *Report of maritime archaeology in Australia and South Africa*. Unpublished report, Department of Archaeology, University of Stellenbosch, Cape Town.
Government Gazette 1986. *Statutes of the Republic of South Africa*. Cape Town: Government Printers.
Hall, M. 1977. The legal protection of archaeological sites: some problems and suggestions. *South African Museums Association Bulletin* 12, 270–7.
Humphreys, A. J. B. 1977. Reply to Dr M. A. Cluver and Mr Martin Hall. *South African Museums Association Bulletin* 12, 283–6.

Kennedy, R. F. 1955. *Shipwrecks on and off the coasts of southern Africa*. Johannesburg: Johannesburg Public Library.

Mazel, A. D. 1982. Principles for conserving the archaeological resources of the Natal Drakensberg. *South African Archaeological Bulletin* **37**, 7–15.

National Monuments Council 1981. *Annual Report No. 12 for the year ended 31 March 1981*. Cape Town.

National Monuments Council 1985. *Annual Report No. 16 for the year ended 31 March 1985*. Cape Town.

Oberholster, J. J. 1980. Conserving our heritage. In *Our heritage*, B. Basset (ed.). Cape Town: Plate Glass.

Rudner, J. 1981. The legal protection of historical shipwrecks in South Africa. *South African Museums Association Bulletin* **14**, 317–20.

Rudner, J. 1982a. The legal protection of prehistoric and historic relics in South Africa. *South African Archaeological Bulletin* **37**, 5–6.

Rudner, J. 1982b. The legal protection of historical relics in South Africa. *South African Museums Association Bulletin* **15**, 74–7.

Rudner, J. 1986a. New legislation on old shipwrecks. Lecture delivered at Shipwreck Symposium held at the SA Cultural History Museum, 1986.

Rudner, J. 1986b. *The War Graves and National Monuments Amendment Act, 1986*. National Monuments Council memo distributed to Members of the Science Committee.

Rudner, J. 1986c. *Proposed extended salvage legislation*. National Monuments Council memo.

Rudner, J. 1986d. *The legal protection of archaeological and palaeontological sites, as well as of historic shipwrecks and other historic objects in South Africa – problems and policies*. Memo prepared for the annual meeting of the National Monuments Council in Pietermaritzburg.

Rudner, J. & P. Pistorius 1987. *Implications of the 1986 Amendment Act: problems and proposed solutions*. National Monuments Council memo.

Sachs, P. & G. Smith 1981. Shipwrecks and salvage on the Eastern Cape Coast. *South African Museums Association Bulletin* **14**, 320–6.

Stewart, C. T. 1984. Conservation education. *South African Museum Association Bulletin* **16**, 142–6.

Van Meurs, L. H. 1985. *Legal aspects of marine archaeological research*. Institute of Marine Law, University of Cape Town, Special Publication No. 1.

CASE STUDIES

21 *The Cultural Triangle of Sri Lanka*

ROLAND SILVA

The Cultural Triangle comprises the area contained within the three ancient capitals of Anuradhapura (5th century BC to 10th century AD), Polonnaruva (10th to 12th centuries AD), and Kandy (16th to 19th centuries AD), and is located approximately at the centre of the island, to the north of the central hills.

Geographically, Sri Lanka was located between the two major ancient empires of Rome and Peking, with a calculated sailing distance of approximately three months from either capital. Longitudinally, Sri Lanka lies almost on the equator, a promontory at the southern tip of the mainland of Asia. Consequently, any trade or communication between the two major empires would have necessitated a call at the island's ports for sustenance. Cosmas Indicopleustes, a Greek writer of the 6th century, highlighted the strategic location of the island when he referred to the main island port as the 'great emporium', a term that he used rarely in his records. The present excavations and other research have demonstrated the truth of this statement: substantial deposits of Roman coins and Chinese ceramics have been found in the numerous historic sites of the island.

In sailing terms, a three-month journey from Rome or Peking was the convenient timespan for ships to return. The monsoon winds change direction at the equator, and the flow of traffic in the north-east or north-west had to take wind changes and other natural factors into account. For this reason Sri Lanka has been blessed with much trade and commerce throughout its history, and with it the benefits of substantial profit. The revenues from this trade were invested in the building of imposing religious and secular monuments: by the time of the collapse of the Roman empire in the 4th century AD Sri Lanka could boast of having in its capital, Anuradhapura, three *stupas* which were the third, fourth and sixth tallest buildings in the world, surpassed only by the pyramids at Giza. The pinnacles of these *stupas* were the focal points of large Buddhist monasteries which could stand comparison with the biggest religious establishments anywhere in the world; some of them housed as many as 5000 monks. The cities of Anuradhapura, Polonnaruva and Sigiriya (now on the World Heritage List) were extensive and densely populated. Anuradhapura, for example, had nearly 150 000 inhabitants, with a monastic population of nearly 14 000, and covered an area of more than 12 square miles (31 km^2). This is the cultural property that the Unesco-Sri Lanka Project of the Cultural Triangle has undertaken to manage and maintain for the sake of all mankind. It is for this reason that the Director General of Unesco, in launching the international appeal for the safeguarding of the Cultural Triangle of Sri Lanka, said in his address to the Member States of Unesco in August 1980: 'The Cultural Triangle must be preserved for the sake of Sri Lanka . . . . It must be preserved for the sake of Asia . . . . It must be preserved for the sake of the world at large since it forms an integral part of man's heritage'.

Strategies for excavation, conservation and the layout of sites

In 1978 the Sri Lanka Government requested Unesco to provide guidance and assistance in managing the archaeological sites in the historic regions of Sri Lanka, subsequently identified as the Cultural Triangle. The General Conference of Unesco in 1978 resolved to launch a campaign to safeguard the monuments and sites of the Cultural Triangle. A Working Group was set up, composed of officials of Unesco and the Sri Lanka Government, which produced a Work Plan that provided for three important areas of activity with infrastructure support. The areas of activity were identified as excavation, conservation, and the layout of the monuments and sites in six designated social institutions from the past. These were:

(a) the monastery of Jetavana, Anuradhapura (3rd century AD) with 3000 monks and the tallest (400 ft (122 m)) *stupa* in the world;
(b) Abhayagiriya monastery, Anuradhapura (1st century BC) with 5000 monks and the second tallest (370 ft (113 m)) *stupa* in the world;
(c) the Water Gardens and the Royal Palace of Sigiriya (5th century AD);
(d) Alahana Pirivena (University), Polonnaruva (12th century AD);
(e) rock-cut painted caves of Dambulla (12th to 18th centuries AD) with more than 20 000 ft^2 (1858 m^2) of wall paintings; and
(f) the Temple of the Sacred Tooth, the Palace, four Hindu Devales and two Buddhist monasteries in the living city of Kandy (16th to 18th centuries AD).

International effort

A permanent Joint Unesco–Sri Lanka Government Committee was established to monitor the ten-year programme, with an initial cost estimate of US$52 million. About 60 per cent of the funds were to be raised from the international community through the campaign launched by Unesco, the Sri Lanka Government undertaking to provide approximately 40 per cent.

The international assistance was to be in two forms: (a) scientific guidance and (b) resources. Such assistance was to be obtained from international agencies on bilateral agreements and international foundations. With these objectives in view, the Cultural Triangle has set up organizations in the potential donor countries in the generally recognized form of charitable companies. Such organizations are exempt from national taxes and enjoy preferential benefits. The membership of such organizations is drawn from persons of standing from the following areas of activity: (a) academics interested in South Asia, (b) foundations oriented towards scientific research, (c) commercial organizations trading with Sri Lanka and (d) Sri Lankan nationals living in these countries.

Organizations of this kind already established on behalf of the Cultural Triangle Project in more than half a dozen countries have provided valuable scientific guidance and technical assistance, and have influenced public opinion to promote bilateral assistance.

National effort

The organization in Sri Lanka itself is based on a distinguished Board of Governors chaired by the Prime Minister. This statutory body is registered under an Act of Parliament and has among its Governors six Cabinet Ministers and senior officials of the country, so as to be able to harness the best resources for cultural preservation. The Board of Governors, which meets every month, is the executive agency of the Cultural Triangle, and its rôle is to define policy, guide the activities and administer the project.

Implementation

The implementation of the project operates through six separate teams of technical personnel covering the disciplines of archaeology, conservation and the layout of sites. Archaeological activity at each site has been allocated to a university with facilities in this discipline. Conservation and layout work has been assigned to professional architectural firms with experience in these fields. Management services are provided by a central agency under the Board of Governors. Each project has 40–50 archaeological graduates and nearly 800 excavation labourers. The conservation work is handled by the architectural firm, with about ten architects supervising the work at each site. The labour force is highly skilled, consisting of masons, carpenters and other craftsmen specially recruited and trained for this work. Other specialized services are provided by professional firms on contract. The supervisory excavation and conservation staff have been provided with two MSc postgraduate training courses oriented towards practical experience: the lecture programmes are adjusted so that this academic upgrading is provided over the weekends. For the purposes of quality control of the conservation work, documentation of the excavated objects, dating of the archaeological material and conservation of paintings and artefacts, laboratories have been set up covering all of these disciplines and guided by a steering committee of university and other academic personnel. Much of the training and equipment for this area of laboratory activity has been provided under a generous UNDP grant.

Excavation

The scientific aspects of excavation have been standardized so that the excavation methods, the documentation of finds and the storage of information have been codified as a result of many academic sessions between the various university directors. The publications which record the research are issued every six months: these cover the primary phase of archaeological research (excavation records and stratification) without comparative studies. This decision was taken deliberately, as it was felt that the publication of many archaeological reports is delayed awaiting the second aspect of such research, covering the area of comparative study. For this reason in the prefaces to all of its publications the Cultural Triangle Project invites researchers all over the world to participate in this major enterprise and assist in the comparative aspects of archaeological work. Without such a decision we would have failed to publish a single report.

Conservation

In terms of conservation, the architectural consultants for the six projects, like the archaeologists, meet monthly to compare conservation methods and to share their experiences. These firms are pledged to observe the conventions not only of the Venice Charter at the international level, but also of the stringent national standards laid down by the Archaeological Department of Sri Lanka. Reports on conservation work are published annually for each of the six subprojects of the Cultural Triangle.

Administration

The administration of the projects and the co-ordination of the scientific work is monitored through two progress meetings each month. Here the archaeologists, the architects, other professionals, the administrators and the financial personnel are all present, together with a representative of the Government Agent for the area. These lengthy meetings result in firm decisions being taken collectively by all of the scientific and administrative personnel present. This system has, to some extent, democratized archaeological and architectural conservation thinking as well. We believe that such a system can also eliminate possible errors of judgement if decisions are taken individually. A form of veto is available to the two chief scientific personnel (archaeologist and architect) by means of which they can independently stop any area of work, whether such work is within their speciality or not, on the condition that there is a possibility of irreparable damage being done to a monument or to the site. This veto has only rarely been applied. A second progress meeting is held in Colombo (away from the site, where professionals discuss theoretical questions) at which both forward-planning and other administrative and financial matters are discussed. The minutes of such meetings are distributed within 48 hours with a defined column tag for action.

Steering committees

A steering committee has been set up for each of the six projects of the Cultural Triangle, intended to keep them on target (a) in terms of the ten-year macro-plan and (b) in terms of the annual micro-plan. The steering committees are not statutory bodies; they consist of people of standing, selected for this purpose and working in an honorary capacity. The Board of Governors initially appointed chairmen for each of the steering committees, and thereafter provided them with guidelines for selecting the remaining members, who are professionals from the following fields: lawyers, architects–engineers–builders, accountants, representatives of the travel trade and religious personalities. The archaeologists, architectural consultants and administrative personnel of the Cultural Triangle are *ex officio* members.

The functions of the steering committees are not only to monitor the work programme identified for each of the projects, but also to build up close links with the public in respect of the scientific programme. These steering committees are encouraged to hold exhibitions, seminars and other promotional activities relating to each specific project. Their assistance is also anticipated in areas of stress or conflict, whether between specialists or with the religious and secular institutions that own these cultural properties. These committees meet every two or three months, and they visit the sites at least every six months. The relationships between these interested advisory groups and the technical activities have been very harmonious and most useful for the project.

Publicity committee

Alongside the steering committees there is a powerful publicity committee chaired by a senior figure from the commercial world. Publicity personnel from most of the commercial undertakings are members of this body; their main task is to keep the project alive and, above all, to raise funds towards the financial targets identified for public subscription. It is a healthy committee to have in any cultural activity. The benefits of such a group can be judged from its results. The Cultural Triangle receives only 15 per cent of its funds from the government; the rest is secured in various ways formulated by the publicity committee, and are then implemented by the Board of Governors. For example, tourist entrance tickets provide nearly one-fifth of the annual budget for the programme formulated by the publicity committee.

Conclusion

Looking back over the experience of nearly five years in implementing the work of the Cultural Triangle, one becomes well aware of the high potential level of resources available for this work, so long as it is properly formulated and implemented. It is also essential for such cultural enterprises to exert influences on national planning, so that it becomes possible to include cultural activity, and within this framework to emphasize the social, economic and other benefits to society; most importantly of all, it should be stated clearly that, in the absence of public involvement in social and cultural activities of this nature, the country may find itself obliged to provide financial and administrative resources to cater for the activities of otherwise idle minds.

Sri Lanka is proud to have undertaken, jointly with Unesco, so massive an international programme, in which the funding and administration of archaeology have reached unprecedented levels, in which heads of government and cabinet ministers have been persuaded to play a part in digging up the past, in which more than 250 young archaeologists and architects have been brought to the fore, in which nearly 5000 workmen have been employed to rescue a former glory, and in which science has been privileged to play its rôle to the full and to produce results within the shortest possible time for the serene joy and the pleasure of the national and international public.

22 Cultural resource management in the USDA Forest Service

EVAN I. DeBLOOIS and KENT A. SCHNEIDER

Introduction

The Forest Service, the largest agency within the US Department of Agriculture, was founded at the beginning of the present century by Presidential action. Originally charged with the management of the Forest Reserves of the USA, these were later renamed National Forests. The agency consists of a Washington, DC, office and nine regional units which collectively manage just over 191 million acres (77 million ha) of public land in the USA. It is organized into a four-tiered line-staff system with a strong emphasis on decentralization of the decision-making process. The four levels of 'line' authority are the Chief, Regional Forester, Forest Supervisor and District Ranger.

Cultural resource management (CRM) is a recent development in the 80-year history of the Forest Service. In spite of directions from the first Chief, Gifford Pinchot, in 1906 at the passage of the Antiquities Act, serious efforts to develop a programme to manage the considerable number of historic and prehistoric properties on National Forest System lands did not begin until 1967, when the first archaeologist was hired. The passage of the National Historic Preservation Act in 1966 was in part instrumental in this action and added impetus to the development of the programme. In 1970 two additional archaeologists were added to the system. It was not, however, until the publication of the first Advisory Council on Historic Preservation regulation in 1974, coupled with the passage of amendments to the Reservoir Salvage Act of 1960 in the same year, that the major growth in the programme occurred. Recognizing the requirements of these legislative mandates, the Forest Service made a strong push to increase its professional staff during the mid-1970s, along with the writing and issuance of internal direction for the programme. By the end of the 1970s the Forest Service employed nearly 160 professional archaeologists, along with several historians and ethnographers.

Because the CRM programme in the Forest Service is largely a response to legislative action, it has resulted from a lot of top-down direction. In most instances the first archaeologists employed were at the Regional Forester's

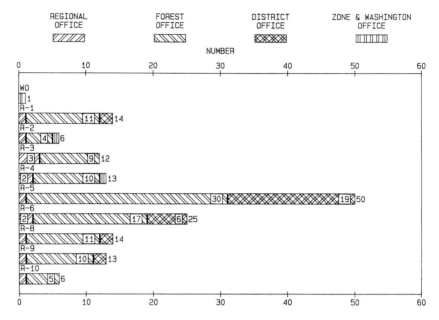

Figure 22.1   Distribution of CRM specialists in the USDA Forest Service.

level of the organization. The almost total absence of national direction for the programme from 1967 to 1975 almost guaranteed a wide variation in the programmes developed in each region. It was not, in fact, until 1978 that the National office hired its first CRM specialist to provide more consistency in programme direction. Although the National Historic Preservation Act was passed in 1966, it was not until 1975 that a task force was assembled to develop internal direction for the agency. These directions, issued as Forest Service Manual chapter 2360, remain largely intact today as the guiding policy direction. Several attempts have been made since 1979 to revise this direction in order to reflect the numerous new regulations and amendments to the governing laws. These efforts are likely to result in a drastic change in the Forest Service's approach to CRM over the next few years.

The current CRM Programme

Federal laws require the Forest Service to find, protect and preserve all significant prehistoric and historic resources before these are damaged or destroyed. In an effort to accomplish this, the Forest Service currently employs approximately 140 full-time cultural resource specialists, mostly archaeologists. There are an additional 35 individuals hired as archaeologists

PART I DATA BY ACTIVITY TYPE	CRM	ENGIN-EERING	FIRE-MGMT	LANDS	MINERALS	RANGE	REC-REATION	S&PF	TIMBER	WATER-SHED	WILD-LIFE	TOTAL	CONTRACT PROJECTS	SP.USE VOLUNT
SURVEYS	242	439	79	551	945	484	265	1	3,145	82	208	6,441	687	—
COMPLETE ACRES	94,200	18,315	26,049	84,501	42,786	27,177	15,762	20	2,054,622	7,859	7,879	2,379,170	218,114	—
CLEARED ACRES	156,362	44,485	39,620	32,801	51,113	32,801	15,457	10	2,845,097	7,961	7,107	3,313,166	234,422	—
SURVEYS W/SITES	140	141	48	188	294	93	96	0	1,318	12	40	2,370	259	—
NEW SITES	1,738	318	177	584	724	260	318	0	6,825	18	85	10,747	1,222	—
SURVEY COSTS	471,810	140,156	64,486	311,478	301,865	140,782	173,406	70	4,150,164	24,955	51,340	5,830,511	728,660	—
EVALUATIONS	100	33	13	82	55	15	155	0	248	2	4	707	35	—
SITES EVALUATED	415	115	92	230	378	23	218	0	1,956	9	14	3,450	573	—
SITES ELIGIBLE	301	58	42	49	153	33	60	0	935	4	2	1,637	143	—
EVALUATION COSTS	131,240	52,715	5,360	104,965	56,114	8,004	61,240	0	369,589	2,300	1,080	812,597	230,535	—
NO EFFECT PROJECTS	115	366	64	459	702	446	218	0	2,726	163	165	5,422	482	—
SITES—NO EFFECT	224	231	114	393	408	246	271	0	4,955	29	92	6,963	911	—
NO ADVERSE PROJECTS	9	32	7	40	64	3	17	0	49	4	3	228	10	—
SITES—NO ADVERSE	54	51	19	101	88	7	31	0	316	6	18	691	72	—
ADVERSE EFFECT PROJECTS	3	6	2	9	5	2	3	0	15	1	0	46	3	—
SITES—ADVERSE EFFECT	4	23	2	20	38	0	16	0	17	3	0	123	5	—
DATA RECOVERY	32	12	2	18	5	1	14	0	55	0	1	140	12	—
SITES W/DATA RECOVERY	65	24	1	19	9	1	13	0	46	0	0	178	28	—
DATA RECOVERY COSTS	79,900	209,364	500	52,099	18,036	720	110,599	0	69,850	0	0	541,068	290,841	—
DOCUMENTATION PROJECTS	63	30	2	52	77	35	10	0	127	2	2	400	1	—
SITES DOCUMENTED	136	32	2	60	89	35	12	0	182	2	2	552	1	—
DOCUMENTATION COSTS	23,306	16,290	100	16,915	16,737	7,423	5,505	0	20,116	200	200	106,792	4,200	—

Figure 22.2 CRM activity in the USDA Forest Service by resource type.

whose primary responsibilities are in other key areas, such as planning. The cultural resource specialists are distributed among nine regions and the national office in Washington, DC. Most of these people are located at the field-going Forest and District levels of the organization, where they are directly involved in project work. Figure 22.1 shows the distribution by organizational level and region of these individuals.

The level of activity in CRM projects continues to expand with the number of staff available. Although the Forest Service has not taken an intensive look at its programme to determine the number of projects needing CRM work compared with the amount of work being done, in a few areas it has discovered a gap between needed expertise and the amount of work to be done. Currently the agency is surveying more than 6000 separate projects annually on more than 2 million acres (810 000 ha) of National Forest System lands. Figure 22.2 shows the amount of activity by resource area for Fiscal Year 1984.

Let us briefly examine the Forest Service and some of its activities in one of the nine regions in order to gain insights into the CRM programme. Region 8, headquartered in Atlanta, Georgia, covers 13 states (Texas through Virginia) and Puerto Rico, and accounts for some 12 million acres (4.8 million ha) of National Forest land. The Forest Service practises 'multiple use management' – concurrent management of all renewable and non-renewable resources which exist on the landbase. Resources managed include recreation, wilderness, wildlife and fish, range, water, cultural resources, and timber. Simultaneous management of these resources, however, can cause contradictions: what is the best management prescription for one resource may not be good for another resource occupying the same parcel of land. Timber management is a case in point. Roads to access the timber must be cut and maintained; timber must be harvested, replanted and managed during its life cycle. During the fiscal year 1985, 419 miles (675 km) of new roads were constructed and 827 miles (1331 km) of old roads were reconstructed to access National Forest land. Reforestation and timber stand improvement activities (planting, seeding and natural regeneration), were conducted on 94 000 acres (38 000 ha). Federal law requires that all significant cultural resources be identified and protected before these activities can be carried out. Because CRM is 'young' in the Forest Service, very little is known about the prehistory or history which evidences as archaeological sites on the landbase. There are 16 full-time cultural resource specialists on the Forests to whom this task falls. The task is both challenging and formidable. To do CRM work for just the timber resource, each archaeologist would have had to survey approximately 6000 acres (2400 ha) of land and 80 miles (130 km) of roads. In addition, survey reports must be written; those significant sites which cannot be protected must receive some mitigation action before the disturbing activities occur. The professional workforce to accomplish just these tasks alone is barely sufficient. Some of the work does not get done; hence some of the significant cultural resources are lost.

Future directions

Regionally and nationally, the CRM programme has continued to expand, slowly at times and some times rapidly. Increases in programme budgets of 30 per cent in a single year have occurred as well as 30 per cent decreases. Still the programme has not reached that level of 'full compliance' required by regulation. Efforts at more-positive management approaches have not ceased entirely, but they are guided to a large degree by organizational or fiscal support. Legal issues have again been emphasized by recent adjudication of several cases in which relatively strict interpretations of the find–protect–preserve and do-it-first laws have underlined the need to meet compliance.

The future of CRM in the Forest Service continues to be uncertain. Pressures on the Agency to reduce its budgets and its numbers of employees have affected all programmes, and they appear certain to increase the problems with meeting legal requirements in CRM. Given recent Congressional action, it appears likely that a major confrontation between the agency's perceived capabilities and currently defined legal requirements will occur within the next two years. The outcome of this conflict remains in doubt. Most likely the size of the CRM programme in the Forest Service will be seriously reduced in proportion to the reductions in other activities. Efforts to expand the programme to current workload levels in other resource management areas, such as timber management, are unlikely to occur. There is, however, some optimism that this period of stress on CRM may provide an opportunity to refashion the programme to reflect a more positive approach to the problems of protection and conservation of important cultural resource values.

What will be needed in the next few years is an increased effort between all categories of archaeologists and other resource managers within and external to the Forest Service to work together and produce a new cultural resource conservation programme that everyone can support and defend in light of efforts to reduce federal deficits. A failure to do so will, most certainly, result in the loss of much of the strength the CRM programme has attained over the past decade.

23 *Cultural resource planning and management in a multiple-use agency*

ROBERT LAIDLAW

Introduction

The Cultural Resource Management (CRM) programme in the US Bureau of Land Management is defined generically in a fashion which addresses both the sociocultural and the cultural material aspects of human interaction and use of lands now under the jurisdiction of the agency. This programme addresses a broad spectrum of specific resource types, including archaeological sites, historic structures, and the cultural values of Native people and other ethnic groups. It is the goal of the CRM programme in the Bureau to accomplish the identification of cultural resources on the public lands, and to ensure their protection, analysis, and interpretation or recovery, or both, in the context of agency actions.

In general, the management, protection and development programmes of the Bureau are designed to respond to and to address current national priorities within a planning and management framework which ensures the consideration of a broad spectrum of resources. The CRM programme as one aspect of this process emphasizes the full consideration and professional review of cultural resource values and issues as a component of decision-making within the agency. Cultural resource issues, legal and compliance responsibilities, and management considerations are developed within the context of the agency's overall management mandate.

Inventory

An essential prerequisite for any planning system is a sufficient database from which reliable and responsible evaluations of resource sensitivity can be derived. In an effort to ensure such a sufficient database, the Bureau has developed a series of *overviews* covering many geographic regions within its jurisdiction. Assembled by in-house professionals or through contract with other researchers, these materials provide a base level of information against which initial resource significance can be evaluated. The overview database supplies a summary of all previous research, known resource values, the potential of the resources for providing insight to major scientific theories or regional models, or both, and an evaluation of resources for public interpretation and other non-scientific aspects of significance. These data, referred to generically as 'Class I inventories', are incorporated in the agency planning process toward the development of long-range protection, stabilization and recovery, and for interpretative plans.

One of the most significant rôles of the cultural specialist within the Federal agency is to assure the consideration and evaluation of cultural resource values which may be affected by agency actions. Bureau responsibilities include the administration of mineral and energy activities, and other actions which have a potential for altering the condition of lands and affecting many categories of resources. The most efficient means of avoiding a loss of significant cultural resource values is to ensure that reliable data are available to agency planners and decision-makers at the initial stages of project design. Such data are available within the Bureau in the form of the Class I documentation. Site-specific information on archaeological and historic resources is also being incorporated into a computer-based information management system in some areas of the USA. These data can be applied in the design of a project to avoid or minimize potential effects on *known* cultural values. Indeed, in most cases the development of project alternatives by the agency incorporates a review of available information to ensure a minimum adverse effect on sensitive resource values.

Overview data are also applied to evaluate potential resource sensitivity and the need for further research. Where Class I data indicate a potential for sensitive cultural resources, subsequent planning and management consideration will often include a *sample field inventory*. This level of inventory of representative landform and ecological communities within a study region is referred to as a 'Class II inventory'. The level of field inventory varies in relationship to the nature of anticipated resource, known cultural–ecological correlations, or temporal and/or fiscal constraints. Field data at this level provide an invaluable tool for determining the location, nature and range of occurrence of specific resource types. Class II level data are most frequently collected as a component of project-specific or resource management planning, working in conjunction with regional specialists, major research facilities and academics.

Specific actions or projects are designed incorporating a consideration of the site data supplied by the cultural resource specialist(s). In many cases this process allows for the development of project alternatives which avoid many potentially significant effects upon cultural resources and, hopefully, minimizes the need for subsequent mitigation.

In those cases where a project action has a potential for disturbing areas of cultural resource value, a Class III or *intensive* field inventory is often undertaken. Such an inventory level ensures the identification and consideration of all cultural resources before any surface disturbance occurs.

Management and planning issues

The inventory structure and the database which results from its implementation are designed to identify and address specific cultural resource sites within the context of regional models of culture dynamics. The information provided by this system ensures a means of identifying research and management needs within the agency, and it establishes a baseline for pursuit of research by other professionals.

This CRM and planning programme is also designed to respond to a profile of agency needs and public interests which far exceed the scope of interest of agency cultural resource specialists. Federally supported historic preservation groups, professional societies, avocational organizations, conservation–preservation groups and others all have an interest in the management of Federally administered cultural resources. The concerns of these groups must also be incorporated into any public agency's management programme for cultural resources. These interests provide the basis for the systematic development of interpretative sites, public education materials and scientific programmes.

An additional and significant component of the CRM programme for the Bureau is the identification and consideration of sociocultural values of ethnic (primarily Native) groups which are associated with lands and resources managed by the agency. Ethnographic overviews designed to identify contemporary Native American use and traditional cultural significance of Bureau lands and resources have been conducted for many areas of the USA. Specific inventories are also initiated in association with individual project actions. Consultation is undertaken with those individuals recognized by the local ethnic community as knowledgeable about folklife values or particular aspects of the community's heritage and cultural legacy. Individuals who are consulted include tribal elders, traditionalists, folklorists and practitioners of native crafts, the healing arts and religious ceremonies. By developing an understanding of the concerns of traditional ethnic communities, the agency gains an understanding of ways of life and ethnographic values which may be affected by agency actions.

Synthesis

Effective planning for resource management must incorporate a strategy for the application as well as the compilation of relevant data. The planning system described here employs ethnographic and archaeological data not only toward the understanding and analysis of identified sites, but also toward the anticipation of site occurrence and subregional resource sensitivity. A qualitative analysis of environmental correlates of site occurrence and distribution has been accomplished for almost all agency-administered lands. Evaluation of these data and their application in the planning process has supported the development and testing of resource sensitivity models which have, in some circumstances, accurately anticipated the occurrence of cultural properties. Although very limited in scope, statistically based models of site occurrence have been applied in several planning efforts.

Conclusion

Essentially the US Bureau of Land Management planning programme is designed to draw upon existing data to identify both subregional and site-specific cultural resource sensitivity, and to ensure that significant resource issues are systematically addressed in the course of all agency undertakings. The system provides an opportunity to refine and supplement hypotheses for large planning areas. Overview (Class I) data, which are employed to develop anticipatory models of site occurrence, are continually being refined and updated through additional sample inventory (Class II) and site- or project-specific investigations.

Modelling of historic and prehistoric land-use patterns on Bureau lands has been facilitated by an increasing body of information on ethnographic and ethnohistoric significance and exploitation of resources. For many areas ethno-archaeological, ethnolinguistic and historic land-use models have provided a complementary basis for identifying and interpreting the material cultural resources.

24 A contractor's perspective of two approaches to cultural resource management in Arizona

JON S. CZAPLICKI

Over the past several years I have served as project director on two large archaeological survey projects for agencies in the US Department of the Interior, the Bureau of Reclamation (Reclamation) and the Bureau of Land Management (BLM: see Ch. 23). Reclamation's Tucson Aqueduct Project (TAP) is the last leg of the Central Arizona Project (CAP), which will bring Colorado River water into central Arizona to alleviate a severe groundwater overdraft problem, and to provide water for municipal, industrial, and agricultural users (Fig. 24.1). The BLM project initially involved survey of public land, which has been determined to meet certain criteria under which it can be disposed of by sale or exchange under the Federal Land Policy and Management Act. Although each agency works under the same public laws for cultural resource management (CRM), the agency's interpretation of and response to the laws can, and often does, differ. Such differences exist to some extent because of the different missions with which each agency is charged. Reclamation is project-oriented, and it deals with cultural resources on a threat-induced basis resulting from land-altering projects like dam construction. The BLM's mission of public land management is a continuous process dealing with planning and overseeing multiple-resource use of public land. Its goal is cultural resource conservation (Meiszner 1982). While threat-induced management is not usually a consideration, it can influence BLM cultural resource management studies.

This chapter first summarizes two public laws and one executive order that relate directly to the survey projects to provide some background for those not familiar with CRM legislation in the USA. It then briefly discusses the projects, compares, from the vantage point of the contractor, how these two agencies managed the cultural resources under their jurisdiction, and it notes several problems that arose during each project. Several suggestions are then presented that may help to remedy some of the problems. Finally, several pertinent comments are provided to lend additional insight to the discussion. These comments were provided by an archaeologist from both

Reclamation and the BLM, and they reflect their personal and professional opinions only; they do not represent official Reclamation or BLM opinions.

Pertinent Federal legislation

Over the past 80 years various laws have been passed by the US Congress dealing with the preservation of or mitigation of damage to archaeological sites (McGimsey & Davis 1977, King *et al.* 1977, Fish 1980). Two of these are the National Environmental Policy Act (NEPA) and the Archaeological and Historic Preservation Act. The 1969 NEPA outlined how Federal agencies such as Reclamation and the BLM were to deal with archaeological resources under their jurisdiction. This Act made protection of cultural resources part of a more comprehensive plan dealing with all aspects of the environment. It requires environmental impact statements (EIS) on all major Federal projects affecting the environment, and stipulates that an archaeologist be involved in the initial planning stages of Federal projects.

In 1974 the Archaeological and Historic Preservation Act required that all Federal agencies conduct appropriate archaeological investigations before undertaking any projects that might result in destruction of significant cultural resources. This law outlined the use of Class I, II and III surveys and the rôle each was to play in designing appropriate mitigative data-recovery plans. A Class I survey is an overview or inventory of the known cultural resources for a particular study area. The Class II and III surveys are sample-oriented and intensive surveys, respectively, designed to acquire data for managerial decision-making and for identifying all significant cultural resources and providing recommendations for mitigating impacts to these resources. This law sought to avoid the loss of irreplaceable archaeological data by requiring proper planning and field investigations, in addition to requiring that project budgets and planning processes provide sufficient time and funds for adequate survey and excavation.

In addition to these laws, Executive Order 11593, Protection and Enhancement of the Cultural Environment, was issued in 1971 and expanded the Federal Government's responsibility for archaeological and historical properties as outlined under the NEPA and the 1966 National Historic Preservation Act. It broadened Federal authority regarding archaeological resources on Federal *and* non-*Federal* land, affected by Federal, Federally funded, or Federally licensed projects, and called for Federal agencies to locate, inventory and nominate all qualified sites under their jurisdiction to the National Register of Historic Places.

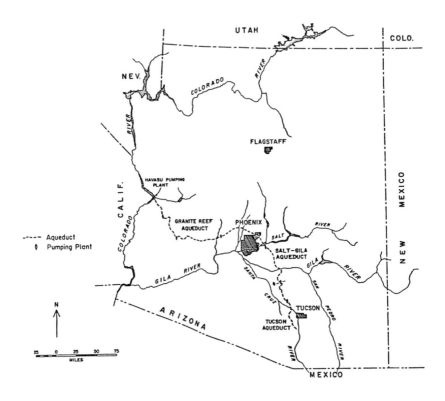

Figure 24.1 The Central Arizona Project aqueduct system.

The Bureau of Reclamation's Tucson Aqueduct Project: scheduled cultural resource management planning

The Tucson Aqueduct (TA) is the final segment of the 531 km CAP (see Fig. 24.1). Reclamation approach to cultural resource management for the TA has been to complete the necessary studies – survey, limited testing and excavation – before initiation of a particular land-altering action, in this case construction of an aqueduct across central and southern Arizona. Cultural resource studies began in 1979 with the Class I overview of the 4015 km^2 project area (Westfall 1979). Early in 1980 a supplemental over-view of an additional 1993 km^2 was completed (McCarthy & Sires 1981). These overviews provided Reclamation archaeologists with an assessment of the known and expected archaeological resources in the project area, outlined basic research questions pertinent to the prehistory of the project area and ranked 11 preliminary aqueduct alignments in terms of their impacts to known and expected archaeological resources.

In 1980 an 18-month contract was awarded to Arizona State Museum (ASM) for Class II and III surveys and mitigation plans for each segment of the TA. This timeframe proved to be overly optimistic and completely inadequate. Because of on-going engineering and alignment planning, political and environmental concerns about the aqueduct, changes in the scope of work and the unexpected size of some of the sites found during survey, which required considerably more effort to record and test, the contract had to be extended by an additional 54 months, to the end of 1985.

Class II sample surveys provided Reclamation with information on the kinds and densities of archaeological sites in the study area, and ranked each of the 14 alternative aqueduct routes (six alternatives in Phase A and eight in Phase B) in terms of their impacts to the archaeological resources. These rankings were ostensibly used in selecting the preferred aqueduct route, but in reality they played a very minor rôle in this decision-making process. Other considerations such as geology, terrain and construction costs were considerably more important; the costs for mitigating the adverse effects of aqueduct construction to the archaeological resources were minor when compared with the cost of moving the aqueduct to avoid them. Consequently, site avoidance was not a viable option for consideration.

Intensive Class III surveys identified all but the very smallest sites located in the preferred aqueduct right-of-way, which consists of two phases each between 60 and 80 km long and varying in width from 122 m to more than 800 m (Figs 24.2 & 3). Since 1982 almost 78 km^2 have been intensively surveyed and 133 sites recorded. Sites range in age from Archaic, Hohokam, pre-Spanish contact, to Historic, and include Archaic camps and Hohokam villages, field houses, farmsteads, a reservoir and agricultural features. Limited testing at selected sites provided additional data for assessing significance and for making mitigation planning recommendations.

Reclamation archaeologists needed information from the Class III surveys on site type, size, location and research potential in order to meet their schedules for completing the draft and final environmental impact statements for each segment of TA and for preparing requests for proposals for the data-recovery projets. Schedules for acquiring these data however were often disrupted by delays beyond the control of Reclamation archaeologists. The delays were usually the result of Reclamation's engineering and construction planning which, although separate from Reclamation's cultural resource planning, were not necessarily mutually exclusive from such planning. To meet these schedules intensive survey had to be carried out before final aqueduct alignments were known. Design plans for sections of the Phase A and B alignments had not been completed at the time of the intensive surveys, which meant that considerably larger survey areas had to be designated by Reclamation archaeologists to ensure that these sections had been surveyed when the alignments were finally determined. On-going engineering and design planning also necessitated realignment of previously surveyed areas. This was a problem especially on Phase B where almost half of the 3370 ha surveyed represent survey of realigned portions of the original right-of-way.

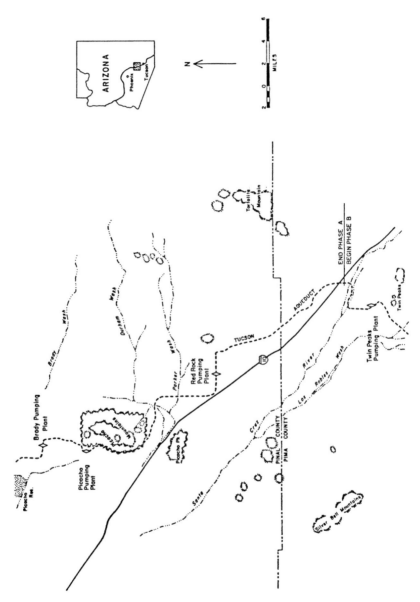

Figure 24.2 Phase A segment of the Tucson aqueduct.

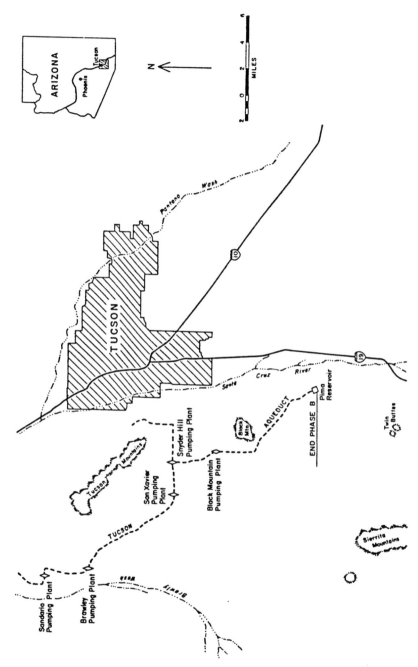

Figure 24.3 Phase B segment of the Tucson aqueduct.

Because of design and engineering delays, sections of the alignment were inadequately identified by Reclamation, or not identified at all. Archaeological survey crews relied primarily on a brushed and staked centreline to guide them during the survey. The staked centreline also provided a reference point for survey transects in the right-of-way, which was up to 800 m wide in some areas. Because design planning for portions of the Phase A and B alignments was not completed, centreline brushing or staking, or both, was absent. When a site was located, it could not be located with reference to a numbered centreline stake (these stakes were generally placed every 100 ft, or about 30 m), and a determination of its location and extent in relation to the construction zone could not be made until after the centreline alignment was confirmed.

On several occasions the centreline was moved after the survey had been completed, which resulted in sites that were originally located in the right-of-way now falling outside the right-of-way. Conversely, some sites that were outside the right-of-way were now located inside the right-of-way and subject to damage by aqueduct construction or by indirect impacts from construction. This would not have been much of a problem if both Reclamation and ASM archaeologists had been told of the centreline realignment; however, centreline realignment was usually discovered only accidentally by the survey crew.

Legal considerations and poor planning by Reclamation real-estate personnel were responsible for yet another problem: the need to have information on the cultural resources for the EIS occasionally preceded the need for Reclamation to acquire access across private property. Because it is standard ASM policy to obtain permission from landowners before entering private property, during the Phase B survey this request was the first indication that landowners had that an aqueduct was planned across their land. Although most landowners understood the need for the archaeological survey on their property, their initial reaction about the proposed aqueduct ranged from indifference to open hostility. Needless to say, the survey crew avoided those areas whose owners were of the latter disposition. In fact, it was at least a year after the start of the Phase B survey before Reclamation officials contacted many of the private landowners to discuss access across their property.

These problems had various effects on the TA survey project. The necessity of providing Reclamation archaeologists with pertinent survey data and recommendations for preparing the EIS and for planning data-recovery projects was very important. The EIS had to be reviewed and approved before construction could begin and, once construction contracts were awarded, delays affecting construction – such as cultural resource studies – would not be tolerated. Therefore it was crucial that contracts for data-recovery excavations be awarded well in advance of construction to ensure that all necessary excavations were completed before the start of construction. Obviously, preparation of the final survey reports was important if Reclamation's cultural resource planning was to stay on schedule and

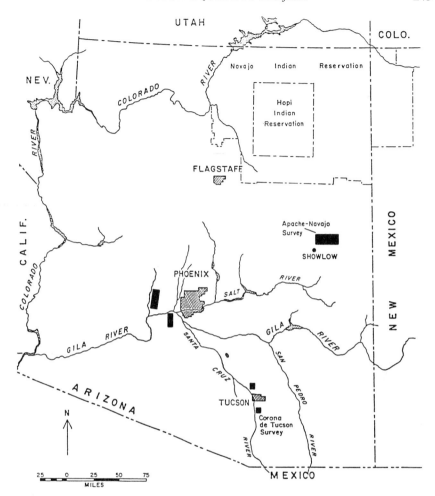

Figure 24.4 Navajo–Hopi Land Exchange: survey parcels in Arizona.

avoid conflicting with construction schedules. As a result of the delays and problems associated with the intensive surveys, survey results and recommendations for mitigation planning had to be submitted before all survey data were analysed and interpreted, and before recommendations for excavation could be carefully considered. Realignment of portions of the aqueduct during analysis and report preparation caused additional delays and usually resulted in modifications to the report to reflect new survey data. Once all survey data were analysed and interpreted, and recommendations for a mitigation plan had been formulated, earlier conclusions had to be re-evaluated and modified. This was a problem particularly during preparation of the Phase A report, where scheduling required that conclusions and

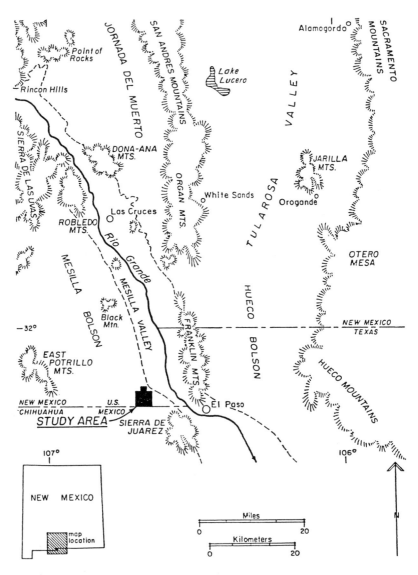

Figure 24.5 Navajo–Hopi Land Exchange: the Santa Teresa survey parcel in New Mexico.

recommendations for data recovery be provided soon after fieldwork was completed.

Another result of the engineering planning delays was the increased cost of the archaeological surveys. The additional areas that were surveyed when the exact alignment was uncertain, and the time required for survey of realigned portions of the right-of-way, increased costs. Although the cost of the Class III survey and testing was minuscule (about 0.1 per cent) compared with the estimated US$534 million cost of the Tucson leg of the CAP, it was still a substantial contract budget. When agency managers and planners are concerned about the cost of archaeology, better-co-ordinated planning would reduce costs.

The Bureau of Land Management's Navajo–Hopi Land Exchange Project: cultural resource management and crisis planning

This project originally was to provide cultural resource information and recommendations for making decisions about disposal or retention of public land in 31 study areas in Arizona. When ASM was awarded a contract early in 1984, expectations were focused on a proposed five-year project involving from 243 to as much as 2022 km^2 of public land. However, with the award of the contract it was learned that the BLM had replaced the land-disposal project with cultural resource investigations for the Navajo–Hopi Land Exchange project. This project represented a considerable change in scope of work and schedule, involving survey of various-sized tracts of public land scattered over Arizona and New Mexico (Figs 24.4 & 5). Initially, little if any excavation was anticipated; land containing significant archaeological resources would be withdrawn from any exchange and retained by the BLM. The land to be surveyed was being transferred to private landowners who were to lose land as part of the Navajo–Hopi Settlement Act, which provided for settlement of the land dispute between the Navajo and Hopi tribes in the Joint Use Area of the Navajo Reservation. The Settlement Act authorized transfer of more than 1000 km^2 of BLM land in Arizona and New Mexico in exchange for state and private lands of equal value which were selected by the Navajo Tribe for relocation purposes.

Although lands transferred to the Navajo Tribe must be within 29 km of the present boundary of the Navajo Reservation, BLM lands almost anywhere in Arizona or New Mexico could be used for exchange purposes. It should be noted that according to the Settlement Act no actions of the land exchange were to be considered a major Federal action under the National Environmental Policy Act of 1969 (42 USC 4321).

The BLM does not usually deal with threat-induced management projects, but the Navajo–Hopi Land Exchange is an exception. The threat in this case was not from construction activities *per se*, but rather from the loss of cultural resources when Federal land was transferred to private ownership.

Once transferred, protection of the archaeological resources would be virtually impossible. Since private development of much of the transferred Federal land is anticipated, many of the resources would eventually be damaged or destroyed, most probably without any attempt at preservation or data recovery.

Since the summer of 1984 three major survey projects have been carried out by ASM for the land exchange. These are the Apache–Navajo survey in the White Mountains of east-central Arizona (4196 ha), the Santa Teresa survey in southwestern New Mexico (2286 ha), and the Corona de Tucson survey south-east of Tucson (1619 ha, Figs 25.4 & 5). The BLM approach to dealing with these survey projects was essentially one of crisis management. Critical deadlines were established for each of the surveys, the completion of which was crucial for the success of the exchanges. The deadlines were established by BLM state office managers, who were negotiating the exchange with little co-ordination with the archaeologist regarding the practicality of deadlines. Logistics, personnel, terrain, weather, access and other factors important in planning an archaeological survey were not seriously considered when the deadlines were mandated. Political, economic and business considerations were apparently the primary concerns. In spite of these difficulties, all three surveys were completed on time; however, as the deadlines came and went, the crisis atmosphere that had prevailed before and during the surveys also evaporated. The deadlines were apparently aribtrary and were not as critical for consummating the exchanges as the BLM had indicated. In fact, it was almost one year after the surveys for Apache–Navajo and Santa Teresa were completed before the exchanges for these parcels occurred.

Although the survey deadlines were met, the rush to complete the surveys compounded logistic problems and brought unnecessary pressure on field supervisors and crew personnel, which increased the potential for missing sites, and permitted only minimum site recording and data collection on which to base recommendations.

The crisis atmosphere that governed these surveys is probably not unusual when decisions affecting archaeology are made by people not familiar with the goals, methods and logistics of archaeological survey. There also appears to have been little consultation between BLM managers and archaeologists about the nature and requirements of the cultural resource studies that were being scheduled.

Originally, excavation was not considered an option for any of the land exchange surveys; the BLM would retain land on which potentially important sites were located and would exchange land containing no sites or sites which were not recommended for preservation or excavation. The need for some excavation became apparent, however, when the BLM found that it could not retain all of the land necessary to protect sites and still proceed with the exchanges. On the Santa Teresa project the survey strategy incorporated a modified data-collection plan that eliminated the need for additional investigations. This was not the case for the other two surveys, however. A data recovery effort was proposed to deal with a limited number of the 69 sites recorded during the Apache–Navajo survey. Excavation of four sites with the best research potential was considered too expensive by the BLM and the land on which these sites were located was excluded from the exchange. Instead, the BLM identified 15 other sites of which nine were to be excavated, three surface-collected and three documented by mapping and photography. Because only very preliminary survey data had been collected for several of these sites, a result of the haste with which the survey had to be completed in order to meet the BLM deadline, a testing programme was recommended by ASM. Budget constraints did not allow for the recommended testing programme, and in fact forced a further reduction in the scope of work. The BLM emphasized that funding for cultural resource studies was minimal and that only a very limited effort would be considered. An appropriate research-oriented data-recovery programme was not considered feasible by ASM, given the levels of effort and funding proposed by the BLM. Furthermore, an adequate sampling strategy to provide even the most basic functional and temporal data necessary for interpretation was not possible. Having determined that spreading a limited amount of money ($100 000) over 15 sites would not yield a professionally acceptable research programme, and after considerable negotiation with the BLM and the State Historic Preservation Office (SHPO), research efforts were again re-focused, this time on five of the nine sites previously considered for excavation. Although the reduced excavation effort further restricted the research orientation, it ensured a more realistic mitigation programme, including publication of the results. Furthermore, it was acceptable to the SHPO. Since additional funding was ostensibly out of the question, contingencies that arose during excavation would have to be dealt with within the limits of the budget. As with the earlier survey, BLM managers established yet another deadline, although they were somewhat more flexible by providing a cushion of several weeks beyond which the excavations were projected to last.

Not surprisingly, the five sites were larger and considerably more complex than surface indications suggested, and they required additional excavation (and funding) in order to satisfy the SHPO that sufficient data would be recovered to address the research objectives. After consultation with BLM archaeologists and the SHPO, the BLM did provide additional funding, despite previous claims that this was not possible.

At the same time that the Apache–Navajo excavations were under way, excavation was being considered for the Corona de Tucson project. Fourteen sites were recommended for some level of excavation and, perhaps because of the lesson learned from the Apache–Navajo excavations, the initial excavation budget was approved without major complaint. Although a testing programme was not included, sufficient money for fieldwork, analysis, and report preparation and publication was provided by the BLM.

Different approaches to cultural resource management

It is apparent that, at least in Arizona, the Bureau of Reclamation and the Bureau of Land Management perceive cultural resource management differently and have their own approach for dealing with archaeological resources. Although the mission of each agency is partly responsible for these differing approaches, it is also apparent that each agency's attitudes towards the importance of archaeological resources, its previous experience in dealing with large contract projects, budget priorities, and co-operation between the agency archaeologists and managerial and planning staff play even more important rôles in how cultural resource projects are planned and, perhaps more importantly, supported by the agency.

Reclamation archaeologists have considerable involvement in the decision-making and planning processes for cultural resource studies such as the TA surveys. Planning for and scheduling of TA archaeological investigations permitted their completion within a sufficient timeframe to avoid crisis planning. Scheduling was usually based on realistic considerations of the nature, amount and cost of the work. The on-going aqueduct engineering and planning – over which Reclamation archaeologists had no control – was responsible for many of the problems which plagued the survey project.

In contrast, BLM archaeologists involved with the Navajo–Hopi Land Exchange seemed to have considerably less involvement in decision-making processes. Most of the decisions on planning, scheduling and budget ceilings, all of which directly affected the archaeological studies, were made by BLM managers. Although such decisions are undoubtedly within managerial jurisdiction, they appear more often than not to have been made without any serious consultation with agency archaeologists. Apparently, political and legal concerns affecting the various proposed exchanges outweighed the need for realistic planning for and scheduling of cultural resource studies.

Although cost is a primary concern for both Reclamation and the BLM, there is a marked difference between how each agency perceives the costs for cultural resource studies. When they are completed, both projects will be comparable in total cost. However, generally, Reclamation was less concerned about project costs unless these seemed out-of-line with expected cost estimates. Here is perhaps the major difference between how each agency views the cost of doing work. The nature of work performed by Reclamation does not favour cultural resource preservation, and avoidance of archaeological resources is usually not a viable option. Consequently, Reclamation archaeologists have considerable experience in planning and budgeting for large survey and excavation projects and, although project costs were an important concern for Reclamation archaeologists (Rogge 1983), cultural resource management budgeting and planning processes ensured sufficient funding and time for survey and testing.

Bureau of Land Management projects are usually geared towards preser-

vation of cultural resources, and surveys are often done by BLM archaeologists. When a project requires a level of survey and excavation beyond
what is usually done within the agency, costs may appear high. Whereas the
surveys were approved with only a minimum of complaint about the cost,
money for the limited Apache–Navajo excavation project was at first only
grudgingly granted. Only when it became apparent that without sufficient
funding the excavation efforts would not meet with approval by the SHPO
did the agency become more realistic.

BLM managers appear to have had virtually no idea about the scope of the
archaeological studies or the potential costs for completing these studies:
BLM archaeologists, while aware of the effort involved in completing the
required surveys and excavation projects, also had little idea of project costs.
This, I believe, is a result of the BLM's lack of experience in routinely dealing
with large projects. Nevertheless, even if BLM archaeologists had the
advantage of this experience, the apparent lack of enthusiasm and support
provided by most BLM managers for the archaeological studies would
remain a problem.

Concluding comments

These two projects indicate that in Arizona the Bureau of Reclamation and
the Bureau of Land Management have different approaches on how best to
deal with the cultural resource studies that they are required by law to
conduct. These differences are in part a reflection of each agency's mission
and the support that each agency provides for cultural resource studies.
Reclamation archaeologists are supported to a much greater degree by their
agency than are their counterparts in the BLM. This support has resulted in a
CRM programme that, although not without its problems, is adequately
funded and noticeably free of crisis planning.

The BLM's mandate for planning and overseeing multiple-resource
management – including cultural resources – on public land distinguishes it
from Reclamation's project-specific orientation. What also distinguishes it, at
least in Arizona, is the minimal amount of agency support for cultural resource
management. The BLM archaeologists involved with the Land Exchange
project were placed in a position in which they had little involvement in the
decision-making process for the cultural resource studies, yet they were
responsible for the successful completion of these studies. Critical decisions
were made by the managers, who did not seem to be well informed about the
archaeology, or about the specific requirements for successfully completing
the survey and excavation projects, or about the cost of doing the work.

As Douglas (1979) points out, it is the managers who are responsible for
managing the cultural resources. In order to manage cultural resources
better, it is important that managers be well informed not only about the
nature and importance of the cultural resources under their care, but also
about the specialized archaeological studies that are an integral part of any

management programme. The only way that managers will begin to acquire a better understanding is if the archaeologists make the effort to educate them. Of course, this assumes that the managers want to learn more about what they are supposed to manage. Managers need to take more time to meet the archaeologists and discuss the archaeological resources, review recommended options for dealing with them and discuss the kinds of studies that are required for compliance. It is also becoming clear that the managers must be encouraged to come into the field in order to gain an appreciation of the archaeology, and of the problems involved in planning and conducting survey and excavation projects. Contract archaeologists must also begin to assume greater responsibility for encouraging communication with the managers, and for making them more aware of particular cultural resource concerns. Better planning and budgeting can come only with better communication about and understanding of why cultural resources are important and how archaeologists deal with them. It should also be emphasized to managers that, in addition to publishing and distributing the results of the research projects, a public information programme can yield the benefit of enhanced public relations for relatively little cost. The value of such programmes is recognized by Reclamation, which encourages, and in some cases even requires, them.

In conclusion, Rogge's (1980, p. 36) caveat that 'no matter how good the technical planning process is, projects are more often than not shaped by political rather than technical considerations' will undoubtedly continue to hold true. Perhaps a better understanding of archaeology by the people responsible for managing cultural resources will help to temper political considerations and permit realistic and cost-effective CRM planning. It might also foster CRM programmes that comply not merely with the intent, but also with the spirit of CRM legislation.

Acknowledgements

The author would like to thank Lynn S. Teague, John Ravesloot and R. Gwinn Vivian for reading earlier drafts of this chapter. Tom Lincoln of the USBR Arizona Projects Office and John Hanson of the BLM Indian Project Office also deserve thanks for taking the time to review it and to provide their personal and professional views on it. Credit for the idea of including these views as an appendix to the chapter goes to John Ravesloot, who felt that the addition of these comments would provide the reader with additional insight into certain aspects of large Federally funded cultural resource studies in Arizona.

Appendix. Views from 'the other side'

Before submitting this contribution to the World Archaeological Congress, the author submitted a draft of the paper as delivered at the Congress to archaeologists in the Bureau of Reclamation and the Bureau of Land

Management, respectively, who were familiar with the agency's project. Their comments are included to provide the reader with some additional insight into the particular nature of the two archaeological survey projects that are discussed in this chapter. These comments do not represent the official opinions of either government agency, they are the personal and professional opinions of these agency archaeologists.

John Hanson, Archaeologist, Bureau of Land Management

In general I thought that the chapter was an accurate assessment of the situation from the contractor's point of view. I would stress the last four words of the previous sentence. My views on the matter are necessarily somewhat different.

I think that generally you may be somewhat misleading in treating the two agencies in generic terms. The CAP and corresponding USBR office in Phoenix is not a typical situation to be found throughout the USBR. In fact, it has been my experience elsewhere that the kind of cultural work being done for CAP is unheard of and generally incomprehensible to other USBR archaeologists, who seem to get no more support from their managers than you suggest is typical of BLM management here in Arizona. I believe the 'Arizona-ness' of the CAP – the intense public scrutiny, the 20 years or more timeframe for completing the project, the fact that the project impacts highly political Indian communities, and so forth – could be stressed to a greater degree.

In a similar vein it seems to me that you portray BLM-Arizona as being typical of the BLM in general. This may in fact be the case, but I am not convinced of that. I think that if your audience is 'world archaeology and archaeologists' it is important to make clear that the agency that you portray none too kindly is, in this case, specific to a particular locale.

You indicate that upon award of the contract ASM learned that the BLM had 'scrapped the land disposal project and replaced it . . .'. In part this is true, and in part it is not. Perhaps the difference is semantics. Exchanges for Navajo–Hopi are, in fact, land disposals, though admittedly not the same as were anticipated for Asset Management (disposal under Section 202 of FLPMA). Procedures under either were to remain the same.

Also, in the interests of clarity I think that some mention of legislatively mandated deadlines involved in the Navajo–Hopi Act should be included to enhance your arguments about crisis planning. The Amendments Act was passed in 1980. It (among other things) gave the Navajos three years to make their selections. The Tribe used all three years before final selections were made. The relocation process (and hence the land exchanges) was to be completed by 8 July 1986. In essence we could not make a move until the selections were finalized. This gave the Bureau three years to do all the background work and complete 215 000 acres (87 000 ha) of exchanges. Most exchanges, even minor ones, take one to two years to complete.

It is also instructive that in 1984 *Congress* made the very real push to exclude cultural resources from consideration. It was in large measure the BLM managers, who are (rightfully) castigated for wishy-washy support of cultural resources later in the chapter, who argued loudly and long that cultural resources not be excluded from consideration that helped to squelch this move.

Although it is of little consequence to the arguments made in this chapter, it is interesting to speculate on the considerations for cultural resources that might have obtained had the situations described been reversed. What if CAP had only three to six years and restricted funding to complete their entire project? I wonder if it is realistic to expect that USBR would have reacted in the far-sighted way that you give them credit for. Suppose, too, that BLM had 20+ years and $3000+ million to complete our land exchanges. I think they would probably have been far less short-sighted than they admittedly have been. Or, to add a piece to Rogge's *caveat* cited on the last page: 'Money (time) talks'.

You make good points with regard to the arbitrariness of the deadlines for Apache–Navajo and Santa Teresa. I think it is important to realize (if not necessarily to state in the chapter) that because we were negotiating with private landowners, the BLM – as the middleman – was to a greater or lesser degree being pushed by Congress and the Commission, on the one hand, and the ranch owners on the other. From the BLM's perspective, political and economic considerations *were* more important than professional consideration for the carrying out of the inventories. I personally do not think the BLM cared about the business considerations. In any event, when the deadlines – arbitrary as they were – were set, they appeared to *be* critical. That they were not was only known after the fact. Again, this is more a point of clarification than disagreement with what you say.

The section entitled 'Different approaches to CRM' gave me more problems than most of the rest of the chapter. The reasons why are difficult to explain, but I shall have a go at it.

Part of the problem lies with an issue that I raised earlier. It comes from detailing actions occurring at a specified time and place, but treating those actions as if they were generic. These are Arizona issues that you are dealing with, each special in its own way. Unlike Gertrude Stein's statement that 'a rose is a rose is a rose', the USBR is not the USBR, etc., and the BLM is not the BLM, etc., except in general terms. I think perhaps you do not give sufficient credence to the importance of each agency's mission in your discussion. I think it is perhaps (along with funding) the most important consideration.

Much of what you say in this section is absolutely correct in my view. This is particularly the case with regards to experience dealing with large contract projects, although BLM's Dolores project in Colorado is a notable exception.

I would not suggest and do not think that either agency is particularly enlightened about CRM at the managerial level. They are not. Managers (decision-makers) in both, I think, tend to view cultural resources as a necessary evil, only to be dealt with seriously when there are no alternatives. I think that a $3000 million budget allows for a more benign attitude at USBR when cultural resources are, by your estimates, utilizing a 'minuscule' 0.1 per cent of the total budget. I would argue that if BLM had that kind of money for Navajo–Hopi, then we would be a lot more flexible, too. For NAHO, as we call it, our total budget has been somewhere in the neighbourhood of $2.5 million, and when we have finished CRM will have consumed about 25 per cent – a fairly *un*minuscule figure. I think it is fair to say that the costs of the projects *were* more important for BLM because we had a much smaller total budget going in. Nevertheless, your comments about the experience of the agencies in dealing with large-scale contracts are well taken. I am not convinced, however, that cost is quite the primary concern for USBR on CAP as it generally is for us on NAHO or anything else.

It may appear that I am being overly sensitive about criticisms of BLM in your chapter. In fact, I find most of your critical remarks to be accurate. My reaction in part is that a very positive picture is painted for USBR and a negative one of BLM. I keep telling myself that this is being written from the contractor's point of view and that this is the way it appears from your perspective.

I am in full agreement with your statements in the final paragraph, but I think that it may be somewhat unfair to pick only on BLM's managers for education. I think an argument could be made that some problems that were encountered by ASM on the TA project could have been lessened had USBR managers known a little more and cared a little more. Archaeologists in USBR may have no control over realty specialists or planning and aqueduct engineering, but you can bet that the managers do.

Thomas R. Lincoln, Archaeologist, Bureau of Reclamation

The differences between Reclamation and BLM are, in fact, derived to a great extent by the agency missions. Reclamation is project-goal-oriented with a philosophy of 'whatever it takes, get the job done'. Reclamation is an agency steeped in tradition. It is a wealthy agency that has a clear record of accomplishment, something it is very proud of. (In fact, a poll taken in 1983 among Washington, DC based Federal programme managers and businessmen ranked Reclamation as the most respected Federal agency.) Reclamation recognizes its environmental commitments and usually pursues them energetically; however, cultural resource programmes are ancillary (and contradictory) to Reclamation's mission, and are given much less emotional energy by programme managers than construction-related projects.

The BLM, of course, is driven by a different set of political realities. Oil, gas, grazing and, increasingly, recreation special interests are prominent in the BLM scheme of things. Simply put, where BLM manages land and resources, Reclamation builds water projects to enhance economic growth by agricultural, industrial and municipal users.

An important point needs to be made about the Arizona Projects Office (APO) approach to its cultural resource programme. It is project-specific and does not reflect Reclamation-wide philosophy or operation. Each office directs its own programme with guidance from 'higher' players, but the burden of operation is clearly a local function. The APO philosophy is to buy off the archaeology, an approach not followed by most other offices. In other words, with all of its monetary resources, the Central Arizona Project is willing to spend up to 1 per cent of its construction costs (as provided by the Archaeological and Historic Preservation Act of 1974) on cultural resource programmes. The Tucson Aqueduct will cost $534 million which makes $5.34 million available for cultural resource studies. By the time our Tucson Aqueduct studies are complete we will have spent about $3.6 million (67 per cent of available funds) which is a bargain when compared with construction costs. During a project design phase our engineers use 10 per cent as an acceptable cost-estimate error rate, so you can see that our $3.6 million is a very reasonable real cost, well within the design–cost error rate.

Finally, we are trained archaeologists, not preservationists. Regardless of what we say, we prehistorians want to dig every site that we can get a shovel into. Reclamation is providing a bounty of dollars, and employs most of the contract archaeologists in Arizona. We are all grabbing as many dollars as possible. In the larger scheme of things, a greater area has been surveyed and more sites inventoried as a direct result of the Tucson Aqueduct archaeological studies. The CAP has gladly paid for these benefits. Federal dollars are a boon right now, but they will not last forever. We are trying to do research-oriented contract archaeology, and as long as the floodgates are open we have a golden opportunity to achieve some of our professional goals. The CAP's goal is being reached, water is being transported across the desert. Along the way it has helped Arizonans and Southwestern archaeologists to understand a bit more of the past.

Designing a large, complex construction project is a dynamic process of which the cultural resource programme and studies are a part. Designing Phase B of the Tucson Aqueduct involved a new Reclamation policy direction implemented in 1981 as an efficiency move. For Phase B the traditional planning process was shelved in favour of the new 'two-stage' planning process. The two-stage process is charged with saving time. This is accomplished through a series of reports which are more flexible and project-specific than previous structured reporting. It also allowed for a reduced level of detail – that is, less data and less data analysis. The operative word here is risk. Reclamation is willing to risk premature design based on potentially uninformed engineering data in order to speed project planning which historically has taken 20 years per project; the two-stage planning goal is to have a project under construction in 7–11 years. Beginning in 1981, the Tucson Aqueduct Phase B used the two-stage process (APO's first use of it) with surprising success at meeting scheduled deadlines. However, it has been an admitted four years of stress and confusion as the alignment shifted with each new round of more refined engineering data. The point to make is that Reclamation got the job done in five years, and the city of Tucson expects water in 1991 on schedule. We may have been inconvenienced, but we suffered no severe mental duress.

References

Douglas, J. G. 1979. Cultural resource management by title only (letter to editors). *Anthropology Newsletter* **29**(8), 23.

Fish. P. R. 1980. Federal policy and legislation for archaeological conservation. *Arizona Law Review* **22**(3), 681–99.

King, T., P. Hickman & G. Berg 1977. *Anthropology in historic preservation: caring for culture's cluster.* New York: Academic Press.

McCarthy, C. H. & E. Sires 1981. An archaeological overview of the middle Santa Cruz Basin: a supplemental Class I cultural resource survey for Reach 3 of the Central Arizona Project – Tucson Division. *Arizona State Museum Archaeological Series* **134**. Tucson: University of Arizona.

McGimsey, C. R., III & H. A. Davis 1977. *The management of archaeological resources: the Airlie House Report.* Washington, DC: Society for American Archaeology.

Meiszner, W. C. 1982. Cultural resource management archaeology: Federal variations. *Contract Abstracts* **3**(1), 44–8.

Rogge, A. E. 1980. The evolution of agency compliance: a case study. *Proceedings, American Society of Conservation Archaeology* **7**, 30–41.

Westfall, D. A. 1979. An archaeological overview of the Middle and Lower Santa Cruz Basin: A Class I cultural resource survey for the Central Arizona Project – Tucson Division. *Arizona State Museum Archaeological Series* **134**. Tucson: University of Arizona.

25 *Stonehenge – past and future*

F. N. GOLDING

Stonehenge is a potent symbol of England. It has been used and abused, as symbols often are. At present it is in a sorry state and change is needed. If we look back we can see that Stonehenge has been treated in ways which reflected the assumptions and values of the time.

What values and assumptions should we now be imposing on the monument as we consider the changes that are needed? What forces need to be met before a solution can be found? This chapter attempts to answer these questions, and to set them in their context. To understand the problems facing us at Stonehenge, one must know something of the monument itself: its location, the number and pattern of visitors, social and economic considerations, and something of the local, regional and national interests which affect decisions.

Most people visualize Stonehenge as the present structure of massive stones. A circle, originally of 30 sarsens (a type of stone found lying on the chalk hills 30 miles (48 km) to the north of Stonehenge), but of which only 17 remain standing, surrounds a horseshoe setting of the remains of five enormous trilithons, each consisting of two vertical sarsens capped originally by a third acting as a lintel. In its final development a continuous line of lintels capped the outer circle of uprights. All of these stones have been carefully shaped and smoothed by pounding with stone hammers, and the monument's builders were capable of such refinements as carving the lintels of the outer circle to maintain a smooth, continuous curve. The stones were fixed together with mortice-and-tenon joints. The stones in the circle of sarsens have an average height of about 13.5 ft (4.1 m) with a further 3–5 ft (1–1.5 m) below the ground. Their average width is 7 ft (2.2 m) and their average thickness is 3–4 ft (1–1.2 m). Their average weight is about 26 tons (26.4 tonnes).

Between the sarsen circle and inner horseshoe was another stone circle of blue stones, and within the sarsen horseshoe was another horseshoe, also of mainly dolerite bluestones. These igneous rocks had been brought by sea, river and overland some 150 miles (240 km) from their source in south-west Wales. The whole structure was surrounded by a ditch and bank, approached by a ceremonial banked Avenue which seems to have curved round to link the monument with the River Avon.

This massive structure, built and modified between about 2000 and about 1100 BC, was not the first ceremonial monument on this site. The original form of Stonehenge, constructed more than a millennium earlier, had been a

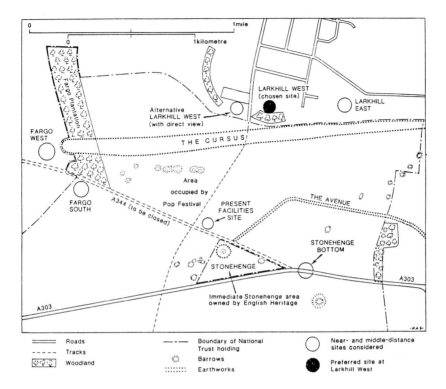

Figure 25.1 Map of Stonehenge and its immediate surroundings.

circular enclosure with a bank and ditch, with just a simple circle of pits and a few carefully sited single stones. Over the centuries it was modified and rebuilt to reach the form described above.

The exact purpose of Stonehenge can never be known. Clearly it was of great religious or ceremonial significance. Its alignment on midsummer sunrise suggests some astronomical awareness on the part of its builders. From the density of monuments around it and the long time over which they were built, one can tell that for its builders and adapters Stonehenge stood in an area of great significance. Even before the first Stonehenge was built, the great Cursus, a ditched and bank enclosure nearly 3 km long, was built to the north of its site. To the north-east lie the great henge monuments of Durrington Walls and Woodhenge. Associated with the many phases of Stonehenge were groups of burial mounds sited within view of and surrounding the 'ritual' focal point.

Despite the activities of the intervening centuries, much of this prehistoric landscape survives (see Fig. 25.1). The Cursus can be seen over much of its length, and many of the burial mounds survive so that, with proper presentation, Stonehenge could be seen as part of its landscape and not as a monument on its own. However, there are complexities of land ownership, land use and land management, which have to be considered as a whole.

First, land ownership. The stones stand on a triangle of land owned by the Department of the Environment. Two sides of that triangle are marked by two major roads, one (the A344) running to the north and one (A303) to the south of the monument. The A303 is the responsibility of a government department, the Department of Transport; the A344 is the responsibility of local government, Wiltshire County Council.

This northern road cuts the Avenue, the ceremonial route by which Stonehenge was originally approached. It also passes within about 2 m of the Heel Stone, a stone standing about 5 m high which was one of the first erected on the site. The triangle is surrounded by 1400 acres (567 ha) in the ownership of the National Trust[1] in which lie the earlier ceremonial monument, the Cursus, the still visible part of the Stonehenge Avenue and several of the barrow cemeteries which ring the ceremonial area. To the north are the buildings of the Larkhill Military Camp, owned by the Ministry of Defence, and the plantations of conifers which have been planted to screen those buildings.

Next, land use and management. Regrettably, the sense of isolation and mystery which should pervade Stonehenge is marred by the sights and sounds of modern life. No village or community can be seen from Stonehenge, but the noise and sight of traffic are constantly present, and intrusively assert the present day.

The land in the ownership of the National Trust around the monument is used for grazing purposes only. Beyond that, open land is used for agricultural purposes, principally the cultivation of grain. Most of the identifiable surviving and visible monuments, such as burial mounds, are fenced off and are not cultivated. However, agricultural use also brings its problems. For example, farmers may wish to build silos for grain storage, and to build them to a height and with a bulk which mars the skyline. Planning permission for buildings is normally given by the local authority, although in exceptional cases the Secretary of State for the Environment may decide. The resolution of the competing needs of archaeology, agriculture and transport demands a determination of priorities which at times inevitably leads to strong differences of opinion.

Although the land on which Stonehenge stands is owned by a government department, its management is entrusted to the Historic Buildings and Monuments Commission for England, generally known as English Heritage. The Commission was established by Act of Parliament in 1983, and it took over its duties on 1 April 1984. Its main duties are to secure the prservation of ancient monuments and historic buildings, to promote the preservation and enhancement of the character and appearance of conservation areas, and to promote the public's enjoyment of and advance their knowledge of ancient monuments and historic buildings and their preservation.

English Heritage can draw on the advice of two specialist committees, including its Ancient Monuments Advisory Committee (a body of distinguished archaeologists and scientists) as well as on its own professional, technical and scientific staff. The functions of English Heritage are extremely wide. It has direct responsibility for the management of some 400 national monuments, including Stonehenge.

Care of the monument today presents comparatively few technical problems. Since Stonehenge came into public ownership in 1919, much has been done to secure the fabric of the monument. Stones which have fallen in historic times have been re-erected and set in concrete. Many of those still standing have also been secured in concrete in order to prevent future collapse. The stones themselves are hard, and suffer little from the weather. Man represents a greater threat than the elements. Although the stones are hard, they are not so hard as to have prevented initials being cut in them, and in recent years there have been a few acts of vandalism, such as paint spraying by football supporters and protest groups. However, generally the stones are treated with great respect.

The sheer volume of visitors presents a greater threat to the stones than vandalism. In the past those stones lying prone were liable to be walked on and the shallow carvings of axes and daggers (presumed to be of Bronze Age date) have been harmed by fingering and rubbing. The magnitude of the problem of management of visitors can be illustrated by reference to the increase in number betwen 1955 and 1975. In 1955 184 000 people visited the monument; in 1965 the figure had risen to 363 000; in 1977 there were over 815 000 visitors. By 1982 numbers dropped to 530 000 people, but the number has been rising since then, and in 1984 nearly 640 000 people visited Stonehenge. In 1985 the number was 655 690.

The number of visitors at the site at any one time is as important as total numbers. During August 1977 as many as 7000 people were visiting Stonehenge in a single day, and some 2000 people in a single hour. All sense of isolation was lost. One was conscious of the bombardment of noise from traffic coming and going, and what one saw was people milling around the stones, rather than the stones themselves. Some thought was given to controlling or influencing the number of people visiting the monument by means of a pricing policy, but the cost of admission has not been used decisively to keep people away.

The crowds which assemble at Stonehenge at the time of the summer solstice cause exceptional management problems and require particular comment. Since the 17th century Stonehenge has been associated in the minds of many people with the Druids and astronomical significance. There was a resurgence of interest in Druidism at the beginning of the present century. In 1905 the Druids assembled at Stonehenge at the time of the summer solstice to pay homage to the Sun and to affirm their faith in that source of life. With some interruption they have appeared there at midsummer ever since. The ceremony has added to the public interest in the solstice, and in 1961 it was felt necessary to protect the monument from potential acts of hooliganism arising from the great numbers at the solstice. Initially the monument was secured by barbed wire. In more-recent years this was replaced by crash barriers and security lighting. Neither approach was totally successful in preventing mass incursions at the time of the sunrise.

In 1974 a group of 'hippies' arrived at the site, expressing their desire to follow the practice of the Druids and to hold their own form of Sun worship accompanied by music. That event began the annual visit to the monument which in recent years, up to 1984, took the form of a 'pop' festival lasting for several weeks and at its peak around the midsummer solstice, attracting as many as 30 000.

The festival brought constant noise and a potential health hazard. Water and toilet facilities at the visitor centre at Stonehenge were totally inadequate to meet the needs of those attending the festival. Arrangements were therefore made to install additional standpipes for water in the fields, and to provide temporary lavatories. A camp layout was determined to ensure access for emergency services, and rubbish collection points were identified. The festival became a nuisance to other visitors, and such a threat to the monuments and existing uses of land in the area that the National Trust, supported by the Commission, announced that the festival would not be allowed to take place in 1985 or in the future on land at or near Stonehenge. In 1985 this led to a violent confrontation between the police and a group of people trying to force their way to Stonehenge in defiance of legal pro-hibitions. In 1986 the situation was peaceful, and Druid groups were allowed to perform their ceremonies close to the monument, but a large-scale police operation was still necessary.

Even without the exceptional pressures and problems caused by the festival, it is generally accepted that the needs of visitors are badly catered for. Facilities are concentrated in a cutting below ground level, but sited on the other side of the A344 road from the stones, so to get to them the visitor goes by way of an underpass and suddenly emerges within a few metres of the stones. The original provision for car parking and for lavatories is now insufficient. Temporary toilets are installed for the summer months. There is a snack bar but no restaurant, and no covered shelter or seating for those who wish to eat or drink. The ticket office has very limited space, and there is little room for the sale of guide-books and other goods. There is virtually no presentational information, apart from half a dozen information posts which the visitors see as they walk round the stones.

Until 1978 visitors were allowed to walk around the stones, sometimes in very muddy conditions, and to touch them, but the fear of erosion of the turf led to the stones being roped off. Visitors can now only walk around outside the stones. Part of their route runs along the line of an old track-way which passed inside the bank and ditch, and it has been possible to provide this section with a hard surface without causing archaeological damage. The remainder of the route is on grass, which suffers heavily from wear by visitors. At present it is not possible for visitors to make a complete circuit of the stones, but lengthy discussions have been in progress with the highway authority to see whether part of the road's grass verge might be taken in order to enable this to be done.

In the summer of 1984 English Heritage conducted a visitor survey: 73 per cent of visitors came from overseas, 53 per cent of the overseas visitors came from the USA, 9 per cent from Germany and 8 per cent from Canada. More than 27 per cent of the visitors had travelled between 76 and 100 miles (120–160 km) on the day of the visit: 58 per cent by car and 25 per cent by coach tour. The main reason for visitors coming was general interest (43 per cent) or an interest in history (22 per cent). Only 1 per cent came for an educational or academic reason as the main reason. The cost of entry was not high (80p for an adult) but, even so, only 18 per cent found the visit very good value for money. Fifty-four per cent spent nothing on brochures.

Eight permanent custody staff, whose numbers are supplemented during the summer season, protect the stones and assist visitors. They patrol the monument day and night, and sell tickets, publications and souvenirs to the public. Catering facilities are licensed to a contractor.

I have described the inadequacies of current arrangements, but I should not like to finish this section on a note of criticism. There has been a long process of putting Stonehenge back into a natural environment since it came into state care. This has involved the removal of 'modern' intrusions such as airfield buildings, cottages and ticket offices. Putting the visitor facilities partly underground and moving the car park further west was part of the process, and what is criticized today was hailed as a great advance at the time: this provides a cautionary lesson for the policy maker.

What has happened at Stonehenge is representative of what has happened at many sites, and the conclusions which one can draw may seem commonplace to many. They are:

(a)   the continuing growth of interest in the heritage, which has been such a strong feature of cultural life in England in the past 30 years, and of visitor numbers has risen far faster than anyone had expected;

(b)   the rise in the standard of living in Europe and North America has given people more leisure time and greater mobility than was taken into account in earlier planning;

(c)   effective planning for visitors must look well beyond the site itself, and is likely to involve public agencies, local communities and amenity societies whose interests are likely to conflict with one another;

(d)   a judgement is essential as to whether a site can be planned flexibly to absorb increasing numbers or whether visitors should be restricted to a predetermined number; and

(e)   it is not sufficient to be expert just in the preservation of a monument: expertise in visitor management is essential.

What then of the future?

On the first day on which the Historic Buildings and Monuments Commission assumed its statutory powers, it announced that it would abandon proposed short-term improvements at Stonehenge and provide a long-term solution instead. Accordingly, it set up a Study Group of officials of those organizations most closely involved. Its terms of reference were 'To consider the possible options for a long-term improvement of the setting of Stonehenge and of the way in which visitors are received and the monument is shown to them'. The Group was also asked to give particular attention to specified key considerations, and to produce a report identifying the possible options. The Study Group reported in December 1984. It identified three main problems: Stonehenge in its landscape, roads, and the siting, nature and extent of visitor facilities. It also identified and examined eight possible sites for the visitor centre, grouped under those which were 'near', 'middle distance' and 'distant' sites.

On receiving the report the Commission stated certain policies which would govern their decision. They were that the Commission:

(a) accepts as its first priority its duty to ensure the long-term conservation and protection of Stonehenge and its surrounding archaeological area for future generations;

(b) recognizes that Stonehenge has long been an important international tourist attraction, and accepts that it must enable Stonehenge to be viewed, understood and enjoyed by visitors from all over the world in a way which is compatible with the main duty of conservation and protection;

(c) will pursue a policy of providing much better interpretive facilities, so that visitors will derive enlightenment and enjoyment from their visits and spend more time at the monument;

(d) believes that the present facilities for visitors intrude on Stonehenge and are unworthy, and that much better facilities should be provided away from the main site;

(e) believes that the sense of isolation can best be achieved by keeping the monument as free as possible from the noise and sight of vehicles. It considers it is not unreasonable to ask able-bodied people to undertake a modest physical effort and walk from the visitor centre to Stonehenge, although the special needs of the disabled and handicapped must be met. The Commission will explore opportunities to make the walk to and from the monument as interesting as possible by explaining the other archaeological features *en route* and showing the importance of Stonehenge in the context of its historic and beautiful landscape;

(f) intends to encourage visitors to visit other important archaeological and historic sites in the area;

(g) believes that the closure of the A344 is vital, if its policies are to be fully successful, although it accepts that this will cause problems for some local residents;

(h) will give the National Trust its full support in its efforts to curtail the pop festival, which has seriously affected the whole area and spoiled visits from *bona fide* tourists;

(i)   is also keen to share the benefits that tourism can bring to local communities, especially in employment and commerce; and

(j)   fervently hopes to secure through consultation the support and co-operation of national and local government, of other organizations, of neighbouring communities and of people in Great Britain and all over the world in order to achieve the policies set out above.

The Commission invited comments from the public before taking a final decision on what course it prefers, and allowed a three-month consultation period. It has, however, stated what its present preferred option is: that facilities should be located at a 'middle distance' site at Larkhill West and be set behind trees. There would be an excellent view of the monument and of the Cursus. The walk from Larkhill to Stonehenge would take about 20 minutes and would pass Bronze Age barrows on the way, following the general direction of the historic approach to Stonehenge, the Avenue.

Stonehenge would be seen first in the distance. It would then be lost from view as the visitor walked down the dip in the approach path, and would then appear again dramatically as one approached nearer to the stones. It would be a walk of pilgrimage, of learning and of beauty.

The Commission proposed to provide a new visitor centre at which up to 1 million visitors per year could be received and catered for, although not all of them might visit the monument. There would be an imaginative information centre which would explain not just the history and significance of Stonehenge, but, in co-operation with others, would identify and explain other important monuments in the immediate neighbourhood of Stonehenge and in the region. The Commission expressed confidence that it could finance the project, and that the capital costs would soon be recovered. It did not propose having a replica of Stonehenge constructed.

There were over 80 responses to the report. The preponderance of opinion favoured the English Heritage proposals, and this support went wider than that of the archaeological and amenity groups, which was perhaps predictable. At the same time a number of respondents repeated views which they had expressed to the Study Group, including Heritage Projects of York. No other respondent supported their proposal for a subterranean visitor centre on the site of the existing car park at Stonehenge, although a number of people supported the idea of a visitor centre to the west of the monument, at Fargo Plantation.

The key to the success of the proposals lies with the Ministry of Defence, which owns the land at Larkhill proposed as the site for the visitor centre, and which would be affected by visitor traffic to and from that centre. Before the consultation period could be considered over it was necessary to see whether agreement could be reached with the Ministry over the English Heritage proposals. This has necessitated difficult negotiations which have gone far beyond the three-month period allowed for consultation, have involved landowners other than the Ministry and, at the time of writing, have still not reached a final conclusion.

However, even when those negotiations are finally over and English Heritage can begin to design its proposals in detail, the story will not be over. As explained above, the statutory procedures relating to land-use planning and to highways will have to be negotiated before work can begin. They will only be negotiated successfully if the final proposals have widespread support. The opening date for a new visitor centre is still some years away.

What conclusions can be drawn from this depressing tale? What live questions does it raise? The first set of conclusions relates to the organization of society. It is clear that a surprisingly large number of institutions, organizations and individuals have to be strongly in favour if any solution to the Stonehenge problem is to be found, even though for many of them that problem will be of low priority or entirely off the agenda. The common good can only be achieved at some voluntary sacrifice of sectional interest.

The second set of conclusions is more tentative. In its approach to Stonehenge, English Heritage has decided that the time has come to turn away from physical encroachment on the monument, and that it is of the utmost importance to reverse it and to retreat from it. It decided that the attempt to use sophisticated technological solutions to try to reconcile 20-minute visits with the dignity of Stonehenge would fail.

Note

1 The National Trust for Places of Historic Interest or Natural Beauty was founded in 1895 as a body which would act as trustee for the nation in acquisition and ownership of land and buildings worthy of permanent preservation.

26 *The Stonehenge we deserve*

PETER V. ADDYMAN

Problems of presentation at Stonehenge

Every generation gets the Stonehenge it deserves, as the merest glance at early illustrations of Great Britain's most famous archaeological monument will show. It is a sad reflection on the Britain of the 1970s and 1980s that the images which will survive of Stonehenge in recent years are those of a monument surrounded by barbed wire, patrolled by warden-like custodians or police with dogs, and approached by a grim concrete neo-brutal bunker from a litter-strewn car park with a visitor reception centre of almost unbelievably bad layout, design and effectiveness. To add to Stonehenge's uncanny ability to reflect contemporary British attitudes, most visitors have to experience the monument herded together in a crowd, walking along worn-out trackways, and see it against a background of pounding traffic on the nearby A344 road.

It was also typical of British ancient monument presentation in the 1970s that visitors found little or nothing to help them to understand or enjoy the monument except guidebooks (which could only be read after the visit) or dry archaeologically based interpretation diagrams which used archaeo-logical language and plans well beyond the comprehension of 70 per cent of the public. On a scholarly level, too, Stonehenge of the 1980s uncannily reflected a general situation. The monument has been excavated to high standards and minutely studied, and is better understood than ever before, yet the excavation report lay incomplete and unpublished after 30 years. At the other end of the spectrum, Stonehenge has become the focus for activities of the harmless eccentrics – latter-day Druids and the like – and the much more disruptive popular festival at the midsummer solstice.

It was heartening that the Historic Buildings and Monuments Commis-sion (HBMC), at its formation in 1984, gave as its most urgent objective the better presentation of Stonehenge. The Commission intended 'to direct sustained efforts to finding a long-term solution as quickly as possible and implementing it'. As these words are written some two years later, there have been few visible changes at Stonehenge, and the reasons for delay again provide a microcosm of the British approach. The reaction of the HBMC to this 'urgent' problem was to set up a committee. This, the Stonehenge Study Group (SSG), invited suggestions, gathered evidence, discussed the problem and reported early in 1985. The HBMC reviewed the options suggested by SSG, chose one, tried to implement it and ran straight into the opposition of local groups and landowners, not least the Ministry of Defence, who owned much land required for HBMC's preferred solution. By October 1985 *The Times* reported Lord Montagu, Chairman of HBMC, as saying that his bargaining with the Secretary of State for Defence had been 'disappointingly long'. Meanwhile HBMC, the police and the National Trust had chosen to confront rather than control the popular midsummer festival, adding an archaeological element to a year in which Great Britain has seen police confrontations with miners, printers and whole local populations. Stonehenge maintained its reputation as a mirror of British life.

Heritage Projects Ltd (HPL), a York-based company set up to develop the experience gained at the Jorvik Viking Centre of presenting archaeology to a wide public, submitted to the SSG and the HBMC a detailed scheme for the imaginative presentation of Stonehenge. The objective set by HPL was the creation at Stonehenge of a cultural, touristic, recreational and educational asset by imaginative presentation which would minimize disturbance to the site and its environs, maximize the number of visitors and benefits to them, and produce a substantial annual income for HBMC. The company was so convinced of the rightness of its scheme that it offered to help to finance the project from non-government non–HBMC sources: that is, at no cost to the British taxpayer. The company was disappointed to have its scheme roundly rejected by HBMC. A quick analysis of the preferred HBMC alternative showed it to be, in HPL's opinion, so heavily flawed and such a missed opportunity that the company presented a critique to HBMC, to its Chairman Lord Montagu, and eventually to Lord Elton, Minister at the Department of the Environment. The criticisms of the HBMC scheme for a visitor centre at nearby Larkhill contended that it was fundamentally flawed because of:

(a)   its distance from the monument;
(b)   its proximity to a sewage farm;
(c)   the need for access through an area of high military security and a military housing estate, unacceptable to the inhabitants, if not to the Ministry of Defence;
(d)   the requirement for substantial new infrastructure, including a widened road between the Interpretation Centre and the monument, tracks for pedestrians across the intervening landscape, and built facilities near the monument; and
(e)   the disruptive effect to the ambience of the monument, and damage to the land itself, resulting from very large numbers of pedestrians crossing the landscape north of Stonehenge.

Indeed, it seemed to HPL that the HBMC scheme provided the worst of all worlds – a centre which would frustrate all visitors except those with substantial time at their disposal, various installations which would endanger precious archaeological evidence and detract from the landscape environment of Stonehenge, a package of developments which would be at best only marginally viable financially and a solution which missed the one real opportunity in Great Britain to involve a wide public in prehistory and harness its support for the conservation of the archaeological heritage.

The real opportunity at Stonehenge

Stonehenge is possibly the best-known prehistoric site in the world, attractive to, and capable of appreciation by, a far greater proportion of the public than any other British archaeological site. It represents an opportunity, present at no other site, to propagate their interest and harness their concern for the preservation of the past. A solution which attracts rather than repels the casual or marginally interested visitor is required to seize this opportunity.

Stonehenge is already a major tourist destination, especially amongst North Americans. It could have a far greater rôle in bringing visitors to its region, provided that easy access, especially for tour buses and private vehicles, is maintained. A solution which requires more than four times the present dwell-time, most of which is devoted to a long walk, effectively prohibits this; what is required is easy and quick access, with the option for long walks for those who desire them.

Stonehenge and its environs are perhaps the most numinous and archaeologically sensitive area in the country. Preservation both of the atmosphere and the below-ground remains is vital. This can readily be achieved by a solution such as the HPL one, which keeps all extraneous activity out of sight, avoids any further desecration of the landscape, and allows people to see both an uncluttered landscape and a good view of the monument itself.

Stonehenge has the potential to produce a huge return on investment, even on the fairly adventurous scale envisaged in the HPL scheme. The company is, therefore, confident that it can be financed by the private sector. The real opportunity provided by Stonehenge is to establish, by imaginative entrepreneurial action, that the national monuments can cease to be a burden and start to be a positive contributor to the economy.

The HPL scheme for Stonehenge

The essence of the HPL scheme for Stonehenge is to return the immediate environs of the monument to something like their pre-20th century condition while providing superb reception and interpretation facilities within a few metres of the monument (see Fig. 26.1). Heritage Projects Ltd takes as an essential prerequisite the absolute necessity not to destroy any more of the buried archaeological evidence in this most sensitive of archaeological areas than has so far been disturbed by the present installations. To this end all of the modern above-ground extraneous features in the immediate area of Stonehenge must be removed, including the A344 road east of the present car park, the fences, built structures and notices.

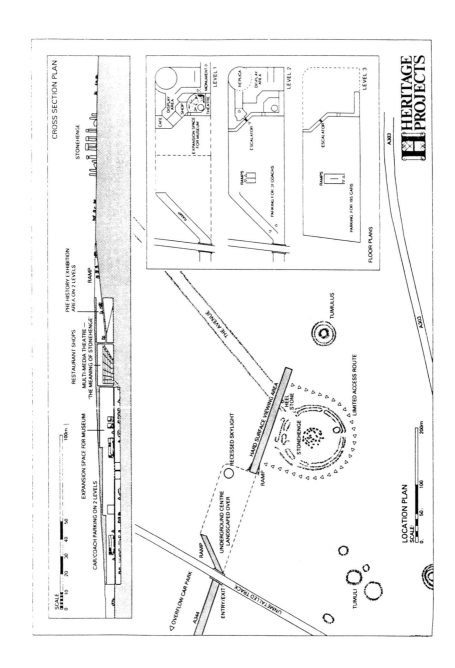

Figure 26.1 The HPL scheme for Stonehenge.

The existing car park and adjacent areas now occupied by the A344, which have already been archaeologically destroyed, should be developed as an underground prehistory centre, providing an introduction to Stonehenge and the surrounding areas, with car and coach parking sufficient for all but especially busy times. Vehicular access to the prehistory centre should be from the west along the course of the A344, reduced in level to be even less visible from the monument than it is at present. The whole area of the prehistory centre should be grassed over except at the point of egress to the monument itself.

The Stonehenge prehistory centre will be a two-level or possibly three-level construction, submerged up to a depth of 10 m or more. Visitors will enter from the car park at the lower level, past well-appointed toilets and refreshment areas. Passing a model of the Heel Stone, they would proceed up to a main concourse, a dramatic and uncluttered lead-up to a scale recon-struction of Stonehenge, with all of the stones in their final-phase positions. Visitors may walk through the model, explore it and even touch it. A graphic explanation relating to the reconstruction and the present condition of the monument will be displayed in a circular exhibition round the walls of the concourse. A second concourse leads visitors to the admissions area, and a second display shows in wider aspect how Stonehenge is situated in a landscape of many other prehistoric sites, and explains how a special prehistory trail may be followed round sites in the vicinity.

Multiple admissions desks minimize queuing at busy periods, and a tiered admissions price system is envisaged, reflecting different levels of visitor participation in what is to come. Stewards will collect prebooked parties following ticketing, and moving ramps will conduct visitors directly to the open air for a short walk to the monument. Those who had elected to approach the monument by foot from a long-distant entry point join the main visitor flow at this stage.

Most people will view the monument from a low-profile hardened pathway on the site of the A344, but there will be a limited-access route around the whole perimeter, as at present. There will be no visible physical barriers, but visitors will be constrained by an audio alarm system or other such device. Well-trained, well-briefed and personable guides will escort visitors and maintain a security function.

Although at busy times the immediate environs of Stonehenge will, as at present, inevitably be crowded, all those who visit the monument, looking out from the crowd, will see the landscape in which it is set in an uncluttered and largely unpeopled state.

Visitors will return to the prehistory centre at the upper level, and enter a third display area specifically designed to answer a variety of questions about the monument and its environs, which their visit has provoked. From a viewing gallery they will be able to obtain another view of the model below. At this point there will be an option to view a multi-media presentation 'The meaning of Stonehenge'. This, using existing planetarium technology, will present the complex constructional sequence of Stonehenge, the legends that have come to be associated with it, and the relationship of the monument to surrounding sites and to prehistory. The 15-minute presentation will involve the use of models, lighting, sound, film and video.

Visitors, whether or not they have seen 'The meaning of Stonehenge', proceed through an area where there are group discussion facilities for school parties, shops, refreshment areas, sequential life-sized sculptures portraying the setting-up of the stones, and finally an egress to the car and coach park.

The HPL scheme is designed to produce a programmed visitor flow through the centre and the monument, to answer particular questions as they occur to the average visitor, but to preserve flexibility so that visitors can use the centre in a self-determined way. The scheme should cater just as well for the perceptive person who wishes to approach the monument without any interpretive help as for the uninitiated general visitor for whom reading is not a congenial or even usual means of obtaining information.

A Stonehenge prehistory park will probably emerge from surveys recently carried out by the Trust for Wessex Archaeology and initiatives taken by the National Trust, which owns much of the land around Stonehenge. The opportunities to present British prehistory through these monuments (to include sites as far as the Winterborne Stoke Cross Roads barrow group) should be a natural adjunct to proposals for Stonehenge itself.

The presentation philosophy

In presenting the HBMC's proposals for Stonehenge, Lord Montagu of Beaulieu, Chairman of the Commission, indicated that the HBMC philosophy was to provide facilities for those who were prepared to devote some time to a visit. 'I cannot put it too strongly', he said, 'we do not want to encourage the 20-minute visitors'. His archaeologist colleagues in the Commission and its Ancient Monuments Advisory Committee have confirmed a view that a Stonehenge returned to its environment, with any necessary visitor facilities kept well away from the monument, best satisfies the archaeological requirements. Such a philosophy fits well into existing minimalist treatment of Great Britain's national monuments, and accords with the approach of the National Trust, which often demands considerable investments of time, energy and intellectual commitment to the exploration of the heritage. It has the additional effect, perhaps attractive in terms of conservation, of cutting visitor numbers down to those who 'really want to go'.

Heritage Projects Ltd takes a quite different approach to heritage presentation. The company believes that visitors to monuments and museums are at present self-selecting – those who are already committed to an interest in the past. It further believes that far more people, given the opportunity, would enjoy and gain immense benefit from such an interest. Indeed, it would go even further, to state that it is important for the nation's psychological health in a time of increasing rootlessness, diversity and

uncertainty – and escalating leisure time – to increase an awareness of origins
and historical process. It believes, therefore, that a quite different philosophy
should be adopted, not necessarily for all historic or prehistoric sites, but
certainly for some where public awareness is already high.

Stonehenge must be the most obvious example of these sites. The
philosophy for these few high-profile sites should be to make it as easy as
possible, and as attractive as possible, for visitors to come, so that those who
are only marginally inclined to indulge can be encouraged rather than
deterred. The interpretive facilities should make no assumptions about
previous knowledge, either of the site or of archaeology. The methods of
communication should be those now normally used – and for much of the
nation these no longer include reading more than the shortest texts. The
ancillary facilities should acknowledge that people would be far more
constrained to take a positive attitude to the past if they have experienced it in
wholly enjoyable and convenient conditions. The objective should be to
harness an interest in the past, making it seem both relevant and revealing,
and inculcating a strong feeling of the worth of both preserving and
presenting it. The company sees no essential conflict between these aims and
the conservation of the monuments themselves.

Heritage Projects Ltd is a commercial company. Part of its philosophy is
that presentation of the past need no longer be a total drain on the nation's
resources. It believes that such projects as a presentation scheme for
Stonehenge not only could, but should, be achieved commercially. Indeed,
it sees such schemes as a vital means of financing the interpretative facilities
on other monuments where visitor numbers will never be large enough to
'justify' investment, but which are just as important a part of the nation's
cultural baggage.

At the time of writing, no-one outside HBMC knows which scheme may
eventually be chosen for Stonehenge. Probably the monument will again
assert its ability to reflect British mores and the result will be a compromise,
but what emerges will be important. It will reflect what the nation can expect
for the 1990s so far as monument presentation is concerned, and HPL hopes
profoundly that, for the sake of archaeology if nothing else, it will partake
more of the popular than the élitist approach.

TRAINING AND QUALIFICATION OF ARCHAEOLOGISTS FOR HERITAGE MANAGEMENT

27 Learning by doing: this is no way to treat archaeological resources

HESTER A. DAVIS

Professional archaeologists condemn anyone who excavates in an archaeological site without having had proper supervised training in excavation techniques, to say nothing of background in culture history, theory, material culture and several other subjects. Sites excavated by inexperienced or unknowledgeable individuals are destroyed, and so is the information those sites contain. However, individuals with no supervised training or experience are being allowed to make life-and-death decisions about archaeological sites in other but equally destructive ways, individuals who are called by what has become a relatively prestigious and professionally recognized name – cultural resource managers. Archaeologists in the real world and in the academic world are ignoring the fact that this is going on and that individuals are being hired to 'manage' archaeological resources who have no background on the considerations that should or even must go into making a decision about the future existence of any particular archaeological site. Why has this situation come about? Can and should archaeologists do something about it? If so, what? And if they agree that something should be done about it, who is going to see that it gets done? It is my intention to offer some answers to these questions.

Let me say first that I do not equate cultural resource management with archaeological research. Cultural resources, for example, include such things as historic battlefields, which may have a below-ground archaeological component, and historic structures, bridges and other engineering features which have significance to the cultural heritage but may have no archaeological component. My concern here is with *archaeological* resource management.

In the USA, historically, there have been some highs and lows with regard to the amount and nature of training for cultural resource managers at academic institutions over the past ten years. In anticipation of a Federal law in 1974, which allowed all Federal agencies to expend money for archaeological research and cultural research management (CRM), several universities instituted one or two courses which covered Federal and state laws, regulations and procedures, and discussed the theory of the management of non-renewable resources and how to decide which ones should be protected, saved, preserved, excavated or destroyed. A very few universities – perhaps a dozen – instituted essentially a graduate emphasis in the subject. For example, the University of Arizona began a Master's degree emphasis called Cultural Resource Management in 1972 or 1973. Idaho State University, Southern Illinois University, the State University of New York at Binghamton and the University of South Carolina did something similar, and many more began teaching one or at most two courses to give students going into what was a greatly increased job market at least some idea of what the real world was like. The professors who were teaching them had been 'learning by doing' only since about 1970. To the best of my knowledge, other countries have lagged behind this calendar.

Andrew Saunders (ch. 15, this volume) indicates that in England, 'learning by doing' CRM is the norm and always has been. In the past six years in the USA, as the job market has decreased, so has the perceived need to provide this kind of additional 'real world' training to people taking graduate programmes in archaeology – even though the jobs that are available involve a lot of management decisions about archaeological resources, and a consequent knowledge of the law at a minimum. At the University of Arkansas, Fayetteville, there are two relevant courses in the graduate anthropology programme, one entitled 'Public Archaeology' and the other 'Cultural Resource Management'. From 1974 to 1984 the Public Archaeology course was required of all archaeology students, but it has not been taught for two years; the Cultural Resource Management course has not been taught for three years. Graduate students are concentrating on other, more 'scientific' and traditional, courses: they are learning statistics and the use of computers in order to do interesting things with their archaeological data, but they are not learning to negotiate with a Federal agency about protecting a site on Federal property, or how to establish the significance of an archaeological site by the criteria established by law. Why is there this change in interest on the part of students, and parenthetically, a change in emphasis on the part of professors who advise them? I know only that these courses have always been considered to be *in addition to* what is required to be an archaeologist. Taking these courses lengthens the time required to complete a degree, by having to study this subject, and in these hard times that is a major consideration in a student's programme.

Perhaps we should not be surprised by this. If we look at anthropology–archaeology graduate programmes historically, the job market has never had much influence on them. Until the mid-1970s the jobs for archaeologists were in museums or in teaching. Archaeologists got jobs doing archaeology for museums, not necessarily building exhibits. If curation or exhibitry was a requirement of the job, then the archaeologist often learned that by doing it, not by having been trained in any academic courses in graduate school. The same is still, unfortunately, true with teaching. In the USA at least, no-one teaches an archaeologist how to teach. Consequently we all know superb researchers who are ghastly teachers. The job market for teaching has remained remarkably stable, although there are not very many positions, but there has been little or no effort to provide teachers of archaeology with instruction in teaching or with supervised experience before releasing them into the real world. Academic institutions support this approach by requiring information on a candidate's research ability first when filling a professorial post; teaching experience is normally a poor second, and supervised training is not required at all. This attitude in academia, of placing subjects other than traditional ones as an add-on and with minor emphasis, is not new, therefore and might have been anticipated by those who want to give students some skills for dealing with the real world.

So to my second question: should archaeologists concerned with the future of archaeological resources be troubled about this situation? Of course they should, but to face it they will have to buck the entrenched academic system. This happened in the USA ten years ago, when it was obvious that the employment available for archaeologists required them to have some acquaintance with those outside forces affecting archaeological sites, and that this was a 'new' situation requiring a 'new' approach. Graduate programmes adapted to meet this situation. Now public archaeology and CRM are a part of almost every archaeologist's vocabulary, even though it may not be a part of their training. The orientation of CRM, of conserving the archaeological resources, is not a fad; given diminishing resources, it is the necessary approach today, and it must be for the future. In the USA the archaeological job market is certainly still largely for people who are going to be doing archaeology under contract for Federal agencies or who are employed to make recommendations for the management of archaeological sites. A student can have one graduate course in the subject and participate at some level in a field project done under contract with, say, the US Army Corps of Engineers, perhaps even have a hand in writing the recommendations for treatment of sites, and will then call him- or herself a cultural resource manager. This is not as it should be, any more than a student with one academic course in field techniques and participation in one field excavation project should call himself an archaeologist.

What should be done? Fighting entrenched academic programmes is not to be taken on lightly, but there are ways of fitting this need into the recognized system within what could be called 'traditional' academic programmes. One of these is instituting an emphasis in applied archaeology; the student learns first to be an archaeologist, and then learns how to apply his or her skills to problems other than excavation. The key to an applied programme, however – something recognized in academia but stolen from medicine (where incidentally life-and-death decisions are also made) – is internships.

The supervised field excavation experience normally required of a student is not called an internship, but it is nevertheless required. Students are taught *under supervision* methods, techniques, applications of theory, and other approaches to recording and interpreting the archaeological record. Learning archaeological field techniques by a student on his or her own or out of a book is not approved. Established internships for cultural or archaeological resource managers would benefit the student, benefit the agency or museum or private entity where the student interns, and certainly benefit the resources by having more-informed decisions, perhaps even wise decisions, made about their future. Students should get academic credit, they could take real-life problems and suggest solutions, but should not have this as the final and ultimate solution without passing the solutions by an experienced supervisor. The student might even earn a stipend, but it could be at a slightly lower rate of pay than a full-time experienced individual. A real-life project given to a student to work on (what can be called 'research' in the traditional problem-solving sense) could be used as a thesis or dissertation. This certainly parallels field excavation projects under a professor (or supervisor), with the report scrutinized by a committee and used as the thesis or dissertation. This system applied to CRM projects should not be too hard for academic archaeologists to understand.

There is certainly nothing in present US academic institutions to prevent this from becoming standard procedure for anyone pursuing a graduate programme in archaeology. It *is* happening in the even more recently developed specialty within history known as 'public history'.

There is a second and side benefit to this suggested internship programme, which few, if any, cultural resource managers are likely to have thought about, much less the average professor. This is the ability through supervised project situations to teach archaeologists how to handle *people*. In purely research-oriented field projects, no-one teaches an archaeologist how to handle an unruly crew or how to 'manage' an individual who is determined to disrupt the field situation; the result is sometimes disastrous, not only to the career of the archaeologist involved, but quite possibly to the archaeological site as well. In supervised management situations with interns, guidance can be given on how to negotiate contracts, when to compromise and what to compromise, how to handle City and County Councils, and, in the USA, how to work effectively with Native American groups. The result of real 'training' in these situations is bound to be to the benefit of the resources – which is, of course, our ultimate goal.

Finally, who is going to see that the present situation gets changed? Every archaeologist has a professional responsibility to work at this. However, those in academic situations can work from within, seeing to it that at least some courses in CRM are *required*, and if indeed this idea of establishing internships seems to be a viable one, working to get such programmes set up with local agencies.

In addition, in the USA and in England there are now professional organizations which screen applications and admit to membership those archaeologists who have the stipulated amount of academic and field training in archaeology. In the case of the Society of Professional Archaeologists (SOPA) in the USA, after having met those basic and 'traditional' requirements, an individual must also apply for approval or certification in one or more specialized emphases: fieldwork, collection research, administration, teaching, and so on. Cultural resource management is one of these emphases. The additional requirements to be certified in this emphasis do not include supervised training; there is only a requirement that the individual show evidence of having had major responsibility for a certain number of 'management' projects. Supervised experience is required in field excavation techniques, in underwater and historic archaeology emphases, but not in CRM. The damage which can result to archaeological resources from having an untrained inexperienced archaeologist make unwise management decisions can be as devastating as the difference between a trained experienced archaeologist and a person with a shovel in his hand looking for treasure. We have now had about 15 years of CRM experience in the USA. Learning by doing in the real world of managing cultural resources should be considered unprofessional and unethical. In the USA at least, 99 per cent of the employment available to archaeologists for the next few decades is probably going to be oriented towards the best treatment of archaeological sites for the public good. A site with unique scientific information will not be preserved for that reason alone, if a road or a power plant must be built there and nowhere else. Archaeologists know that potential information is in that site, and they must be a part of the decision as to what happens to it. However, they cannot do that if they do not know when the law is on their side, if they do not know the art of compromise and if they cannot communicate with the profit-oriented businessman. These techniques and the strong commitment to the resources must be learned in formal and informal training situations, not on the job.

Reference

Saunders, A. 1989. Heritage management and training in England. In *Archaeological heritage management in the Modern World*, H. F. Cleere (ed.), ch. 15. London: Unwin Hyman.

28   *A suggested training scheme for archaeological resource managers in tropical countries*

JOHN ALEXANDER

Preparation for undertaking the teaching of a higher-degree course (MPhil) in archaeological resource management at Cambridge has led to the writing of this chapter. My especial concern is with the problems of tropical countries; although there are a number of aspects of the subject that are common to all parts of the world, the experience and proposals relating to the temperate regions of the world and reported in other chapters in this book are not in every case applicable in tropical countries. Nevertheless, the common objective is to train intelligent and academically able young men and women who care for the past and who will be prepared to devote their lives to conserving the material evidence and recording what is to be lost.

In the selection of recruits for this work in the tropics, there are three qualities that are to be looked for in particular: orderly minds, a liking for being out-of-doors in all weathers – perhaps candidates should be drenched in rain and plastered with mud before being interviewed – and the ability to work with all kinds of people, from officials and soldiers to villagers. The problem with people of this calibre in tropical countries is that, if they are well trained and able, they will immediately be lost to archaeology because other needs in their countries will call them to become administrators, legislators or diplomats. This often happens, so selectors must try to choose candidates who are intellectually committed to the recording and preservation of the past, and who will accept something less than the glittering prizes that other kinds of career can offer. Even the top levels of the archaeological research management structures in any country will never be as financially rewarding as other types of career.

The best moment for selecting candidates is probably towards the end of a first-degree course, since a formal academic training is essential, although the actual subject of the first degree is less important. Selectors should advertise widely among both arts and sciences faculties, since a mixture of skills and attitudes within a management hierarchy cannot be other than an advantage. Directors of antiquities departments might well try to influence universities to allow a wider range of subjects to be studied in combination with archaeology and history, the more traditional source areas for recruitment into antiquities services.

The most suitable and economical method of training graduates for this kind of archaeological management is probably a one-year course following a first degree. It should preferably be an examined course, and it should be organized if possible both in a university environment and within the country, or at least the region, in which the candidates are going to work. It is extremely important for such a course to be internal to the country, since it is essential that a manager should thoroughly understand the organization and the administrative structure of that country and the statutory status of antiquities of all kinds. The one-year course should provide training in four areas of expertise.

The first is obvously *the identification of archaeological resources*, divided, as in most countries, into portable objects, above-ground structures (buildings and earthworks) and below-ground remains. Future managers must be trained to recognize all three categories in the field, and to deal with them. This will require three different types of skill and, in a one-year course, three separate series of seminars and practicals.

The specifically tropical problems in field identification are the speed of growth and density of vegetation and, very often, the large areas of difficult country involved. There are no simple answers to these problems, but candidate managers must be trained to recognize them from the first and encouraged to find ways of coping with them. It may also be the case that the survey and excavation seasons are very short, because of rain or heat, or that certain areas have to be watched to see where there have been clearances which provide conditions that exist for no more than two or three years.

The second area of expertise in which training is necessary is *planning of conservation*. It is not possible to preserve everything, so archaeological resource managers must select what is to be saved from destruction, by region, by period and by type of monument. The most important aspect of their training is their ability to select, one of the most difficult judgements of all (see Saunders, ch. 15, this volume). Character as well as knowledge must be considered when choosing people who will be capable of taking these decisions on a logical and caring basis; this is not an easy skill for which to provide training, but it is essential for the benefit of future generations.

There are, of course, two types of selection: by preserving an area from destruction or by recording the archaeological evidence from that area before it is destroyed. The one-year training course must prepare candidates for both types of decision-making – on the one hand, what should be saved permanently for the future on or in the ground and, on the other, what can be saved by survey and excavation before destruction is allowed for a pipeline, a new town or an agricultural plantation. Some of the special problems in decision-making of this kind relate to the fact that many structures, town walls, buildings, etc., are made of wood and mud-brick and so are difficult to maintain. The problems of conserving them are considerable and require specially trained craftsmen. Earthworks can become overgrown with vegetation very quickly, and they are expensive to keep cleared. It has also proved difficult to save even recent monuments such as town walls or cemeteries from being utilized as quarries for building materials if the local inhabitants are determined upon it.

The third part of any training course is *the administration of remains* that have been selected for preservation. Once the decision has been taken to save objects, buildings or areas, it must then be decided how they are to be administered. Portable objects are obviously the concern of museums, the training of the managers of which demands different skills and a separate university course. Buildings or other kinds of monument and considerable areas reserved for their archaeological potential and for future work require managerial decisions, so they must be included in the one-year course.

Many countries now impose 'restriction of use' arrangements in such cases, and also set aside archaeological zones as parts of national parks, so consideration must be given to the question of national reserves. Once again, the special problems in the tropics are those of the maintenance of timber, clay and thatched buildings in humid conditions and the rapid vegetation growth which necessitates regular clearance of sites. There is also a problem of erosion if sites are cleared too much or too often. The pressure of local agricultural needs can be very considerable, and a lack of informed and supportive local opinion can be a serious disadvantage. A manager will very often need to be able to convince local people that areas are worthy of preservation in this way: this problem is similar to that encountered in wildlife conservation.

The fourth element in any training course will be *the recording of evidence before destruction*. This is often treated under the heading of 'rescue' or 'salvage' work, and certainly the problems of carrying out surveys and excavations of remains of all periods are common to all parts of the world. A special feature in tropical areas is that this type of work is often more difficult than elsewhere: the distances involved and the types of country and vegetation may call for especially robust transport, which may be difficult to procure and expensive to operate. Expense is, of course, a major constraint throughout the world, but it is particularly severe in tropical countries, which often have major problems in this respect.

The suggested one-year course to prepare people to cope with these problems would best be organized in the following way. First, there should not be too many lectures, since this type of training cannot be conducted through endless lecture courses. Within a single year's training there should not be more than two courses of lectures continuing throughout the year with one or two lectures in each course each week.

One of the courses should be on *Management Theory*, describing the techniques in use in, say, civil engineering and wildlife conservation. Within that course there should be emphasis on Critical Path Analysis, on which there is a considerable literature and which is a very valuable tool for resource managers. A second part of the course would develop a knowledge of decision-making processes and of local archaeological and administrative hierarchies. Students must learn how different government departments in their country articulate, and how their administration, both central or federal and local, can link with archaeological resource management. Students must also acquire experience in office organization and the handling of the bureaucratic side of their work; if possible, computing studies and the mechanical handling of complicated information should be included.

The second lecture course to run throughout the year should be on *Conservation Practice* – that is, the legislative framework within the students' country, its financial practices and, in general terms, how to write and argue cases for financial and other forms of support for projects. There should also be discussion of local information networks and of ways of discovering when and where destruction is likely to take place.

These two courses should be examined by written papers, and constitute the core of the course. Other elements of training might be dealt with in a series of seminars on *Archaeological Practice*, running in parallel with the lecture courses – probably not more than one per week, but with candidates preparing papers for it weekly. The recording of building in local materials in vernacular use, such as clay, wood or stone, and the surveying of earthworks should form part of that course. It will also be important for area surveying of various kinds and of all archaeological periods, including the recognition of successive landscape utilizations by hunter–gatherer, subsistence-farming and other communities, to be taught. Seminars on the preparation of reports for publication will also be necessary.

The third part of the course should be a series of *Practical Exercises* in which candidates record standing buildings and carry out surveys, ideally in the field, but if that is not possible in sandtables; the sandtable of military training is not inappropriate for this type of work, where the problems of, for example, pipeline archaeology could be demonstrated. The practical exercises should also include regular sorting of material. Managers must know in detail the practice in the recognition of stone, clay, metal and other small objects likely to be found in surveys, and training must enable them to recognize material of this kind from all periods from the Palaeolithic onwards. A practical competence in the use of aerial photographs, place-name surveys, etc., would also be taught in this part of the course.

The fourth part of the course should be devoted to *Facility Visits*, which would cover visits to and discussions with museum curators in their storerooms, government officials in their offices, architects in their drawing offices, and experienced archaeological resource managers carrying out their duties.

The final component of the course should be a *Project*, decided at the beginning of the year and carried on throughout it. This piece of work might count for as much as one-third of the examination. The student would have to conduct, probably in his home region, *either* a survey of a small area which would assess its archaeological potential and produce in support a register of sites and finds and a report on their current condition, *or* a register and report on the standing buildings in a similar area, and an outline policy for the conservation of those that merited preservation, *or* a report on museum holdings in a particular area, with an analysis of the lacunae in them and how these might be filled.

At the end of the year the candidate's progress would be tested by two written papers, assessments of their practical work and an examination of the formally presented project.

Although what is advocated here is applicable to any part of the world, the preparation of the managers of archaeological resources in the tropics should not be carried out by talking about general principles. Managers of this kind are more akin to engineers than they are to university teachers or to most government administrators. They must be competent and confident enough to deal on equal terms with other professional workers, and to find their way through legal, administrative and financial jungles. However, unless they maintain a knowledge of and a liking for archaeological fieldwork, they are likely to find themselves less and less effective as their careers develop.

Reference

Saunders, A. 1989. Heritage management and training in England. In *Archaeological heritage management in the modern world*, H. F. Cleere (ed.), ch. 15. London: Unwin Hyman.

29 Policies for the training and recruitment of archaeologists in India

B. K. THAPAR

Early history

The beginnings of archaeological studies in India go back to the last quarter of the 18th century, when the Asiatick Society was founded in 1784 at Calcutta with the avowed purpose of enquiring among other things 'into the History – the Antiquities, Arts, Sciences and Literature of Asia'. In the present context it would be inappropriate to follow the evolution of the conscious antiquarian thought that developed during the following century. Much of it was marked by dilettantism, confined largely to the translation and interpretation of ancient texts and inscriptions, topographical and architectural surveys, descriptive accounts of monuments, the copying of murals, etc. However, among these, six pursuits deserve special attention, providing – however summarily – a perspective for the present study: (a) the exploration of historical sites and the collection of antiquarian objects, including inscriptions of peninsular India by Colin Mackenzie between 1800 and 1821; (b) unlocking the mystery of the Brahmi and Kharoshti scripts by James Princep in 1834–7; (c) detailed architectural surveys of monuments by James Fergusson in 1829–47 and by James Burgess in 1871–89; (d) the systematic field survey of northern India, following in the footsteps of the Chinese pilgrim Huen Tsang, and of the Central Provinces, Bundelkhand and Malwa by Alexander Cunninghan in 1861–85 and of Orissa by Rajendra Lal Mitra in 1860–9; (e) Stone Age (Palaeolithic and Neolithic) discoveries by Bruce Foote and others from 1863 onwards; and (f) the organization of epigraphical studies by Alexander Cunningham and James Burgess with the publication in 1877 of the first volume of *Corpus Inscriptionum Indicarum*, embodying carefully edited texts of all the available inscriptions of Ashok and his grandson, with translations and lithographic facsimiles, and the subsequent appointment of J. F. Fleet as Government Epigraphist in 1883 and the starting of a quarterly publication, *Epigraphia Indica* in October 1888.

By the end of the 19th century, therefore, Indian archaeology had reached a stage of development at which meaningful research could be carried out in the fields of art and architecture, archaeological fieldwork and epigraphy. The last two decades of that century, in particular, witnessed an intellectual ferment in the understanding of Indian archaeology as a whole, set in motion by the provocative writings of Rudolf Hoernle and George Bühler. A professional approach was now needed, and that could be provided only by a properly staffed organization. Although such an organization, known as the Archaeological Survey of India, was constituted as early as 1861 with Alexander Cunningham as the Archaeological Surveyor (later in 1871 designated as Director General), it was not until 1902, when John Marshall (knighted in 1914) was appointed Director General that archaeology achieved its proper place in the scheme of knowledge. Lord Curzon (Viceroy 1899–1905), who evinced a single-minded devotion to the cause of archaeology, was clear-sighted enough to visualize that 'it is in the exploration and study of purely Indian remains, in the probing of the archaic mounds, in the excavation of old Indian studies and in the copying and reading of ancient inscriptions that a good deal of the work of the archaeologists will in future lie'. In a speech delivered before the Asiatic Society on 6 January 1900 he had announced: 'It is in my judgement equally our duty to dig and discover, to classify, reproduce and describe, to copy and decipher and to cherish and conserve'. Such was the task that he had mapped out for the reconstituted Archaeological Survey of India.

Unfortunately, however, all of the human and material resources required to implement this task could not be made available to the new Director General. The whole country was divided into five circles, with an Archaeological Surveyor in charge of each. In addition, a separate officer was appointed to look after Islamic architectural remains in northern India. How to fill these posts was the next question. The Director General himself was experienced, having worked in Greece, southern Turkey and Crete, and had been infused by the spirit of Schliemann and Dörpfeld. As early as 1898 the 11th Congress of Orientalists had discussed a proposal to form an Indian Exploration Fund which was to sponsor excavation of Indian sites by trained European experts. Curzon, to whom the proposal was referred, promptly ruled it out: 'The last thing that we want', he observed, 'is the continental expert with a spade in hand. Let us excavate our own sites'.

In the accomplishment of his colossal task, therefore, Marshall during the initial period secured the assistance of Henry Cousens, Alexander Rea, J. P. Vogel, T. Bloch, Aurel Stein, A. H. Longhurst and D. B. Spooner, none of whom was an accredited archaeologist by training. The first Indian Officer to join the Archaeological Survey was D. R. Bhandarkar, an eminent orientalist. However, these arrangements fell short of the requirements. In 1912, therefore, the government thought of decentralizing the Survey by abolishing the post of Director General and replacing it by a Professor of Archaeology, to be attached to a proposed Oriental Research Institute. The proposal raised a storm of protest in India and abroad, and was accordingly dropped. With a view to encouraging Indian talent and enlisting its assistance in archaeological fieldwork, Marshall therefore instituted a system of scholarships, including those for Sanskrit scholars, affording intensive professional training in various fields of Indian archaeology. It was through this system that he was able to attract men like D. R. Sahni, K. N. Dikshit and M. S. Vats, all of whom subsequently rose to the supreme position of Director General of the Survey, D. R. Sahni being the first Indian to hold that post (from 1931 to 1935). The seed of training was thus sown by Marshall. By a Resolution dated 14 June 1921, the Government of India had decided that 60 per cent of the service henceforth would be filled only by Indians. The immediate result of this was an increase in the strength of the Survey and the setting up of a separate Exploration Branch to speed up the work of exploration and excavation. By the time Marshall relinquished his charge in September 1928, the Archaeological Survey had grown into a massive organization, covering such functions as conservation, excavation, epigraphical studies, museums and publications. It consisted of a staff which was trained on the job.

However, a serious criticism of Marshall and his staff is that the methods used by them in the excavation of sites were behind those advocated and employed in the West since the time of Pitt Rivers. The reason is not difficult to find: it lies essentially in quality. Neither Marshall nor any of his staff had received a thorough grounding in and more-concentrated experience of scientific standards under closely critical observations. The charge may thus be largely true, but the fact should not be overlooked that those standards of scientific excavation had during that period hardly penetrated to the shores of the Mediterranean; east of Suez they were almost unknown.

Specialized training

The system Marshall bequeathed to his successors remained almost unchanged and the Survey's activities, which had fallen into disrepute, were severely criticized in February 1939 by the eminent British archaeologist Sir Leonard Woolley, who was invited by the government to review the entire archaeological work in the country and to make suggestions on the future plan of work. In his report Woolley *inter alia*, emphasized the need for specialized training and comprehensive planning. Another fruitful suggestion was that non-official institutions, both foreign and Indian, should be encouraged to take part in archaeological fieldwork. One of the significant results of the Woolley Report was the appointment of Mortimer Wheeler (knighted in 1952) as Director General of the Survey in the spring of 1944. He was required to undertake the total reorganization of the Archaeological Survey of India, a task which was then regarded as a matter of great urgency.

Wheeler's first task therefore was to convert the activities of the Survey to a new and modernized phase of archaeological research and methodology. He accordingly made an urgent appeal to the Vice-Chancellors of the Indian universities for the recruitment of young university graduates to carry out organized research in archaeological technology. He had decided to provide facilities for training at Taxila where, besides the ancient metropolitan site, there was a well-kept museum. This training camp came to be known as the

Taxila School of Archaeology in 1944. The response was astonishing in quantity and quality alike. Over 60 young graduates, coming from all parts of India, gathered at Taxila to receive training in modern methods of archaeological fieldwork. This was the first organized phase of training, which was continued by Wheeler at all of the subseqeuent excavations that he undertook in India: Arikamedu (1945), Harappa (1946), and Brahmagiri and Chandravalli (1947). He brought to his task the scientific methods of archaeological excavation which he had developed in England in the 1920s and 1930s, based on the earlier techniques of Pitt Rivers.

During the four years of his stay in India Wheeler trained over 100 students. The training consisted of the technique of excavation and its supervision, and the preparation of proper field records, along with surveying, photography, and administration. Lectures were given on subjects such as publication, epigraphy, numismatics, and special archaeological and anthropological topics. He did not claim that this training produced fully qualified field archaeologists or skilled recorders or photographers, for whom long experience is necessary, but it could and did attempt to provide the basic essentials of that discipline. He was strongly of the view that archaeological research must be extended outside the confines of a government department into the activities of the universities and learned institutions of India. 'Archaeology like other sciences', he affirmed, 'can flourish only on a basis of healthy emulation and informed criticism'. He therefore urged that 'the Indian universities like other universities throughout the world must enter the field and join the fray'. Another chapter in the history of archaeological fieldwork in India was thus added, and with it terminated the monopoly of the Archaeological Survey of India in exploration and excavation.

In the 1950s field research projects in archaeology were initially set up in six universities where some trained staff was already available. More universities have subsequently established composite departments of Ancient Indian History Culture and Archaeology, with the result that the number of universities offering courses in archaeology is now over two dozen. This number, however, belies the real position, since several of these appear to exist in little more than name. Most do not undertake fieldwork but confine their activities to teaching theory alone, considering archaeology as merely an adjunct. There is thus a marked imbalance in the growth of field archaeology in these universities; only a few have fully equipped departments and trained staff to undertake field research. What is needed is more fully trained professionals. The pace of progress in training which Wheeler had initiated had regrettably slackened with the ostensible reduction in the training facilities.

Courses for professional training in heritage management

The Constitution of India, which came into force in 1950, listed archaeology as a concurrent subject, with the result the allocation of functions relating to archaeology became the charge of both the Union and the State Governments. As a result all the State Governments were also required to establish Departments of Archaeology in order to fulfil their constitutional obligations. The increase in archaeological activities in the country led to a growing demand for fully trained archaeologists. None of the universities, much less the State Departments of Archaeology, could offer facilities for training in all branches of archaeology, including conservation.

Realizing the need for integrated training in archaeology, the Central Advisory Board of Archaeology passed a resolution urging the government to open a School of Archaeology under the Archaeological Survey. The government acceded to this resolution, and the School was opened in 1959, providing a 20-month postgraduate diploma course in Indian archaeology. The courses covered prehistoric, protohistoric and early historical archaeology, art and architecture, palaeography, theory and methods of excavation and exploration, publication, the preservation of monuments, including chemical preservation, museum methods, and antiquities legislation, as well as practical training in surveying, drawing, photography, preparation of casts and taking impressions, etc. During the period of training students are also taken around important groups of monuments in the country to obtain first-hand knowledge of their art and architecture and to familiarize themselves with problems of conservation. In addition, the school runs refresher courses in conservation for the benefit of the in-service staff. In 1967 the duration of the course was reduced to 12 months. Fifteen postgraduate students are admitted for each course, of whom nearly 40 per cent are in-service trainees from the Archaeological Survey of India and the State Departments of Archaeology. This diploma course also attracts foreign students from neighbouring countries such as Afghanistan and Nepal. The school is headed by a Director and the teaching staff is mainly drawn from the Survey, though scholars from universities and organizations such as the Anthropological Survey, the Zoological Survey, the Birbal Institute of Paleobotany and the National Physical Laboratory who have specialized in some branches of archaeology are also invited to deliver lectures. At the end of the course the students are examined in all of the subjects; they are also required to submit a dissertation on a subject of their own choice in any branch of archaeology. Evaluation is based on the marks obtained in the written papers plus the performance in *viva voce*. Students obtaining marks of less than 50 per cent overall or less than 40 per cent in each subject do not qualify for the diploma.

The syllabus of the course is fairly comprehensive. It is the only facility in the subcontinent for full-time excavators, archaeologists, scientists, conservators, epigraphists and administrators to provide the would-be professional archaeologists with technical expertise, theory and experience. This diploma, although awarded by the government, is not so far recognized by any university in its academic framework, but its possession is now an accepted research qualification in the field of archaeology.

An Expert Group appointed by the government in 1983 to review the functioning of archaeology in India recommended, *inter alia*, that the diploma course should be extended to two years so that students could receive more-intensive field training, extending to a minimum period of ten months covering excavation, conservation, etc. The two-year course was put into operation in 1986.

The Expert Group also stressed that the archaeology of India must be studied in a wider perspective. Realizing the need for developing specialization in the archaeology of the neighbouring countries, the Group recommended that the existing School of Archaeology should be upgraded to an Institute of Archaeology with expanded functions. The government has accepted this recommendation. The functions and activities of the Institute of Archaeology are to be twofold: research and teaching, including training. For the latter, it would take over the functions of the School of Archaeology by expanding its activities to the teaching and practising of West Asian, South-East Asian and Central Asian archaeology, including fieldwork. It will have eight main faculties (without prejudice to further development): Indian archaeology, South and South-East Asian archaeology, West Asian and Central Asian archaeology, Environmental archaeology, Archaeological technology, Conservation (both structural and chemical), Documentation and recording, and Underwater archaeology. Of these, only the faculties of Indian archaeology and Conservation are as yet operative. For activities relating to research, the Institute will offer fellowships to scholars for advanced study and research in various branches of archaeology. The Institute will also run short refresher courses for in-service staff. Such courses will aim to survey existing methods and add new ones, and as such will serve as a stimulus for further improvement.

The Institute of Archaeology is housed in a separate building (24 Tilak Marg, New Delhi–110001) from the Archaeological Survey. The diploma course starts in October each year. The announcement in the course is made in June through advertisements in leading newspapers. Applicants have to take a written test followed by a *viva voce*. Selected candidates receive a stipend for undergoing the course.

Recruitment

In India the employment potential for archaeologists is very limited, being confined to the requirements of the Archaeological Survey of India, the State Departments of Archaeology and, to some extent, the universities. Among these, the Archaeological Survey is the largest employer and absorbs most of the graduates, depending on the vacancies in a particular year. The State Departments are inadequately funded, and are accordingly poorly staffed. Their demand for trained diploma holders is, therefore, very low, and the position in respect of the universities is similar.

Recruitments to the various cadres of the Archaeological Survey of India is carried out by different agencies such as the Union Public Service Commission, the Staff Selection Commission, etc., depending on the grade of the post. It is gratifying to record that the present Director General of the Archaeological Survey is a graduate of the first intake of the School of Archaeology (1959–61); many of his colleagues in the Survey and in the universities have also graduated from the School. State Departments have similar Commissions for recruitment of their staff. Recruitment to the university cadre is through special selection committees constituted for the purpose. A representative of the employing institution and one or two experts in the field are normally associated with these selections.

30 Archaeology and conservation training at the international level

N. P. STANLEY PRICE

Introduction: conservation and archaeological management

The idea that archaeological resources, like other substantial assets, require active management has received wider recognition during the past 20 years. Two related trends in particular seem to be responsible: first, the much-increased rate of destruction of archaeological sites through changes in land use and, secondly, the rapid growth in world tourism, especially in areas hitherto not much frequented.

Both of these trends have had an adverse impact on the preservation of archaeological sites.[1] However, they should not be allowed to obscure a more fundamental truth – that sites are subject in any case to deterioriation as a result of natural agencies. This is all the more true once the sites have been excavated.

Management of archaeological sites therefore requires a policy developed in awareness of conservation philosophy and of the technical measures needed to implement that policy. It demands an understanding of the values ascribed to individual sites, their historical and environmental context, the nature of the material remains, the factors causing deterioration and the measures to reduce their effect.

In other words, awareness of the principles of conservation should, I suggest, be required of a manager of archaeological resources. This opinion is gaining wider acceptance, at least among conservators. An international meeting in 1983 of conservators concerned with training (the Working Group on Training in Conservation and Restoration of the ICOM Committee for Conservation) agreed:

> that the recommendation be made to international and national associations concerned with art history, architecture, anthropology, archaeology, ethnography, librarianship and related professions to formally recognize that no training in these disciplines be considered complete without at least an introduction to the basic principles of conservation, not in the sense of conservation practice, but with the aim of generating an awareness of conservation and instilling an understanding of its

function and importance to other disciplines, both in terms of preservation and in the acquisition of new knowledge.

Among archaeologists, the truism about excavation being destruction has long prompted a proper insistence on the need to document fully all phases of the excavation. Less often mentioned is the concomitant need to conserve what has been found. This is often realized only later, when finds from earlier fieldwork are re-excavated from museum basements or when sites long considered 'dug' are revisited to answer different questions. The processes of deterioration since excavation are then only too evident and the remedial measures far more costly than the preventive measures that should have been taken at the time of excavation.

There is a common misconception that this is not the excavator's responsibility, and that funds devoted to conservation are funds lost to further research. This betrays an erroneous view of conservation. The information to be derived from excavating is the greater, the more the excavator is aware of material decay processes and of the appropriate preventive measures (see various papers in ICCROM 1986).

What opportunities are there for archaeologists to acquire this knowledge of conservation principles? As for formal training, the record at the national level is poor. Very few university degree courses in archaeology include conservation; if they do, it is usually an option. Conversely, few of the degree courses in historic preservation in the USA include archaeology. More options exist in short, post-experience courses, but these are often specialized in one material, or conservation is treated solely as a technique.

A similar situation existed in the field of architecture some 20 years ago, when perhaps the majority of building restoration projects were carried out by architects unaware of the principles of conservation. A number of international initiatives taken at that time have improved the situation today. A notable milestone was the Second International Congress of the Architects and Technicians of Historical Monuments, in Venice, in 1964. This led to the drafting of a set of principles (the Charter of Venice) to guide the conservation and restoration of monuments and sites, the establishment of a specialized body (ICOMOS) to promote those principles, and the setting-up of an international training course in architectural restoration, organized jointly by ICCROM and the University of Rome.

Since it was first held in 1965, this course has been completed by over 800 participants from some 80 countries. Many of these have been influential in establishing postgraduate or diploma courses in architectural conservation in their own countries; more than 40 such courses now exist (ICCROM 1982). Moreover, conservation is now included in the syllabus of several professional training curricula for architects.

In view of the undoubted advances in architectural conservation due to international initiatives, it is worth examining the nature of international training and its relevance to archaeologists. A final section looks at international agreement on ethical standards.

International training in conservation

The following account concentrates on ICCROM, which is the most active organization in this field. However, it should be recalled that it works closely with other international organizations concerned with training in conservation, including Unesco, ICOM, ICOMOS and IIC. (Since these bodies with similar initials are often confused, they are briefly described in the Appendix.)

The conservation training activities of ICCROM can conveniently be divided into three types according to geographical scope:

(a) regular international courses held annually, usually in Rome;
(b) regional courses organized with other centres, serving one geographical region; and
(c) local, national courses organized at the request of one country.

National courses

To take these in reverse order, national courses may be 'refresher' courses for conservators with several years' experience, or introductions to conservation for those, for example museum curators, with professional training in other fields. ICCROM co-operates in providing teachers and teaching material; this is then often donated to the country as a nucleus for future courses organized independently of ICCROM.

The initiative to organize a national course sometimes comes from a former participant of one of ICCROM's international courses in Rome. Because of his or her familiarity with the format and style of the Rome courses, the practical organization of a national course is greatly facilitated. In turn the national course is used to select promising candidates for further training abroad, either in Rome or elsewhere.

Sometimes training at national level forms part of a long-term project of technical assistance at one site. For example, at Göreme, in Turkey, and on various sites in Thailand and now in Burma, conservators of mural paintings have been trained on-site during successive annual seasons; several are later selected to attend the Rome course in mural painting conservation to broaden their experience.

Recent courses organized by ICCROM in the archaeological field include one on conservation on excavations for Chilean archaeologists, a course on site conservation and maintenance on Easter Island, and a seminar for museum technicians at Moenjodaro.

Regional courses

Regional courses have many of the features of the international courses (see below). The participants come from different countries, but they have the advantage that all have a similar cultural, and sometimes linguistic, background. This reduces problems of adaptation to a different environment, both cultural and climatic.

Recent regional courses have included one on the preservation of mud-brick in Peru, principally for those working in Latin America. ICCROM also provides teachers for the SEAMEO–SPAFA courses on art and archaeology in South-East Asia, and for the Unesco Regional Centres, for example for the annual course on architectural recording and survey held in Baghdad.

Regular international courses

There are at present four regular international courses held annually in Rome: one on architectural conservation, which lasts five months; one on mural paintings conservation and another on the scientific principles of conservation, each of which lasts four months; and a three-week course on preventive conservation in museums.

The scientific principles course is concerned with the structure of materials, their deterioration and conservation. Both this and the architectural conservation courses are relevant to archaeologists, a point taken up below.

These courses are well established at ICCROM, the first dating from 1965 and the latest from 1975. There is, therefore, a great deal of accumulated experience in organizing courses of this kind. With the aim of decentralizing international training activity, two more specialized courses have been organized biennially under Unesco sponsorship. Since 1976 an international course on the conservation of stone has taken place every two years in Venice, while another on wood conservation technology was held in Norway in 1984 and repeated in 1986, under the sponsorship of Unesco and the Norwegian Ministry of the Environment.

Why international training?

With this summary of training activity in which ICCROM is involved, it is time to ask a leading question. What do international courses achieve that cannot be achieved equally well, or better, at a national level or, where national facilities are inadequate, through bilateral agreement between countries? Their rôle in providing training that is not otherwise widely available has already been mentioned. However, what other advantages are there for those taking part?

It should be emphasized first that these courses are not for beginners, but for those already qualified and actively working in some aspect of conservation, including archaeology. The benefits for a participant include the broader conception of the theory and practice of conservation provided by an international course, the establishment of a common technical vocabulary for describing conservation practice, and the chance to update and expand knowledge of techniques.

For these benefits to be realized, much care has to be taken in designing and running these courses. Their main characteristics have been described in a paper by Mora & Torraca (1983) under the headings (1) choice of participants, (2) syllabus, (3) lecturers, (4) style of teaching and (5) organization. Experience has shown repeatedly that technical conservation principles can be taught to a mixed international audience if certain guidelines are followed. Here only a few points will be mentioned.

Participants are accepted whatever their training, whether in the arts, the crafts or the sciences. However, an absolute requirement is that they have at least four years' experience of professional work devoted to the cultural heritage, preferably in or on behalf of government bodies. Preference is also given to those involved in teaching in their own country. All are subject to competitive selection procedures held annually.

The extremely varied professional and cultural backgrounds of the trainees underlines an essential objective of the course, the establishment of a common terminology for describing conservation practice. To take an example, early in the curriculum of the Architectural Conservation Course, each participant is asked to make a case study of the Ara Pacis monument in Rome, and to propose alternative solutions to the one adopted in the 1930s for its rescue, restoration and display. The ideas presented are always astonishingly diverse (see Linstrum 1981, for a similar experience), but all can be communicated and discussed, given a common terminology.

The diversity of background is also viewed positively as a means of comparing different values with regard to tradition and conservation. Each participant is asked to give a talk illustrating his or her own experience in conservation. It is instructive to observe how quickly new concepts are absorbed and how they modify personal accounts of conservation work.

This, then, is one important objective. Another is to enable trainees to update their knowledge and to be exposed to current thinking in the subject. To this end specialist teachers are invited to cover each topic. More than 80 per cent of lectures are given by non-ICCROM staff, many of them being invited from abroad.

To gauge whether new concepts have been absorbed coherently, some method of assessment is required. The assessment system has to acknowledge that course participants are professionals with an average age between 30 and 40 years, for whom a formal written examination would be inappropriate. Different courses use different methods. The Architecture course requires the preparation of a project, for example a local case study of conservation; the Mural Paintings course uses a combination of theoretical and practical on-site evaluation; whereas the Scientific Principles course holds a series of written review papers for which participants are allowed to use their own notes taken during lectures and practical work. Only if an adequate level of comprehension throughout the course is attained is the ICCROM Certificate of Attendance awarded.

The 70 or so people who complete an ICCROM course in Rome each year automatically become part of an informal network that facilitates other aspects of ICCROM's work. There are now some 1500 former trainees in over 100 countries. They act as contacts who can report on current conservation work in their countries, and who can obtain less-widely circulated publications for ICCROM's library, as specialists to take part in technical field projects, and, above all, as teachers who initiate local training activities and influence the insertion of conservation in teaching curricula.

Archaeologists and international training

It was pointed out above that rarely are conservation principles included in the training of archaeologists. The increased attention given to conservation in the training of architects has also benefited archaeology, especially in those countries in which the restoration of archaeological sites is in the hands of architects.

The regular training courses at ICCROM are of direct relevance to archaeologists and, indeed, several have attended them. Both the Architectural Conservation course and the course in Scientific Principles of Conservation provide an exposure to the philosophy and principles of conservation that should, I suggest, be familiar to the archaeologist who is aware of the duty to preserve.

Nevertheless, none of these courses, nor the regional courses mentioned earlier, are solely archaeological in orientation. What is needed are short, post-experience courses that are directed to the particular problem of archaeological material. The hope would be that, as experience has shown in the architectural field, these would eventually influence the designers of archaeology degree courses to include conservation as an integral element.

The demand for short, post-experience courses is likely to increase with the emergence of the management of archaeological resources as a professional subdiscipline. Not only conservation principles, but other topics such as management methods and financial accounting, should form part of course curricula. At present there are few opportunities of this kind, though mention should be made of the annual Management Development for Archaeologists course held at Brunel University, in England, and the short courses run by the US National Park Service (NPS). The latter, covering a range of topics in cultural resource management, are designed primarily for in-service NPS employees but applications from others are considered (National Park Service 1984).

Ethics and professional qualifications

If post-experience courses at national and international levels are to increase, how are they to be evaluated as contributions to the professional qualification of archaeologists? There are two steps here: first, establishing what constitutes a professionally qualified archaeologist, and, secondly, assessing different training components for their contribution to professional qualification.

Similar questions have preoccupied conservators, who for some years have had regular meetings of international working groups on training. Conservators and restorers have been attempting to define their profession and to establish criteria as to who may call themselves conservator–restorers. One goal is to agree on ethical standards; the other is to establish a system whereby different forms of training can be evaluated relative to one another. When these have been agreed upon at a national level, a more ambitious goal is to achieve international agreement on the same.

In conservation much has been achieved in the way of agreement on ethical standards. The Codes of Ethics adopted by different national associations of conservators reveal a core of ethical principles common to conservation worldwide. Conservators have therefore moved on to make a concerted attempt to find a definition of their work that is internationally acceptable. There now exists a document (ICOM 1985) entitled 'The conservator–restorer: a definition of the profession', which has been officially approved by the International Council of Museums and has received widespread circulation.

Agreement on definition of the profession ought to facilitate the evaluation of different training schemes. This is easier at national level where conservation training is organized by the state. Where it is not, as in many countries including the UK, it remains an elusive ideal after many years' discussion. So long as this is the case, international consensus appears a distant prospect.

Agreement has to be reached not only on the status of different national training schemes, but also on the relative value of international courses, internships and field experience. The aim, it should be emphasized, is not to standardize training; this would be undesirable even if feasible. Rather, the purpose is to establish a system whereby the components of different training schemes can be evaluated as qualifications for the professional conservator–restorer.

The introduction to the ICOM document referred to above states: 'definition of the profession of conservator–restorer is appropriate and timely and should result in the profession achieving parity in status with other related disciplines such as those of the curator, the archaeologist and the scientist'.

The statement rather flatters archaeology which, although well established as a discipline, has less than conservation does in the way of written codes of ethics. Much had long been taken for granted in this respect until the explosion of rescue archaeology in the 1970s. With the emergence of contract archaeology, and in the USA of competitive tendering for contracts, there arose an urgent need for some means of checking the credentials of archaeologists offering their services.

This has led to the founding of self-regulating professional associations, for example the Society of Professional Archaeologists (SOPA) in the USA and the Institute of Field Archaeologists (IFA) in the UK. These have established rules of membership based on professional qualifications and drawn up codes of ethics to which all members must subscribe. They recognize that archaeologists may be qualified mainly in one or two fields of expertise within archaeology, and that that expertise may have been acquired through a variety of theoretical and practical training.

The move towards professional associations of archaeologists with written codes of ethics has implications for the international regulation of archaeology. For instance, an archaeologist applying to work abroad might be required to show membership of his or her national professional association, or to meet the professional criteria laid down in the host country. This raises the question of whether there in fact already exists a consensus of what constitutes the professional qualification of an archaeologist. If it does, to what extent is it universal, regardless of the disparities in financial and professional resources for archaeology around the world?

In this respect it is worth recalling that there has long existed a series of guidelines for the conduct of archaeological fieldwork. I refer to the *Recommendation on international principles applicable to archaeological excavations* adopted by Unesco's General Assembly in 1956. Although not well known among archaeologists, this document has been very influential in determining the form of national legislations on archaeology, especially those enacted in non-European countries (O'Keefe & Prott 1984). The terms of permits for foreign archaeologists frequently echo the guidelines of the 1956 Recommendation.

The Recommendation is now outdated in some respects. It needs to be rewritten in contemporary idiom and updated to bring it into line with current thinking and to give greater emphasis to conservation (Stanley Price 1984). The text drawn up in 1956 exhibits the flexibility required of a Recommendation to encompass the diversity of national conditions. The extent to which a revised version could be more specific would reveal how universal agreement is on the standards of professional archaeology. This represents a worthwhile goal for world archaeology in the 1990s.

Notes

1   This chapter, at the Editor's request, refers specifically to sites, although I consider archaeological resources to include movable objects, for which similar arguments apply.
2   The views expressed here are the author's and not necessarily those of ICCROM, by whom he was employed when this chapter was written.

References

ICCROM 1982. *International index on training in conservation of cultural property*. Rome. (New edition in preparation.)
ICCROM 1986. *Preventive measures during excavation and site protection*. Rome.

ICOM 1985. *The conservator–restorer: a definition of the profession*. Working group on training in conservation and restoration, ICOM Committee for Conservation. (Text reproduced in, for example, *ICOM News* **39** (1986), *ICOM Committee for Conservation Newsletter no. 4* (1986), *ICCROM Newsletter* **12** (1986).)

Linstrum, D. 1981. Education for conservation. In *Nessun futuro senza passato. Atti ICOMOS VI Assemblea Generale*, Vol. I, 679–89. Rome. Italian National Committee.

Mora, P. & G. Torraca 1983. A project for an international course on wood conservation technology. In *The conservation of wooden cultural property. International Symposium on Conservation of Cultural Property*, Tokyo, 297–301.

National Park Service (USA) 1984. Training and development opportunities. *Courier* (The National Park Service Newsletter), Special Issue, Fall.

O'Keefe, P. J. & L. V. Prott 1984. *Law and the cultural heritage*. Vol. 1: *Discovery and excavation*. Abingdon: Professional Books Ltd.

Stanley Price, N. P. 1984. Conservation on excavations and the 1956 Unesco Recommendation. In *Conservation on archaeological excavations*, N. P. Stanley Price (ed.), 1–10. Rome: ICCROM.

Unesco 1956. *Recommendation on international principles applicable to archaeological excavations*, Paris. (Text reproduced in Stanley Price (1984).)

Appendix. ICCROM, ICOM, ICOMOS and IIC

ICCROM

ICCROM is an autonomous scientific intergovernmental organization founded by Unesco in 1959. At present it has 73 Member States and 64 Associate Members – public and private non-profit cultural institutions. Its work is funded by contributions from Members and from other sources such as contracts from Unesco and cultural foundations for specific activities.

Its full title is the International Centre for the Study of the Preservation and the Restoration of Cultural Property. This was abbreviated in earlier years to 'the Rome Centre' and 'the International Centre for Conservation'. Since 1977 it has been known for short as 'ICCROM' (which is not an acronym).

Address: ICCROM, Via di San Michele 13, I–00153 Roma, Italy.

ICOM

ICOM, the International Council of Museums, is a non-profit organization dedicated to the improvement and advancement of museums and the museum profession. Like ICOMOS (see below), it is a non-governmental organization, generating its own activities through its members, of which there are more than 8000, both institutions and individuals, in 120 countries.

Address: ICOM Secretariat, Maison de l'Unesco, 1 rue Miollis, F–75732 Paris Cedex 15, France.

ICOMOS

ICOMOS, the International Council on Museums and Sites, is a non-governmental organization devoted to the conservation, protection and *mise en valeur* of monuments, historic areas and sites. It has a membership of 2900. Like ICOM, many of its activities are carried out through national and international committees. In 1985 a new International Committee on Archaeological Heritage Management was established.

Address: ICOMOS, 75 rue du Temple, F–75003 Paris, France.

IIC

IIC, the International Institute for Conservation of Historic and Artistic Works, was founded in 1950 and is incorporated as a limited company in the UK. It has more than 3000 members in more than 65 countries, and promotes contact between museum personnel and conservators through publications, congresses and regional groups.

Address: IIC, 6 Buckingham Street, London WC2N 6BA, UK.

Fuller notes on these organizations will be found in the *ICCROM Newsletter* **12** (1986); further information can be obtained by writing to the addresses given above.

31 The rôle of the professional institution

PETER V. ADDYMAN

The need for a professional archaeological institution in Great Britain

So long, so all-pervasive and so remarkably effective has been the rôle of the amateur in British archaeology that until relatively recently it seemed inconceivable that anyone could habitually earn his living by being an archaeologist. O. G. S. Crawford, founder editor of *Antiquity*, and himself the first professional archaeologist in the Ordnance Survey, saw, for instance, an advertisement for an archaeologist in *The Times* in 1913 – and even in 1955, in his autobiography, could write of it 'I should imagine that it was the only one ever to appear there' (Crawford 1955, p. 90). Certainly by 1955 there were many archaeologists in Great Britain, but they were university lecturers who were also archaeologists, museum curators who also excavated, and civil servants whose duties included archaeological work. The subject was at best an academic discipline – though there were still some in 1955 who would have disputed that – and more often it had the status of a hobby. It was certainly not a profession for any but a few. Now, 30 years later, there are probably more than 2000 people in Great Britain who might classify themselves – probably with some pride – as professional archaeologists, and *The Times* frequently carries the advertisements which lead them to their professional positions.

The change has come about for a number of reasons. The first and most important, perhaps, is a change in the nation's perception of the material evidence for its past: from something of marginal importance and antiquarian interest to something of real worth, relevant to both the present and to the future. A second reason is the rapid development of archaeology as a discipline and as a science with specialisms well beyond the scope of all but the most determined amateur. A third reason is the increasing pace of development and change in an overcrowded Britain, which has threatened to destroy – and indeed has destroyed – more archaeological evidence in the past 30 years than had been destroyed in the previous 300 years. A fourth reason emerged from the third: universities, seeing the need for archaeologists in a time of crisis, expanded courses and established new ones to provide the trained graduates for what, perhaps for the first time, were full and permanent positions as professional archaeologists. Such posts proliferated during the 1970s, at a time when government spending on rescue archaeology in Great Britain increased by tenfold and more than 100 professional excavation units were established throughout the British Isles.

These rapid developments inevitably brought tension and misunderstanding, as new bodies sought to find a place in a long-established scheme of things, new professionals began to carry out work that had long been the preserve of the amateur or the university-based scholar, and institutions with a long and distinguished history were confronted with brash new organizations and individuals in a hurry. The very nature of rescue archaeology, moreover, brought archaeologists into contact with the real world, away from the sun-swept downlands of earlier research projects and far from the ivory towers of Academe. They were expected to treat with architects, quantity surveyors, developers, planners and other professionals, and to observe professional standards of their own. Such other professionals, in their turn, encountering archaeologists, as often as not met enthusiasts who were green in the world of business, commerce and professional behaviour or – worse – they mistook amateurs of little experience or status for archaeologists of professional standing.

Moves towards the formation of a British archaeological institution

By the early 1970s it was evident that some order was needed in a situation of increasing confusion. The Council for British Archaeology (CBA), the one organization which can credibly claim to represent the full range of bodies concerned with the protection and interpretation of Great Britain's past, was a natural sounding-board for the issue. Its Working Party on Professionalism in Archaeology, set up in 1973, proposed that consideration be given to the establishment of a professional institution for archaeologists, analogous to those existing in other professions. A Steering Committee was formed to explore the possibility of founding a 'British Archaeological Institution'. By 1975 the Steering Committee had encountered such opposition to its proposals that the CBA reluctantly abandoned the attempts to form a professional institution. Some of the worries came from amateur archaeologists, who perhaps feared increasing exclusion from a discipline that, uniquely among scholarly pursuits, had been a legitimate preserve for those qualified by experience rather than paper qualification. Others did not recognize archaeology as a profession, and regretted a tendency to make it one. Yet others failed to see the need for another body in a field already catered for by specialist societies and existing professional institutions such as the Museums Association. Moreover, many people had the gravest suspicions about the mechanics by which a British Archaeological Institution would be set up – inevitably by a group of first members who would have to constitute themselves an Institute.

While such soul-searching was in progress in Great Britain a similar process was going on in the USA (see Davis, ch. 27, this volume). Here the proliferation of contract archaeology in the wake of forward-looking conservation legislation had led to the emergence of archaeological consultancies and a very commercial, but not always very professonal, approach. To provide a self-regulating body for a rapidly expanding new profession there was very similar wide-ranging discussion in the Society for American Archaeology, and a similar working party. Similar difficulties were encountered over the means of formation of a new body. Eventually, in 1975, the working party took the step of constituting itself the Society of Professional Archaeologists (SOPA), and set about the contentious task of establishing rules, procedures, a code of practice and the formulation of standards – and the challenging task of recruiting members.

Such a move took nearly a decade longer in Great Britain. It began with the formation of a new, and this time independent, steering committee early in 1979, and establishment of an Association for the Promotion of an Institute of Field Archaeologists (APIFA) later that year. The APIFA eventually attracted 500 members, which indicated the strength of support for its aims. It spent the years between 1979 and 1982 taking opinions on the form a professional institution should take, drawing on the growing experience of SOPA in the USA and on that of other professional institutions in the UK. Eventually APIFA encapsulated what it considered to be the consensus of opinion into a Memorandum and Articles for a new Institute of Field Archaeologists (IFA), which set out the nature and form of the new body. It also prepared a draft Code of Conduct to define the standards of conduct and self-discipline required of an archaeologist, formulated various procedures for the day-to-day running of the new Institute, gathered together a substantial foundation fund, sought nominations from members of APIFA for a first Council for the new Institute, carried out elections and finally, in December 1982, handed over responsibility for the new Institute to this Council. The gestation period of IFA had, therefore, in one way or another, been a full ten years.

The Institute of Field Archaeologists

Aspiring members of IFA were reminded that the fuller understanding of man's past is part of society's common heritage, and it should be widely available. Because of this, and because it is irreplaceable, archaeologists had a corporate and an individual duty to help to conserve the archaeological heritage. They should regard it as a finite resource, and use it economically in their work. Their work should be conducted in such a way as to produce reliable information, and the results should be disseminated. The objectives of IFA were explained as the advancement of the practice of field archaeology and allied disciplines, the definition and maintenance of proper standards in training and education in field archaeology, in the execution and supervision of work and in the conservation of the archaeological heritage, and the dissemination of information about field archaeologists and their areas of interest. Under these objectives and aims some 500 archaeologists have so far sought admittance to the Institute, either as full members, or as associates or students, and at the end of the 1985/6 working year membership in all categories was 520.

Membership of the Institute carries with it the presumption of competence as an archaeologist, and great care has therefore been taken to admit only those who have proved their competence. The usual criteria for admittance – academic qualifications plus a period of satisfactory practice – have been demanded. The special nature of archaeology, a discipline in which some of the most distinguished practitioners have had no formal academic training at all, is recognized, and such people can be admitted on an assessment of their performance. All those admitted, in whatever category of membership, undertake to observe the Institute's Code of Conduct. The Institute's membership list therefore now presents to the nation a cadre of archaeological practitioners whose competence has been assessed by their peers and vouched for, and who have voluntarily undertaken to observe a code defining the highest ethical standards in the practice of their profession.

It is self-evident that no-one can be equally competent in the practice of all branches and specialisms of a subject as diverse as archaeology. The Institute has therefore sought to identify, both for purposes of admitting members and for purposes of advising the public, a series of areas of competence within the discipline. It is the intention to provide a Professional Register under which the specialisms of members and their achievement within these areas of competence can be recorded.

Although standards of British field archaeology are thought to be high, the Institute believes that the training of field archaeologists is, and always should be, one of its major concerns. Since 1970 the number of single-honours courses in archaeology in British universities has risen to more than 25, and the estimated number of graduates from 60 in 1972 to 270–280 in 1985. Similarly, the number of joint-honours graduates increased from 30 to 150. Not all of these courses contain a strong vocational element in their training, and not all are of an even standard in the practical professional training they provide. There are only a handful of postgraduate courses which provide professional training rather than research training. In these circumstances the Institute has undertaken a survey of what is available, with the purpose of identifying the strengths and weaknesses, and encouraging better provision. The Institute does not see itself as providing such training, though (a personal opinion) it may in due course have a rôle in assessing its eventual effectiveness.

If the Institute has an educational rôle at all, it lies in the improvement of its members' skills, practices and awareness. Two main methods of achieving this seem to have emerged in the Institute's early years: by the sponsorship and organization of conferences and seminars, and by various publications, including its newsletter *The Field Archaeologist* (ISSN 6265–9921) and a series of Technical Papers. The subjects of the conferences held in conjunction with other bodies have so far included such topics as *Archaeological excavation in the 21st century* and *Machine-based and machine-assisted post-excavation techniques*. For the future the Institute has in preparation annual multitheme national conferences on archaeology.

The Institute has identified one special field in which it considers it might help its membership at a time of rapid change. It has therefore set up a special Working Party on Computer Usage in Archaeology; *Current Issues in Archaeological Computing* (British Archaeological Reports), M. A. Cooper and J. D. Richards (eds) is an IFA-derived publication on the subject.

One of the main functions of a professional institution is to advise and mediate on relations between its members and the users of the profession's services. The IFA has addressed its responsibilities in this field in a number of ways. It is developing a policy of presentation of both the Institute and the profession to users and the public at large, through open and positive public relations. Secondly, it is supporting measures to establish codes of practice in various fields, such as that recently promulgated by the British Archaeologists and Developers Liaison Group (Code of Practice 1986). Thirdly it is prepared to investigate problems which may arise from use of archaeological services by the public.

It seems inevitable that some problems which emerge from relationships between the profession and its users will involve complaint or dispute. The Institute exists both to advise its members and to safeguard the public in such instances. It also seems possible that, from time to time, disputes or complaints may arise between individual members of the Institute, or regarding practices unacceptable under the Institute's Code of Memorandum and Articles. In its early years the Institute has devoted much thought and careful consideration to the regulation of such problems and the establishment of procedures for dealing with those of them which fall within its competence.

Archaeology in Great Britain has long been a friendly and quite informal pursuit involving a plethora of different organizations and *ad hoc* arrangements, and a variety of funding systems. As increasingly large numbers of people have come to depend on it for their livelihood, and increasingly large, expensive and physically disruptive excavation projects have been mounted, it has become evident that existing *ad hoc* arrangements both for the employment of archaeologists and for the regulation of archaeological work are inadequate. The IFA therefore initiated discussion of these issues by forming a joint working party, with other organizations, on archaeological contracts. This working party has chosen not to concern itself with the far more contentious issue of 'contract archaeology' – the competitive tendering for archaeological work which has become a norm in the USA – perhaps in the hopes that it will not emerge in Great Britain and the spectre may go away.

Other professional institutions in Great Britain and the problems of regionalism

The Institute's inauguration has been, in the event, welcomed and supported by other bodies and institutions in Great Britain: even those who opposed the CBA's moves in the 1970s now seem to see the Institute's virtues. In the meantime, however, and in its absence, a number of other professional archaeological organizations have grown up. The Association of County Archaeological Officers came into being in 1973. The Standing Conference of Unit Managers (SCUM, latterly renamed SCAUM) was founded in 1976, as was the Society of Museum Archaeologists. The Archaeology Section of the UK Institute of Conservation was formed in 1978, as was the Association of Archaeological Illustrators and Surveyors. Whether any of these organizations could have been subsumed in a single professional institute, and whether they would now wish to be, is a matter for debate. Certainly the Institute might possibly – and usefully – develop specialist sections, and it has also begun to form regional groups. These seem especially relevant for parts of the UK with a separate identity and often separate legislative provision, such as Northern Ireland, Scotland or Wales.

The future for professional institutions in the provision of cultural resource management services

Now that IFA exists in Great Britain it seems inconceivable that we could have done without it. Perhaps this is because British archaeology has, in the past decade, suddenly grown up. No longer is it a remote subject which can safely be left to harmless and devoted scholars. It has become part of the activities of everyday life, with the same potential for good and for disruption as any modern discipline, and for which some sort of self-regulation was needed before society imposed it from outside.

References

Crawford, O. G. S. 1955. *Said and done*. London: Weidenfeld & Nicolson.
Davis, H. A. 1989. Learning by doing: this is no way to treat archaeological resources. In *Archaeological heritage management in the modern world*, H. F. Cleere (ed.), ch. 27. London: Unwin Hyman.

Index

Aboriginal Land Rights (Northern
    Territory) Act (Australia), 87
Aboriginal Sacred Sites Act (Australia), 81,
    85
Aboriginal Sacred Sites Protection Authority
    (Australia), 81
Aboriginal sites
    conservation, 87–9
    definitions, 82
    excavation, 85
    and land rights, 81, 83, 84, 87
    legislation, 80–3, 85–6
    public access, 87
Aboriginal and Torres Strait Islanders
    Heritage Protection Act (Australia),
    82
Aborigines
    cultural identity, 6
    involvement in CRM, 83–7
    Tasmanian, 87–9
Abu Simbel (Egypt), 34
Accra (Ghana), 126
administration of monuments and sites
    Canada, 146–9
    China, 103, 106
    India, 7–8
    Spain, 188–92
Administrative Bureau of Cultural Relics
    (China), 103
Agbodrafo (Togo), 123–4
Ahlo (Togo), 124
Airlie House Report (USA), 52
Akrowa (Togo), 124
Ambohimanga (Madagascar), 130
Ambositra (Madagascar), 130
Amendments Act (USA), 251
American Society for Conservation
    Archaeology (ASCA), 43, 56–7
ancient monuments, definition, 165
Ancient Monuments Act (Ireland), 173
Ancient Monuments and Archaeological
    Areas Act (UK), 152–3, 165, 166,
    168–9
Ancient Monuments (NI) Act (Northern
    Ireland), 172–3
Ancient Monuments Protection Act (UK),
    1, 7, 153, 172
Andafiavaratra (Madagascar), 141
Aneho (Togo), 124

antiquities
    legislation, 1–2, 24–5, 82, 156, 207
    protection of
        Australia, 83
        China, 102–3
        Denmark, 1, 4
        Ecuador, 142–3
        GDR, 31
        Ghana, 125
        India, 1
        Italy, 1
        Madagascar, 130–2
        Nigeria, 120
        Philippines, 111–13
        Scandinavia, 24–5
        South Africa, 210–12, 213–14
        Spain, 189–90
        Sweden, 1, 25
        Togo, 123
        United States, 1
        USSR, 31
    trade in, 144
        Philippines, 109, 111, 113
        South Africa, 207, 210–12, 214
        and see treasure hunting
Antiquities Act (Nigeria), 121
Antongona (Madagascar), 130
Anuradhapura (Sri Lanka), 221, 222
Anyang (China), 103
Apache-Navajo survey (USA), 246, 247,
    249, 252
APIFA see Association for the Promotion of
    an Institute of Field Archaeologists
archaeological heritage
    definition, 72
    main threats, 71
    and politics, 23–4
    significance, 48–9
archaeological heritage management, 15–17
    definition, 72
    history, 1–5
    ICAHM promotion of, 73–4
    and land-use planning, 12–13
    legislation, 5
    and property rights, 11
    rationale, 5–10
    training, 16
    and see cultural resource management,
        heritage management

Archaeological and Historic Preservation
    Act (USA), 3–4, 237, 254
Archaeological Institute of China, 106
archaeological resource management training
    tropical countries, 280–4
    USA, 275–6
    and see cultural resource management
        training, heritage management
        training
archaeological resources, 48–9
Archaeological Resources Protection Act
    1979 (USA), 38
Archaeological Survey of Canada, 146
Archaeological Survey of India, 286, 287,
    291
Archaeological Survey of Northern Ireland,
    174
archaeologists
    internships, 277–8
    and the job market, 267–8, 290–1
    supervision of, 277–8
archaeology
    holistic, 55–6
    and legislation, 5
    Marxist, 195
    methodology, 38, 40–2
    New, 24, 195
    universal, 55–6
    world, 55–6
Architectural Association (England), 161
Arizona State Museum, 239, 245
Armagh (Northern Ireland), 176, 178
artefacts *see* antiquities
ASCA *see* American Society for
    Conservation Archaeology
Asiatick Society, 285
Association for the Promotion of an Institute
    of Field Archaeologists (APIFA), 304
Aswan Dam (Egypt), 34
Athens (Greece), 3
Australia
    conservation, 87–9, 93–6
    cultural resource management, 83–7
    heritage protection, 79–80
    legislation, 80–3, 85–6
    rescue archaeology, 85
    sites and monuments record, 79–80
    training, 83–7
Australian Archaeological Association, 83–4,
    88
Australian Heritage Commission, 79
Australian National Parks and Wildlife
    Service, 87
Avdeevo (USSR), 204

Baguida (Togo), 123

Ballygroll (Northern Ireland), 180
Banco del Pacifico (Ecuador), 142
Banpo (China), 107
Bassar (Togo), 124
Batangas (Philippines), 111
Beijing (China), 103, 106, 107
Belfast (Northern Ireland), 176
Biskupin (Poland), 32
Black, Murray, 88
Brazil, 3
Bulgaria, 30, 31, 32, 36
Burgess, James, 285
Burra Charter, The, 92–101
Bushmen Relics Protection Act (South
    Africa), 207

Cache River Project (United States), 12
Cadw (Wales), 155
Camp-Massu (Togo), 124
Canada
    administration, 146–9
    CRM, 150
    legislation, 147–8
    salvage archaeology, 146–7
    training, 150
Cape Town (South Africa), 212, 216
Carrickfergus (Northern Ireland), 176, 178
Casa de la Cultura (Ecuador), 143
Cashel (Northern Ireland), 178
CBA *see* Council for British Archaeology
Central Bank of Ecuador, 141, 142
Centre International de Developpement,
    cultural study, 59–60
Changan (China), 107
Charter for Archaeological Heritage
    Management (ICOMOS), 74
Charter for the Conservation of Places of
    Cultural Significance (Australia), 92–6
Chernigov (USSR), 32
China
    administration, 103, 106
    excavation, 105–6
    Institute of Archaeology, 103, 105, 106
    legislation, 102–6
    property rights, 103
    protected sites, 103
    public involvement, 107
    surveys, 106–7
    training, 103, 105–6
    Xian, 30
Chinese Academy of Social Sciences, 106
Cochasqui (Ecuador), 143
Coleraine (Northern Ireland), 176, 178
Cologne (FRG), 2
Commission for Excavations and Research
    (Madagascar), 132

Commission for Sites and Historic
    Monuments (Madagascar), 130
conservation, 4–5
    Aboriginal remains, 87–9
    Burra Charter, 93–6
    Cultural Triangle Project, 224
    definitions, 52, 53, 54, 93
    and excavation, 293
    ghana, 126–7
    international recognition, 292–3
    international training, 294–7
    Madagascar, 131, 132–6, 139–40
    Nigeria, 122
    sub-Saharan Africa, 118
    training, 294–7
    USSR, 204
    and see preservation, reconstruction
conservation areas (South Africa), 213
Conservation Areas (UK), 153
consultation on archaeological work,
    principles for (Australia), 86
Convention on the Means of Prohibiting and
    Preventing the Illicit Import, Export,
    and Transfer of Ownership of
    Cultural Property (Unesco), 83
Coobool Creek (Australia), 88
Corona de Tucson survey (USA), 246, 247
corporate CRM (Canada), 149
Cotocollao (Ecuador), 143
Council for Archaeology and Ancient
    History (GDR), 31
Council for British Archaeology (CBA), 303
Crawford, O. G. S., 302
Crocodile River (South Africa), 213
Crowther collection of Aboriginal remains,
    88–9
Cuenca (Ecuador), 143
cultural continuity, 7–8
cultural identity, 8, 24, 33, 35–6, 144–5
    Aboriginal, 6
    Third World, 60
Cultural Properties Protection and
    Preservation Act (Philippines), 111,
    113
cultural property, definition, 112–13
cultural resource management, 4–5
    Australia, 83–7
    Canada, 150
    definition, 52
    objectives of, 28
    and professionalism, 28
    and US Bureau of Land Management,
        232–5, 248–9
    and US Bureau of Reclamation, 248–9
    US development, 52–4
    and USDA Forest Service, 227–31

and see archaeological heritage
    management, heritage management
cultural resource management training, 4–5,
    83–7, 150
    and the job market, 276–7
    USA, 16, 275–6
    and see archaeological resource
        management training
cultural significance, definitions, 97–9
Cultural Triangle Project (Sri Lanka), 222–6
culture
    definition, 33, 59
    and development, 59–63
Cunningham, Alexander, 285, 286
Curzon, Lord (Viceroy of India), 286
Czechoslovakia, 32

Dambulla (Sri Lanka), 222
data
    collection of, 41–4
    selection of, 41–7
Datong (China), 103
Decrees (Nigeria), 119, 121, 122
Delhi (India), 7
Denmark
    antiquities protection, 1, 4
    heritage management and land-use
        planning, 12–13
    legislation, 25
Department of the Environment Northern
    Ireland, 179–80, 181
development
    and Third World Archaeology, 60–3
    and Third World cultures, 59–63
Downpatrick (Northern Ireland), 176, 178
Druids, 259–60

Ecuador
    antiquities protection, 142–3, 144
    legislation, 142
    museums, 141, 142, 143
    public involvement, 143
    training, 145
education, 9
    ecological museums, 66–9
    USSR, 197–8
    Venezuela, 66–9
    and see training
Egypt, 34
Eldena (GDR), 34
England
    finance, 158–9, 169
    legislation, 152–3, 164–7
    preservation, 158, 168–9
    professionalism, 302–7
    property rights, 156, 166–7

rescue archaeology, 156, 158, 169
scheduling, 164–7
site interpretation, 159, 256–7, 261–4,
   265–71
training, 160–3, 297, 302–3, 305
and see United Kingdom
English Heritage, 153–4, 157–9, 161, 166,
   167, 169
and Stonehenge, 258–9, 261–4, 270
Environmental Assessment Act (Canada),
   147
Environmental Impact Assessment (United
   States), 4
environmental protection, 3–4
excavation, 11–12
   Aboriginal sites, 85
   China, 105–6
   and conservation, 293
   Cultural Triangle Project, 224
   definition, 186
   role in heritage management, 12
   urban, 176
excavation licences/permits, 113, 173, 176,
   188, 198, 211, 214
Executive Order 11593 Protection and
   Enhancement of the Cultural
   Environment (USA), 237

Fergusson, James, 285
field survey, 28 *and see* surveys
fieldwork, guidelines for, 299
finance
   England, 158–9, 169
   Madagascar, 130
   and methodology, 47–8
   Navajo-Hopi Land Exchange Project,
      246–7, 248–9, 252, 253, 254
   Nigeria, 121–2
   rescue archaeology (England), 169
   Toronto International Airport (Canada),
      147
   Tucson Aqueduct Project (USA), 248
   United States, 3–4
   USSR, 199–200
Foote, Bruce, 285
Fudan University (China), 106

Gdansk (Poland), 36
Georgian Academy of Sciences (USSR),
   197
German Democratic Republic, legislation,
   31, 32
Ghana
   conservation, 126–7
   legislation, 125
   Museum and Monuments Board, 125

property rights, 125
training, 118
Great Serpent Mound (USA), 7
green bans, 79
Gross Raden (GDR), 32
Guayaquil (Ecuador), 143, 145
Gwolu (Ghana), 126

hadivory, 139
Hempel, C. G., on methodology, 40–1
heritage management
   Denmark, 12–13
   India, 7–8, 286–90
   United States, 12–13
   USSR, 204–5
   and see archaeological heritage
      management, cultural resource
      management
heritage management training
   England, 160–3, 302–3, 305
   India, 286–90
   Italy, 16
   Poland, 16
   and see archaeological resource
      management training
Heritage Projects Ltd, 266
   and heritage presentation, 270–1
   Stonehenge scheme, 267–70
Higher Council for Archaeological
   Exploration and Excavation (Spain),
   190
Higher Council for Rock Art (Spain), 190
Historic Buildings and Monuments
   Commission *see* English Heritage
Historic Monuments Act (NI) (Northern
   Ireland), 178
Historic Monuments and Arts Objects
   Department (Madagascar), 130
Historic Preservation Act 1974 (USA),
   3–4
historical heritage, definition, 184
Historical Heritage Law (Spain), 184–90
Historical Monuments Commission (South
   Africa), 207–8
historical sites, definition, 212
history, contribution of CRM to, 28
holistic archaeology, 55–6
huaqueros, 141
human inhumations, 212–13
human remains
   Australia, 87–9
   South Africa, 213
Hungary, 31, 36

ICAHM *see* International Committee on
   Archaeological Heritage Management

ICCROM *see* International Centre for the
    Study of the Preservation and
    Restoration of Cultural Property
ICOM *see* International Council of
    Museums
ICOMOS *see* International Council on
    Monuments and Sites
ICRC *see* Institute for the Conservation and
    Restoration of Cultural Property
IFA *see* Institute of Field Archaeologists
IIC *see* International Institute for
    Conservation of Historic and Artistic
    Works
Ilafay (Madagascar), 130
Imperial Archaeological Commission
    (USSR), 195
Inch Abbey (Northern Ireland), 180
India
    antiquities protection, 1
    archaeological job market, 290–1
    British in, 7–8
    Delhi, 7
    early history of archaeology, 285–7
    heritage management, 7–8, 286–90
    Indus Valley, 36
    Institute of Archaeology, 290
    School of Archaeology, 289
    training, 286–90
Ingapirca (Ecuador), 143
Institute for the Conservation and
    Restoration of Cultural Property
    (ICRC), 190
Institute for the History of Material Culture
    (USSR), 195
Institute of Advanced Architectural Studies
    (England), 161
Institute of Archaeology (China), 103, 105,
    106
Institute of Archaeology (India), 290
Institute of Archaeology (USSR), 195, 197,
    199
Institute of Field Archaeologists (IFA),
    298–9, 304–7
Institute of Palaeovertebrate Studies and
    Anthropology (China), 106
International Centre for the Study of the
    Preservation and Restoration of
    Cultural Property (ICCROM), 72,
    300
    training courses, 294–7
International Committee on Archaeological
    Heritage Management (ICAHM), 5,
    70–5
International Council on Monuments and
    Sites (ICOMOS), 70–5, 80, 293, 301
    Burra Charter, 92–101

Charter for Archaeological Heritage
    Management, 74
Charter for the Conservation of Places of
    Cultural Significance, 92–6
    objectives for legislation, 90–2
International Council of Museums (ICOM),
    5, 72, 300
    Committee for Conservation, 292–3
International Institute for Conservation of
    Historic and Artistic Works (IIC), 301
internships for archaeologists, 277–8
interpretation of sites, 13–15
    England, 159, 256–7, 261–4, 265–71
    GDR, 32
    Madagascar, 133–4, 136, 139–41
    Northern Ireland, 180
    Sri Lanka, 222, 225–6
    Stonehenge, 256–7, 261–4, 265–71
    USSR, 202–4
inventories
    Spain, 191
    US Bureau of Land Management, 232–4
    USSR, 202
    and see sites and monuments records,
        surveys
Investigation and Excavation of Ancient
    Cultural Ruins and Ancient Tombs
    (China), 102
Ireland, site types, 171
Irish Church Act, 172
Istanbul (Turkey), 7
Italy
    antiquities protection, 1
    and Ecuadorean antiquities, 144
    Pompeii, 30
    professionalism, 16
    training, 16

Jiling University (China), 106
job markets
    India, 290–1
    USA, 276–7
Jordan, 30, 36
Jorvik Viking Centre, York (England), 14

Kakadu National Park (Australia), 87
Kamina (Togo), 124
Kamir-Blur (USSR), 204
Kandy (Sri Lanka), 221, 222
Karoo formations (South Africa), 210
Kasanlyk (Bulgaria), 30, 32
Keeping Place, 89
Keran (Togo), 124
Khakasii (USSR), 202
Khersonese (USSR), 203
Kiev (USSR), 32

Kostenki (USSR), 204
Kow Swamp (Australia), 88
Kpalime (Togo), 124
Krasnoyarsk (USSR), 201–2
Kurnell (Australia), 79
Kutikina Cave (Australia), 82
Kyffhauser (GDR), 32

Lal Mitra, Rajendra, 285
land rights, 81, 83, 84, 87 *and see* private
      property, property rights
land-use
   and archaeological heritage management,
      12–13
   Denmark, 12–13
   FRG, 10
   Stonehenge, 257–8
   United States, 12–13, 230
   USSR, 202
Lascaux (France), 32
lavaka, 139
Law of Archaeological Excavations (Spain),
      182
Law of the Enlightenment (Spain), 182
Law of Protection of Cultural Relics
      (China), 105
Law on Protection of Cultural Relics of the
      People's Republic of China, 105
Law of the Spanish Historical Heritage, 186,
      188
legislation, 24–6
   Aboriginal sites, 80–3, 85–6
   antiquities, 1–2, 24–5, 82, 156, 207
   and archaeological heritage management,
      5
   Canada, 147–8
   China, 102–6
   Denmark, 25
   Ecuador, 142
   England, 152–3, 164–7
   environmental protection, 3–4
   German Democratic Republic, 31, 32
   Ghana, 125
   ICOMOS objectives, 90–2
   Madagascar, 128, 130–2
   Nigeria, 120–1
   Northern Ireland, 172–4, 178–9
   Philippines, 111–15
   Scandinavia, 11
   South Africa, 207–15
   Spain, 182–92
   Sri Lanka, 224–5
   Sweden, 25
   Togo, 118–19, 123
   United Kingdom, 1
   United States, 1, 38, 227–8, 237, 245

USSR, 201, 222
Lenin, V. I., on protection of monuments,
      36
licenced excavations *see* excavation licences
Lipe, W. D.,
   and CRM, 4–5
   and data collection, 43–7
listing of sites (Madagascar), 131, 133
Liujiaxia (China), 103
Lome (Togo), 123
London (England), 2
Londonderry (Northern Ireland), 176, 178
Longmen (China), 103
Luoyang (China), 103, 107

Mackenzie, Colin, 285
Madagascar
   antiquities legislation, 130–2
   conservation, 131, 132–6, 139–40
   finance, 130
   legislation, 128, 130–2
   listing of sites, 131, 133
   site interpretation, 133–4, 136, 139–41
   sites and monuments record, 130, 133
   training, 136, 138–41
   University, 138–9
management agreements, 168
Marinduque Island (Philippines), 109
Maritime Museum Advisory Committee
      (South Africa), 215–16
Marshall, Sir John, 286–7
Marxist archaeology, 195
Meroe (Sudan), 30
methodology, 38, 40–2, 47–8
Mexico, cultural continuity, 8
Mikulcice (Czechoslovakia), 32
Mondiacult Declaration, 33
Montagu Cave (South Africa), 211
Most (Czechoslovakia), 3
Mungo, Lake (Australia), 89
Murray River Valley (Australia), 88
Museum of Indian Archaeology (Canada),
      150
museums, 32
   econological, 65–9
   Ecuador, 141, 142, 143
   open-air, 32, 203–4
   USSR, 198, 203–4
Museums and Monuments Board (Ghana),
      125
Mycenae (Greece), 30

Nalerigu (Ghana), 126
Natal Drakensberg (South Africa), 210
National Aboriginal Sites Authorities
      Committee (Australia), 84–5

National Classification Commission
(Madagascar), 131
National Commission for the Control of the
Export of Items from the National
Heritage (Madagascar), 132
National Commission for Museums and
Monuments (Nigeria), 119–22
National Designation Commission
(Madagascar), 132
National Environmental Policy Act (NEPA)
(USA), 3, 237
National Estate (Australia), 79–80
National Heritage Act (England),
153–4
National Heritage Memorial Fund
(England), 155
National Historic Preservation Act (USA),
38, 49, 227
National Institute for the Cultural
Patrimony (Ecuador), 143, 145
National Institute of the Cultural Patrimony
of Ecuador, 145
National Liberation Council Decree 387
(Togo), 125
National Monuments Council (South
Africa), 208–9
National Monuments Record (England), 155
National Museum, Division of Monuments
and Sites (Togo), 123–5
National Museum Week (Philippines), 112
National Patrimony Law (Ecuador), 143
National Trust (Australia), 79
National Trust (England), 155, 260
Native and Historical Objects and Areas
Preservation Act (Australia), 82
Natural and Historical Monuments, Relics
and Antiques Act (South Africa),
207–8
Natural Historical and Monuments Act
(South Africa), 207
nautical archaeology, 213–16
Navajo-Hopi Land Exchange Project, 243,
244, 245–7, 248–9, 252, 253, 254
Navajo-Hopi Settlement Act (USA), 245
Navan Fort (Northern Ireland), 180
NEPA see National Environmental Policy
Act (USA)
New Archaeology, 24, 195
New Project Areas (USSR), 198, 200–2, 205
New World Conferences on Rescue
Archaeology, 5
Nigeria
antiquities protection, 120
conservation, 122
finance, 121–2
legislation, 120–1

National Commission for Museums and
Monuments, 119–22
property rights, 121
tourism, 122
training, 118
Northern Ireland
archaeological survey, 173–6
Department of the Environment, 179–80,
181
excavation licences, 173, 176
legislation, 172–4, 178–9
property rights, 178–9
public involvement, 173–4
publications, 175, 178
rescue archaeology, 176–7
site interpretation, 180
site types, 177–8
sites and monuments records, 171, 174–5
tourism, 180
Notse (Togo), 124
Novgorod (USSR), 32
Nubia (Sudan), 12, 30, 32

Olbia (USSR), 203
Old Nisa (USSR), 204
Ontario Energy Board (Canada), 148
Ontario Environmental Assessment Act
(Canada), 147–8, 149
Ontario Heritage Act (Canada), 147, 148
Ontario Planning Act (Canada), 148, 149
Opole (Poland), 32
Ordinance No. 20 (Ghana), 125
Ordnance Survey (UK), 155

Padroes, 211
Parks Canada, 146
past
awareness of, 5–6
respect for, 6–7
Pecos Pueblo (USA), 44–5
Pedjikent (USSR), 204, 205
permits see excavation permits
Petra (Jordan), 30
Philae (Egypt), 34
Philippines
antiquities protection, 111–13
antiquities trade, 109, 111, 113
excavation permits, 113
legislation, 111–15
Ministry of Tourism, 114, 115
National Historic Institute, 114, 115
National Museum 113–14, 115
problems implementing legislation,
112–15
salvage archaeology, 113–14
site destruction, 109, 111

training, 114–15
treasure hunting, 109, 111
Pinchot, Gifford, 53
Planning Act (Canada), 148
Planning (NI) Order (Northern Ireland), 181
Plettenberg Bay (South Africa), 211
Pliska (Bulgaria), 32
Plovdiv (Bulgaria), 30
Poland 31, 32, 36
    professionalism, 16
Polannaruva (Sri Lanka), 221, 222
politics and archaeological heritage, 23–4
Pompeii (Italy), 30
Preservation of Ancient Relics Regulations
    (China), 102
preservation
    England, 158, 168–9
    problems in tropical countries, 281
    and see conservation, reconstruction
Presidential Decrees (Philippines), 111–12,
    114
Preslav (Bulgaria), 32
Princep, James, 285
private property, 11, 24–6
    and see land rights, property rights
proclamations (South Africa), 209–10
professionalism, 16–17, 56–7, 278–9, 297–9
    and cultural resource management, 28
    England, 302–7
    Italy, 16
    Poland, 16
    USA, 304
Programa de Antropologia (Ecuador), 145
Prohibition of Export of Precious Cultural
    Relics and Books (China), 102
property rights
    China, 103
    England, 156, 166–7
    Ghana, 125
    and heritage management, 11
    Navajo-Hopi Land Exchange Project,
        245–6
    Nigeria, 121
    Northern Ireland, 178–9
    South Africa, 209–10, 214–15
    Spain, 183, 184, 191–2
    and see land rights, private property
Protecting Relics from Capital Construction
    (China), 103
Protecting Revolutionary Relics from
    Agricultural Production and
    Construction (China), 103
Protection and Administration of Cultural
    Relics (China), 104
Protection of Movable Cultural Heritage Bill
    (Australia), 83

Protection and Use of Cultural and
    Historical Monuments (USSR), 201
Protection of Wrecks Act (England), 165
Provisional Regulations on Protection and
    Administration of Cultural Relics
    (China), 104
public, definitions of, 10
public access, 31–3, 87, 282
    Stonehenge, 259–61, 266
public archaeology, 4–5
    training course, 276
public involvement in archaeology, 6–7,
    24–5
    Aborigines, 83–7
    China, 106
    Ecuador, 143
    Northern Ireland, 173–4
    South Africa, 210
    Sri Lanka, 225
    Stonehenge, 261–3
    United Kingdom, 4, 155–6, 261–3
    United States, 53, 57
    USSR, 173–4
publications
    China, 107
    Institute of Field Archaeologists, 305–6
    Northern Ireland, 175, 178
    USSR, 198–9

Qin Shi Huang (China), 107
quantum mechanics, and archaeology 39–40
Quito (Ecuador), 141, 143

Raininboay estate (Madagascar), 134
raths and cashels (Northern Ireland), 179
re-use of building materials, 34
Real Alto (Ecuador), 143
reconstruction, 13–14, 32
    definitions, 93
    USSR, 204
    and see conservation, preservation
Redundant Churches Fund (England), 155
relocation of monuments, 32
rescue archaeology, 10, 12, 169
    Abu Simbel, 34
    Australia, 85
    England, 156, 158, 169
    Northern Ireland, 176–7
    Philae, 34
    South Africa, 213
    USSR, 200–1
    and see salvage archaeology
research design, 44, 45–6
    and see methodology
Reservoir Salvage Act (USA), 227
restoration, definitions, 93

Romania, 31
Rome (Italy), 6
Royal Australian Historical Society, 79
Royal Commissions on Ancient and
    Historical Monuments (United
    Kingdom), 155
Rumicucho (Ecuador), 143
Russian Academy for Material Culture, 195
Russian State Archaeological Commission,
    195

Saalburg (FRG), 14
Salango (Ecuador), 143
salvage archaeology, 44, 45, 114
    Canada, 146–7
    Navajo-Hopi Land Exchange Project,
        245–7, 249
    Philippines, 113–14
    South Africa, 213–15
    Tucson Aqueduct Project, 238–45
    and see rescue archaeology
Samarkand (USSR), 201
Sanmenxia (China), 103
Santa Elena (Ecuador), 143
Santa Teresa survey (USA), 246, 252
Scheduled Monument Consent, 166
scheduling, 26, 120, 158, 164–7, 178–9
    and see proclamations
Schlachtenberg (GDR), 32
School of Archaeology (India), 289
Scientific Council on Problems in the Field
    of Archaeology in Central Asia and
    Kazakhstan (USSR), 205
Scientific and Methodological Council for
    the Protection of Historic and
    Cultural Monuments (USSR), 203
Scottish Development Department, 155
shell middens (South Africa), 211
shipwrecks, 213–15
Shul'gan-Tash (USSR), 204
Sigiriya (Sri Lanka), 221, 222
sites and monuments records, 167
    Australia, 79–80
    Madagascar, 130, 133
    Northern Ireland, 171, 174–5
    United Kingdom, 153
    USSR, 202–3
    and see inventories, surveys
site interpretation see interpretation of sites
skeletal remains, Aboriginal, 87–9
Society of Professional Archaeologists
    (SOPA), 278–9, 298–9, 304
SOPA see Society of Professional
    Archaeologists
South Africa
    antiquities protection, 210–12, 213–14

antiquities trade, 207, 210–12, 214
excavation licences, 211
human remains, 213
legislation, 207–15
property rights, 209–10, 214–15
public involvement, 213
rescue archaeology, 213
salvage archaeology, 213–15
shipwrecks, 213–15
South African Historical Wreck Society, 214
South African National Society, 207
South-East Asian Ministers of Education
    Organization Special Project in
    Archaeology and Fine Arts
    (Philippines), 115
Southern Rhodesia see Zimbabwe
Spain
    administration, 188–92
    antiquities protection, 189–90
    excavation licences, 188
    heritage administration, 188–92
    inventories, 191
    legislation, 182–90, 192
    property rights, 183, 184, 191–2
Sri Lanka, 221–6
    legislation, 224–5
    Cultural Triangle, 221–2
    public involvement, 225
    site interpretation, 222, 225–6
Stare' Mesto (Czechoslovakia), 32
State Academy for Material Culture
    (USSR), 195
State Administrative Bureau of Cultural
    Relics and Archaeological Data
    (China), 105, 106
State Historic Preservation Office (USA),
    247
stewardship, 53–4
Stonehenge, 14–15
    care and protection, 259–61
    date, 256–7
    description, 256–7
    and Druids, 259–60
    and English Heritage, 258–9, 261–4, 270
    and Heritage Projects Ltd, 267–70
    land-use, 257–8
    and National Trust, 260
    pop festival, 260, 266
    presentation, 14–15, 261–4, 265–71
    site interpretation, 256–7, 261–4, 265–71
    tourism, 2–3, 10, 259–61
Stonehenge Study Group, 262, 265
Stop Work Order (Canada), 147
Sudan, 12, 30, 32
surveys
    China, 106–7

Navajo-Hopi Land Exchange Project,
    245–7
Northern Ireland, 173–6
Tucson Aqueduct Project, 239–45
USA, 246
and see field survey, inventories, sites and
    monuments records
Sweden, 1, 25
Swedish Royal Proclamation, 1
Szczecin (Poland), 36

Tamberma (Togo), 124
Tanais (USSR), 203
Tananarivo (Madagascar), 130, 134, 141
Tashkent (USSR), 200, 203
Tasmania, 87–9
Taxila School of Archaeology (India), 287–8
Third World archaeology
    and development, 60–3
    and tourism, 60, 62
    ways of raising awareness, 63
Tilleda (GDR), 32
Togo
    antiquities protection, 123
    categories of sites, 123–4
    legislation, 118–19, 123
    National Museum, Division of
        Monuments and Sites, 123–5
    tourism, 124
Togoville (Togo), 123
Toronto International Airport site (Canada),
    147
tourism, 2–3, 9
    Nigeria, 122
    Northern Ireland, 180
    pressure on sites, 32
    Stonehenge, 2–3, 10, 259–61
    sub-Saharan Africa, 119
    Third World, 60, 62
    Togo, 124
Town and Country Planning Act (UK),
    152–3
training, 15–17
    archaeological resource management,
        275–6, 280–4
    Australia, 83–7
    Canada, 150
    China, 103, 105–6
    conservation, 294–7
    cultural resource management, 4–5, 83–7,
        150
    Ecuador, 145
    England, 160–3, 297, 302–3, 305
    Ghana, 118
    heritage management, 16, 286–90
    ICCROM, 294–7

India, 286–90
    internships, 277–8
    Italy, 16
    Madagascar, 136, 138–41
    Management Development for
        Archaeologists, 297
    Nigeria, 118
    Philippines, 114–15
    Poland, 16
    tropical countries, 280–4
    United States, 16, 275–6
    and see education
treasure hunting, 3
    earliest, 141
    North Andean Area, 141
    Philippines, 109, 111
    and see antiquities, trade in
Treasure Trove, 1, 25, 156
Tsinjoarivo (Madagascar), 130
Tucson Aqueduct Project, 236, 238–45, 248

Ukraine (USSR), 202
UN Environmental Programme (UNEP), 3
underwater archaeology, 113, 213–15
UNEP *see* UN Environmental Programme
Unesco, 36
    Convention on the Means of Prohibiting
        and Preventing the Illicit Import,
        Export, and Transfer of Ownership
        of Cultural Property, 83
    Convention on treasure hunting, 3
    and cultural property, 5
    Cultural Triangle Project, 222–3
    Mondiacult Declaration, 33
    preservation, 34–5
    protection of cultural monuments, 31
    World Heritage Convention, 35, 130–1
United Kingdom
    public involvement in archaeology, 4,
        155–6, 261–3
    sites and monuments records, 153
    and see England
United States
    antiquities protection, 1
    archaeological management training, 16
    archaeological resource management
        training, 275–6
    Bureau of Land Management, 232–5, 236,
        245–9, 251–3
    Bureau of Reclamation, 236, 238–40,
        248–9, 253–5
    CRM development, 52–4
    CRM training, 16, 275–6
    Department of Agriculture Forest Service,
        227–8
    finance, 3–4

United States *cont.*
    heritage management and land-use
        planning, 12–13
    inventories, 232–4
    job market, 276–7
    land-use, 12–13, 230
    legislation, 1, 38, 227–8, 237, 245
    Pecos Pueblo, 44–5
    professionalism, 304
    public involvement, 53, 57
    publications, 198–9
    surveys, 246
    training, 16, 275–6
universal archaeology, 55–6
USSR
    administration, 31, 197–8, 204–5
    ancient monuments protection, 31
    antiquities protection, 31
    conservation, 204
    education, 197–8
    excavation licences, 198
    finance, 199–200
    heritage management co-ordination,
        204–5
    Institute of Archaeology, 195, 197, 199
    inventories, 202
    land-use, 202
    legislation, 201, 202
    museums, 198, 203–4
    New Project Areas, 198, 200–2, 255
    public involvement, 173–4
    publications, 198–9
    reconstruction, 204
    rescue archaeology, 200–1
    site interpretation, 202–4
    sites and monuments records, 202–3

    training, 294–7
Uzbekhistan (USSR), 200

Venezuela
    cultural resources, 64–5
    ecological museums, 65–9
    education, 66–9
Venice Charter, 13–14, 74, 293
Vergina (Greece), 30
Vohemar (Madagascar), 133
Volga-Don project (USSR), 201
Vyborg (USSR), 203

War Graves and National Monuments Act
        (South Africa), 208
War Graves and National Monuments
        Amendment Act (South Africa),
        212–13
Western Australia Aboriginal Heritage Act,
        81
Wheeler, Sir Mortimer, 287–8
Williamsburg (USA), 14
Woolley, Sir Leonard, 287
world archaeology, 55–6
World Heritage Convention, 35, 130–1
World Heritage List, 126, 221
Wrocław (Poland), 36

Xi'an (China), 30, 103
Xianyang (China), 103

Yerebuni (USSR), 204
Yungang (China), 103

Zhoukoudian (China), 107
Zimbabwe, cultural continuity, 8